A History of Women in Christianity to 1600

# A History of Women in Christianity to 1600

*Hannah Matis*

WILEY Blackwell

*Registered Offices*
John Wiley & Sons, Inc., 111 River Street, Hoboken, NJ 07030, USA
John Wiley & Sons Ltd, The Atrium, Southern Gate, Chichester, West Sussex, PO19 8SQ, UK

For details of our global editorial offices, customer services, and more information about Wiley products visit us at www.wiley.com.

Wiley also publishes its books in a variety of electronic formats and by print-on-demand. Some content that appears in standard print versions of this book may not be available in other formats.

*Library of Congress Cataloging-in-Publication Data*
Names: Matis, Hannah W., author. | Wiley-Blackwell (Firm), publisher.
Title: A history of women in Christianity to 1600 / Hannah Matis.
Description: Hoboken : Wiley-Blackwell, 2023. | Includes bibliographical
  references and index.
Identifiers: LCCN 2022031402 (print) | LCCN 2022031403 (ebook) | ISBN
  9781119756613 (paperback) | ISBN 9781119756620 (adobe pdf) | ISBN
  9781119756637 (epub)
Subjects: LCSH: Women in Christianity–History–Early church, ca. 30–600 |
  Women in Christianity–History–Middle Ages, 600-1500. | Women in
  Christianity–History–16th century.
Classification: LCC BV639.W7 M335 2023 (print) | LCC BV639.W7 (ebook) |
  DDC 270.082–dc23/eng/20221110
LC record available at https://lccn.loc.gov/2022031402
LC ebook record available at https://lccn.loc.gov/2022031403

Cover Design: Wiley
Cover Image: © Michael Cook, *An Idle Tale* (2013), private collection

Set in 9.5/12.5pt STIXTwoText by Straive, Pondicherry, India

# Contents

# 1

# A History of Women in Christianity

An Introduction

> I argue below that the writing of history must come to terms gracefully with the incomplete, that it must be a conversation open to new voices, that its essential mode is a comic one. I suggest that the pleasure we find in research and in storytelling about the past is enhanced both by awareness that our own voices are provisional and by confidence in the revisions the future will bring.
>
> Caroline Walker Bynum, *Fragmentation and Redemption: Essays on Gender and the Human Body in Medieval Religion*

In the 1130s, a man wrote to the mother of his child with an early attempt at a history of women in Christianity. Women have a special and favored status in the church, he argues, "For if you turn the pages of the Old and New Testaments you will find that the greatest miracles of resurrection were shown only, or mostly, to women, and were performed for them." The man was the scholar Abelard; the woman was the learned Héloïse, his lover and his wife (Abelard and Héloïse 2003, pp. 56–62). After the brutal assault and castration of Abelard instigated by Héloïse's uncle, however, whatever hopes they may have had of the marriage were in ruins. Both had taken monastic vows, Abelard had buried himself in his teaching, and they had not seen one another for a decade. When they did meet again, it was in the midst of moving Héloïse's community of nuns to Abelard's new experiment in monastic life, the oratory of the Paraclete, and it is entirely possible, even likely, that they had had no real time to speak about the past.

When Abelard publicized their story, however, in an open letter now known as the *History of My Calamities,* Héloïse wrote to him, ostensibly requesting an account of his welfare. Her first letters represent the distillation of 10 years of unresolved grief, sexual frustration, and despair. They are also a hopeless and impossible demand for her former husband, and their former life, to return. Abelard's reply, his small history of women in Christianity, is both an *apologia* for women's status within the church and an attempt to console his distraught partner in reform. But it also was an effort to manage the strength of Héloïse's emotions, even to control them, by her husband-turned-spiritual director. Certainly to Héloïse, Abelard's deliberately detached response felt like avoidance: she took monastic vows first, she bitterly reminded Abelard in her answering letter, but not because she was aware of a shred of religious vocation in herself at that time. She did it for him.

The exchange between Abelard and Héloïse, nearly nine hundred years ago, neatly encapsulates one of the chief dilemmas in writing a history of women in Christianity: to what extent is the creation of any narrative history of this kind just one more effort, however well-intentioned, at the appeasement and control of women within and by a patriarchal religious tradition? Even if, or

*A History of Women in Christianity to 1600*, First Edition. Hannah Matis.
© 2023 John Wiley & Sons Ltd. Published 2023 by John Wiley & Sons Ltd.

precisely insofar as, the history of women in Christianity is an uplifting story, to what extent does it remain, in the poet Audre Lorde's famous phrase, a master's tool which cannot dismantle the master's house? Even if one recognizes the extent to which Christianity, historically, has been not only an opiate, as Marx believed, but the refuge of the oppressed and a crucible for resilience and political resistance, has that also been true for women? What does one make of churches and religious spaces overwhelmingly inhabited, supported, and maintained by women, yet which deny women positions of leadership and authority and have often exploited women's faith, hope, and love? There are no straightforward answers to these questions, and it is not always clear that they can even be answered or addressed satisfactorily by a book of this kind, but they have framed and shaped this project from its conception and at every stage of its development (Murray 1979; Grant 1989; Douglas 2005; Hayes 2011; Turman 2013; Walker-Barnes 2014; Jennings 2020; Pierce 2021).

On a very basic level, this book attempts to name the names of women in the Christian tradition – significant figures, but also, in some cases, the only names we have – and survey them in roughly chronological order, from the origins of Christianity through the Reformation, ending at the seventeenth century. It attempts, first and foremost, to situate women within the particularity of their regional and historical context. It aims thereby to give the reader a sense of the normative experience of the ordinary laywoman, from whom, not least, so many of us trace our biological descent. This also creates a baseline against which the achievements of the extraordinary individual might be better understood. Particular attention is given to those women who were able to write, but a historical survey of this kind is also able to be generously inclusive about non-literate women, as well as those women in the church whose achievements were political, institutional, and administrative rather than more obviously "religious." In the premodern world, "church" and "state" were not separate or even clearly defined categories, and certainly were not experienced as such by ordinary people; this book ends exactly when such modern definitions and distinctions were coming into being. As one enters the early modern period, both the quantity and the quality of historical sources changes. There are more glimpses of non-aristocratic women who are neither royal nor canonized in the documentary record, and more non-textual sources survive to illustrate the rhythms of women's daily lives. In the last two chapters in particular, therefore, I have had to be particularly selective about whom and what to include for the sake of clarity, at exactly the moment when a broader field of choice exists.

It is virtually impossible, of course, for a single book to be completely comprehensive, not least because new discoveries continue to be made into the present moment. It is equally impossible to give equal, and sometimes even sufficient, treatment to everyone. Necessarily this is a work of synthesis, building on the meticulous scholarship of recent years, some of it very recent indeed. In the last 20 years in particular, interest in, and the pace of research on, women in the Christian tradition has increased to an exponential degree. Nevertheless, within the academy, much of this work is comparative and thematic in nature, and is often divided between scholars of early and world Christianity, Late Antiquity, the European Middle Ages, and the early modern world. The differing perspectives of history and theology, the nature of historical periodization, the selective lens of confessional history, not mention the numerous languages of both primary and secondary sources and the cost and availability of academic books and articles beyond research libraries, have all contributed to a situation in which much of this scholarship is unknown in the wider church and difficult to navigate for the beginning student. Where possible, I have referred to translations in English of the primary sources discussed here, which in turn can direct the student to the best critical editions of the primary sources available in their original languages. With some exceptions, the secondary scholarship cited in these pages is, likewise, in English, not because this represents anything like an exhaustive account of what exists, but because this book is intended as an introductory resource.

Particularly in recent years, there have been several efforts to provide broad surveys of women in Christianity across the whole of its history, including treatments specifically of nuns and religious women (Kavanagh 1852; Tucker and Liefeld 1987; McNamara 1996; Malone 2001–2003; MacHaffie 2006; Pui-lan 2010; Moore 2015; Tucker 2016; Muir 2019). There are also more specialized works which concentrate on women's religious experience within discreet historical periods (Parks et al. 2021; Cooper 2013; Cohick and Hughes 2017; Bitel and Lifshitz 2008; Dronke 1984; Stjerna 2009). Out of necessity, broad treatments must be selective; likewise, they often adopt a thematic approach to this material, which tends to flatten and decontextualize women's historical experience, particularly across wide swathes of time. On the other hand, surveys which distinguish between the ancient, medieval, and early modern world are always weakest at their edges, in times of disruption and transition; moreover, they often neglect the extent to which women adapted earlier models of devotion and forms of religious life to respond to immediate economic and social pressures. One era which has particularly suffered in both broad and topically focused surveys is the late European Middle Ages, often dismissed as decadent or chaotic, but which should be understood on its own terms as one of the most creative and transformational eras for women's vernacular devotion and in pioneering new forms of women's religious life. The influence of late medieval devotional practice was so pervasive it extended, in different ways, both to women evangelicals and to women in early modern Catholicism – praying in one's native language and praying the rosary, respectively – but this period should not be understood merely as a prelude to the Reformation.

In fact, many of the women named in this book are venerated across multiple Christian traditions. It is all the more important, therefore, to situate them firmly in the times and circumstances in which they lived. In creating a narrative chronological survey, I attempt to discern overarching themes and recurring problems within the history of Christianity which emerge through a focus on women's religious experience. The book concentrates on the premodern and early modern world, including the European Middle Ages, partly because this is my own area of expertise, but also because women's experience in the millennium before the Reformation has often been treated as monolithic in broad surveys of women in Christianity, and often as uniformly "Catholic" by Protestant scholars when such confessional boundaries did not yet exist. By surveying sequentially the first sixteen hundred years of women in the Christian tradition, it is my hope to give greater attention to more obscure figures in the tradition, but also to give the reader a clear sense of their sheer variety. Two well-known visionary women reformers and theologians, Hildegard of Bingen and Catherine of Siena, both western Europeans working in the Latin Christian tradition, were nevertheless working in different languages and within different socio-political contexts, in very different religious communities and at very different moments in the life of the institutional church. The differences between Catherine of Siena and a fifteenth-century Ethiopian saint like Krestos Sämra are, of course, exponentially greater.

Surveying the history of women in the premodern and early modern church, this book underscores the difficulty of imposing simple or static labels and definitions on women's religious experience. Far more often, the institutional certainties of later generations are projected anachronistically back upon a messy and ad hoc experimental reality. This is perhaps most clear in the cases of women saints who have been linked with, and to some extent coopted into, the histories of particular monastic orders, but general terms like "nuns" or "deaconesses" were always fluid, contested, and negotiated offices and identities rather than static known quantities, and were always dependent on contingent local factors. The history of the church is littered with efforts to order and regulate women's religious life, most of which were impracticable failures; an old joke runs that not even the Holy Spirit knows how many women's orders there actually are.

Beyond naming names, this book examines the complex and often contradictory discourses and traditions which have crystallized around women in Christianity. It is one of the principle arguments of this book that these discourses and traditions are, in fact, complex and contradictory, in the same way that the bible does not present a united and monolithic front to the world, but represents a patchwork of texts and a plurality of voices accumulated, like sedimentary rock, over long stretches of time (Barton 2019; Fentress-Williams 2021; Schmid and Schröter 2021). An abiding tension exists between those traditional discourses invoked by church authorities to control and regulate women's religious practice, and those which empowered their religious experimentation. Frequently, both were operative simultaneously, as demonstrated in the conflicted and ambivalent response of many clergy toward women visionaries. Male theologians, historians, and writers have frequently used women rhetorically to "think with" over the course of the Christian tradition: to polarize, to motivate, to shame, and to titillate their readers, and occasionally, to act as models for ideal Christian practice. In these discourses, women are more often added "spice" than essential staple; they are rarely, if ever, described neutrally, and yet these ancient discourses established around women's religious experience, uncritically repeated, continue to shape practice into the present.

This book examines women's choices in historical context: the ways and means by which they engaged with their faith, what was realistically possible, what was allowed, and, more often than one might think, what women did in the teeth of opposition. This book describes the origins and the nature of the resistance that women encountered in the church more or less constantly, while recognizing as well that the most proscriptive and misogynistic legislation passed by both church and state often failed spectacularly to be enforced, and perhaps was only ever intended as rhetorical bluff in the first place. As the great proponent of women's ordination within the Orthodox tradition, Elisabeth Behr-Sigel, once cautioned, "We must be very careful, however, not to give way to an unhealthy masochism and to caricature the teaching and practice of the church in the past as though it is *nothing more* than a sad story of the oppression of the weak by the strong and of women by men" (Behr-Sigel 1991, p. 96, emphasis mine). Ultimately it is women's choices that most interest me, and these varied enormously over the course of the history of the church, depending on a woman's lifecycle, her social status, where she lived, the political climate of the time in both church and state, and the vagaries of illness and chance. It goes without saying that one need not approve of the choices that were made in order to attempt to understand them.

In these ways this book attempts to avoid what Chimamanda Ngozi Adichie has called "the danger of a single story" (Adichie 2009). Women in the Christian church have always been engaged in complex processes of negotiation, for themselves and others, their roles multiple and intricate and their identities the result of ongoing, creative self-fashioning and the navigation of networks of interpersonal relationships. Beyond their immediate families, some of the most important of these relationships were with the clergy. Clergy and ordained monks provided women with the sacraments, acted as confessors, supported or discouraged religious life and vocation, acted as the main line of defense in western Europe in protecting women from the inquisition, and were historically a religious woman's main point of access to the Christian theological tradition and to literacy generally. Much of what is known about religious women in the Christian tradition is refracted through the prism of the male clerical confessor, for better and for worse (Clark 1998). A woman's relationship with her confessor, teacher, or parish priest could range from the exploitative and manipulative to the symbiotic and constructive, and on occasion, as with Lady Catherine and Mr. Collins from *Pride and Prejudice*, to the downright servile. Power dynamics did not work only in one direction.

With some significant exceptions, therefore, women's relationships with clergy were essential elements in their religious identity, but across the history of Christianity, precisely because of its importance, the relationship was not a static one. Clerical identity itself evolved, like women's own status, often in tandem or in contrast with secular and lay masculinity. So did the nature of ordination within the church. Many previous efforts at telling the history of women in Christianity have centered on the search for historical precedents for women's ordination and eucharistic ministry (Muir 2019; Kateusz 2019; Malone 2001–2003; Witt 2020). This is, of course, important, but it is also necessary to remember that ordination itself within the church, even sacramental ordination, does not have a simple or easy definition, applicable to all times and places, and particularly not in the premodern church. Inevitably, this book traces women's de facto participation in worship and liturgy, which is greater than some might suppose, or the exercise of their office in ways that were sometimes defined as ordained, such as an abbess's hearing of confession. However, it also emphasizes the importance of women, like Dante's Beatrice, as lay contemplatives within the Christian tradition, and as lay theologians whose insights have resonated in the later traditions and practice of the church. The hope remains that contemplation, within the Christian tradition and beyond, can be, not a quietist, but a profoundly liberating activity (Coakley 2002, 2013, 2015). This book does not argue for a woman's distinctive, essentialist, or complementarian religious vocation, and certainly not one connected to her motherhood or lack thereof. It does argue for the particular historical importance and contribution of widows throughout the history of the church, not only as a group of the most vulnerable in society, but also, if circumstances were favorable, as the single most autonomous subset of the female population, who often proved to be mature and competent administrators of, and donors to, churches and religious communities.

Any attempt to explore the history of women in Christianity encounters the same tensions and connections between individual and collective experience found also in the history of monasticism. Individual spiritual experiences, interspersed with long stretches of silence and solitude, are only comprehended as extraordinary and only impact the wider Christian tradition insofar as other people *know* about them – preferably literate people with standing in the church who are able to record their encounters with, and impressions of, a particular individual, and in such a manner that survives in the historical record. Needless to say, with so many cracks to slip through, many, if not most, religious women must have done so. History is incurably biased toward the written document, and another of the running arguments of this book will be how difficult, even well-nigh impossible, it was for many women to find their place in the Christian tradition except through others' intervention. In a male-dominated religious discourse, which in the European west was the particular preserve of the Latin-literate and in the east of the Greek, it is usually only aristocratic women who had the resources and education to make themselves felt. Failing those opportunities, the monastic office and the psalter in particular was an essential mnemonic bridge to Latin literacy – or, at any rate, to degrees of it – for many, and it would be a mistake to underestimate how much women understood of the Christian tradition. Although women in the church would shape and redirect this religious discourse in many profound and subtle ways, and many may well have been more free within the church than they would have been outside of it, it should not be forgotten that women did not control the discourse and were never entirely at liberty within it.

The most obvious example of the nature of the dilemma this creates, for both the modern researcher and the reader, is the degree to which the history of women in the Christian tradition is inextricably bound together with the history of the saints. Hagiography, or the lives of the saints, self-consciously encourages the reader toward imitation, to go and do likewise, and many women readers have been introduced to women in the Christian tradition with the understanding, explicit or implicit, that they should somehow be "like" the saints and martyrs – or better yet, like the Virgin Mary. This is a rather more complex business than people often realize. Even setting the martyrs to one side, many women in the hagiographical tradition engaged in practices of asceticism, such as extended or habitual periods of fasting, that to modern eyes look psychologically disordered, if not outright dangerous. Does the study of these women implicitly encourage these behaviors and practices, a question directly addressed by Bynum (1987)? On the other hand, dismissal of hagiography by previous generations of data-driven historians has had knock-on effects in marginalizing the study of religious women generally and in perpetuating essentialist stereotypes about the nature of women's piety in particular. From a more secular perspective, the dangers of attempting clinically to diagnose the state of a woman's mental health a thousand years and more in the past are manifold, not least because the descriptions in our sources are not themselves scientific, clinical, or objective, and were not meant to be. Precisely because, in the premodern church, asceticism was taken as a sign of authenticity, hagiography may often describe women's asceticism in rhetorical terms. And of course, what women themselves thought they were doing and what their confessors saw, or wanted to see, did not necessarily align.

On the one hand, it is very dangerous to lump together "female saints" as a monochrome and monolithic category, even if that is what many sources do (Newman 1997, p. xix). On the other hand, the discourses of the Christian tradition carried real weight, and perpetuated patterns of women's religious experience that could both hinder and help in a conservative society that looked to the past to guide the present. If women could establish precedents for themselves in certain roles, such as queens or reforming abbesses, it became that much easier for other women who followed to make similar choices. The empress Matilda, Hildegard, and Claire of Assisi all had their imitators. Ironically, this is true even if a woman's actual historical existence is questionable, as in the case of a semi-legendary figure like Thecla or Brigid of Kildare. Women refer to one another and invoke each other, sometimes in surprising ways; this book also aims to show these spiritual lineages and connections where they can be seen to exist.

Particularly in the premodern world, of course, this influence was not only intellectual but was believed to extend powerfully into the spiritual realm. For royalty and the nobility, sanctity in the family was an important political card, often and deftly played. In a monastic context, a powerful and miracle-working founding female saint offered an important precedent for an abbess's authority throughout the history of the foundation or of an order generally, for example, in the case of the Merovingian queen Radegund or the late medieval mystic Bridget of Sweden. When saints were believed to have geographical zones of influence, even a kind of spiritual jurisdiction, people often described visionary experiences in which they were in a female saint's presence or under her sometimes terrifying authority.

Likewise, many regarded women in a religious community as having particular influence or powers of intercessory prayer, while their religious vocation brought renown by extension to their families without and preserved and memorialized them within. The rhetoric, both in monastic vocations and in conventional marriage, is that such commitments must be entered into by women's free choice. In reality, many women either married or entered a religious community at the behest of their families, usually driven by economic necessity of one kind or another. In other words, even if one leaves out incidents of rape and sexual abuse – a dangerous if – women's virginity or lack thereof was rarely a simple matter of the exercise of a woman's free choice. Modern readers will be divided over whether devotion to the Virgin Mary empowered women to have a sense of self-worth independent of their sexual market value or perpetuated damaging and realistically impracticable ideals of sexual purity, and the honest answer is surely a conflicted and contradictory mixture of the two (Warner 1976).

Throughout the history of Christianity, women show themselves to be aware of these religious and cultural discourses, many knowing how to present themselves and play to social expectations, even protecting themselves with them and flouting them simultaneously. It is an essential part of women's complex negotiation of their identity, for themselves and in their relationships with clergy and religious authority. As already noted, practices of asceticism and practical charity, but also different forms of visionary experience, must be understood in the context of these discourses and traditions. It is very difficult to do this without seeming to "debunk" or to cast doubt on the experiences of many religious women, who have often been dismissed or marginalized as less reliable witnesses in the first place (Lowe 2003). In many cases, for example, it is impossible to know whether, or to what degree, a holy woman's devoted and intimate care of lepers as described by her confessor is literally and historically true but modeled on an earlier saint's example, is depicted in a rhetorically stylized but essentially accurate manner, or is wildly exaggerated for dramatic and pious effect. At all times, modern readers must be aware that they are not the designated audience to whom many religious women are "performing." Religious women are overwhelmingly concerned with the ancient and medieval equivalent of the church vestry, the internal politics of insular small towns and market guilds, the private and public opinions of their cousins, neighbors, siblings, parents, spouses and children, scribes and confessors, abbots, bishops, popes, inquisitors, government bureaucrats, kings and queens, and many other actors whose names are completely lost to modernity. Many are "difficult women," problematic not only in their own time but also, and perhaps even more so, in our own, and influential precisely for that reason (Lewis 2020).

Whatever account is written here of women's experience within Christianity, it is incomplete, biased, contingent, and compiled through a methodology of often reading sources slightly against the grain of their authors' intentions. Nevertheless it would seem to add insult to injury to refuse to try to understand these women simply because they do not answer all of our questions in precisely the way that we in the modern world might want. To the general reader, the most urgent and pressing concern will, no doubt, be with the overall trajectory of the narrative presented here: will the status of women be seen to improve over time? According to some criteria, yes, but according to others, it is more difficult to judge. It would be dangerous to underestimate the sheer amount of continuity in gender roles existing across such a broad space of time, geography, and culture, in favor of cheap and easy optimism, privileged by race and class, that neglects the vast majority of women's experience (Bennett 2006, pp. 54–81). The book adopts what may seem a deliberately arbitrary chronology, with chapters breaking neatly at the turn of the century or half-century. This is for the general reader's ease of navigation, not because centuries are particularly significant markers of change in and of themselves. Even such disruptive moments and movements as the Reformation will be seen not to "improve" the status of women so much as they transform the nature of certain choices possible to women, particularly women of a certain social class and education, in certain places. The research and writing for this project was largely completed during the coronavirus pandemic, which revealed, among many other things, the fragile nature of women's employment and socio-economic equality even in the present day. The brunt of the pandemic's impact was felt most strongly in such professions as nursing and teaching, historically done by women generally and women's religious orders in particular, and which as a consequence remain chronically underpaid and under-supported. Even in grim circumstances, however, hope should be understood not as a simplistic upward trajectory but as a duty to future generations, to make the world, however we find it, better (McCaulley 2020; Brown 2018, pp. 175–181; Glaude and Eddie 2020).

Women's religious experience consists, not of a select few moral exemplars from one narrow confessional stream, but in dizzying breadth and variety within the Christian tradition. Over the course of reading and researching for this project, there has not been a day when I was not surprised and delighted by something I encountered for the first time. I have been guided throughout this project by Caroline Walker Bynum's deceptively gentle invitation for history, even in dealing in such weighty matters as religion and gender, to be in the "comic" mode. "Comic" history is free to delight in incongruity, irony, and the unexpected, without being bound to the grim teleological inevitability of the "tragic." As Bynum counsels, history is not necessarily "comic" in the sense of being funny, although it certainly can be, nor is it trivial or lacking in conscience. Comic history is, however, history with a sense of its own proportion. If the approach provided by this book helps readers to better access the work of other scholars, to introduce readers to more obscure names within the Christian tradition and to further and richer possibilities for learning, I will be well pleased. And no one will be happier than I if this book is swiftly made redundant.

## References

Abelard and Héloïse (2003). *The Letters of Abelard and Heloise* (trans. B. Radice). London: Penguin, 1e, 1974.

Adichie, C.N. (2009). The danger of a single story. TED.com. https://www.ted.com/talks/chimamanda_ngozi_adichie_the_danger_of_a_single_story?language=en

Barton, J. (2019). *A History of the Bible: The Book and Its Faiths*. London: Allen Lane.

Behr-Sigel, E. (1991). *The Ministry of Women in the Church* (trans. S. Bigham). Crestwood: St. Vladimir's.

Bennett, J.M. (2006). *History Matters: Patriarchy and the Challenge of Feminism*. Philadelphia: University of Pennsylvania Press.

Bitel, L. and Lifshitz, F. (ed.) (2008). *Gender and Christianity in Medieval Europe: New Perspectives*. Philadelphia: University of Pennsylvania Press.

Brown, A.C. (2018). *I'm Still Here: Black Dignity in a World Made for Whiteness*. New York: Convergent Books.

Bynum, C.W. (1987). *Holy Feast and Holy Fast: The Religious Significance of Food to Medieval Women*. Berkeley: University of California Press.

Bynum, C.W. (1991). *Fragmentation and Redemption: Essays on Gender and the Human Body in Medieval Religion*. New York: Zone Books.

Kavanagh, J. (1852). *Women of Christianity, Exemplary for Acts of Piety and Charity*. London: D. Appleton and Company.

Clark, E.A. (1998). The lady vanishes: dilemmas of a feminist historian after the "linguistic turn". *Church History* 67 (1): 1–31.

Coakley, S. (2002). *Powers and Submissions: Spirituality, Philosophy and Gender*. Oxford: Blackwell.

Coakley, S. (2013). *God, Sexuality, and the Self: An Essay "on the Trinity"*. Cambridge: Cambridge University Press.

Coakley, S. (2015). *The New Asceticism: Sexuality, Gender and the Quest for God*. London: Bloomsbury.

Cohick, L.H. and Hughes, A.B. (2017). *Christian Women in the Patristic World*. Grand Rapids: Baker Academic.

Cooper, K. (2013). *Band of Angels: The Forgotten World of Early Christian Women*. New York: Overlook Press.

Douglas, K.B. (2005). *What's Faith Got to Do with It? Black Bodies/Christian Souls*. Maryknoll: Orbis Books.

Dronke, P. (1984). *Women Writers of the Middle Ages*. Cambridge: Cambridge University Press.

Fentress-Williams, J. (2021). *Holy Imagination: A Literary and Theological Introduction to the Whole Bible*. Nashville: Abingdon Press.

Glaude, J. and Eddie, S. (2020). *Begin Again: James Baldwin's America and Its Urgent Lessons for Our Own*. New York: Crown.

Grant, J. (1989). *White Women's Christ and Black Women's Jesus: Feminist Christology and Womanist Response*. Atlanta: Scholars Press.

Hayes, D.L. (2011). *Standing in the Shoes My Mother Made: A Womanist Theology*. Minneapolis: Fortress Press.

Jennings, W.J. (2020). *After Whiteness: An Education in Belonging*. Grand Rapids: Eerdmans.

Kateusz, A. (2019). *Mary and Early Christian Women: Hidden Leadership*. London: Palgrave Macmillan.

Lewis, H. (2020). *Difficult Women: A History of Feminism in 11 Fights*. London: Jonathan Cape.

Lowe, K.J.P. (2003). *Nuns' Chronicles and Convent Culture in Renaissance and Counter-Reformation Italy*. Cambridge: Cambridge University Press.

MacHaffie, B.J. (2006). *Women in Christian Tradition*. Minneapolis: Fortress Press.

Malone, M.T. (2001–2003). *Women and Christianity*, vol. 3. Orbis: Maryknoll.

McCaulley, E. (2020). *Reading While Black: African American Biblical Interpretation as an Exercise in Hope*. Downers Grove: Intervarsity Press Academic.

McNamara, J.A.K. (1996). *Sisters in Arms: Catholic Nuns through Two Millennia*. Cambridge: Harvard University Press.

Moore, R. (2015). *Women in Christian Traditions*. New York: New York University Press.

Muir, E.G. (2019). *A Woman's History of the Christian Church: Two Thousand Years of Female Leadership*. Toronto: University of Toronto Press.

Murray, P. (1979). Black theology and feminist theology. *The Atlanta University Center Robert W. Woodruff Library. October 25, 1979. The Society for the Study of Black Religion Collection*. https://radar.auctr.edu.

Newman, B. (1997). *Sister of Wisdom: St. Hildegard's Theology of the Feminine*. Berkeley: University of California Press, 1e, 1987.

Parks, S., Sheinfeld, S., and Warren, M.J.C. (2021). *Jewish and Christian Women in the Ancient Mediterranean*. Abdingdon: Routledge.

Pierce, Y. (2021). *In My Grandmother's House: Black Women, Faith, and the Stories We Inherit*. Minneapolis: Broadleaf Books.

Pui-lan, K. (ed.) (2010). *Women and Christianity: Critical Concepts in Religious Studies*, vol. 4. New York: Routledge.

Schmid, K. and Schröter, J. (2021). *The Making of the Bible: From the First Fragments to Sacred Scripture* (trans. P. Lewis). Cambridge, MA: Belknap Press.

Stjerna, K. (2009). *Women and the Reformation*. Oxford: Blackwell.

Tucker, R.A. (2016). *Extraordinary Women of Christian History: What We Can Learn from Their Struggles and Triumphs*. Grand Rapids: Baker Books.

Tucker, R.A. and Liefeld, W.L. (1987). *Daughters of the Church: Women in Ministry from New Testament Times to the Present*. Grand Rapids: Academie Books.

Turman, E.M. (2013). *Toward a Womanist Ethic of Incarnation: Black Bodies, the Black Church, and the Council of Chalcedon*. New York: Palgrave Macmillan.

Walker-Barnes, C. (2014). *Too Heavy a Yoke: Black Women and the Burden of Strength*. Eugene: Cascade.

Warner, M. (1976). *Alone of All Her Sex: The Myth and Cult of the Virgin Mary*. London: Picador.

Witt, W.G. (2020). *Icons of Christ: A Biblical and Systematic Theology for Women's Ordination*. Waco: Baylor University Press.

## 2

# Filling the Hungry with Good Things

Women in Christianity to 200

It is impossible to tell the story of Jesus and his followers without mentioning the women. According to the gospel accounts, it is Mary's consent which precedes Jesus's conception, while the first witness to the resurrection of Jesus is Mary Magdalene, called, in later medieval tradition, "the apostle to the apostles." From the beginning of his ministry, Jesus had defined his mission in the words of the prophet Isaiah: "to preach good news to the poor," the coming of the kingdom of God. This kingdom was to be characterized by healing, freedom from slavery, and cancellation of debts which traditionally belonged to the Jewish year of Jubilee. Jesus's ministry would be only one of several movements within Judaism at the time which sought the restoration of the fortunes of the Jewish people. In comparison with his contemporaries, a distinguishing feature of Jesus's teaching might be said to be his love of a good party, and a good wedding in particular (Levine 2014, pp. 14–15). In his parables he frequently refers to himself as a bridegroom, a narrative which defined the entire nature and history of the church which followed as an expectant bride. In the gospel accounts of Jesus's efforts to redefine the terms and boundaries of where, how, and to whom the kingdom of God would reveal itself, women were distinctive and essential participants in his message and his partners in dialogue.

The Old Testament had described certain women as being particular supporters of its prophets, as in the case of the widow from Sidon who gave her family's last meal to Elijah, and whose son Elijah raised from the dead (1 Kgs 17). Elijah's disciple and successor Elisha performed similar miracles for women who asked for his help (2 Kgs 4). The Ethiopian church in particular venerates the Queen of Sheba, there known as Makeda, who journeyed to meet Solomon and asked him pointed questions (2 Chron 9). In all, the Talmud recognizes seven women as prophets in their own right: Sarah, Miriam, Deborah, Hannah, Abigail, Huldah, and Esther (Levine and Brettler 2017, p. 340). In Luke's gospel, women proclaim Jesus's coming with similarly prophetic authority: Anna speaks from the Temple, while Mary's Magnificat strongly evokes the Old Testament song of Hannah over the birth of her son Samuel. In contrast with the bumbling figures of the disciples, women in the gospels are often described as intuitively grasping Jesus's power and significance, sometimes because they are in such desperate straits they seem to have little other choice (Arlandson 1997, pp. 120–150). The Syro-Phoenician woman persists in the face of the disciples' resistance and even, ostensibly, Jesus's own, until her moral claim on him has been made sufficiently plain to everyone. The woman with the hemorrhage has run out of both money and doctors; the woman at the well seems to have run out of husbands. Like the widow from Sidon, many women in the gospels respond to Jesus's preaching with enormous generosity. Jesus's ministry was made possible through the financial support of Joanna, Susannah, Mary Magdalene, and Martha and Mary of Bethany. Women remain at the cross when the disciples have scattered, women tend and prepare Jesus's shattered body for burial, and women are first to the tomb (Fiorenza 1994, p. xliv).

At the same time, the gospel writers seem to be embarrassed by this aspect of the story they are manifestly telling. Women in the gospels come into focus for moments only, and even then they are, more often than not, nameless. The notoriously overlapping and conflicting accounts in the gospel writers of Mary Magdalene, Mary of Bethany, and the woman with the alabaster box have ensured that, while her deed may be remembered forever, her name was not (e.g. Matt 26; Mk 14–16; Lk 7–8; Jn 11–12, 19–20). According to the gospel of Matthew, because of a dream she had had, Pontius Pilate's wife tried to persuade her husband to release Jesus (Matt 27:19). Later called Procla in the Christian tradition, she remains unnamed in the gospel account. Women are certainly present among the crowd in Galilee who are described as witnesses to Jesus's resurrection; they are almost certainly members of the pairs of evangelists that Jesus sends out into the country-side, and which set the precedent for the male and female evangelistic teams which were often used in the early church (Lk 10:1–20). Certainly Mary, but probably other women as well were present in the early gatherings of the church in Jerusalem and at Pentecost. However, they are generally not named alongside the Twelve.

At the same time, we know precious little about many of the men whose names do appear in the gospels, later Christian traditions about them notwithstanding. In the gospels, the Twelve are frequently treated together as a single and undifferentiated group. The Acts of the Apostles is something of a misnomer: few of the Twelve even make an appearance (Lee 2011, p. 69). After his election, what more is known about Matthias? Any reader of the gospel accounts of Jesus's ministry is, therefore, presented with something of a paradox: within the Christian tradition, many of its most moving and poignant moral *exempla* belong to women whose names are unknown and about whom there are differing or conflicting traditions. On the other hand, little is known about the ostensible leaders of the early Christian community in Jerusalem from James onward, and even less about its everyday practices or governance.

Jesus ordained no one. Those whom he commissioned at the conclusion of the gospel of Matthew are not clearly named or identified in any kind of formal way (Witt 2020, p. 97). Although the title of apostle clearly implied close proximity to Jesus in early Christian accounts, it was clearly so loosely defined that Paul could make a later case for his own inclusion in the group. Junia – without question a woman's name – has often been "masculinized" as Junias, a name that does not appear anywhere in the classical tradition. Junia is described as Paul's relative and "prominent among the apostles," but precisely because Paul assumes the general recognition of his readers, he unfortunately does not include many further details about her (Rom 16:7; Epp 2005; Pedersen 2006). Moreover, what relationship the apostolate had with the developing ministerial offices of the church is unclear; Philip, for example, was described both as an apostle and as a deacon alongside Stephen, and appointed as "one of the seven" to the Gentiles (Brinkhof 2018).

## Named Women in the Letters of Paul

The earliest accounts of the Christian church found in Paul's letters already describe something of a *fait accompli* upon which Acts later elaborates: the expansion of the teachings of Jesus beyond their linguistic, religious, and cultural birthplace. The decision of the church in Jerusalem to admit uncircumcised Gentiles probably did not represent as significant a draw for women converts as has sometimes been argued. Moreover, it risks caricaturing Jewish practice as more misogynistic, and as more distinct from early Christian groups, than it actually was (Fiorenza 1994, pp. 205–226;

Lieu 2016, pp. 115–128). From the beginning, Paul's letters assume that both Jews and Gentiles, men and women, were drawn to early Christian teachings, and he acknowledges the active participation, patronage, and even governance of small house churches by women.

The most extensive list of named individuals by Paul is that found at the conclusion of his letter to the Romans. In pride of place, Paul begins by recognizing Phoebe, a deacon of the church at Cenchreae, and probably the bearer of Paul's letter, "for she has been a benefactor of many and of myself as well" (Rom 16:1–2). He then greets Prisca (or Priscilla) and Aquila, "who work with me in Christ Jesus and risked their necks for my life," describing the reach of a ministry to the Gentiles which included the discipling of the teacher Apollos and extended almost as widely as Paul's own (Rom 16:3–4; I Cor 16:19; Acts 18:26; 2 Tim 4:19). "Greet Mary, who worked very hard for you" (Rom 16:6). He then thanks Andronicus and Junia, "who were in Christ before I was" and who were imprisoned alongside Paul. It is at least a possibility that "Junia" is a Romanized version of "Joanna the wife of Chuza," the wife of Herod's steward and the benefactor of Jesus's ministry, who is described in the gospel of Luke as being one of the women at the tomb (Rom 16:7; Luke 8:3, 24:10; Bauckham 2002, p. 104). "Those workers in the Lord, Tryphaena and Tryphosa," Rufus and his mother, who is "a mother to me also," "Philogus and Julia," and "Nereus and his sister" are all greeted and recognized by Paul, and emphasize the interdependence of "brothers and sisters" within the Christian community (Rom 16:12–15).

In the same vein, in the letter to Philemon, Paul would greet his friend alongside Apphia "our sister," before launching into a veritable rhetorical tour de force by which Paul claims full personhood for, and kinship with, that ultimate non-person, a runaway slave (Philem 2; Ruden 2010, pp. 177–200). In the letter to Philippians, his somewhat exasperated fondness for Euodia and Syntyche is apparent. He reminds the broader community of their central importance within the church and that he and they have a shared history in which they "struggled beside me in the work of the gospel" (Phil 4:2–3). Paul clearly remained in communication with "Chloe's people" about the church in Corinth, and in the letter to the Colossians greeted Nympha "and the church in her house" (I Cor 1:11; Col 4:15). Whether or not Paul was the author of 2 Timothy, describing Timothy's own faith and vocation as an inheritance from his grandmother Lois and mother Eunice is in keeping with Paul's recognition of women in his letters (2 Tim 1:5; Acts 16:1). If 2 Timothy is pseudonymous, it is perhaps even clearer evidence that Paul's greetings to, and recognition of, individual women in leadership roles within his congregations were understood at the time to be telltale hallmarks of his writing.

To some extent, later New Testament books fill out the picture suggested by Paul's letters, and provide some historical context for the kind of woman who found herself drawn to early Christian teachings and the kind of role she often played within its early communities. As in Jesus's ministry, women financially supported, patronized, and hosted house churches. The "elect lady" of the Johannine epistles is clearly the head of one such community (2 Jn 1). In the book of Acts, Peter raised from the dead a woman named Tabitha, or Dorcas, who was known for her charity and particularly her ministry to widows. She is called a "disciple" (*mathētria*, the feminized form of *mathētēs*), a word that does not appear anywhere else in the New Testament (Acts 9:36–43; Lee 2011, p. 63). When Peter escaped from prison, he went to the house church of Mary, the mother of John Mark, where he was greeted by the maid Rhoda in a kind of comic reenactment of the flustered women at Jesus's tomb (Acts 12:12–17). Paul and Luke deliberately sat down to talk with the women who had gathered at the place of prayer outside the gates of Philippi. Lydia, who was there and is described as a "worshiper of God," urged Paul, Luke, and their companions to stay in her house (Acts 16:13–15). One of Paul's first converts in Athens was "a woman named Damaris" (Acts 17:33). Philip is described as having four unmarried daughters who prophesied, although

Luke does not record any of their names (Acts 21:9; Fiorenza 1994, pp. 162–168). The author of the Apocalypse attacks the "Jezebel" who is the head of the church in Thyatira, "who calls herself a prophet" (Apoc 2:20–23).

## Jews and God-Fearing Women in Hellenistic Society

Many of these women were Jewish; of the Gentiles, many were plainly familiar with, and drawn to, Jewish religious customs and beliefs. There would have been many opportunities even for Greek-speaking women to have come into contact with Jewish religious practices. Under the ruling dynasties which had established themselves in the wake of Alexander the Great's conquests, cities were the essential political unit of the Hellenistic world. In addition to a certain quantity of Greek immigration eastwards, many new cities were established with non-Greek citizens, particularly in Asia Minor and Syria, but which used Koinē Greek as the common language and established Greek social and cultural institutions. Nevertheless, Hellenization did not prevent, and was not even antithetical to, a huge amount of regional and local diversity, including the spread of Jewish communities across the Mediterranean (Waterfield 2018, pp. 407–414; Errington 2008, pp. 131–142). In Syria, Aramaic remained as much a lingua franca as Koinē; Jewish communities in Egypt and Palestine did not seem to make or maintain neat distinctions between Jewish and Hellenistic culture, with the exception of religious practice (Grabbe 2008, pp. 125–165). This is perhaps best exemplified in the thriving Jewish community in Alexandria in Egypt, which produced the Septuagint, the revered translation of the Old Testament into Greek which Paul and other early Christians would have known. Paul himself seems to have had at least a nodding acquaintance with Stoicism and Epicureanism, and assumed it among his readers (Wright 2013, pp. 197–278; Long 1993, pp. 138–67). The synagogue itself, despite its later role as the crucible of Jewish identity, was at the time a Hellenistic Jewish invention (Schama 2013, pp. 121–138; Kovelman 2005; see Figure 2.1).

   After the Seleucid ruler Antiochus IV attempted to suppress Jewish religious practice in 167 BCE, the Maccabean revolt established the Jewish Hasmonean dynasty, which in turn was annexed by the expanding Roman Empire in 63 BCE, dashing Jewish hopes for lasting political independence. After the catastrophic siege of Jerusalem and the destruction of the Temple in 70 CE, further significant numbers of Jewish refugees settled abroad, most notably in Spain, and many were enslaved as prisoners of war throughout the Roman Empire. Sputters of further Jewish unrest prompted occasional, piecemeal Roman legislation, culminating eventually in the Bar Kochba rebellion and the war between 132 and 135 CE. Paul would arrange to meet with Priscilla and Aquila in Corinth because Emperor Claudius had ordered all Jews to leave Rome (Acts 18:1–3). At the end of the first century CE, Domitian's decision to tax all Jews within the empire may have acted to cohere the "God-fearers" as a group. A term which began as an insult, its members seem to have been, if anything, predominantly female (Cohick 2009, pp. 186–193). Nevertheless, it would be a mistake to see the "God-fearers" as having anything like a clear or closely defined membership at this time (Parks, Sheinfeld, and Warren 2021).

   In Jesus's own lifetime, how far Hellenistic social customs with regard to women were adopted within Jewish society in Palestine is difficult to say. It is also impossible to know how often proscriptive language in the Mishnah against, for example, women learning Torah was ever actually enforced in practice, particularly after the destruction of the Temple (e.g. Sotah 21b). An inscription from 28 BCE names a Jewish woman named Marin as a priestess (*hierissa)* in a temple in Leontopolis, which may reflect Hellenistic practice (Brooten 1982; Sawyer 1996, pp. 74–75). One of

**Figure 2.1**    The courtyard of the synagogue of Sardis. *Source:* Quintucket / Wikimedia Commons / CC BY-SA 4.0.

the great scholars of the Talmud was the woman Beruriah, who lived in the second century. There seem to have been women present even among the Essenes, as the Dead Sea Scrolls attest (Ilan 2010). The so-called "Babatha archive," a collection of second-century papyrus documents in the possession of a Jewish woman named Babatha who lived near the Dead Sea, records a mixture of Jewish, Greek, and Roman legal and financial practices, as well as records of Babatha's first marriage, widowhood, and second, polygamous marriage (Hylen 2019, pp. 76–77; see Figure 2.2). In the Apocryphal literature itself, the occasional misogyny of a writer like Ben Sira should be weighed against the women who actually appear in Tobit, Susannah, Judith, and in Greek-inspired romances like *Joseph and Asenath*. Certainly Jewish marriage customs seem to have shifted from the use of a bride price to a dowry as a result of Hellenization, and divorce was clearly a matter of some ongoing debate within the Jewish community in Jesus's time.

Jesus's teachings on divorce, when it came to the technicalities recorded by the gospel writers, are largely in keeping with the rabbinical discussions of the day (Matt 5:27–32; Mk 10:2–12; Lk 16:18, 24:10). Divorce could not be said to benefit women where a woman could be left without visible financial means of support – not least, if a marriage produced no children – or where divorce and remarriage were instruments in forming political alliances, as was often the case in the Roman republic. Divorce for barrenness may well have been the cause of the multiple marriages of the Samaritan woman at the well, sometimes called Photeine in the Orthodox tradition, who shows no signs of being a prostitute, as is often argued (Jn 4:1–42; Cohick 2009, pp. 114–128; Talbot 2001, VIII–IX). But Jesus's disapproval of divorce also seems to reflect his particular reading of Genesis and marriage as a reflection of the original created order, a reading which underscored most early Christian teachings on marriage, in particular those of Paul (Satlow 2017, pp. 608–611; Levine 2017, p. 762; Schmid and Schröter 2021, pp. 198–199).

Athenian society of the fifth century BCE had traditionally maintained a deep and gendered division between the public, outdoor, male world of war, athletics, and political participation and the

**Figure 2.2**    The Babatha scroll, found in the Cave of Letters, Israel. *Source:* Nadav1 / Wikimedia Commons / Public domain.

private, domestic sphere proper to women. Women could not represent themselves in court; they had no political voice, and did not participate in either the theater or the games. In public, respectable women were customarily veiled, although the type of veil often varied (Llewelyn-Jones 2001). Women traditionally married men significantly older than themselves who were intended to act within the marriage *in loco parentis*. Even within the home, women were ostensibly supposed to remain in their own quarters, occupied with spinning or weaving, the ubiquitous "working in wool" of which the *Odyssey*'s Penelope is only the most famous example. Women were banned from the drinking parties, the *symposia*, around which most male society revolved. The women who were present by definition were neither veiled nor respectable: most famously the *hetairae*, the cultivated, educated, and often exotically foreign courtesans of classical Athens, as well as the more common musicians, prostitutes, and slaves. Part of the seemingly universal appeal of Greek culture was that it was, at least for men, a drinking culture (Davidson 2016).

Hellenistic society may have spread these traditional attitudes abroad but, at the same time, it made Greek education much more widely accessible to an increasing number of non-Greek women. The sheer dynastic complexity of the Hellenistic successor kingdoms created opportunities for several prominent queens and consorts, such as Berenice II of Egypt, and the regionalism and local diversity of the Hellenistic world contribute to the impression of women being increasingly politically and economically visible in this period. This may be an illusion, a political strategy on the part of their families, but it also formed part of a tradition of gender separation and complementarity ubiquitous in the Greek-speaking world (Waterfield 2018, pp. 415–417; van Bremen 1996). In the mystery cults which swept the eastern Mediterranean and, eventually, the entire Roman Empire, the veneration of the Egyptian goddess Isis seems ultimately to have eclipsed that of her brother Osiris (Brenk 2009). These cults drew many of their members from women who may have been looking for a socially acceptable alternative to the *symposia*.

In the *symposia*, Plato's philosophical dialogues had enshrined a social and cultural institution which was, by definition, already closed off to ordinary women. Plato's Socrates has nothing good to say about marriage; his wife is the target of some of his most pointed snubs. Plato's hierarchical, elitist sensibility was further buttressed in Greek philosophical circles by Aristotelian science, in which the philosopher argued for the inherent physiological, mental, and spiritual inferiority of women. Women were, Aristotle concluded, incomplete and unfinished men: less rational, more given over to chaotic displays of passion, their bodies essentially soft and passive rather than hard and active, heavier matter less shaped by, and farther from, the spiritual Forms (Aristotle 1972, Bk. I, Sections 19–20; Bk. II, Section 3). Greek doctors in the Hippocratic tradition up to the time of the Roman Galen in the second century CE imagined a woman's body as different from a man's, colder and more prone to retaining fluid, which was best regulated through menstruation, intercourse, and breastfeeding. Galen was himself profoundly influenced by Plato, and like Aristotle considered a woman to be colder and fundamentally defective by nature, the nourishment she was incapable of processing passing instead to the developing fetus. Some Aristotelian science denied that women played any role in the conception of a child other than to become a channel or conduit of men's creative energy; Galen argued, however, that it was the heat, or lack thereof, in a woman's womb which determined the relative sex of a child (Fleming 2000).

In *The Republic*, only with the eradication of the nuclear family could Plato envision a woman free enough from its overwhelming claims to receive a different kind of education and to take on a more egalitarian role within the state (Satz and Okin 2013, p. 42). This would be a particularly resonant idea for Christian ascetic and monastic thinkers in later centuries, who often depicted their communities as little cities. Aristotelian social and political thought embraced a strongly hierarchical understanding of the family, while Aristotelian philosophy and science systematized and perpetuated commonplace discourses of misogyny, alongside its more populist forms in both Athenian and Roman comedy (McClure 2018). Greek philosophy was immensely influential in educated Roman circles, popularized by the likes of Cicero and through the ubiquitous Greek slaves who tutored the scions of the Roman aristocracy. Aristotelian misogyny appeared to be rational, scientific, and couched in monotheistic language, and was profoundly influential on later Christian thought (Sawyer 1996, pp. 111–112). A woman who acted bravely or demonstrated superior mental or physical self-control was displaying traits that were understood as essentially masculine, and she was often described using masculine language, the so-called "virile woman."

## Women in the *Pax Romana*

Traditional Roman society was agricultural rather than naval and mercantile, revolving around extended kin groups working family farms. The head of the family, the *paterfamilias*, in theory had the power of life and death over all of his dependents (Ruden 2010, p. 193). In practice this right was seldom exercised, not least because women frequently outlived their fathers, but the symbolic resonance remained. Soon after the birth of a child, slave or free, it was the father's decision whether or not to recognize it as his own, signified by lifting it up in his hands; if he did not, the child would be exposed (Cohick 2009, p. 35). Although common-law marriage, as well as divorce, was the normal practice, a father's authority extended over his daughter even after her marriage. Roman wives remained under the control of their fathers rather than their husbands, and could, at least in theory, have their marriages dissolved by their fathers even against their consent. Of several kinds of traditional Roman marriage, *sine manu,* or "out of hand," dowry practice was one common form, in which whatever property a woman brought to a marriage remained under her father's control, and would revert to her birth family with the dissolution of the marriage. Any children born, however, remained with her husband; a woman had no claim to her children on her own (Arjava 1996, pp. 123–156).

Traditional Roman society, its sexual mores in particular, revolved around honor and shame: in one of Rome's foundational narratives, the raped Lucretia took her own life rather than cause her family dishonor. The Vestal Virgins, shut away from all male contact, were the sacred and traditional guardians of one of the oldest temples in Rome. As with Greek women, respectable Roman women were veiled in public and were barred from representing themselves in court, acting as witnesses for cases or guarantors for loans, or having any form of political participation. In the Roman republic, the cosmopolitan overlay of Greek religion, philosophy, and culture over the underlying Roman bedrock further established a division between the private, inward-looking space of the home and the outdoor, urban, and civic areas of the forum, the Senate, and the courts, understood as masculine spaces in which a woman's voice was not to be heard. If she were, verbal and sexual abuse would inevitably follow (Beard 2014, 2017). Central to a Roman woman's honor was her "modesty" (*pudicitia*) in dress, speech, and action: composed of both active and passive elements, it was always a complex and negotiated performance (Hylen 2019, pp. 42, 60; Wilkinson 2015).

The political breakdown of the Roman republic and the establishment of the Roman Empire under Augustus threatened to upset an already rapidly changing society. Born Octavian, the nephew and adopted son of Julius Caesar, Augustus came to the throne as a result of the naval battle of Actium in 31 BCE and the defeat of the alliance between Mark Antony and Cleopatra. Cleopatra, of course, had already had two children by Julius Caesar. Augustus, meanwhile, portrayed himself not only as the true heir of his uncle's legacy but as the representative of conservative Roman values, in contrast with the exotic Eastern luxury of the Egyptian queen. Cleopatra was, in fact, Greek, her dynasty descended from Alexander the Great's general Ptolemy, but the propaganda reassured Roman traditionalists already concerned by the spectacle of Roman matrons gallivanting about in translucent imported silks. Virgil's tragic Dido, the African queen of Carthage, represents everything that was alluring but also dangerously distracting for dutiful Roman masculinity (Beard 2016, pp. 303–313, 337–385).

It was Roman masculinity that was arguably in crisis as a result of Octavian's coup, and certainly in a state of considerable instability and transition. Over his long reign, as "first among equals" Augustus gradually marginalized the Senate as an organ of real political power, while over time its military significance would dwindle. The success of Augustus's careful self-fashioning as chief priest (*pontifex maximus*) and chief defender of the society he was manifestly transforming rested in part on a gendered rhetoric by which, as *paterfamilias* of Rome, he reminded women of their traditional responsibilities (Rüpke 2018, pp. 119–120). In 18 BCE and 9 CE, Augustus passed the *lex Iulia* and then the *lex Papia Poppaea,* a series of laws which mandated marriage and incentivized women to bear children for the empire. If a Roman woman bore three children, the formal legal requirement for male guardianship, her *tutela,* would be removed; a freed woman had to bear four children. The legislation penalized marriages that crossed class boundaries, and if a woman committed adultery, divorce was mandatory. There was no punishment for male adultery (Arjava 1996, pp. 77–78; Bleicken 2015, pp. 430–441).

In practice, however, the Augustan reforms would be inadvertently responsible for enabling, if not actually creating, the "new woman" of the Roman Empire in the first century. In fact, no emperor in the entire Julio-Claudian dynasty ever succeeded in passing on political control directly from father to son. Augustus himself never had a son and was succeeded by the child of his wife Livia's first marriage. He was forced to exile his own daughter for adultery, and in fact, seems to have enjoyed exacting a hefty profit from those honoring the law more in the breach than in the observance. The early empire is marked by a series of increasingly prominent imperial women, culminating in Nero's mother, the formidable Agrippina. Agrippina essentially acted as a co-emperor in the early years of Nero's reign, issuing coins with her face on them as well as her son's, before he ordered her murder in 59 CE (de la Bedoyère 2018; see Figure 2.3). Ultimately, more aristocratic women were emancipated through the Augustan reforms than through almost any other single measure in the history of the empire, and the political and economic circumstances of the time magnified further their impact on Roman society.

As the borders of the Roman Empire continued to swell and the plunder flowed in triumphal processions into the city, a few Roman women found themselves catapulted to positions of almost unprecedented wealth. The distinctions in class between aristocrats, let alone between a great aristocrat and an ordinary householder, became increasingly stratospheric. All of Roman society worked as a series of nesting and intersecting pyramids of client and patron relationships, with profound ramifications for religion and politics as well as trade and urban planning. Despite their ostensibly private and domestic role, women in Roman society seem to have participated fully in the Roman patronage system, ceding legal and political roles where necessary to designated male representatives acting in their names (Arjava 1996, pp. 112–114). Not least, women were able to take out and issue loans even if they could not act as guarantors for them. For aristocratic women in particular, their domestic "invisibility" could paradoxically become a great strength (Cooper 1996, p. 14).

**Figure 2.3** Agrippina the Younger and her son, the emperor Nero. *Source:* Carlos Delgado / Wikimedia Commons / CC BY-SA 3.0.

As a result, some women were able to thrive in the economic boom that resulted from Rome's conquest economy, sheltering under the umbrella provided by state-sponsored Mediterranean trade during the *Pax Romana*. Some of these women were attracted by Christian teachings: Lydia from Thyatira, for example, who is described as a merchant in the expensive purple or murex-dyed cloth. Lydia's rather geographical name may be a nickname carried over from her business dealings, even an indication that she was a freed slave. She was baptized "with her household" before inviting Paul and his companions to her home, an illustration of how women converts were instrumental in bringing others into the faith (Acts 16:15). Likewise, "Chloe's people" probably also signifies either a group from her household or her clients, while Phoebe the deacon, "a benefactor of many," may have been chosen as Paul's emissary to the Romans precisely because of her existing clientage and connections in the city (Mowczko 2018). Within the Roman Empire, Christian teachings seem to have appealed to this kind of newly influential woman whose particular status within the traditional class system of the Roman Empire was ambiguous and in transition. It may have been a significant influx of merchants which popularized the use of the codex, or the book, in early Christian circles, although the book may have caught on purely on its own technological merits (Boyle 1984, pp. 238–239; Brown 2007). It seems to have been women of means and influence, widowed and engaged in charitable works, that the author of I Timothy was encouraging toward remarriage (I Tim 2:9–15; Maier 2021).

The ongoing conquests of the Roman Empire brought not only vast quantities of goods through the capitol city but people as well: large numbers of slaves, captured as prisoners of war. Within the Roman Empire, even more became enslaved through debt, and worked as agricultural labor on huge senatorial estates or were sold into slavery as children to pay for their families' debts. Still others were kidnapped, born as the children of slaves, or were infants exposed and abandoned by their parents (Harper 2011, pp. 67–99). The bill of sale for a 10-year-old girl from Galatia survives: 280 silver denarii, when a denarius was a day's pay for a skilled laborer, a very difficult sum for one individual to raise or save on their own (Cohick 2009, p. 257). Inscriptions from Herculaneum record women slaves bought, sold, or given as surety for loans (Wallace-Hadrill 2011, pp. 143–44).

In a broad sense, slavery erased personhood in the ancient world; slaves by definition had no legal or political rights. As a consequence, while people understood slaves to have a sex – their perpetual sexual availability could be said to be one of their defining characteristics – they could not be said to have gender in Roman society, strictly speaking, because their slave status trumped any pretensions they might ordinarily have had to honor. Slave women in particular were defined by their lack of any kind of sexual honor (Osiek and MacDonald 2006, pp. 96–97). Slave marriages were not officially recognized, although the epigraphic evidence suggests that slaves themselves occasionally entered into such relationships; their children were routinely sold. That they were often treated very badly indeed is so customary it is difficult to find explicit evidence of it in classical literature (Ruden 2010, p. 192; Hopkins 1978).

At the same time, slave owners in the Roman Empire seem to have freed a huge percentage of their slaves. Most traditionally, slaves received manumission on the event of their owners' deaths, but Roman slave owners increasingly granted it during their lives; the possibility of future freedom could act as a guarantor of good behavior from the unfree. Moreover, in a society which functioned through interlocking pyramids of patron–client relationships, and in which an extensive clientage translated into political power, freed slaves could become clients of their former owners and form part of their entourage. These freed slaves formed a kind of service class; imperial freedmen often worked, in effect, as junior civil servants, and many freed slaves ran the street-level shops in Roman cities. They may not always have been much better off financially than they were before their manumission (Mouritsen 2011; Bond 2016, pp. 42–51; Newitz 2021, pp. 100–102).

Neither slaves nor former slaves in the Roman world, therefore, were defined or limited as a group by particular racial or ethnic characteristics, and they represented a fluid and diverse cross-section of the population. In the early years of the empire, when Roman citizenship was usually confined to the Italian peninsula, the boundaries between slaves and free citizens of suspect provincial groups could sometimes collapse. Crucifixion, for example, was a punishment usually reserved for slaves and political opponents of Rome of low social status. As time went on, however, freed slaves in Roman cities like Pompeii and Herculaneum became an increasingly visible presence, so much so that they may even have outnumbered freeborn citizens; like exotic Eastern imports, they triggered conservative anxieties about the degradation of Roman traditional society (Wallace-Hadrill 2011, p. 145). Freed slaves' children would be free themselves, powerfully motivating their parents, who already had nothing to lose when it came to social status. As a group, freed slaves seem to have been particularly vociferous in creating funerary inscriptions to commemorate their own names and those of their relatives (Mouritsen 2011, pp. 127–128). Roman *insulae*, its urban housing, seem to have consisted not of nuclear families but of extended households of individuals, probably ranging in status from freeborn to unfree, intimately connected to one another as neighbors and as clients and patrons of various kinds (Wallace-Hadrill 2003). Assertive, ambitious, and class-conscious, alongside the "new women" of Augustus's reforms, freed slaves in particular represent a group within Roman society to whom the more egalitarian and reformist aspects of Paul's teachings might be said to appeal.

## Pauline Paradoxes: Defining the Body of the Christian Community

It is impossible to understand the sexual morality of the ancient Mediterranean – and in turn, Paul's reorientation of Christian sexual morality – without recognizing the complex structural linkages between empire, slavery, extreme poverty, and prostitution (Glancy 2002). A Roman citizen who went to his local slave market and bought a child, male or female, could in his active sexual domination claim to mirror and ratify the conquests of the deified emperors and their empire (Williams 1999). Rome itself became something of a byword for male sexual adventure; in addition to the ranks of the official temple prostitutes, many desperately poor women had little other choice as a last resort. Many were slaves. One estimate places the cost of a prostitute in Rome as roughly equivalent to the cost of a loaf of bread. Most did not live very long (Harper 2013, pp. 45–52).

As a response, Paul advocated for sexual renunciation and celibacy as a particularly praiseworthy practice. He himself may well have been a widower (Ramelli 2021; Williams 1999, p. 12). Paul's attempt to reinvent gender and sexuality according to his understanding of Christian identity would be one of the most, if not the most, distinctive aspects of his teaching. In light of the grace of God, Paul could argue that "there is no longer Jew or Greek, there is no longer slave or free, there is no longer male and female," although this may be a form of an early Christian confession that did not originate with Paul himself (Gal 3:28; Wire 1990, pp. 122–128). In Galatians and in his epistle to the Romans, Paul's continual address to his "brothers and sisters" represents a deliberate rhetorical tactic, invoking the restoration of the "male-and-female" Edenic ideal, lost through human sin, which had become his preferred way to describe the church (Lampe 2003). Paul usually stressed the interdependence and mutuality of the genders rather than the rule by men over subordinate women, and he usually emphasized nurture, care, and love rather than the more aggressive, traditional Roman masculine virtues. Nevertheless, he did not explicitly call for either the abolition of slavery or the elimination of all existing gender hierarchies within the family.

Moreover, Paul was also trying to maintain his authority, at distance, over small and diverse churches whose members included prominent women whose ideas or religious background did not necessarily track with his own. That his language around gender and sexuality was new, even for Paul, is apparent in the vague, difficult, and even contradictory terminology that he does use, something that is often lost in modern English translations (Harper 2013, pp. 86–107; Ruden 2010, pp. 33–35). As a result, as with his position on slavery, Paul's language about women and gender shuttles back and forth between genuine innovation and cultural commonplace.

While early Christian gatherings may have been ridiculed by Roman aristocrats as a religion of women and slaves, in reality Christianity attracted converts from across the social spectrum. In a class-dominated society in which such distinctions were, if anything, widening, early Christian gatherings in house churches drew in converts at least in part because of their egalitarian appeal and their ability to break through social taboos. Precisely because these gatherings were taking place in private homes, many of which were owned by women, women's participation was protected and even privileged to some extent. Fourth-century catacomb depictions of these love feasts, such as those in the catacombs of Marcellino, Pietro, and Priscilla, reveal a pattern of women breaking bread and raising cups in a way that does not tend to appear in traditional Greek or Roman art, with call-and-response toasts of "Agape!" and "Eirēne!" "Love!" and "Peace!" (Tulloch in Osiek and Macdonald 2006, pp. 164–193; see Figure 2.4). Cana was sometimes depicted as such a meal. Generally, it seems clear that distinctions in house churches between a traditional commemorative funerary banquet, a family meal, a religious libation, and the celebration of the Eucharist were more than a little blurry (Cohick and Hughes 2017, p. 84; al-Suadi and Smit 2019).

House churches meant the close, communal worship of people who ordinarily might never have met in Roman society, much less have been brought into relationship. Paul's letters show him attempting to create a distinctive kind of religious community in this complex space. Each house church was different, however, and as a consequence, Paul's strictures on the participation of women in Christian worship throughout his letters have a distinctly improvisatory quality. Perhaps what is most striking about the epistle to the Corinthians, for example, is what it reveals about the experience of being in an early church: that both men and women were present together in worship, that both prophesied, and that women taught and were taught alongside men, and that at least some people had renounced sexual relations. Not surprisingly, people did not always know how to behave together, or did so in ways that reflected their previous religious experiences and practices.

**Figure 2.4** Fresco detail from the catacomb of SS. Marcellino e Pietro, Rome. *Source:* Unknown author / Wikimedia Commons / Public domain.

Paul's first letter to the Corinthians was sent to a wealthy, cosmopolitan community, containing both Greek and Jewish members, in which it had been reported to Paul that certain women were prophesying unveiled. It should already be apparent, as in the modern Islamic world, that veiling was an immensely complicated and multivalent concept in the ancient world, its meaning subject to ongoing negotiation. The most common associations an unveiled woman would have had for Paul's readers would have been with prostitution, slavery, and the priestesses of certain temple cults. The women of Corinth who were prophesying unveiled may have been imitating pagan religious practice, such as that of Apollo's oracle (Fiorenza 1994, pp. 229–232; Osiek and MacDonald 2006, p. 26). Archeological excavations have revealed the presence of cults to Apollo, Isis, and Demeter in the city, suggesting strong local traditions of women acting as oracles and priestesses (Marshall 2017, pp. 43–71). Unbound hair was also associated with the public performance of grief and emotional disorder. Just before her martyrdom, the woman Perpetua in the arena made sure to neaten her clothes, to tidy, and to pin up her hair (Heffernan 2012, p. 134).

In the end, Paul's advice to the Corinthian community was both complex and contradictory. In his letter, he both acknowledged women's expression in prophetic roles and controlled and limited the means by which he thought they should appear in the new, interdependent "body" of the community (Marshall 2017, pp. 215–220). Paul began his discussion by introducing the highly complicated concept of "headship," which in English is translated, "Christ is the head of every man, and the husband is the head of his wife." This may be functional and descriptive rather than proscriptive in intent (I Cor 11:1–16; Westfall 2016, p. 80; Witt 2020, pp. 121–143). Certainly Paul's statement reflected widespread Platonic influence on Greek and Jewish discourses on gender, in which women were described as originating from men; the most original point Paul made was to subordinate husbands to the ultimate authority and judgment of God (Levine and Brettler 2017, pp. 340–341). Paul underscored the mutual interdependence of the genders: "for just as woman came from man, so man comes through woman; but all things come from God" (I Cor 11:1–12). At the same time, his overall message certainly suggests that he believed an orderly Christian community was a hierarchical one, and vice versa. Likewise, Paul's subsequent advice about headcovering was broadly in keeping with both Jewish and Gentile practice at the time. However, his practical directives were, to say the least, scattered and impressionistic. In verse 10, he cautioned women against tempting the angels with their unveiled heads, which probably suggests the Corinthian women prophets were claiming a kind of angelic authority or inspiration (Wire 1990, p. 127). Paul's blanket injunction against women prophesying unveiled seems to have been intended to create a baseline for practice that did not exacerbate social and class distinctions within the church, his concern in the rest of the chapter. Nevertheless, his means for creating unity in the congregation at Corinth was the regulation of women's prophetic practice.

This need to contain the Corinthian women prophets' religious expression most likely underlies Paul's notorious injunction, in the same letter, for women to be silent in church (I Cor 14:33b–36). Certainly, it must be read in the context of the entire letter; after all, Paul has just finished describing occasions in which women were prophesying in a leadership role within the community, which he does not forbid per se. Paul had spent a significant portion of the preceding chapter counseling many other people, men and women, to be silent, to wait for one another, and to worship in an orderly manner. For this reason, later exegetes such as John Chrysostom understood the passage to apply not as a universal principle but to certain particular women who were disrupting the course of worship, perhaps by asking their husbands to explain aspects of Christian teaching with which they were unfamiliar (Behr-Sigel 1991, p. 68). One way to resolve this and other contradictions in I Corinthians is to argue for the presence of non-Pauline interpolations in the text, in one form or another, although all modern interpretations are impossible to prove (Peppiatt 2015).

In any case, the pointedness of Paul's directives, suggesting his underlying fear that certain women in Corinth were subverting his authority, passed into the later Christian tradition.

In Ephesians 5, Paul's instructions to husbands and wives argue for the mutual interdependence of individual men and women within a marriage, so strongly, in fact, that the grammar of the passage becomes almost hopelessly entangled. Paul was both imitating and subverting an already existing genre within classical literature: that of the household code, derived, not least, from Aristotle. What distinguishes the Ephesians passage most sharply from other examples of its kind is the weight of responsibility that Paul placed upon the husband within a marriage, defining his duty to his wife as one of Christ-like self-sacrifice (Witt 2020, pp. 104–108; Levine and Brettler 2017, p. 395). Nevertheless, precisely because Paul wanted marriage to mirror the relationship between Christ and the church, Paul's "code" remains an essentially hierarchical model. Likewise, Paul's brief injunction in Colossians, for wives to be subject to their husbands, and for husbands to love their wives, occurs after his exposition of his model of mutual love and interdependence which he envisioned for the whole community; moreover, Paul instructed his letter to be read in the woman Nympha's house church, probably in Laodicea (Col 3:18–19 and 4:15). However, located in the same passage as, "Slaves, obey your earthly masters in everything," it is easy to see how, in later Christian interpretations, the implicit hierarchy of Paul's injunctions tended to eclipse his more radical expressions of mutuality. Paul's public recognition of women's contributions to early Christian communities, and his efforts to define their nature and practice, thus always existed alongside more conventional statements of a hierarchical relationship between the genders.

## The Pastoral Epistles

The Pastoral letters, the epistles to Timothy in particular, use even more barbed language to describe and delineate the status and roles of women within the church. Whether or not the letter is genuinely Pauline, I Timothy seems to have been sent to the church in or near Ephesus, a place where the cult of Artemis, in that part of Asia Minor depicted as a fertility goddess, was famously strong (I Tim 1:3; see Figure 2.5). As with Paul's first letter to Corinth, it represents a reaction against the prominent place of women in that particular community. Certainly it rejects any patronage and influence wielded by women, and it unilaterally condemns women teaching men, which Paul had not done even in his letter to the Corinthians. Moreover, I Timothy rationalizes women's subordinate position as a punishment for Eve's sin, with the promise that they "should be saved through childbearing" and their continued good behavior (I Tim 2:11–15). Notably, the author's advice that these women should marry and bear children runs counter with Paul's advice elsewhere.

The tone of I Timothy in general is rhetorical and polemical, using gendered language very deliberately to polarize and motivate its more neutral and passive readers, a technique Roman rhetoric taught as a matter of course. In this reading, the frivolous young widows "who live for pleasure" are the author's rhetorical foil for what the rest of the letter describes as the proper kind of sober church leadership and governance (Maier 2021, p. 61). However, even here, the language of I Timothy and the rest of the Pastoral Epistles does not exclude women from church leadership as much as English translations might suggest, particularly when male pronouns are introduced which do not exist in the original Greek. I Timothy clearly describes parallel moral qualifications for both male and female deacons. In verse 12, "Married only once" might be better translated as "monogamous," and it is probably a reference to the *univira*, literally "one-man-woman," a small and highly respected subset of widows within the Roman population (Witt 2020, pp. 317–327; Lee 2011, pp. 121–130).

**Figure 2.5** The Lady of Ephesus, Ephesus Archaeological Museum. *Source:* Gargarapalvin / Wikimedia Commons / CC BY-SA 3.0.

The Pastoral Epistles may represent the beginnings of a masculine takeover of an increasingly institutionalized church. However, a certain amount of caution is necessary. These texts are by definition proscriptive, even aspirational, and as with any premodern law code, may not reflect social reality in Ephesus, much less universally or generally across the Mediterranean. Critics like the pagan Celsus argued that women, often lower-class or mercantile types, were playing a significant role in early Christian groups; although this was no doubt a rhetorical ploy, it does not seem to be entirely without foundation (MacDonald 2003). Of the leaders of Christian communities named by Celsus, five were women: Helen, Marcellina, Salome, Mariamne, and Martha. Marcellina and Salome became infamous as the leaders of a heretical group in Rome, the Carpocratians, condemned by Irenaeus, the bishop of Lyons (Lewis 2021, pp. 118–122; Miller 2005, pp. 17–18). Mariamne is a charismatic presence in the apocryphal *Acts of Philip*, where she is described as his sister and an evangelist in her own right; Mariamne was perhaps intended to be Mary Magdalene (Kateusz 2019). Ignatius, the bishop of Antioch and one of the great apologists for the status of the bishop within the church, nevertheless also greets Tavia and her household in Smyrna, "whom I boast is established in faith and love both fleshly and spiritual," and Alke, "a name dear to me." That he says nothing more rather underscores the fact that she was generally known in the Christian community; this may be the same Alke who was mentioned in the *Martyrdom of Polycarp* as having a pagan brother who was resistant to the faith (Schoedel 1985, pp. 247, 253; Trevett 2006, pp. 217–226).

## Thecla, an Early Christian Superhero

In this way, proscriptive Pauline discourses about orderly Christian worship existed alongside and were subverted by the prominent, visible role played by women, both in Paul's letters and in those of bishops like Ignatius who modeled their ministry after his example. Even more than Mariamne, the most dynamic and thrilling early Christian woman of the time was the probably legendary virgin-martyr Thecla. At this distance, disentangling Thecla's martyr-cult, its official life of Thecla, and the stories which surrounded her legend from the apocryphal *Acts of Paul and Thecla*, is a hopeless task; likewise, whether shrine or *Acts* came first is uncertain. Tertullian knew of the *Acts of Paul and Thecla*, meaning the text must have been written before 200 CE, and claimed it was written by a *presbyter*. Since the cult preceded some of the most intense periods of persecution for the Christian church, any historical evidence may well have been destroyed (Voicu 2017). The later, fifth-century life describes Paul's conversion of Thecla and his granting the apostolate to her, as well as permission to baptize. In Seleucia in Syria, she founded a double monastery of celibates, both men and women, which continued to exist at the purported site of her grave. Despite the fact that the shrine had no body, both Gregory of Nazianzen and the Spanish pilgrim Egeria visited the shrine in the late fourth century; Egeria describes the woman Marthana as the abbess of the mixed community at that time. In the fifth century, two women ascetics from Syria, Marana and Cyra, were said to have left their enclosure only twice in 42 years, once to visit Thecla's shrine (Theodoret of Cyrrhus 1985, pp. 183–185).

*The Acts of Paul and Thecla* gives the reader a much more stirring narrative. According to the *Acts*, Paul traveled to Iconium (present-day Konya), where the beautiful Thecla rapidly became a devotee of Christian teaching, despite the fact that, because she was listening through a window, she only heard Paul's voice. Her mother, Theocleia, went to Thecla's fiancé, Thamyrus, with her concerns, and they pleaded with Thecla. She ignored them, however, and bribed the jailer to let her visit Paul in prison, where she sat at his feet and continued to listen to his teaching. When this became known and she and Paul were called before the authorities, her distraught mother called for her disobedient daughter to be burned alive. But like a female Daniel, and with similar powers over wild beasts, Thecla survived being stripped naked, burned, and fed to the lions, and even found a foster-mother in one of the bystanders, Queen Tryphaena. When thrown into a pool filled with ferocious seals, Thecla baptized herself in the water and the seals did not harm her. All further efforts at torture failed, until the exhausted Roman authorities simply released her. Thecla then rejoined Paul, handed over Tryphaena's gifts to her to be given to the poor, and continued her ministry. In her advanced age, after an attempted gang rape by a group of thugs, she vanished through the rock wall of her cell and was never seen again (Clark 1983, pp. 78–88; Miller 2005, pp. 156–166; Cohick and Hughes 2017, pp. 1–25; Streete 2009, pp. 79–102).

It is just possible that *The Acts of Paul and Thecla* were written by a woman. Certainly the story was written in the style of the ubiquitous Greek romances of the day, and like them, it became immensely popular, as much as any contemporary action-hero or comic-book heroine today (Cooper 1996, pp. 20–44, 50–51). Depictions of Thecla, often surrounded by wild beasts, were extremely common in early ascetic communities, often appearing on pilgrim flasks, and seem to have been carried as talismans against rape and violence (see Figure 2.6). Thecla became a very popular personal name for girls, and she was a model frequently invoked in early Christian hagiography (Davis 2001).

Thecla looms so large in the landscape, not least because of her resonance with later monasticism, that she almost blots out early forms of devotion to the Virgin Mary. However, it is also in this period, perhaps as early as the mid-second century in Egypt or Syria, that an anonymous author composed the so-called "Protoevangelium" of James (the title was added later), clearly with an eye to responding to the pagan attacks and polemics of the likes of Celsus (Osiek and MacDonald 2006, p. 53; Schmid and Schröter 2021, pp. 254–255). As a consequence, the author of the *Protoevangelium* describes Mary's background as aristocratic and even priestly. After her miraculously premature birth to Anna and Joachim, the young Mary is described as being raised in the Temple, entering the

**Figure 2.6** Thecla with wild beasts and angels, Nelson-Atkins Museum of Art, Kansas City. *Source:* Ancient World Magazine.

Holy of Holies twice, and is present in the Temple grounds when the annunciation from Gabriel occurs (Miller 2005, pp. 296–301). Devotion to the Virgin seems to have been both powerful and widespread, centering particularly on Jerusalem; Ignatius of Antioch, for example, has a particular devotion to the Virgin. It may have been the Virgin and not the Magdalene who was intended as the heroine of the apocryphal *Gospel of Mary* (Shoemaker 2016, pp. 74–86; 2018, pp. 137–180).

## Prophecy and Secret Knowledge: Women in Gnosticism and Montanism

Despite later Protestant historiography which depicted Marian devotion as an aberration of true Christian teaching, Mary does seem to have been a powerful presence in early Christian circles. Some of the people most fascinated with her in this early period also seem to have had some gnostic leanings, which may explain the reticence of many later Christian writers to acknowledge these texts and traditions. As with Marcellina and Salome, there seem to have been some women among the gnostic teachers (Brakke 2010, pp. 48–49). A veritable thicket of gnostic tradition sprang up around the figure of Mary Magdalene as chief among the disciples, or as Jesus's wife or lover (Schaberg and Debaufre 2006; Pardee 2020; Fiori 2020). Other teachers used Christian texts now considered canonical, alongside or interpreted according to gnostic teachings. As with the pseudonymous or apocryphal texts, these sometimes represented adaptations of existing but lesser-known traditions.

Gnostic thought frequently described feminine beings and personifications, such as Nōrea and the figure of Wisdom, and often included male–female pairs (Brakke 2010, pp. 57, 64–67). As a consequence, it is tempting to associate gnostic circles with women's leadership or with a particularly elevated understanding of women's sacramental participation, particularly in contrast with the patriarchal emphasis of proto-orthodox clergy. However, caution is advisable (Lewis 2021). Gnosticism may have been perfectly correct in its assessment of the increasingly patriarchal bent of bishops like Ignatius and Irenaeus. Its impish "feminism" probably represents a rhetorical gambit to annoy and provoke church authority rather than any real commitment to elevate women's status – Mary Magdalene used to cut Peter and Paul down to size. Most gnostic teachers do seem to have been men, and their use of feminine personifications and archetypes were usually part of a gendered hierarchy within their larger mythology, and may well have acted as a substitute for concrete engagement with actual women. "Woman is the work of Satan" is a gnostic teaching, after all (Fiorenza 1994, p. 271). Given gnosticism's exclusive, inner-circle ethos, and the gnostic rejection of flesh, matter, and the body, it does not seem likely that most ordinary women would have found a comfortable haven in gnostic circles.

Gnostic texts and teachings, however, continued to circulate in a way that filled many bishops of the early church with concern. Certain priests and teachers of the church at this time, such as Clement of Alexandria, began to agitate strongly in favor of traditional marriage in a way that suggests they were concerned about women's asceticism, Thecla-style (Osiek and MacDonald 2006, pp. 138–139; Miller 2005, pp. 262–267; Clark 1983, pp. 47–55). Conversely, the increasing prominence of women's asceticism, either in exclusively female communities or in dual-gender communities, such as Thecla's monastery or the Therapeutae and Therapeutridae described by Philo in Alexandria, may well have been a response to the aspirations of Christian bishops and their sidelining of earlier women's involvement in church communities (Eusebius 2019, Bk. II, Sections 17–23; Taylor 2021).

Prophecy remained a powerful tool by which certain women could subvert and trump more institutionalized and hierarchical church authority. It is perhaps no coincidence, therefore, that around 165 CE, North Africa and certain parts of the eastern Mediterranean saw the appearance of Montanism, the "Phrygian heresy" or "New Prophecy" of one male teacher, Montanus, and two women prophetesses, Maximilla and Priscilla. These women adopted celibate lifestyles, alongside the practice of ecstatic, apocalyptic prophecy, in which Maximilla described her own role as that of an interpreter of the Holy Spirit: "Do not hear me but hear Christ" (Trevett 1996, pp. 151–172). The Montanists seem to have appointed not only women *presbyterae* but also women bishops on occasion. One funerary inscription in Usak, Turkey, from as early as around 200 CE and possibly connected with Montanism, reads "Ammion, *presbytera*" (Tabbernee 2021; Madigan and Osiek 2005, pp. 169–170).

Montanism spread around the Mediterranean and had a surprising degree of longevity in the ancient world. Montanist teachings did not advocate for its adherents to separate from society, and its house churches continued to remain under the jurisdiction of their local bishop. The North African teacher Tertullian could complain that women in his congregation were using the example of Thecla as a precedent for baptizing others during a moment in his career when he seems to have become a Montanist himself (Tertullian 2006, Bk. I, Section 17; Madigan 2021, pp. 264–269). The martyr Perpetua, who died in 203 in Carthage, is described as a living and embodied conduit of the power of the Holy Spirit. Perpetua's vivid and intimate visions of Christ and the spiritual world recorded in the *Martyrdom of Felicity and Perpetua* portray her, not least, as acting as a mediator in ecclesiastical disputes between male clergy. Whether Perpetua was an acknowledged Montanist prophetess or was merely impacted by aspects of Montanist practice as a leader of her local Christian community is perhaps an anachronistic distinction to make (Heffernan 2012, p. 131). Nevertheless, the Montanist emphasis on prophetic leadership, which could be exercised by women on occasion, became the focus of attacks by the episcopate and determined the course of future debates around women's participation and sacramental ordination in the church (Miller 2005, pp. 36–38; Fiorenza 1994, pp. 306–309).

One consequence of the spread of gnostic and Montanist teachings seems to have been the firming up of congregational widows (*ontōs chērai*) as an institutionalized and recognized group within some churches (Thurston 1989, pp. 44, 69–71, 90). As bishops increasingly shouldered the role of patrons of their local church, replacing the earlier, house-church model, the role of the widow became more complex and distinct from that of the deaconess, who particularly worked with catechumens being prepared for baptism. The Pastoral Epistles had already outlined the proper moral qualifications of a Christian widow, suggesting that she hold a kind of public or authoritative status within the community. Polycarp once described widows as "altars of God," an image repeated often in later church tradition, suggesting the degree to which their role was defined by both charity and intercession. They were not supposed to marry a second time; Tertullian disapprovingly records a case of a virgin veiled as one of the widows. In Alexandria, both Clement and Origen saw widows as holding authority, even a kind of office, within the church, while Origen permitted women to teach in the context of a private home. The *Didache*, or the *Teaching of the Apostles*, forbid widows to participate in either teaching or baptism with a vehemence that suggests widows were doing both on occasion, and as a group distinct from the deaconesses (Madigan and Osiek 2005, pp. 106–116). *The Shepherd of Hermas* notes that the woman Grapté would pass along its revelations "to the widows," suggesting both that they were a recognizable group within the church, and that Grapté had a form of teaching authority (Trevett 2006, pp. 154–159).

By the end of the second century, the office of the bishop had become centrally important, partly as a means of preserving and defending doctrine, and more poignantly, to offer leadership to churches that were beginning to attract unwelcome attention from the Roman authorities. Precisely as the Christian community emerged into public spaces and farther away from private, enclosed house churches, women's leadership and their socio-economic role as patrons of private churches became one casualty in the ascent of the episcopate. Women's roles as *presbyterae*, and in positions of public leadership generally, became polarized and weaponized in the debate against gnosticism and Montanism. However, particularly in the Greek East, traditions of gender complementarity within the church were so deeply engrained that women continued in positions of leadership as widows, deaconesses, and even as *presbyterae*, as tomb inscriptions suggest. Ultimately, it cannot be said that the only evidence of women's ordained leadership within the church belongs to the gnostics and the Montanists, that they were distinct groups, or that the totality of the evidence can be easily dismissed as "heretical." The evidence is too geographically widespread, and reflects the diversity of Christian practice that existed at such an early date.

However much bishops may have wanted to regulate and control women's voices, they soon found they needed them. Despite the taboo on women's voices being heard in public, martyrdom very quickly became the exception to the rule in the later Christian tradition. That women, even slave women, could act with bravery and integrity was evidence of the power of the Holy Spirit working in them and of the power of the gospel. In a famous letter to the emperor Trajan, Pliny the Younger records the interrogation and torture of two slave women he describes as *ministrae* of a local Christian church (Pliny 2003, Bk. 10, letter 96; Madigan and Osiek 2005, pp. 26–27; Cook 2018). The Orthodox Church commemorates the martyrdom of Holy Sophia (*Agia Sophia*) and her three daughters, Faith, Hope, and Charity (*Pisti, Elpida, and Agapi*) under the emperor Hadrian around 126 CE. Not surprisingly, in later Christian tradition the historical Sophia has become hopelessly confused, historically and liturgically, with the figure of Holy Wisdom from the book of Proverbs (Marker 2007, pp. 15–16). One of Origen's protégés, the virgin Potamiaena from Alexandria, was martyred with her mother under Septimius Severus, converting the soldier who executed her (Eusebius 2019, Bk. VI, Section 5; *Acts* 1954, vol. II, pp. 132–135; Miller 2005, pp. 45–46). Near Pergamum, the woman Agathonicê, witnessing the execution of two of her fellow Christians, joined them with the cry, "Here is a meal that has been prepared for me! I must eat and partake of this glorious repast!" (*Acts* 1954, vol. II, pp. 26–29; Miller 2005, pp. 43–45). In the Greek colony of Lyon in southern Gaul, Blandina the slave was hung on a stake to be eaten by the wild beasts. As her fellow Christians watched, "she was seen to have the form of a cross. . .for in her contest they saw with their external eyes, through the sister, the one who was crucified on their behalf" (Eusebius 2019, Bk. V, Section 41; *Acts* 1954, vol. II, pp. 62–85; Behr 2006, pp. 121–122).

# References

Musurillo, H. (ed.) (1954). *Acts of the Christian Martyrs*, vol. 2. Oxford: Clarendon Press.

Al-Suadi, S. and Smit, P.-B. (ed.) (2019). *The T&T Clark Handbook to Early Christian Meals in the Greco-Roman World*. London: Bloomsbury.

Aristotle (1972). De generatione animalium I (with passages from II.1–3). In: *De partibus animalium I and De generatione animalium I (with passages from II.1–3)* (trans. D.M. Balme). Oxford: Clarendon Press.

Arjava, A. (1996). *Women and Law in Late Antiquity*. Oxford: Clarendon Press.

Arlandson, J.M. (1997). *Women, Class, and Society in Early Christianity: Models from Luke-Acts*. Peabody: Hendrickson.

Bauckham, R. (2002). *Gospel Women: Studies of the Named Women in the Gospels*. Grand Rapids: Eerdmans.

Beard, M. (2014). The public voice of women. *London Review of Books* 36: 6.

Beard, M. (2016). *SPQR: A History of Ancient Rome*. London: Profile Books.

Beard, M. (2017). *Women and Power: A Manifesto*. New York: Liveright Publishing Corporation.

de la Bedoyère, G. (2018). *Domina: The Women Who Made Imperial Rome*. New Haven: Yale University Press.

Behr, J. (2006). *The Mystery of Christ: Life in Death*. Crestwood: St. Vladimir's Seminary Press.

Behr-Sigel, E. (1991). *The Ministry of Women in the Church* (trans. S. Bigham). Crestwood: St. Vladimir's.

Bleicken, J. (2015). *Augustus: The Biography* (trans. A. Bell). London: Allen Lane.

Bond, S.E. (2016). *Trade and Taboo: Disreputable Professions in the Roman Mediterranean*. Ann Arbor: University of Michigan Press.

Boyle, L. (1984). *Medieval Latin Paleography: A Bibliographic Introduction*. Toronto: University of Toronto Press.

Brakke, D. (2010). *The Gnostics: Myth, Ritual, and Diversity in Early Christianity*. Cambridge: Harvard University Press.

van Bremen, R. (1996). *The Limits of Participation: Women and Civic Life in the Greek East in the Hellenistic and Roman Periods*. Amsterdam: J.C. Gieben.

Brenk, F. (2009). "Great Royal Spouse who Protects her Brother Osiris": Isis in the Isaeum at Pompeii. In: *Mystic Cults in Magna Graecia* (ed. G. Casadio and P.A. Johnston), 217–234. Austin: University of Texas Press.

Brinkhof, J.H.A. (2018). Philip, one of the seven in acts (6:1–6; 8:4–40; 21:8). In: *Deacons and Diakonia in Early Christianity* (ed. B.J. Koet, E. Murphy and E. Ryökäs), 79–90. Tübingen: Mohr Siebeck.

Brooten, B.J. (1982). *Women Leaders in the Ancient Synagogue: Inscriptional Evidence and Background Issues*. Brown Judaic Studies 36. Atlanta: Scholars Press.

Brown, M. (2007). The triumph of the codex: the manuscript book before 1100. In: *A Companion to the History of the Book* (ed. S. Eliot and J. Rose), 179–193. Malden: Blackwell.

Clark, E.A. (1983). *Women in the Early Church*. Collegeville: Liturgical Press.

Cohick, L.H. (2009). *Women in the World of the Earliest Christians: Illuminating Ancient Ways of Life*. Grand Rapids: Baker Academic.

Cohick, L.H. and Hughes, A.B. (2017). *Christian Women in the Patristic World*. Grand Rapids: Baker Academic.

Cook, J.G. (2018). Pliny's tortured *ministrae*: female deacons in the ancient church? In: *Deacons and Diakonia in Early Christianity* (ed. B.J. Koet, E. Murphy and E. Ryökäs), 133–148. Tübingen: Mohr Siebeck.

Cooper, K. (1996). *The Virgin and the Bride: Idealized Womanhood in Late Antiquity*. Cambridge: Harvard University Press.

Davidson, J.N. (2016). *Courtesans and Fishcakes: The Consuming Passions of Classical Athens*. London: Fontana Press.

Davis, S.J. (2001). *The Cult of St. Thecla: A Tradition of Women's Piety in Late Antiquity*. Oxford: Oxford University Press.

Epp, E.J. (2005). *Junia: The First Woman Apostle*. Minneapolis: Fortress Press.

Errington, R.M. (2008). *A History of the Hellenistic World, 323–30 BC*. Malden: Blackwell.

Eusebius of Caesarea (2019). *The History of the Church: A New Translation* (trans. J.M. Schott). Oakland: University of California Press.

Fiorenza, E.S. (1994). *In Memory of Her: A Feminist Theological Reconstruction of Christian Origins, 10th anniversary edition*. New York: Herder and Herder.

Fiori, E. (2020). The vine and the net-caster: Mandaean and Manichaean transformations of the Magdalene. In: *Mary Magdalene from the New Testament to the New Age and Beyond* (ed. E.F. Lupieri), 79–104. Leiden: Brill.

Fleming, R. (2000). *Medicine and the Making of Roman Women: Gender, Nature, and Authority from Celsus to Galen*. Oxford: Oxford University Press.

Glancy, J.A. (2002). *Slavery in Early Christianity*. Oxford: Oxford University Press.

Grabbe, L.L. (2008). *A History of the Jews and Judaism in the Second Temple Period. Volume 2: The Coming of the Greeks: The Early Hellenistic Period (335–175 BCE)*. London: Bloomsbury.

Harper, K. (2011). *Slavery in the Late Roman World, AD 275–425*. Cambridge: Cambridge University Press.

Harper, K. (2013). *From Shame to Sin: The Christian Transformation of Sexual Morality in Late Antiquity*. Cambridge: Harvard University Press.

Heffernan, T.J. (ed.) and trans.(2012). *The Passion of Perpetua and Felicity*. Oxford: Oxford University Press.

Hopkins, K. (1978). *Conquerors and Slaves*. Cambridge: Cambridge University Press.

Hylen, S.E. (2019). *Women in the New Testament World*. Oxford: Oxford University Press.

Ilan, T. (2010). Women in Qumran and the Dead Sea Scrolls. In: *The Oxford Handbook of the Dead Sea Scrolls* (ed. T.H. Lim and J.J. Collins). Oxford: Oxford University Press.

Kateusz, A. (2019). *Mary and Early Christian Women: Hidden Leadership*. London: Palgrave Macmillan.

Kovelman, A. (2005). *Between Alexandria and Jerusalem: The Dynamic of Jewish and Hellenistic Culture*. Leiden: Brill.

Lampe, P. (2003). The language of equality in early Christian house churches: a constructivist approach. In: *Early Christian Families in Context: An Interdisciplinary Dialogue* (ed. D.L. Balch and C. Osiek), 73–83. Grand Rapids: Eerdmans.

Lee, D. (2011). *The Ministry of Women in the New Testament: Reclaiming the Biblical Vision for Church Leadership*. Grand Rapids: Baker Academic.

Levine, A.-J. (2014). *Short Stories by Jesus: The Enigmatic Parables of a Controversial Rabbi*. New York: Harper Collins.

Levine, A.-J. (2017). Bearing false witness: common errors made about early Judaism. In: *The Jewish Annotated New Testament*, 2e (ed. A.-J. Levine and M.Z. Brettler), 759–763. Oxford: Oxford University Press.

Levine, A.-J. and Brettler, M.Z. (ed.) (2017). *The Jewish Annotated New Testament*, 2e. Oxford: Oxford University Press.

Lewis, N.D. (2021). Women in gnosticism. In: *Patterns of Women's Leadership in Early Christianity* (ed. J.E. Taylor and I.L.E. Ramelli), 109–129. Oxford: Oxford University Press.

Lieu, J. (2016). *Neither Jew nor Greek? Constructing Early Christianity*. London: Bloomsbury.

Llewelyn-Jones, L. (2001). *Aphrodite's Tortoise: The Veiled Women of Ancient Greece*. London: Classical Press of Wales.

Long, A.A. (1993). Hellenistic ethics and philosophical power. In: *Hellenistic History and Culture* (ed. P. Green), 138–167. Berkeley: University of California Press.

MacDonald, M.Y. (2003). Was Celsus right? The role of women in the expansion of early Christianity. In: *Early Christian Families in Context: An Interdisciplinary Dialogue* (ed. D.L. Balch and C. Osiek), 157–184. Grand Rapids: Eerdmans.

Madigan, K. (2021). The meaning of *presbytera* in byzantine and early medieval Christianity. In: *Patterns of Women's Leadership in Early Christianity* (ed. J.E. Taylor and I.L.E. Ramelli), 261–289. Oxford: Oxford University Press.

Madigan, K. and Osiek, C. (2005). *Ordained Women in the Early Church: A Documentary History*. Baltimore: Johns Hopkins University Press.

Maier, H.O. (2021). The entrepreneurial widows of I Timothy. In: *Patterns of Women's Leadership in Early Christianity* (ed. J.E. Taylor and I.L.E. Ramelli), 59–73. Oxford: Oxford University Press.

Marker, G. (2007). *Imperial Saint: The Cult of St. Catherine and the Dawn of Female Rule in Russia*. DeKalb: Northern Illinois University Press.

Marshall, J.E. (2017). *Women Praying and Prophesying in Corinth*. Tübingen: Mohr Siebeck.

McClure, L. (2018). Introduction. In: *Making Silence Speak: Women's Voices in Greek Literature and Society* (ed. A. Lardinois and L. McClure). Princeton: Princeton University Press.

Miller, P.C. (2005). *Women in Early Christianity: Translations from Greek Texts*. Washington D.C.: Catholic University Press.

Mouritsen, H. (2011). *The Freedman in the Roman World*. Leiden: Cambridge University Press.

Mowczko, M. (2018). What did Phoebe's position and ministry as diakonos of the church at Cenchrea involve? In: *Deacons and Diakonia in Early Christianity* (ed. B.J. Koet, E. Murphy and E. Ryökäs), 91–102. Tübingen: Mohr Siebeck.

Newitz, A. (2021). *Four Lost Cities: A Secret History of the Urban Age*. New York: W.W. Norton and Co.

Osiek, C. and MacDonald, M.Y., with Janet H. Tulloch (2006). *A Woman's Place: House Churches in Early Christianity*. Minneapolis: Fortress Press.

Pardee, C.G. (2020). The gnostic Magdalene: Mary as disciple and reader. In: *Mary Magdalene from the New Testament to the New Age and Beyond* (ed. E.F. Lupieri), 50–78. Leiden: Brill.

Parks, S., Sheinfeld, S., and Warren, M.J.C. (2021). *Jewish and Christian Women in the Ancient Mediterranean*. Abingdon: Routledge.

Pedersen, R. (2006). *The Lost Apostle: Searching for the Truth about Junia*. San Francisco: Jossey-Bass.

Peppiatt, L. (2015). *Women and Worship in Corinth: Paul's Rhetorical Arguments in 1 Corinthians*. Eugene: Cascade Books.

Pliny (2003). *The Letters of the Younger Pliny* (trans. B. Radice). London: Penguin.

Ramelli, I.L.E. (2021). Colleagues of apostles, presbyters, and bishops: women *syzygoi* in ancient Christian communities. In: *Patterns of Women's Leadership in Early Christianity* (ed. J.E. Taylor and I.L.E. Ramelli), 26–58. Oxford: Oxford University Press.

Ruden, S. (2010). *Paul among the People: The Apostle Reinterpreted and Reimagined in His Own Time*. New York: Image Books.

Rüpke, J. (2018). *Pantheon: A New History of Roman Religion*. Princeton: Princeton University Press.

Satlow, M.L. (2017). Marriage and divorce. In: *The Jewish Annotated New Testament*, 2e (ed. A.-J. Levine and M.Z. Brettler), 608–611. Oxford: Oxford University Press.

Satz, D. and Okin, S.M. (2013). *Women in Western Political Thought*. Princeton: Princeton University Press.

Sawyer, D.F. (1996). *Women and Religion in the First Christian Centuries*. London: Routledge.

Schaberg, J., with Melanie Johnson Debaufre (2006). *Mary Magdalene Understood*. New York: Continuum.

Schama, S. (2013). *The Story of the Jews: Finding the Words, 1000 BC–1492 AD*. New York: Ecco.

Schmid, K. and Schröter, J. (2021). *The Making of the Bible: From the First Fragments to Sacred Scripture* (trans. P. Lewis. Cambridge, MA: Belknap Press.

Schoedel, W.R. (1985). *A Commentary on the Letters of Ignatius of Antioch*. Philadelphia: Fortress Press.

Shoemaker, S. (2016). *Mary in Early Christian Faith and Devotion*. New Haven: Yale University Press.

Shoemaker, S. (2018). *The Dormition and Assumption Apocrypha*. Leuven: Peeters.

Streete, G.P.C. (2009). *Redeemed Bodies: Women Martyrs in Early Christianity*. Louisville: Westminster John Knox Press.

Tabbernee, W. (2021). Women office holders in Montanism. In: *Patterns of Women's Leadership in Early Christianity* (ed. J.E. Taylor and I.L.E. Ramelli), 151–179. Oxford: Oxford University Press.

Talbot, A.-M. (2001). *Women and Religious Life in Byzantium*. Aldershot: Ashgate.

Taylor, J.E. (2021). Gendered space: Eusebius on the Therapeutae and the "Megiddo church". In: *Patterns of Women's Leadership in Early Christianity* (ed. J.E. Taylor and I.L.E. Ramelli), 290–301. Oxford: Oxford University Press.

Tertullian, S.D. (2006). *De baptismo et de oratione: Latin and German*. Turnhout: Brepols.

Theodoret of Cyrrhus (1985). *A History of the Monks of Syria* (trans. R.M. Price). Kalamazoo: Cistercian Publications.

Thurston, B.B. (1989). *The Widows: A Woman's Ministry in the Early Church*. Minneapolis: Fortress Press.

Trevett, C. (1996). *Gender, Authority, and the New Prophecy*. Cambridge: Cambridge University Press.

Trevett, C. (2006). *Christian Women and the Time of the Apostolic Fathers (AD c. 80–160): Corinth, Rome, and Asia Minor*. Cardiff: University of Wales Press.

Voicu, S.J. (2017). Thecla in the Christian east. In: *Thecla: Paul's Disciple and Saint in the East and West* (ed. J.W. Barber, J.N. Brewer, T. Nicolas and A. Puig i Tàrrech), 47–68. Leuven: Peeters.

Wallace-Hadrill, A. (2003). *Domus* and *insulae* in Rome: families and housefuls. In: *Early Christian Families in Context: An Interdisciplinary Dialogue* (ed. D.L. Balch and C. Osiek), 3–18. Grand Rapids: Eerdmans.

Wallace-Hadrill, A. (2011). *Herculaneum: Past and Future*. London: Frances Lincoln.

Waterfield, R. (2018). *Creators, Conquerors, and Citizens: A History of Ancient Greece*. Oxford: Oxford University Press.

Westfall, C.L. (2016). *Paul and Gender: Reclaiming the Apostle's Vision for Men and Women in Christ*. Grand Rapids: Baker Academic.

Wilkinson, K. (2015). *Women and Modesty in Late Antiquity*. Cambridge: Cambridge University Press.

Williams, C. (1999). *Roman Homosexuality: Ideologies of Masculinity in Classical Antiquity*. Oxford: Oxford University Press.

Wire, A.C. (1990). *The Corinthian Women Prophets: A Reconstruction through Paul's Rhetoric*. Minneapolis: Fortress Press.

Witt, W.G. (2020). *Icons of Christ: A Biblical and Systematic Theology for Women's Ordination*. Waco: Baylor University Press.

Wright, N.T. (2013). *Paul and the Faithfulness of God*, vol. 2. Minneapolis: Fortress Press.

# 3

# From Agnes to Sant'Agnese

Women as Witnesses, 200–350

In the Piazza Navona in Rome, if one moves past Bernini's extravagant baroque fountains and enters Borromini's church dominating the square, in a side chapel one may see preserved the tiny, delicate skull of a 13-year-old girl. The skull belongs to Agnes, martyred according to Christian tradition around 301 CE. Turned over to the Roman authorities by a thwarted suitor, Agnes was stripped naked, only to have her hair miraculously grow to preserve her modesty, while the fire lit to burn her went out at her prayers. Eventually, her throat was cut, like the lamb which remains her symbol in Christian iconography. Small but formidable, the rest of Agnes's body remains preserved with her freed slave and sister-martyr, Emerentiana, in the much older church of Sant'Agnese fuori le mura, "outside the walls" on the Via Nomentana and the traditional center of the saint's cult. Together, these women saints and the fourth-century church built around their relics form the heart of a veritable early Christian pilgrimage complex, including the nearby catacombs and the great mausoleum turned baptistery of Constantina, the daughter of the first Christian Roman emperor, Constantine I (r. 306–337) (Masson 2009, pp. 193–194, 362–367; Clark 1983, pp. 106–114; Visser 2000; see Figures 3.1–3.2).

From two executed teenage girls to the blossoming of a martyr's cult so important it attracted the patronage of the Roman imperial family is a vast leap, even more so given that it happened in only a few decades. Christianity's surreal somersault from persecuted minority to publicly recognized religion, awash with imperial donations, to the faithful felt like an act of divine deliverance as momentous as the parting of the Red Sea. Working in Constantine's court, early Christian historians interpreted the emperor's conversion in 312 as only the final flourish in a long, triumphant drama in which the power of God was seen to be working miraculously through the bodies of the martyrs, many of them women. Stories of Jewish martyrs found in the books of Maccabees had contrasted the woman who lost her seven sons and remained resolute in her faith with the bestial, fruitless rage of the tyrant Antiochus Epiphanes (2 Macc 7). Taking up language from Paul and the epistle to the Hebrews, Christian writers described the martyrs as spiritual athletes in competition with Satan and the demons, running to win an eternal crown (Eph 6:12; Heb 11–12). Against such a vast and cosmic backdrop, the Roman Empire's judicial machinery could sometimes seem strangely irrelevant, as the martyr stories portrayed Roman officials as mere tools of demons. A polemical, triumphant narrative of Christian identity crystallized around the martyrs which, while it derived in part from the letters of Paul, might well have been unrecognizable to earlier generations and even to Paul himself (Lieu 2016, pp. 223–243). Not only did the martyrs' stories describe a commitment to Christian belief that was so fervent and so complete a young girl would be willing to die for it, it created a narrative and a history of true Christian belief as a new identity, separate from that of demonic, "pagan" Rome.

*A History of Women in Christianity to 1600*, First Edition. Hannah Matis.
© 2023 John Wiley & Sons Ltd. Published 2023 by John Wiley & Sons Ltd.

**Figure 3.1**  The skull of Agnes, Sant'Agnese in Agone, Rome. *Source:* Michaelphillipr / Wikimedia Commons / CC BY-SA 3.0.

**Figure 3.2**  The mausoleum of S. Costanza, Rome. *Source:* Parish of Santa Agnese fuori le Mura / Wikimedia Commons / CC BY-SA 2.0.

## The Third-Century Crisis and the Transformation of the Empire

The third century CE was a historical moment of almost unprecedented vulnerability for the Roman Empire, a time of extreme crisis and transformation as great as anything that occurred two hundred years later. The causes were multifactorial, stemming, not least, from fluctuations in climate and the spread of disease. The Roman emperor Septimius Severus was himself North African, his dynasty drawing to Rome a generation of provincial aristocrats from beyond the old vested interests of Italy. In 212, his son Caracalla granted universal Roman citizenship to all who lived within the boundaries of the empire. Even more than the Christian martyrs, however, the wild beasts of the arena were themselves harbingers of the diseases that inevitably resurfaced in a world interconnected by trade. In the 240s, the eastern and most populous half of the empire saw drought so extreme it appears to have affected the flooding of the Nile, an almost unheard-of occurrence. The so-called "plague of Cyprian," named after the martyred bishop of Carthage who described the disaster in his sermons, originated in Ethiopia and struck in the 260s, killing as much as half the population of Alexandria in Egypt. Although the identity of the pathogen is not known for certain, it may well have been a kind of pandemic influenza not so very different in its effects from COVID-19 (Harper 2017, pp. 2–4, 122–145). Meanwhile, the silver currency was so devalued that inflation spiraled out of control and the copper coinage virtually collapsed. Whole regions of the empire broke away from Rome's control, including the wealthy trading cities of Syria under the leadership of the glamorous queen Zenobia of Palmyra, who claimed to be a descendant of Cleopatra (Watson 1999, pp. 57–88). Beyond Syria, a reinvigorated Persia posed an ongoing and even more critical threat on the empire's eastern border. In 260, the emperor Valerian was captured by Persian forces at Edessa and carried off into captivity, an unprecedented blow for Roman military prestige.

The Roman Empire which re-emerged from the Third-Century Crisis found its nature subtly changed. Not least, the *Pax Romana* was definitively over: Roman citizens now lived with the constant presence of, and the no less constant tax burden of maintaining, a professionalized army and fortified frontiers in Syria and along the Rhine and Danube rivers. Traditional avenues of promotion, political and military, for young Roman aristocrats were increasingly closed off, in comparison with the opportunities garnered by the *cursus honorum* in previous generations. Those who could sought refuge on private estates, and cultivated highly personal experiences in religion and philosophy; for these few it was a much more "introverted" age (Brown 1971, pp. 49–54). For the rest, slaves made up a tenth of the population and as much as a fifth of the labor force on the enormous senatorial estates; by one estimate, one tenth of the population owned another tenth, with another huge percentage surviving on subsistence-level day wages (Harper 2011, pp. 67–99). Not inherently decayed from an earlier Augustan ideal, this period, which saw its military, political, economic, and religious life reinvented and transformed, should be understood on its own terms. Now customarily called Late Antiquity, the era remains a matter of vigorous scholarly debate, particularly concerning when it should be said to end and its relationship with the early medieval world which followed (Johnson 2012; Herrin 2020, pp. xxxiii–xxxv).

The emperor Aurelian (d. 275) brought new stability to the empire and was largely responsible for ending the Third-Century Crisis. A decade later, Diocletian further reorganized the empire's administration and governance to reflect straightened circumstances and metastasizing paperwork. Diocletian's Tetrarchy consisted of four emperors, two senior and two junior, which in theory gave increased mobility and responsiveness to the Roman army as it faced threats from both east and west. In a far cry from the distinctive individual portraits of earlier emperors, one famous statue of the Tetrarchy emphasizes the interchangeability of the four rulers. In its political ideology, the Tetrarchy made much of the respect and submission of junior to senior emperors, and drew heavily on the cults of Jupiter and his heroic son, Hercules (Williams 2000; Rees 2004). Amidst looming disaster and wholesale reorganization for Roman society, it was, therefore, a particularly sensitive moment for a Christian to reject and refuse to participate in the traditional sacrifices to the gods and divinized emperors. Roman persecution of the church was at its most intense in the reigns of the emperors Decius (r. 249–251), Aurelian, and Diocletian, and to a lesser extent, under Diocletian's junior emperor in the western empire, Maximian.

## Martyrdom, Memory, and Place

By definition the martyr does not control the final version of their story. It is extraordinarily rare to have an early account like that of the North African Perpetua, which records her visions in detail before ending with an account of her martyrdom and that of her companions by wild beasts in 203 (Moss 2012, pp. 29–43; Gold 2018). Even in this case, it is impossible to pinpoint how much of the text is genuinely from Perpetua's point of view or written by someone who knew her well and had heard a first-person account of her visions, and how much was written and added later. Precisely because Felicity and Perpetua, as well as Cyprian, became some of the most famous saints of Christian North Africa, many later versions of the martyrdom were adapted and circulated from this early text. Onlookers in the Carthage arena were described as dipping cloths into the blood of those who had been killed; the martyrs' bodies became the locus of Christian worship, whether in the catacombs or buried in tombs, traditionally located outside of Roman cities. In the late fourth century in North Africa, Augustine describes his mother, Monica, leaving small offerings of bread and wine near the graves of the martyrs, around whom stories, passions, and legends continued to be told, retold, and embellished over time (Augustine 1997, pp. 135–136; Brown 1981, pp. 28–30). In Egypt, numerous saints' shrines emerged at around the same time, spawning entire building complexes to house and feed the numerous pilgrims, who gave votive offerings of all kinds (Frankfurter 2018, pp. 104–144).

However much they were later deplored as pagan superstition, the resonance of these Christian feasts with the meals eaten at a house church, as depicted in catacomb art, and with the celebration of the Eucharist, is clear. As with the Eucharist, celebrated over the relics of the martyrs often kept traditionally in a Christian high altar, the place of the martyrs is, first and foremost, a monumental act of memory by the Christian community: religious, but also social, political, architectural, esthetic, and liturgical. According to later Christian doctrine, the Eucharist and the martyr were both "incarnational" and "iconic" in nature, physical bodies which recalled Jesus's example and through which passed the power of the Holy Spirit. Sanctifying the space in which they were kept, physical relics and the stories attached to them became extremely important in shaping local Christian identity – martyrs turned patron saints. In this early period and for centuries after, sainthood was, first and foremost, a matter of popular acclaim. Like Sant'Agnese off the Via Nomentana, individual saints became intimately associated with place, space, and a kind of spiritual jurisdiction. Ineluctably, communal memory shaded over into local and civic identity, even down to the urban quarter and the neighborhood. Communal memory could be both plastic and fragmented by the trauma caused by betrayal and torture, and local identity in the ancient world encompassed many religious subcultures, not all of them Christian (Frankfurter 2018, pp. 74–76). In many cases, what primarily survived was the memory of a woman martyr's name, perhaps with a slim story about when and how she died. In some cases, the popular veneration, or cult, of a particular saint is indisputably ancient; usually the stories told about them are considerably less so.

## *Christiana sum*: Women, Martyrdom, and Christian Identity

Precisely because of its importance in shaping later, local identity, the range and extent of Roman persecution is often exaggerated in the history of Christianity. It was only briefly coordinated or universal imperial policy, and was always, even at its worst, implemented by individual Roman officials at the local level with varying degrees of zeal or even interest (Fox 1986, pp. 549–608; de Ste. Croix 2006; Corke-Webster 2020). Many of the stories told about the martyrs, both the *acta* and the hagiographies or saints' lives, were written decades or even centuries later. They are often patently legendary; some scholars would go so far as to say that Christian martyrdom is an entirely rhetorical construction from start to finish (Moss 2013). Within the Protestant tradition, non-biblical early Christian saints and martyrs occupy a profoundly ambivalent place – Protestant primitivism standing in tension with deep misgivings around the overly enthusiastic popular veneration of the saints. On the other hand, where saints' cults continued among Christian communities in the Middle East, many saints were valued as intercessors by Muslims and Christians of many denominations. Into the present day, miracle-working icons, such as that of George the martyr at his shrine in Lod, now in Israel, attract pilgrims of both faiths (Dalrymple 1998; Ferg 2020).

Early Christian identity in its first three centuries was not so fixed or defined always to exist at the expense or destruction of its older heritage, whether Jewish or Gentile; Paul did not think that he had ceased to be a Jew after his vision of Jesus. The martyr stories, however, dramatized a polarized spiritual landscape in which Christian faced off against pagan, and where there could be no common ground between the two. Perpetua had a vision of her spiritual life as a great ladder, around which the demons lurked, waiting for souls to stumble and fall. For Perpetua, her new faith represented the complete transformation of her identity, which then inevitably determined the rest of her actions: as she told her furious father, a jug cannot choose to be anything other than it is. *Christiana sum*, "I am a Christian" (Heffernan 2012, p. 126). Under Maximian, the Thessalonikan martyrs refused outright either to sacrifice to the emperor or to eat sacrificial food, the latter a practice where Paul had once permitted the believer some latitude in the name of Christian freedom. When interrogated in turn by the Roman prefect, the women Agapê, Chionê, Cassia, and Philippa all refused to sacrifice, saying: "I believe in the living God . . . and I refuse to destroy my conscience . . . I believe in the living God . . . and I refuse to do this . . . I wish to save my soul . . . I would rather die than partake." Their sister Irenê, who had hidden scripture in her house, chose to be burned alive rather than comply (*Acts* 1954, pp. 280–293).

The human cost of what it would have meant for an ordinary person to choose between renouncing his or her beliefs and going up against the full and crushing weight of Roman authority would have been considerable. Perhaps even more traumatizing for those who survived would have been the circumstances of an arrest: the division of the church community and the betrayal of its scriptures and its leaders by its own members. Most stories of Christian martyrdom stem from after 250 CE; many of these date from "The Great Persecution," the decade between 303, Diocletian's first edict targeting Christians, and 313, Constantine's legalization of Christianity. The remembrance of past violence against Christian communities, however scattered and transitory in nature, therefore virtually coincided with ambitious claims on the part of the new men who came to populate the imperial court and the new capital at Constantinople (Muehlberger 2019, pp. 190–192). For courtiers such as the church historian Eusebius and the chronicler Lactantius, the martyr stories dramatized a shift in political power, and were a means by which they could dissociate themselves from generations past and usher in a new and Christian triumphal narrative. Ironically, in the process Christian writers did much retroactively to systematize and thereby to create "paganism" from the mélange of religious practices which existed in the ancient world.

The stories of the martyrs heavily emphasize the contrast between the ordinary Christian believer who ought to be helpless and the power that they manifestly displayed, during and after death, further testament to the Holy Spirit working and suffering through their bodies. If the Christian believer was a woman, this contrast could be made all the more powerful. As a consequence, in these stories gender plays a pivotal and rhetorically complex role. That women and slaves like Blandina, Perpetua, and Felicity could die bravely, even nobly, was a revelation which publicized Christian belief to a new audience beyond the circles of God-fearers and Jews. In North Africa, Tertullian famously declared, "the blood of the martyrs is seed," not least because persecution drove urban Christians into the rural hinterlands of the empire. As Christians discovered the element of public theater always inherent in Roman executions, martyrdom became a means by which to flip a very fixed and gendered script, and to tell its victims' stories in such a way as to appropriate for themselves the power of the Roman state (Castelli 2004, pp. 39–68). As a consequence, Christian martyr texts are some of the few occasions in the classical world in which a woman speaking, even arguing, in public space is described in a positive way. In the account of the Thessalonikan martyrs' trial, their interrogation shades into catechism; the text itself frames their story with numerous quotations from scripture–including, of course, Paul's epistle to the Thessalonians. Alongside Felicity and Perpetua, one of the earliest of the North African martyrs was the woman Crispina, executed in Tébessa, now in Algeria, in 304. A mother with children, her later *acta* describe her in court in very articulate debate with the Roman authorities (*Acts* 1954, pp. 302–309). As in Egypt, a veritable pilgrimage complex was later built over an earlier church dating from the first half of the fourth century, dedicated to her and to other local martyrs, who came to be known as her companions (Conant 2019).

Augustine would preach a sermon on Crispina's saint's day eulogizing her example, in which he describes how, like Perpetua, "she gave up even her weeping children who mourned her, heartless mother as she seemed to them" (Augustine 2004, Section 137.7). When applied to women, rhetorical depictions meant to stress the super-human strength of the martyr's resolve often describe them as ignoring or neglecting their children, as well as their husband's or their father's authority. Perhaps even more troubling to modern readers is the extent to which these "unnatural" women are portrayed as actively desiring martyrdom, even voluntarily seeking it out. Perpetua, the nursing mother, gave up her infant and described how the pain of her lactating breasts miraculously ceased; the power of God working through her was so in control of the arena and its wild beasts that Perpetua had to guide her executioner's sword to her own throat. Her fellow martyr was the pregnant slave Felicity, who prayed that she might go into labor early so that she could die with her friends, described as her newfound family. These hagiographical texts often depict women, in their heroic quest to win a martyr's crown, in masculine terms and by male descriptors. Perpetua has a famous vision in which she enters the arena to fight an Egyptian gladiator, and just as she squares up to do battle, "I became a man"; it is as if she cannot imagine the scene in any other guise (Heffernan 2012, pp. 129–130).

In martyrdom, women transformed or transcended their gender as most Romans understood it, their physical suffering and violation transformed into occasions for glory rather than shame (Cobb 2008; Petersen 2011; Streete 2021; see Figure 3.3). At the same time, the inescapable focus of these stories are the bodies of the women, fixed in the public eye: what was done to the body, what it suffered, what power made itself manifest through the body, and what miracles occurred through the physical relics that remained after its death (Miller 2009; Hunt 2012, pp. 63–77; Frank, Holman, and Jacobs 2020, pp. 1–12). In ancient sources, the body was frequently described as a garment for the soul; the beauty, or ugliness, of the soul was made manifest in the physical body, and was fully revealed through the drama of martyrdom. Likewise, Christian believers responded to the relics of

**Figure 3.3** Mosaic, Sant'Apollinare Nuovo, Ravenna. *Source:* Chester M. Wood / Wikimedia Commons / CC BY-SA 4.0.

the martyrs by kissing or touching them, hoping for the healing of their physical bodies through contact with those who had suffered in a similar fashion. Some stories or artistic depictions of martyred women, particularly those who suffered graphic torture, invited the fascinated gaze of the believer not very differently from that of an arena spectator or even the executioners themselves. Others described the beauty or desirability of the martyr and then promptly veiled her from sight. In the tale of Agnes, her hair miraculously grew to cover her nakedness; before her burning, the Roman prefect ordered the Thessalonikan Irenê to be exposed in a brothel, only for her to be preserved from harm. Regardless, women martyr's bodies were never rhetorically neutral territory.

## Martyrdom as Christian Genre Literature

Many of these early texts are populist in tone, like *The Acts of Paul and Thecla* describing events in simple, visceral, action-packed narratives. Eusebius preserved many traditions of Christian martyrdom which he had collected from elsewhere, and was in part responsible for the impression that martyrdom was a ubiquitous element of early Christian experience. In comparison with the writers of his own day, however, Eusebius seems to have particularly emphasized the stoic self-control of the Christian martyrs rather than their skills, like those of Crispina, in triumphant verbal fencing; he also exaggerates the near-bestiality demonstrated by their pagan Roman persecutors. Perhaps most strikingly, he actively encouraged the Christian avoidance of persecution where possible. This suggests that even as the tales of the martyrs were crystallizing as a literary genre, Eusebius was working to make it harmonize more closely with the mores of aristocratic Roman society, and thereby to broaden its appeal (Corke-Webster 2019, pp. 175–211).

Many later writers of Christian martyrdom clearly knew the conventions of classical romance and milked them for full rhetorical effect. The result is religious difference expressed as sexual soap opera. As seen in *The Acts of Paul and Thecla* and in the tale of Agnes, a trope of later hagiography is the jealous and slighted pagan male suitor, who betrays the beautiful Christian virgin to torture and death. The modesty of virgin saints like Agnes stands in marked and polemical contrast with the capricious brutality of the Roman authorities, governed entirely by their passions and appetites, and who are goaded to even further extremes of rage when their tortures fail to have any effect. The juxtaposition between the self-possessed virgin and the slavering pagan executioner could be made even more strong and poignant, and the saint more appealingly aristocratic, if the women could be said to be the daughters of high-ranking Roman officials or pagan priests, sleeper agents coopted to the Christian cause. Many of these writers, such as Jerome (d. 420), were themselves caught up at the time in complex debates around aristocratic women's asceticism and the importance of women's virginity, and allied virginity to martyrdom in a set of polemical discourses which would have lasting impact within the Christian tradition. Ironically, if anything, Christian hagiography only preserved and perpetuated classical Roman beliefs in the "intact" body of the virgin as a particularly potent conduit of divine power.

## Deaconesses, Missionaries, and Martyrs in the Provinces

When Roman officials did target Christians, they understandably sought to punish those who held authority within the church, who had received the laying on of hands and were, in a very real sense, the memory of the Christian community. Bishops, then, were frequent martyrs, but the stories also record the names of martyrs who were deaconesses in the church. Given the fluidity of the definition of the term, particularly in relation to the later growth of monasticism, it is often very difficult to know what sort of memory of women in office it is preserving. When a martyr-deaconess was credited with popularizing Christian belief within a region, she was forever associated with local identity in that area; conversely, the use of a deaconess's title could also be a rhetorical signal of the strength of her later, local cult. In 230, the deaconess Tatiana was said to have been martyred in Rome by the regent Ulpian after a series of tortures strongly reminiscent of those faced by Thecla; her relics were taken to Romania and Poland, and she continues to be venerated alongside the woman Eupraxia in the Orthodox Church (Blackburn and Holford-Stevens 2000, p. 33). Eusebius describes Apollonia as a deaconess of Alexandria martyred under Decius; in the course of her execution her teeth were knocked out, and she remains the patron saint of toothaches (Eusebius of Caesarea 2019, Bk. VI, Section 41). Using the conventions of later, monastic literature, Symeon Metaphrastes tells the highly colored story of the young Antiochene woman Justa, who converted her pagan father and, in fending off a jealous suitor, "became instantly like Joseph, that most chaste and most courageous man" (Symeon 2017, p. 13). When the thwarted suitor commissioned a magician, Cyprian, to summon demons to afflict her, Justa remained unharmed, and the remorseful Cyprian tearfully converted before Justa's bishop, eventually becoming a deacon and then a bishop himself. One of his first actions was to enroll ". . .the truly noble virgin Iousta, whom he renamed Ioustina, among the deaconesses and [he] entrusted her with the governance of their convent, appointing her as their spiritual mother" (Symeon 2017, p. 33). In 268, she was said to be beheaded alongside Bishop Cyprian, not to be confused with Cyprian of Carthage.

Eulalia of Barcelona was said to be crucified in 305, but very little else is known about her, and she is often confused with Eulalia of Mérida who was martyred around the same time. Christina, called "the Great Martyr" in the Orthodox Church, is virtually unknown, except that she was venerated in Bolsena, north of Rome, from the fourth century (Blackburn and Holford-Stevens 2000, pp. 75, 305). The Great Martyr Anastasia died under Diocletian in the town of Sirmium, the capital of the Roman province of Pannonia, now Sremska Mitrovica in Serbia. The sixth-century *Liber ad Gregoriam* makes her out to be Roman and lists her name alongside two other Roman women martyrs, Felicity and Symphorosa. However, it is more likely that Anastasia was a local Serbian saint. Said to be martyred under Diocletian were Julia and Devota, now the patron saints of Corsica; Devota has the slightly dubious honor of being the patron saint of Monte Carlo. Also in the reign of Diocletian, the child saint Cyricus was said to have been tortured alongside his mother, Julitta, who had tried to keep him safe. Cyricus and Julitta were later venerated in Greek, Syriac, Armenian, Georgian, and Coptic hagiography; translated into Arabic, the cult became extremely popular in Ethiopia from at least the tenth century, where the saints were known as Qirqos and Iyäluta. Usually a marginal figure in the literary tradition, in Ethiopian illuminated depictions of their passion, Iyäluta assumes a much more prominent role

(Pisani 2015, p. 190). Also extremely popular in Ethiopia is the Armenian martyr Hripsime, known as Arsema in the Ge'ez language. Her legend describes her as a woman living in a religious community in Rome under the leadership of another woman, Gayane, before she caught the eye, of all people, of the emperor Diocletian. Refusing to marry him, she, Gayane, and their companions traveled to Vagharshapat, where they were tortured and executed; the seventh-century cathedral at Etchmiadzin is dedicated to her (Zarian, Zarian, and Ter Minassian 1998; see Figure 3.4).

Eudokia or Eudoxia of Heliopolis, sometimes called "the Samaritan," was said to have been martyred as early as the reign of Trajan; like Justa, her life describes the conversion of a wealthy woman using the tropes of a much later monastic literature. Nino, wonderfully nicknamed "the Illuminatrix," was a Christian slave woman who in 334 converted the Georgian king Mirian III (284–361) and his household to Christianity; she was said to have been ordained a deaconess by the patriarch of Jerusalem (Kateusz 2019, pp. 54–58; Blackburn and Holford-Stevens 2000, p. 51). The virgin Euphemia was martyred in Chalcedon in 303; her reputation and her cult would be forever linked with the council that would meet in her city a hundred and fifty years later. The Syrian church venerates the martyr Candida, a Christian woman taken prisoner by the Persians in the third century and resettled in their territory. Legendarily beautiful, she was martyred for refusing to convert to Zoroastrianism, after, so the story goes, rejecting the advances of Shapur I (Brock and Harvey 1998, pp. 63–64).

Lucy, a martyr of Syracuse in Sicily from around 304, was said to have had her eyes miraculously restored after her torture. Lucy remains the patron saint of the blind, and on the western medieval calendar, her feast day used to be the darkest night of the year. After the Fourth Crusade in 1204, her relics were taken to Venice; she became a favorite saint of Dante Alighieri and, by extension, of C.S. Lewis (Blackburn and Holford-Stevens 2000, pp. 497–498). Another very young girl, Faith, was executed in the Gaulish town of Agen, now in Conques in southern France. Recorded in the martyrology of Jerome, the saint who is recorded in her passion may have been

**Figure 3.4** Cathedral of St. Hripsime, Etchmiadzin. *Source:* Vahagn Grigoryan / Wikimedia Commons / CC BY-SA 3.0.

confused with an earlier, third-century martyr. Faith, or Foy as she was later called, first attracted early medieval veneration, including the striking Carolingian gold reliquary which still survives in Conques, and became an important saint on one of the most important medieval pilgrimage routes to the shrine of the apostle James in northern Spain, Santiago de Compostella (Sheingorn 1995, pp. 33–38, 277–278, n. 3; Green 2001). Said to be martyred under Diocletian, the early medieval life of Afra of Augsburg describes her as a converted prostitute, a well-established trope in later, monastic literature.

## Saints and Legends

Many, although not all, of these legendary saints are now removed from the contemporary church's calendar. Nevertheless, they remain important for their impact on the history of Christian devotion, particularly for their influence on other, later Christian women who bore their names or chose them in religion, as well as in the history of Christian art and iconography. The virgin saint Barbara, said to be martyred around 306, was imprisoned in a tower until her father was miraculously struck by lightning (Symeon 2017, pp. 153–181). As well as for lightning strikes, Barbara would later be invoked for fever in the Middle Ages, and was often depicted alongside her tower. Agatha of Sicily was perhaps the most famous virgin martyr of many who were said to have had their breasts cut off; she is often illustrated holding them before her on a platter. The patron saint of gardeners, Dorothy of Caesarea, was ridiculed by a pagan lawyer before her execution around 310; he later converted abruptly when an angel brought him a basket of heavenly roses and apples.

Margaret of Antioch may represent a confusion with another Antiochene martyr saint, but the entire story may be a complete fabrication. The legend of Margaret, or Marina, of Antioch records that a beautiful virgin, the daughter of a pagan priest, was raised a Christian in secret by her nurse. When she refused marriage with a Roman official, he arrested her and tortured her in a variety of ways. Back in her prison cell, demons began to materialize, including, finally, a dragon emerging from thin air, sometimes understood as a personification of Satan. The dragon swallowed Margaret, but when the girl made the sign of the cross, the beast exploded and she emerged unharmed. Not surprisingly, the story of Margaret and her dragon proved immensely popular in the western church, although the legend seems originally to have been Greek, gaining notoriety in the west particularly after the Crusades. Margaret had a particularly lively cult in England in the late Middle Ages, where, as a kind of hagiographical retelling of Eve and the snake in Eden, she was often invoked by women in childbirth (Dresvina 2016, pp. 13–24; Heyes 2020).

Catherine of Alexandria remains a hugely important focus of veneration in the Orthodox Church, where she is perhaps most famous for the ancient monastery in the Sinai desert named for her, which guards her relics. In the *Ecclesiastical History*, Eusebius refers to a nameless woman from Alexandria desired by the emperor Maximian. She refused him, and although he could not bear to execute her, he did send her into exile and confiscate everything she owned. This may be the source of Catherine's story; certainly, her life is later, and her cult may be even later than that. According to her legend, a noble girl (Catherine is sometimes claimed to be the daughter of Constantine) converted to Christianity as the result of a miraculous dream, and was even accorded the particular honor of being secretly married to Christ, an important episode for women in subsequent centuries who chose her name in religion. In one of the most popular episodes of the life, the learned Catherine debated the pagan philosophers of Alexandria, who were confounded by the knowledge given to her by the Holy Spirit. The furious emperor ordered Catherine ground to death by a spiked millstone – the origin of the Catherine wheel – which an angel destroys; she was finally beheaded (Marker 2007, pp. 29–54).

## *Maria orans*: Proclamation and Liturgy

Perhaps because of their association with women martyrs, the Christian art of the catacombs contains many of the earliest and most powerful images of women acting in liturgical roles, such as the images of women raising cups in the frescoes of SS. Marcellino e Pietro (Stevenson 1978). The most famous of these is the *orans* pose: Latin for "praying," this is a declamatory posture with arms raised, elbows bent, and palms forward. It is, not least, a reminder that the ancient world did not practice either prayer or confession as private, interior activities but as public, communal proclamation and witness. Originally borrowed from classical paganism, more specifically from depictions of Augustus's wife Livia, the *orans* pose was baptized into Christian use. The famous fourth-century wooden doors of S. Sabina in Rome, which include perhaps the first depiction in Christian art of the crucifixion, show Christ on the cross, arms bent in *orans*. Surviving examples of fourth-century Roman Christian gold-glass, in which gold leaf was inserted between layers of glass at the bottom of a vessel, depict various biblical scenes, Peter and Paul, and women martyr-saints like Agnes, *orans*.

The woman most depicted in Christian art in *orans*, of course, is the Virgin Mary (see Figure 3.5). The iconographic tradition from the so-called "Six Books Dormition Apocrypha," a fourth-century text purporting to be a letter of James on the death of Mary, places Mary, *orans*, beneath the figure of Christ in majesty, enthroned (Shoemaker 2018, pp. 181–194). Later Ethiopic and Arabic manuscripts from this tradition also depict Mary, *orans*, blessing the rest of the apostles effectively as

**Figure 3.5** The Orans of Kyiv, Saint Sophia Cathedral, Ukraine. *Source:* Google Arts & Culture / Wikimedia Commons / Public domain.

their bishop. It is customary even today in icons of the Pentecost to depict Mary seated – the position of authority in classical art – surrounded by the apostles as they receive the Holy Spirit. The mosaic of the personified *Ecclesia ex gentibus* in the west end of the church of S. Sabina shows a woman with raised "blessing fingers." The seventh-century mosaic in the S. Venantius chapel of the Lateran baptistery in Rome depicts Mary wearing a pallium, and describes her with the title of *archepiscopa*. Even more common, particularly in later Byzantine church plate such as chalices and processional crosses, is the pairing of Mary with Christ in parallel eucharistic roles (Shoemaker 2016, pp. 130–165; Kateusz 2019; Kateusz and Confalonieri 2021). Mary is also often portrayed bearing a censer, a resonant image of fragrant self-offering much taken up in later Christian exegesis, theology, and hymnody.

As the inevitable target for polemical attacks from non-Christians, it became particularly important to describe and to protect the Virgin Mary in a confessional environment. The bustling border town of Nisibis in Syria had significant populations of Jews as well as pagans and the wandering Manichaeans, who were persecuted by the Persians. There, the deacon Ephrem the Syrian (c. 306–c. 373) composed in Syriac some of the most eloquent hymns ever written to the Virgin Mary, whom he describes as a new Eve. Unlike Eve, deceived by the serpent, Mary's "unclouded eye" of faith became the conduit or the mirror by which light reached a darkened world. For Ephrem, Mary was the "luminous" pearl of great price, fished from the depths of the sea, whose womb was the bridal chamber in which the vastness of God was somehow contained. Mary is absolutely central in Ephrem's thought, standing at the nexus of his understanding of the doctrine of the Incarnation, the nature of faith, and virginity (Ephrem the Syrian 2013; Brock 1985, pp. 71–79, 106–114). As dazzlingly creative as he was, however, Ephrem was working in a congregational context where trained choirs of both men and women would have sung these works, which served both for their own education and for that of those who heard them (Harvey 2020). The sophistication of Ephrem's Marian piety speaks to the existence of some level of popular devotion to the Virgin within the Syriac church, without which that piety would have been incomprehensible, and certainly, Ephrem's lasting importance within the Syriac tradition did much to foster it in later centuries.

Over the course of the fourth century, almost certainly because of the increasing importance of Jerusalem as a site of Christian pilgrimage, the veneration of Mary seems to have gathered real momentum alongside and as part of the cult of the saints (Shoemaker 2016, p. 14). In Rome, the wooden doors of S. Sabina also contain one of the first depictions of the Dormition or Assumption of Mary: her death and the subsequent raising of her body to heaven by angels. In later, medieval Christian pilgrimage, the doctrine of the Assumption helped to explain why, of all the saints and martyrs, there was no site of Mary's grave and no physical relics of her body (Warner 1976, pp. 221–223, 278–280, 291–294). The church of the Kathisma, or the "Seat," of the *Theotokos* dates from the fifth century and is the earliest church dedicated to Marian veneration, said to be the place where Mary rested before she gave birth; another fifth-century church was built nearby, most likely to commemorate the place where she rested on the way of the flight into Egypt (see Figure 3.6). An early chapel dedicated to Mary near the garden of Gethsemane, which certainly existed by the fifth century, claimed to be the site of her tomb (Shoemaker 2002, pp. 78–107). In light of subsequent Christological speculation, it became important for the faithful doctrinally to "protect" Mary's body, which, after all, had been the sole source of Christ's own, from the touch of physical decay. As for the other martyrs and saints, it was believed that the life-giving Spirit acted miraculously to preserve her, as another forerunner of the resurrection of the body. Nevertheless, there remained and remains to this day a great deal of doctrinal ambiguity around Mary's physical death.

**Figure 3.6** The church of the Kathisma. *Source:* Hagai Agmon-Snir / Wikimedia Commons / CC BY-SA 4.0.

## The New Holy Places

Well before the great theological debates of the fifth century, however, Marian devotion gained an unexpected adherent in the emperor Constantine and his family. Constantine's dream and subsequent conversion is one of the most intensely debated events in Christian history. Whatever his personal motives, alongside aggressively Christian courtiers like Eusebius, for the rest of his reign Constantine had to reckon with the continued existence of pagan religion among many of his aristocratic elites, particularly in the city of Rome itself. In his court ideology, Constantine continued to use some elements of pagan iconography, presenting himself politically with a certain calculated ambiguity (Drake 2017; Fox 1986, pp. 609–662; Barnes 2011). At the same time, however, in founding the city of Constantinople Constantine was establishing a new capital for the eastern empire that was not only more defensible and strategic, but was also Christian from the beginning. In the long term, this had the effect of politically sidelining Rome, now inconveniently distant from both the Persian frontier and the forts along the Rhine and Danube. After appropriating and re-dedicating several monuments around the city, Constantine would not visit Rome again (Barnes 2011, pp. 85–89; Holloway 2004).

In his persona as Christian emperor, Constantine issued a raft of new divorce legislation modeled on biblical principles, which, not surprisingly, proved impracticable in the long term (Clark 1993, pp. 21–26). In Constantinople, Constantine constructed the Church of the Holy Apostles, which contained relics of all 12 apostles, with space reserved for his own body. Necessarily, however, such an important prophet of God must have come from somewhere. However, his own mother, Helena (b. 248), seems to have been of embarrassingly ordinary birth. Said to be the daughter of a tavern- or stable-keeper, Helena is sometimes said to be from Britain, where the young Constantine began his ascent to the throne (Cohick and Hughes 2017, pp. 110–113). The latter part of the emperor's reign would see his court theologians routinely borrow elements of Marian devotion in order to describe Helena. In 324, she was formally proclaimed "Augusta." In 326, when she was nearly 80 and in the wake of ferocious debate at the Council of Nicaea over the full divinity of Christ, the empress traveled to Jerusalem, where, like her son, she was said to receive a miraculous dream. Helena's dream concerned the hidden location of the True Cross, now dramatically discovered for the veneration of the faithful. By the fourth century, the True Cross would become the most precious relic in Jerusalem, treasured in the Church of the Holy Sepulchre and revealed only in Holy Week (Coon 1997, pp. 97–103; Edwards 2015, p. 170; Kelley 2019, pp. 22–23). Over the course of her pilgrimage to the Holy Land, Helena would found other churches as well, setting a precedent for the donations of other imperial and aristocratic women on pilgrimage in Jerusalem. In particular, Helena would establish the Eleona, the church on the Mount of Olives, the Church of the Nativity at Bethlehem, and a shrine to Mary *Theotokos* or "God-bearer," establishing patterns of Christian pilgrimage in the Holy Land from the 330s (Jacobs 2004, pp. 152–158; Cooper 2013, p. 139). These acts of generosity were meant to demonstrate imperial support for Nicene Christianity in Jerusalem, partly in the teeth of the nearby Arian diocese of Caesarea, and cemented a firm association between Nicene Christianity, Mary as God-bearer, and the person of the empress herself (Cohick and Hughes 2017, pp. 124–125; Muehlberger 2019, p. 38).

For better or for worse – it could not exactly refuse, even if it had wanted to – the church became the recipient of large numbers of public buildings, most famously the basilicas or royal halls which were consecrated as churches, where the relics of the martyrs were now moved, or "translated." A symbiotic relationship now developed between the bishop of Rome and the powerful presence of the bodies of the martyrs. In the fourth century, Jerome's patron and friend, Pope Damasus I, put up a large number of inscriptions around the city, which served to hallow catacombs, like those near Agnes's church, as intrinsically Christian holy places, something which was not an inevitable association or development (Sághy 2015). Martyrs and ancient sites of Christian worship existed in an intimate relationship, with existence of the former often popularly assumed amidst the presence of the latter. Perhaps the oldest church in Rome, and certainly where the bishop of Rome lived before the conversion of Constantine, is S. Pudenziana, built into a second-century Roman bath complex. Pudentiana is said to be the daughter of the same Pudens mentioned in the second letter to Timothy; it is also possible that her name is actually a misreading of a male saint's name (Masson 2009, pp. 412–414). Nevertheless, one of the most striking features of the church is its fourth-century mosaic, in which an enthroned Christ, against a backdrop of the heavenly Jerusalem and the four living creatures, is surrounded by the apostles and two veiled women casting down their martyrs' crowns. One is traditionally identified as Pudentiana, but if this is mistaken, it is nevertheless a triumphant early depiction of women's martyrdom (see Figure 3.7). Pudentiana is traditionally associated with her sister-martyr, Praxedes or Prassede, whose ninth-century church is just up the road. Both are situated very near to the largest and most ancient church in Rome dedicated to Mary, the fifth-century basilica of S. Maria Maggiore (Goodson 2010). Across the Tiber is the early medieval church of S. Cecilia in Trastevere, built over a Roman house and next to the catacombs of Praetextatus, with its third-century Christian art, from where her relics were translated. The date of Cecilia's martyrdom has been variously assigned. According to legend, she was first sentenced to die in her own bath house, but when the steam failed to kill her, she was beheaded. She was said to live for three days afterwards notwithstanding, and when her coffin was opened in the sixteenth century, her body was found to be incorrupt. Through the Spirit's intervention, Cecilia was able to hear the "music of the spheres" and was later named the patron saint of music (Blackburn and Holford-Stevens 2000, pp. 469–471; Masson 2009, pp. 486–487).

**Figure 3.7** Apse mosaic, S. Pudenziana, Rome. *Source:* Sixtus / Wikimedia Commons / Public domain.

## Asceticism and the New Martyrs

For all that Constantine's conversion left the church astounded at its own good fortune, it also posed a deep conundrum: with Christianity now declared a legal religion, where would the power of God be made so clearly and apparently manifest as in the bodies of the martyrs? Over the course of the fourth century, asceticism and monasticism emerged as the natural heirs of the martyrological tradition, employing the same discourses of spiritual combat and athleticism. To some extent, martyrdom and asceticism had always existed in relationship in the early Christian tradition. Beyond any general expectations surrounding Christ's immediate return, many early Christian communities understood the practice of their faith to lie, not in the immediate expectation of Christ's return, but in paradoxically life-giving acts of renunciation which anticipated the life to come (Wright 2019, pp. 135–152). Jesus's teachings regarding wealth and money were clear, whether or not any churches succeeded for long in holding property in common; Paul's teachings on sexuality were likewise uncompromising. Ancient philosophy, Stoicism in particular, had never been a purely intellectual exercise but had always involved the training of the whole self (Nussbaum 1994, pp. 316–358). Many ascetic practitioners in the early Christian tradition taught that spiritual and even angelic aid would be proffered to the believer through ascetic practices and through the reading and prayerful interpretation of scripture. The "noetic exegesis" taught by Origen, the third-century Alexandrian ascetic and biblical scholar, and the writings of the fourth-century writer Evagrius of Pontus, would be extremely powerful throughout the development of monasticism even when Origen's teachings became deeply controversial (Stefaniw 2010). In particular, the ascetic's memorization and recitation of the psalter, sometimes in its entirety on a daily basis, became a common practice in the Egyptian desert. For the enclosed woman, particularly if she were already well educated, this tradition licensed and even encouraged the extensive study of scripture as an ascetic practice.

For the Syriac church, which spread beyond the empire's borders into Persian territory in the subsequent centuries, sexual renunciation, asceticism, and the profound emptying of the self became, not optional extras, but central tenets of the church (Brown 2012, p. 266). Ephrem the Syrian, as well as many of the men and women of his congregation, practiced a form of life that scholars now consider to be "proto-monastic" in nature. The "sons" or "daughters of the covenant" made up a central core of consecrated Christians in a given church community, the *bnay qyama* (Brock 1985, pp. 133–139). Both in the Syrian church and throughout the Greek-speaking eastern empire, church buildings were customarily segregated by gender. In some parts of the Greek world, parallel groups of ordained deacons and deaconesses ministered, respectively, to both parts of the church. It sometimes occurred that men and women agreed to live in celibacy in the same house. On some occasions, these would have been married couples who had decided to live chastely. In other cases, however, this appears to have been a pragmatic solution to the problem of how to support both single clergy and unmarried women who wanted to live a celibate life but who did not have any other economic means. The potential for exploitation, however, was such that the practice, sometimes called syneisacticism, was generally frowned upon by church authorities (McNamara 1996, pp. 37, 62–65). Canons in the 314 Council of Ancyra ruled, on the one hand, for disciplinary measures against people who backed out of their vows of virginity, suggesting that these decisions were publicly witnessed within the church by the fourth century and carried real weight in the church community, and also against the practice of syneisacticism (Elm 1994, pp. 25–28).

Traditional stories of the beginnings of monasticism tend to focus on Athanasius's depiction of Anthony – and therefore on men, on the desert, and on the region of Egypt in particular. In fact, monasticism seems to have taken shape concurrently in different regional forms in both Egypt and Syria (Brown 2008, pp. 208–209). Women were always a constant presence alongside men as practitioners, whether or not men publicly admitted to it. But women's monasticism of necessity was usually urban, particularly early Egyptian monasticism based in Alexandria. It was usually practiced in individual houses, often by women alone or in small groups for whom enclosure in the family home was a natural extension of aristocratic Roman practice. As early as 235, Origen, who was rumored to have castrated himself for the sake of the kingdom, lived for two years in Caesarea in the house of "Juliana the virgin." Clearly wealthy and well-connected, Juliana possessed books by Symmachus the bible translator, instrumental in helping Origen to produce his edition of the Old Testament, the *Hexapla* (Elm 1994, pp. 29–30; Palladius 2015, p. 133). An important martyr of the Coptic church is the virgin Dimyānah, the daughter of Diocletian's provincial governor and a secret Christian. According to the Coptic Synaxarium, Dimyānah asked her father for a house where she might pray and read scripture; she gathered around her a community of some 40 other women. When she encouraged her father to recant his public paganism she was arrested and martyred (Farag 2014, p. 123; Beshara 2019, pp. 60–66). The wealthy fourth-century pilgrim Melania the Elder met with the hermit Alexandra, who had shut herself into the tomb-cave complexes still being discovered beneath the modern city of Alexandria; she cannot have been the first (Palladius 2015).

In Asia Minor in 312, a man named Theodotus was taken prisoner by Roman authorities for attempting to bury seven Christian women who had been martyred together, and who seem to have been living together as consecrated virgins before their ordeal. One of the women, Tekousa, was named as a *presbytera* and is therefore considered a Montanist prophetess, although it is difficult to be certain (Elm 1994, pp. 51–58). By the mid-fourth century, the canons of Hippolytus describe the presence of unenclosed, dedicated virgins in Christian communities who were veiled but not ordained as deaconesses. A fourth-century papyrus from Panopolis in Egypt describes the children of a former magistrate, Aurelius Mikalos and his sister, "Didyme, ever-virgin" (Mathieson 2014, p. 240). Around 400, the Jew Aurelius Jose, son of Judas, took out a lease on some land belonging to "Aurelia Theodora and Aurelia Tauris . . . apotactic nuns" from Oxyrhynchus. What "apotactic" means is unclear, although it probably designates some form of religious life in common or in a shared house; obviously it did not prevent the women from leasing property without any men acting on their behalf (Mathieson 2014, pp. 242, 248–249). In all likelihood, it has been argued, it was a house of religious women like these with whom Antony left his sister, before setting out for the desert on his own (Elm 1994, pp. 229–230; Athanasius 1980, Sections 2–3). The existence of these *canonicae* (or *kanonikai*) suggests that a form of life was taking shape in which women were starting to live together in individual households or as a small ascetic community, although no rule yet existed (Clark 1993, p. 103). Much later, the Byzantine writer Symeon Metaphrastes recounts the stirring tale of the martyr Eugenia of Alexandria, said to be the daughter of the proconsul of Egypt in the reign of Commodus. Eugenia disguised herself as a man to join an ascetic community, eventually being elected abbot. When she rejected the advances of a wealthy widow, Eugenia was brought before the authorities – in this case, her father – to whom she revealed her identity. All were later martyred together according to the novel, which combines many of the tropes of Greek romance with those of Christian martyrdom (Symeon 2017, pp. 184–261). In particular, the cross-dressing virgin saint was a trope that appeared again and again as a feature of later monastic hagiography (Hunt 2012, pp. 63–77; Cooper 2013, pp. 228–233; Swan 2001, pp. 81–82).

Monasticism emerged in tandem with the tensions between the Nicene and Arian parties within the church, and was polarized and indelibly shaped by that conflict even after the Council of Nicaea in 325. A rare survival of an Arian, or homoian, text is *On Virginity*, by Basil of Ancyra (d. 358). The bishop described a spiritual journey in which certain consecrated women, as in martyrdom, "became male" through the practice of self-denial and asceticism. He did not describe the existence of a shared rule which shaped their practice – which he surely would have done had it existed – and they did not seem to be enclosed in one particular dwelling. However, Basil did describe a process by which a consecrated virgin would undertake a novitiate of some length, a public examination, probably by the bishop, a public vow, and perhaps a procession in church (Elm 1994, pp. 113–131). Basil did not seem to accord a consecrated virgin any formal role within the church's clerical hierarchy other than as a visible presence; nevertheless, for him to have written the treatise at all suggests the active encouragement of consecrated women by Arius and other teachers within Alexandria.

A similar text, *De virginitate*, was later ascribed to the great champion of Nicene orthodoxy: Athanasius of Alexandria, the author of the *Life of Antony*. The treatise assumes that a consecrated woman will be living according to a religious form of life enclosed within her house, and even suggests that she "eucharistize" her dinner, making a sign of the cross three times over her plate as she says a prayer (Berger 2021). In the *Lausiac History*, Palladius claimed to have met a woman who, like Origen and Juliana, sheltered Athanasius himself during one of his several periods in exile over the course of a turbulent career (Palladius 2015, pp. 131–133). But the firmest evidence for Athanasius's support of religious women is in his letters. Read in tandem with his other theological treatises and the *Life of Anthony*, Athanasius's letters to women suggest that the bishop both wanted to harness the power and prestige of monks, male and female, to the Nicene cause, and worried over the disturbing appeal of other, Arian models of life for religious women (Elm 1994, pp. 331–357). Only the power of a Christ fully God could empower men and women in this way, went the Athanasian argument. Instead of models like those of Basil of Ancyra, Athanasius's distinctive approach elevated the Virgin Mary as the ideal model for women in the religious life as the place where the full power of divinity entered the created world. In this period, Mary, it must be remembered, was understood first and foremost as the girl from the *Protoevangelium* of James: raised and to some extent enclosed in the temple before Gabriel's visitation (Brown 2008, p. 273; Demacopoulos 2007, pp. 39–42). What was said about Mary could be reasonably extrapolated to other saints and martyrs, and from thence to the individual Christian woman. In a similar vein, it is possible that the gold-glass depiction of Agnes, *orans*, from the Catacomb of Pamphylus may also be intended as an anti-Arian argument (Cohick and Hughes 2017, p. 87). To the fourth-century bishop and chronicler Epiphanius of Cyprus, the enclosed virgin also offered a polemical contrast to the specter he conjured of the scandalous public ministry of gnostic and Montanist women (Kim 2015, pp. 41–43).

## Macrina and the Household Community

It is in this fluid and contested world that monastic life within the Roman household was given its most definitive shape yet by Macrina the Younger (c. 327–379). Named for her grandmother the martyr, Macrina the Elder, Macrina was given the nickname "Thecla" very young. Indeed, she grew up not so very far away from Thecla's shrine in Seleucia. Born to an aristocratic family with estates in several Roman provinces, Macrina was the eldest of her widowed mother Emmelia's 10 children. Famously, her siblings included Basil "the Great," bishop of Caesarea, and Gregory of Nyssa, who between 380 and 383 recorded much of what is known about Macrina's life and teaching. The entire family, along with their mutual friend, Gregory Nazianzen, and his sisters, were both Nicene and heavily invested in the new monastic movement. During their travels the young Basil and Gregory Nazianzen spent a considerable time at Thecla's shrine and monastic community, while Gregory of Nyssa may well have visited as well during a period of his later exile (Gregory of Nyssa 2008, pp. 18–19). In his youth, Basil seems to have been far more deeply interested by Arian ascetic teaching than he later wanted to admit. In the same vein, in his later works the great monastic teacher does not ever credit or even refer to his elder sister, who according to Gregory of Nyssa tartly dressed down a sophomoric Basil on at least one memorable occasion.

If the chronology Gregory of Nyssa outlines in his life of Macrina is correct, then after a major earthquake, Emmelia and Macrina moved the family to the more remote country estate of Annisa, with the intention of establishing a *martyrion* in the manner of Thecla's shrine. Macrina's younger brother Peter, ordained a priest by Basil, then appears to have taken the momentous step of becoming a solitary ascetic. Following her brother's tragic and untimely death and that of her fiancé, in the 340s Macrina made the unprecedented decision to remain in Annisa and become a "virgin widow" (Gregory of Nyssa 2008, pp. 44–46). Having supported her mother through the grief of losing Peter, Macrina became the head of a double monastery which included both men and women on the estate. Her mother had already taken the step of freeing the family slaves, and gradually the religious community at Annisa would take in more and more sisters, or *parthenoi*, of lower social status. However, the community also included the senator's daughter Vetiana, as well as at least one named deaconess, Lampadion. In his *Great Asceticon*, Basil the Great would later outline a model for monastic life which included both men's and women's communities – although not under a woman's leadership. However, it was Macrina who first took the momentous step of bringing together the aristocratic Roman estate, with its inbuilt structures of social patronage, with the ascetic Christian community. Gregory of Nyssa describes how Annisa continued to function within the late Roman landscape as a source of aid for the surrounding countryside, not least in the miracle stories which quickly sprang up around the memory of his sister.

Macrina could not have anticipated that it was a model of Christian community that would outlast the Roman Empire in the west.

Like Gregory of Nyssa, Gregory Nazianzen would eulogize his sister Gorgonia, the widow and deaconess, as well as the life of another of his sisters, Theosebia, whom he also describes as a deaconess (Ramelli 2021, pp. 43–45). Macrina, by contrast, was never ordained, although Gregory of Nyssa attributes to her the treatise which he records as *On the Soul and the Resurrection* – a clear instance of a woman teaching, and teaching a bishop, even if he is her little brother (Miller 2005, pp. 22–29, 192–207; Gregory of Nyssa 2008). There is some evidence that the Cappadocian fathers, influenced by the more radical teachings of Origen, Evagrius, and other ascetic teachers around the resurrection of the body and the nature of the angelic life, could at least suggest the transformation of late Roman understandings of gender through asceticism and embrace the intellectual and spiritual authority of an extraordinary woman (Stefaniw 2010; Muehlberger 2013, pp. 133–145). How such a woman could fit into the established church hierarchy, however, posed a much more complicated problem – perhaps another reason why Basil never mentions Macrina. The innate power of the ascetic Macrina certainly eclipsed the authority of the deaconess who lived among the community in Annisa, and suggests how the role of the deaconess would often be subsumed into a group of women living a monastic life.

Both martyrdom and asceticism demanded, in their different ways, that the Christian woman might be required to separate herself from society. In so doing, both necessarily argued for the pagan and even demonic nature of that society, promising to the believer the power of the Holy Spirit to overcome in their spiritual struggle. In this period, asceticism was without question the path to a kind of liberation for women from the social expectations of marriage, even if it was achieved at the cost of demonizing women's sexuality. No doubt, the upheavals of the period may also have lent urgency to women choosing such practices, particularly if their homes and communities were already under suffocating economic pressure. However, as monastic authors continued to focus on women's virginity as the culmination of their spiritual and ascetic practice, Christian discourse by 350 had subtly narrowed the field of sanctity from what had existed in 200: after the legalization of Christianity, only women from a particular social class realistically had the opportunity or the ability to refuse marriage. The heir of Felicity and Emerentiana, the slave and the freed slave, was now Macrina.

## References

Musurillo, H. (ed.) (1954). *Acts of the Christian Martyrs*, vol. 2. Oxford: Clarendon Press.

Athanasius (1980). *The Life of Anthony and the Letter to Marcellinus* (trans. R.C. Gregg). Mahwah: Paulist Press.

Augustine (1997). *The Confessions* (trans. M. Boulding). New York: New City Press.

Augustine (2004). *Expositions of the Psalms, 121-50* (trans. M. Boulding). Hyde Park: New City Press.

Barnes, T. (2011). *Constantine: Dynasty, Religion, and Power in the Later Roman Empire*. Oxford: Wiley.

Berger, T. (2021). Women's liturgical practices and leadership roles. In: *Patterns of Women's Leadership in Early Christianity* (ed. J.E. Taylor and I.L.E. Ramelli), 180–194. Oxford: Oxford University Press.

Beshara, A. (2019). *Egyptian Women in the Coptic Orthodox Church of Egypt*. Meadville: Christian Faith Publishing.

Blackburn, B. and Holford-Stevens, L. (2000). *The Oxford Book of Days: Being a Voyage through the Calendar*. Oxford: Oxford University Press.

Brock, S. (1985). *The Luminous Eye: The Spiritual World Vision of Saint Ephrem the Syrian*. Kalamazoo: Cistercian Publications.

Brock, S. and Harvey, S.A. (1998). *Holy Women of the Syrian Orient*, updated ed. Berkeley: University of California Press.

Brown, P. (1971). *The World of Late Antiquity, AD 150–750*. New York: W.W. Norton and Co.

Brown, P. (1981). *The Cult of the Saints: Its Rise and Function in Latin Christianity*. Chicago: University of Chicago Press.

Brown, P. (2008). *The Body and Society: Men, Women, and Sexual Renunciation in Early Christianity*, rev. ed. New York: Columbia University Press.

Brown, P. (2012). *Through the Eye of a Needle: Wealth, the Fall of Rome, and the Making of Christianity in the West, 350–550 AD*. Princeton: Princeton University Press.

Castelli, E. (2004). *Martyrdom and Memory: Early Christian Culture Making*. New York: Columbia University Press.

Clark, E.A. (1983). *Women in the Early Church*. Collegeville: Liturgical Press.

Clark, G. (1993). *Women in Late Antiquity: Pagan and Christian Lifestyles*. Oxford: Clarendon Press.

Cobb, L.S. (2008). *Dying To Be Men: Gender and Language in the Early Christian Martyr Texts*. New York: Columbia University Press.

Cohick, L.H. and Hughes, A.B. (2017). *Christian Women in the Patristic World*. Grand Rapids: Baker Academic.

Conant, J.P. (2019). Memories of trauma and the formation of a Christian identity. In: *Memories of Utopia: The Revision of Histories and Landscapes in Late Antiquity* (ed. B. Neil and K. Simic), 36–56. London: Taylor & Francis.

Coon, L.L. (1997). *Sacred Fictions: Holy Women and Hagiography in Late Antiquity*. Philadelphia: University of Pennsylvania Press.

Cooper, K. (2013). *Band of Angels: The Forgotten World of Early Christian Women*. New York: Overlook Press.

Corke-Webster, J. (2019). *Eusebius and Empire: Constructing Church and Rome in the Ecclesiastical History*. Cambridge: Cambridge University Press.

Corke-Webster, J. (2020). The Roman Persecutions. In: *The Wiley-Blackwell Companion to Christian Martyrdom* (ed. P. Middleton), 33–50. Chichester: Wiley.

Dalrymple, W. (1998). *From the Holy Mountain: A Journey in the Shadow of Byzantium*. London: Flamingo.

Demacopoulos, G. (2007). *Five Models of Spiritual Direction in the Early Church*. Notre Dame: University of Notre Dame Press.

Drake, H.A. (2017). Constantine and religious extremism. In: *Constantine: Religious Faith and Imperial Policy* (ed. A.E. Siecienski), 11–26. London: Routledge.

Dresvina, J. (2016). *A Maid with a Dragon: The Cult of St Margaret of Antioch in Medieval England*. Oxford: The British Academy.

Edwards, M. (2015). *Religions of the Constantinian Empire*. Oxford: Oxford University Press.

Elm, S. (1994). *Virgins of God: The Making of Asceticism in Late Antiquity*. Oxford: Clarendon.

Ephrem the Syrian (2013). *The Harp of the Spirit: Poems of Saint Ephrem the Syrian*, 3e (trans. S. Brock). Cambridge: Aquila Books.

Eusebius of Caesarea (2019). *The History of the Church: A New Translation* (trans. J.M. Schott). Oakland: University of California Press.

Farag, L.M. (2014). Monasticism. In: *The Coptic Christian Heritage: History, Faith, and Culture* (ed. L. Farag), 116–131. London: Routledge.

Ferg, E. (2020). Early Christianity and Saint George. In: *Geography, Religion, Gods, and Saints in the Eastern Mediterranean*, 135–186. London: Routledge.

Fox, R.L. (1986). *Pagans and Christians in the Mediterranean World from the Second Century AD to the Conversion of Constantine*. London: Penguin.

Frank, G., Holman, S.R., and Jacobs, A.S. (2020). *Garbed in the Body: Embodiment and the Pursuit of Holiness in Late Ancient Christianity*. New York: Fordham University Press.

Frankfurter, D. (2018). *Christianizing Egypt: Syncretism and Local Worlds in Late Antiquity*. Princeton: Princeton University Press.

Gold, B.K. (2018). *Perpetua: Athlete of God*. Oxford: Oxford University Press.

Goodson, C.J. (2010). *The Rome of Paschal I: Papal Power, Urban Renovation, Church Rebuilding, and Relic Translation, 817–824*. Cambridge: Cambridge University Press.

Green, H. (2001). *Little Saint*. London: Souvenir.

Gregory of Nyssa (2008). *Macrina the Younger, Philosopher of God* (ed. A.M. Silvas). Turnhout: Brepols.

Harper, K. (2011). *Slavery in the Late Roman World, AD 275–425*. Cambridge: Cambridge University Press.

Harper, K. (2017). *The Fate of Rome: Climate, Disease, and the End of an Empire*. Princeton: Princeton University Press.

Harvey, S.A. (2020). Training the women's choir: ascetic practice and liturgical education in late antique Syriac Christianity. In: *Wisdom on the Move: Late Antique Traditions in Multicultural Conversation: Essays in Honor of Samuel Rubenson* (ed. S.A. Harvey, T. Arentzen, H.R. Johnsén and A. Westergren), 203–223. Leiden: Brill.

Heffernan, T.J. (ed.) and trans.(2012). *The Passion of Perpetua and Felicity*. Oxford: Oxford University Press.

Herrin, J. (2020). *Ravenna: Capital of Empire, Crucible of Europe*. London: Allen Lane.

Heyes, M. (2020). *Margaret's Monsters: Women, Identity, and the Life of St. Margaret in Medieval England*. Abingdon: Routledge.

Holloway, R.R. (2004). *Constantine and Rome*. New Haven: Yale University Press.

Hunt, H. (2012). *Clothed in the Body: Asceticism, the Body, and the Spiritual in Late Antiquity*. Farnham: Ashgate.

Jacobs, A.S. (2004). *Remains of the Jews: The Holy Land and Christian Empire in Late Antiquity*. Stanford: Stanford University Press.

Johnson, S.F. (ed.) (2012). *The Oxford Handbook of Late Antiquity*. Oxford: Oxford University Press.

Kateusz, A. (2019). *Mary and Early Christian Women: Hidden Leadership*. London: Palgrave Macmillan.

Kateusz, A. and Confalonieri, L.B. (2021). Women church leaders in and around fifth-century Rome. In: *Patterns of Women's Leadership in Early Christianity* (ed. J.E. Taylor and I.L.E. Ramelli), 228–260. Oxford: Oxford University Press.

Kelley, J.L. (2019). *The Church of the Holy Sepulchre in Text and Archaeology*. Oxford: Archaeopress.

Kim, Y.R. (2015). *Epiphanius of Cyprus: Imagining an Orthodox World*. Ann Arbor: University of Michigan Press.

Lieu, J. (2016). *Neither Jew nor Greek? Constructing Early Christianity*. London: Bloomsbury.

Marker, G. (2007). *Imperial Saint: The Cult of St. Catherine and the Dawn of Female Rule in Russia*. DeKalb: Northern Illinois University Press.

Masson, G. (2009). *The Companion Guide to Rome*. Revised by John Fort, 9e. Suffolk: Boydell & Brewer.

Mathieson, E.A. (2014). *Christian Women in the Greek Papyri of Egypt to 400 CE*. Turnhout: Brepols.

McNamara, J.A.K. (1996). *Sisters in Arms: Catholic Nuns through Two Millennia*. Cambridge: Harvard University Press.

Miller, P.C. (2005). *Women in Early Christianity: Translations from Greek Texts*. Washington D.C.: Catholic University Press.

Miller, P.C. (2009). *The Corporeal Imagination: Signifying the Holy in Late Ancient Christianity*. Philadelphia: University of Pennsylvania Press.

Moss, C. (2012). *Ancient Christian Martyrdom: Diverse Practices, Theologies, and Traditions*. New Haven: Yale University Press.

Moss, C. (2013). *The Myth of Persecution: How Early Christians Invented A Story of Martyrdom*. New York: HarperOne.

Muehlberger, E. (2013). *Angels in Late Antique Christianity*. Oxford: Oxford University Press.

Muehlberger, E. (2019). *Moment of Reckoning: Imagined Death and Its Consequences in Late Antique Christianity*. Oxford: Oxford University Press.

Nussbaum, M.C. (1994). *The Therapy of Desire: Theory and Practice in Hellenistic Ethics*. Princeton: Princeton University Press.

Palladius of Aspuna (2015). *The Lausiac History* (trans. J. Wortley). Kalamazoo: Cistercian Publications.

Petersen, A.K. (2011). Gender-bending in early Jewish and Christian martyr texts. In: *Contextualizing Early Christian Martyrdom* (ed. J. Engberg, U.H. Eriksen and A.K. Petersen), 225–256. Frankfurt am Main: Peter Lang.

Pisani, V. (2015). Passio of St Cyricus (Gädlä Qirqos) in North Ethiopia: elements of devotion and of manuscripts tradition [sic]. In: *Veneration of Saints in Christian Ethiopia* (ed. D. Nosnitsin), 161–199. Wiesbaden: Harrassowitz Verlag.

Ramelli, I.L.E. (2021). Colleagues of apostles, presbyters, and bishops: women *syzygoi* in ancient Christian communities. In: *Patterns of Women's Leadership in Early Christianity* (ed. J.E. Taylor and I.L.E. Ramelli), 26–58. Oxford: Oxford University Press.

Rees, R. (2004). *Diocletian and the Tetrarchy*. Edinburgh: Edinburgh University Press.

Sághy, M. (2015). The bishop of Rome and the martyrs. In: *The Bishop of Rome in Late Antiquity* (ed. G. Dunn), 37–56. London: Routledge.

Sheingorn, P. (trans.)(1995). *The Book of Sainte Foy*. Philadelphia: University of Pennsylvania Press.

Shoemaker, S. (2002). *Ancient Christian Traditions of the Virgin Mary's Dormition and Assumption*. Oxford: Oxford University Press.

Shoemaker, S. (2016). *Mary in Early Christian Faith and Devotion*. New Haven: Yale University Press.

Shoemaker, S. (2018). *The Dormition and Assumption Apocrypha*. Leuven: Peeters.

de Ste. Croix, G.E.M. (2006). *Christian Persecution, Martyrdom, and Orthodoxy* (ed. M. Whitby and J. Streeter). Oxford: Oxford University Press.

Stefaniw, B. (2010). *Mind, Text, and Commentary: Noetic Exegesis in Origen of Alexandria, Didymus the Blind, and Evagrius Ponticus*. Frankfurt am Main: Peter Lang.

Stevenson, J. (1978). *The Catacombs: Rediscovered Monuments of Early Christianity*. London: Thames & Hudson.

Streete, G.P. (2021). *Violated and Transcended Bodies: Gender, Martyrdom, and Asceticism in Early Christianity*. Cambridge: Cambridge University Press.

Swan, L. (2001). *The Forgotten Desert Mothers: Sayings, Lives, and Stories of Early Christian Women*. New York: Paulist Press.

Symeon Metaphrastes (2017). *Christian Novels from the Menalogion of Symeon Metaphrastes* (ed. S. Papaioannou) ed. and translator. Cambridge, MA: Harvard University Press.

Visser, M. (2000). *The Geometry of Love: Space, Time, Mystery, and Meaning in an Ordinary Church*. London: Viking.

Warner, M. (1976). *Alone of All Her Sex: The Myth and Cult of the Virgin Mary*. London: Picador.

Watson, A. (1999). *Aurelian and the Third Century*. London: Routledge.

Williams, S. (2000). *Diocletian and the Roman Recovery*. New York: Routledge; First edition, 1985.

Wright, N.T. (2019). *History and Eschatology: Jesus and the Promise of Natural Theology*. Waco: Baylor University Press.

Zarian, A., Zarian, A., and Ter Minassian, A. (1998). *Vagharshapat: Edjmiatzin, Hrip'simè, Gayanè, Shoghakat*. Venice: Oemme.

# 4

# Romancing Stones

Women in Christianity, 350–500

Two old practitioners of the new wisdom coming out of the Egyptian desert thought it would be a good joke to humiliate the woman they had traveled so far to visit. "According to nature I am a woman, but not according to my thoughts," Amma Sarah snapped in response. "It is I who am a man, you who are women" (Ward 1975, pp. 229–230). It is probably too much to hope that that was the only time in which Sarah had to defend her chosen vocation to visitors who had come to stare. Any woman who chose to renounce the world alongside Antony and the other Egyptian fathers was entering a spiritual battlefield in which the most obvious lines of engagement were all drawn by gender. As with the women martyrs of a previous generation, the only way for a woman in this context to claim respect and legitimacy for herself was, in effect, to repudiate her own gender and appropriate that of her critics. Sarah's bald and uncompromising remarks are some of the only things known about her, beyond an anecdote in which she is recorded as wrestling with her own sexuality in much the same heroic terms as the desert fathers. It is not surprising that one of her other recorded teachings is a prayer, not to become "a penitent at the door" of every one of her potential critics, but to retain purity of heart toward all.

The training, even mastery, of desire and the inner tranquility which resulted, which Christian asceticism promised to the practitioner, clearly appealed to both men and women. As it developed in Syria and Egypt, the monastic tradition sought, not simplistically to divide soul from body, but to help the soul to inhabit the body in a deeper and more integrated fashion, partly through rooting out the destabilizing forces of the passions (Nussbaum 1994, pp. 359–401; Miller 2005, pp. 247–249; Swan 2001, pp. 32–70; Williams 2021). Another woman teacher, Amma Theodora, noted dryly that the minute one attempts to live in this way, "in peace," the soul finds itself beset by myriad temptations and the dragging lassitude of depression, *accedie*. She and a contemporary, Amma Syncletica, both described the ongoing burden of what modern readers might well describe as mental illness, a recurring obstacle in the long psychological battles of monastic life. The only way to make progress, Theodora argued, was through humility; likewise, Syncletica approved of constructive penitence but, in the face of self-mockery and despondency, recommended consistent, regular prayer and psalmody. All rejected distraction and change for change's sake; Syncletica in particular counseled against the pitfalls of a too flamboyant ascetic practice (Ward 1975; Bongie 2003, Sections 40, 86, 94, 100; see Figure 4.1).

Ironically, of course, if Sarah and the other women ascetics of the desert had not attracted notice from the men around them, even such fragments of their teaching that were recorded would have been lost. What has been preserved was indelibly shaped by the particularly gendered perspective of the desert literature. Because these and other texts survived, and because of the wisdom many over the centuries have found in this tradition and through its practices, the vehemence of the

*A History of Women in Christianity to 1600*, First Edition. Hannah Matis.
© 2023 John Wiley & Sons Ltd. Published 2023 by John Wiley & Sons Ltd.

**Figure 4.1** Syncletica of Alexandria. *Source:* Anonymous / Wikimedia Commons / Public domain.

misogyny expressed, both in the desert fathers' teaching and in the asceticism of Late Antiquity, has come to seem a normal part of the Christian tradition. Harder to recapture for a modern reader is the abiding fragility and ambiguity behind the uncompromisingly gendered language, and the experimental and fluid nature of ascetic teaching. In the early years of the desert, it has been argued, misogyny was a rhetorical tool which played a structural role in maintaining city and desert, women and men, as distinct and separate spheres of activity (Brown 2008, p. 243). In much messier reality, however, Antony never moved so far away that the faithful could not find him again. Whether sincere or not, the perennial complaint of the early monastic hermits was that their renown had brought the distractions of the city out into the desert. Despite the stark divisions between the genders in the monastic literature, behind every ascetic aficionado in Late Antiquity stood another, more ambivalent figure: that of the city woman with her dangerous but necessary patronage, who supported Antony and the other monks with donations of food, who sought their spiritual counsel, and who brought them their sick and asked for their intercession. "Many people, then, have found salvation in a city," Syncletica taught, "while imagining the conditions of a desert. And many, though on a mountain, have been lost by living the life of townspeople" (Bongie 2003, Section 97).

## Wars and Rumors of Wars

The city was radically changing around the desert in ways which impacted how the ascetic woman would be remembered in an increasingly Christian society. Between 350 and 370, the central Asian steppe saw its worst drought in two thousand years, forcing westwards nomadic pastoralists, desperate to feed their flocks and herds, disrupting not only grazing patterns but also traditional definitions of tribal identity (Harper 2017, p. 192). These non-Greek speakers, the "barbarian" tribes from which much of western Europe traditionally traces its identity, were not pure racial or ethnic entities but loose conglomerations of peoples who spoke common languages: a Goth, it has been argued, was the ancient historical equivalent of an American. Moreover, many of these people became ready muscle for recruitment into the Roman army, taking long terms of service within the empire, which made them intimately familiar with Roman ways of life. These groups were not literate in their own languages and did not have their own systems of writing or written traditions of recorded history. As a consequence, much of what is known about them comes from much later, Roman sources driven by external rhetorical agendas: the Germanic woman and the desert mother had that much in common (Goffart 2005; Curta 2001, 2005, 2021).

For Constantine and his successors, far more dangerous than the western frontier was the Persian military threat in the east. As a consequence, from the Council of Nicaea onwards, the political pressure on the emperors to create religious unity among the Christian community was considerable, if ultimately not achievable in practice. Meanwhile, the Persians stoked theological squabbles in the Christian east by sheltering and patronizing schismatic groups, alongside the still-numerous communities of Jews in Syria, the Iraq, and Arabia. The church in Syria venerates a group of Persian martyrs from the fifth century, largely converts to Christianity from Zoroastrianism and targeted not so much by the king as by the Zoroastrian clergy. Martha was the daughter of a Christian craftsman, a resettled refugee, who took a vow of virginity. Likening herself to Isaac, before her execution she said, "But I *do* have wood and fire, for the wood is the cross of Jesus my Lord, and I *do* have fire too – the fire that Christ left on earth." Like Martha, Tarbo was a martyred "daughter of the covenant," living in a kind of house community with her sister and her maid, also committed to virginity; they were accused of witchcraft and executed. A group of five such "daughters of the covenant" from the place where modern-day Kerkuk now stands were executed under Shapur, including the fittingly named Thekla. The story of their martyrdom was translated into Greek, and their cult spread as far as Crete (Brock 2020). Anahid seems to have been a prominent convert who had been healed of multiple illnesses through the prayers of another convert-turned-monk; she continued to be miraculously healed despite the various tortures inflicted upon her (Brock and Harvey 1998, pp. 63–99). It may have been as a result of this brief spate of Persian persecution that Syriac-speaking Christians began to settle along the Coromandel coast in India by the end of the fifth century. More likely, converted Sassanian merchants, traveling on trade routes extending along the coast of the Indian Ocean, brought the faith with them, by the sixth century making the claim that they had been evangelized by the apostle Thomas (Andrade 2018).

Within the empire, until the end of the fourth century there continued to be significant numbers of pagans who were not resigned to the emperors' new preference in religion. For a brief moment under the reign of Julian (r. 361–363), a Roman emperor who had been raised as a Christian reconverted to paganism. Publia was a widow from Antioch, the city where Ephrem spent the last years of his life as a refugee. Theodoret of Cyrrhus called her a deaconess, and like Macrina, she founded a monastery in her house. When she and the other women pointedly sang psalms against idolatry as the emperor passed by, Julian "commanded one of his bodyguards to strike her on either side of the face, and to bloody her cheek with his hands" (Madigan and Osiek 2005, pp. 48–50). The deaconess Susanna, sometimes called Susanna Eleutheropolis, is an even more highly colored pastiche of the tropes of martyrdom and asceticism starting to become fixtures of the literature in this period. Said to be the daughter of a Jew and a pagan priest, when she became a Christian she freed her slaves, dressed herself as a man, and joined an ascetic community in Jerusalem under the name of John. In a twist common to the literature, another devout woman then fell in love with

"John" and Susanna had to reveal herself to the visiting bishop, who made her a deaconess and the abbess of the women's community in his diocese. She remained there until her martyrdom (Madigan and Osiek 2005, pp. 55–56).

Not surprisingly, Julian's premature death in battle with the Persians was hailed by Christians as another act of divine deliverance, but it also marked a watershed moment. Constantine had encouraged Christian polemicists like Eusebius and Lactantius, but he and his successors had also permitted the continuation of traditional "pagan" religious observances. This older, pagan generation, many of whom had been Julian's supporters and who had taken for granted that the traditional religion would always remain as a part of their political reality, were muscled aside in the later fourth century by a group of younger men. For this next, ambitious generation, the successors of Eusebius and Lactantius, their Christian beliefs were part and parcel of what was replacing the world of their elders, which they could see had irrevocably changed. It would be this next generation who supported the new and aggressively Christian dynasty established by the general Theodosius, who made Christianity the official religion of the empire in 380 CE. Many of these young men, the aristocrats in particular, were also seeking by joining the clergy to escape the heavy tax burden of Diocletian's reorganization of the empire. By and large, they became the bishops of the fourth- and fifth-century church, carrying over the inherited civic and social responsibilities of their class into the practice of their pastoral office.

In this context, the ongoing fascination with Egyptian monasticism in the west can be seen as a kind of "youth culture," both a movement of social protest and also an emerging political platform (Watts 2015, pp. 149–165). This can be seen most clearly in the glittering career of Ambrose, bishop of Milan, and the voluminous correspondence of the equally aristocratic ascetic, Paulinus of Nola. In the eastern empire, by contrast, the episcopate became so staffed by governmental functionaries that it came to resemble a kind of civil service, forfeiting much of the charisma the office had once possessed in the days of Ignatius of Antioch. As the episcopate became ever more closely linked to imperial and military authority, the ascetics of the Syrian and Egyptian desert were sought out by ordinary people to perform miracles and wonders precisely because they had obviously placed themselves beyond the established religious and political hierarchy. In the eastern church, the monk and the bishop would often be antithetical and competitive, rather than mutually supportive, offices (Brown 1971).

## A Woman Alone

Because of the temptations their gender posed to most monks, many women who sought to live an ascetic life became solitaries out of necessity. On occasion, women disguised themselves as men, sometimes for decades, with their sex often discovered only on their deaths. Marina the harp-player lived in a cave near the Dead Sea, said to be kept alive by a miraculously refilling basket of lentils (Cyril of Scythopolis 1991, pp. 256–257). Palladius records the story of a woman, his neighbor, whom he never met and whose name he never knew. One day, she had a vision of their local martyr, who warned her she would die that day. The woman emerged from seclusion, brought some simple food to the martyr's shrine, gave away the only book she owned, and died that evening (Palladius of Aspuna 2015, pp. 128–129). The Syriac life of another Marina tells the stirring tale of a woman disguised as a monk who, like Susannah, attracted the notice of the local innkeeper's daughter. When the girl became pregnant she named Marina as the father of the child; instead of revealing her identity, however, Marina accepted both the charge and the baby, living for four years outside the gates of her monastery, which she pleaded to reenter. Both she and her adoptive son were readmitted, and she accepted the most menial position in the community for the rest of her life, the true story only discovered on her death (*Life of St. Mary* 1996, pp. 7–12).

In the case of the first Marina, one wonders if she had a little, less supernatural help from family or friends. Likewise, the tale of the second Marina illustrates just how entangled the life of a monastery could become with its local community. Another fifth-century Syriac story told the poignant tale of Maria, the niece of the monk Abraham of Qidun. Her family were innkeepers who, as in the story of Marina, supported Abraham and his monastic community. However, Maria's parents died and, in desperate circumstances, the girl turned to prostitution. Abraham had a dream, however, and sought out the girl, who confessed her earnest desire to escape her present life and returned with the old man to the desert, where she died. Her lament, recorded in acrostic form, closely echoes the language of the psalter: "Receive the weeping and tears of my wretched state, Lord; wipe out the bill which I wrote through the Murderer's guile. May he be ashamed because your compassion has wiped it out, so that it can never again be exacted" (Brock and Harvey 1998, pp. 27–39; Cloke 1995, pp. 73–76).

An entire sub-genre of Christian hagiography stems from this later period which centers around the figure of the reformed prostitute. Like the martyr literature of previous generations, these stories were the romances of the desert, and as such, were immensely popular (Brown 2008, p. li; Ward 1987). According to the conventions of the genre, unlike Maria these women had become prostitutes, not through debt or poverty, but through a combination of personal desire and avarice. Most are described as very wealthy. Pelagia the Harlot, for example, may possibly have been – or was intended to be – the famous (unnamed) courtesan mentioned by John Chrysostom in the late fourth century. Her fifth-century Syriac life describes how the gorgeously dressed Pelagia, riding a donkey at the head of a group of mimes or actors, happened to pass through the same town as the bishop of Antioch, who lamented that no one spent as much time on the state of their soul as Pelagia had done on her makeup. Nevertheless, she came to church the following Sunday and was moved to convert by his preaching. On her persistent request, she was baptized immediately through the sponsorship of the "head deaconess" Romana, who took Pelagia into her home. But Pelagia took some of the bishop's clothes and, dressing herself as a man, transformed herself into the monk Pelagios, who lived on the Mount of Olives until her death (Brock and Harvey 1998, pp. 40–62). The lives of Thaïs or Mary of Egypt follow a similarly dramatic trajectory, whereby the wealthy prostitute is transformed into the penitent who has mastered her desires and renounced her ill-gotten gains (*Life of St. Mary of Egypt* 1996, pp. 65–93; Coon 1997, pp. 77–94; Cloke 1995, pp. 194–202; Ward 1987; see Figure 4.2). In the new Eden of the desert, Antony was described as the new Adam, inevitably casting women as new Eves. The repentant woman, however, cast aside the trappings of her dangerously alluring femininity and modeled herself on the Virgin Mary, who succeeded where Eve failed, and on Mary Magdalene. For their readers, whether their allure remained even after their conversion is a more complicated question, just as artistic depictions of the penitent Mary Magdalene across the Christian tradition often remain deliberately erotic (Coon 1997, p. 17; Burrus 2010).

## Women in Community

Over time, women began to live not only as solitaries but in monasteries of their own, although finding traces of them in the archeological record is fiendishly difficult (Brooks Hedstrom 2017, pp. 67–70). The Egyptian Talida, or Talis, lived in a religious community, it was said, of 60 women in the village of Antinoë in the Thebaid, which had 12 women's communities in all by 410 (Elm 1994, p. 328). Much beloved, she was said to remark she needed neither locks nor keys to

**Figure 4.2** Mary of Egypt. *Source:* Anonymous / Wikimedia Commons / Public domain.

keep the women of her community close. Palladius records that a woman he had met in that community, named Taôr, had been in the monastery for 30 years and refused any new clothing, saying, "I am not in need – lest I be forced to go hence." Palladius adds, she remained very beautiful (Palladius of Aspuna 2015, pp. 127–128; Beshara 2019, p. 47). In the monastic community at Bawit, there is a depiction of an "Ama Rachel, the mother of the *heneete*" (Brooks Hedstrom 2017, p. 220). Other women, like Antony's unnamed sister or Pachomius's sister Maryam, entered religious life because their closest male relative had done so, and remained closely affiliated with men's communities. Palladius describes Pachomius's community at Tabennesi as consisting of some four hundred women, separated from the men's house across the river, and visited only by a priest and a deacon on Sundays. Nevertheless, a visiting hermit was able to visit the community when he was told by an angel that the holiest person in the region was a woman there, a holy fool who pretended to be mad (Palladius of Aspuna 2015, pp. 79–81). Anba Amun, said to be the founder of Egyptian monasticism in Nitria, established his wife there in a house of her own. In this way, traditions of syneisacticism continued within coenobitic, or community-based, monasticism. Even when strict isolation between the genders was maintained, however, women's religious communities of this kind continued to be dependent on male religious clergy for the sacraments, and the women's houses were often subordinated to the abbot's authority.

Perhaps the largest double monastery of its kind in Egypt, containing both communal houses and satellite hermitages, was the White Monastery in Sohag in Upper Egypt north of Luxor, which through much of the fifth century was ruled by the extraordinarily long-lived abbot, Shenoute (d. 464; see Figure 4.3). Written in an ornate Coptic, Shenoute's letters which survive demonstrate the extent to which he sought to model himself on the apostle Paul, and the monastery on the traditional household, with its separate quarters for men and women. Shenoute kept the women's portion of the community enclosed and private, governed by a female elder, the *chello*, and a "mother," who at one time was Shenoute's own sister, Tachom. The women, as so often, were engaged in making textiles from flax and linen. They were, in fact, a kind of local industry, while the monastery itself provided food relief during famine and to the destitute. Shenoute's long tenure as abbot of the lively community and his continuous efforts to secure his own authority suggest the complexity of life in a large monastery and the kinds of issues that were likely to emerge in a women's community in particular. Ensuring an equal distribution of goods was chronically difficult. Women stealing extra food, particularly on behalf of an elderly family member, was perhaps the most frequent crime, punished by beatings on the soles of the feet. Shenoute attempted to curb gossip and too much contact between the men's and women's houses, a particularly difficult task when so many people were related to one another. Precisely insofar as Shenoute kept his distance from the women, he fretted that Tachom and the others kept secrets from him and,

**Figure 4.3** Shenoute of Sohag. *Source:* The Metropolitan Museum of Art / Wikimedia Commons / Public domain.

in a host of small ways, resisted his authority (Krawiec 2002; Elm 1994, pp. 298–310).

Where women fit in the realigning world of Late Antiquity remained a matter of ongoing negotiation. The recent military disasters of the empire had fostered a certain amount of general skepticism in the capacity of the empire's traditional civic structures to support the poor. In its place was an increased emphasis on the nuclear household, even if that household was eventually turned into a monastery or the monastery modeled on the household (Brown 2008, p. 306). From the beginning of the fourth century, young men no longer looked to "marry up" into socially more powerful and prestigious families, signaling the end of old-fashioned Roman *sine manu* marriage practices. This next generation of young men sought to make their own fortunes rather than to rely on those of their in-laws, and if anything, like the young Augustine, sought concubines of lower social status who were not likely to encumber their careers (Cooper 2007, pp. 146–156). It was the end, therefore, of the ambiguous freedom of the Roman wife who belonged within her father's remit rather than that of her husband. From around 400, literary descriptions of relations between a husband and wife within a marriage relied much more heavily on the language of submission and even used analogies of masters and slaves.

## The Virgin and the Widow

Small wonder, then, that Christian writers found it easy to satirize the drudgery of married life, and to glorify by contrast the liberty of the Christian virgin. The virgin would become such an important and contested figure within the church of Late Antiquity precisely because, in a time of transition, she stood simultaneously for both tradition and change; as such, she was both reassuring and profoundly disturbing (Cooper 1996). Because the virgin's charismatic power was seemingly innate, linked with her physical body, the virgin simply *was*: she did not require further credentials, and she did not have to be incorporated or accommodated into an existing clerical or ecclesiastical hierarchy within the church. Now that the episcopate was a prize coveted by aristocratic families, the virgin posed no direct competition. If she herself were aristocratic and wealthy, a virgin living enclosed in her family home had in many ways chosen a profoundly traditional path, one in which her elective privacy could be seen as part of her modesty, her *pudicitia*. By extension, her asceticism even advanced the prestige of the more public members of her family.

Particularly when women's religious communities grew to some size and offered food or poor relief, deaconesses like Romana were increasingly elided with the structures of monastic life. In later centuries, "deaconesses," now often widows, administered the community and, over time, became an office nearly indistinguishable from that of an abbess. In Antioch, the young heiress Olympias (d. 408) was a close friend of another religious woman, Theodosia, cousin to Gregory Nazianzen, and she may have deliberately modeled her way of life on Macrina. Like Macrina, Olympias maintained her status as a "virgin widow," although in her case her marriage seems to have actually occurred, whether or not it was ever consummated. When her husband died, the emperor Theodosius pressured her to marry, not least to return her considerable fortune to circulation. She refused, however, even when the emperor froze her finances, until eventually Theodosius weakened. At 30, Olympias became a deaconess in Constantinople and established her own religious community, where she became a spiritual mentor to many, not least to John Chrysostom (Elm 1994, pp. 178–181; Cloke 1995, pp. 94–96; Mayer 1999). According to the *Lausiac History*, John Chrysostom's own aunt, Savinianê, was a deaconess in his native city of Antioch (Palladius of Aspuna 2015, p. 103).

A very real tension existed between ascetic women's marginalization from the ecclesiastical hierarchy and their potentially destabilizing presence in, or absence from, the local church community. In the fifth century, regular clergy in Rome began to fret over the power ascetic teachers were gaining as private spiritual directors of wealthy aristocratic women. What, after all, did the enclosed virgin do with her time? Who did she read, and were the books heretical? Was the virgin's apparent *pudicitia* mere artifice, covering up overweening spiritual conceit, and making her physical virginity a fraud? Who did she think she was? The very veiling of a virgin could be construed as a form of (her) flirtation (Wilkinson 2015, pp. 117, 127). The criteria by which one could judge the authenticity or calculation of women's ascetic performance drove ongoing and furious discussion within the church. The monk Jovinian, who was attacked not least by Jerome and Ambrose for his critiques of women's asceticism and for denying the perpetual virginity of Mary, seems in part to have rebelled at the ways that monasticism, far from making everyone equal, was in fact creating a new kind of hierarchy, a spiritual *cursus honorum* (Hunter 2007, p. 64). What no one could argue with was that the presence of religious women in the church was now too obvious and influential to be ignored (Brown 2008, p. lviii).

## The Ascetic Patroness

In the fourth and fifth centuries, a small group of aristocratic women fashioned a new role for themselves in the church: that of the ascetic patroness. As a secluded practitioner herself and a benefactress of others, the ascetic patroness ideally encouraged various different religious authorities to compete with one another to support her vocation, to act as her personal spiritual director, or to make her the dedicatee of theological works. This role did not necessarily require her to retain her own personal virginity, particularly if she were asking on behalf of young daughters or dependents. Many of these women, in fact, were very wealthy widows. Some, although not all, were themselves marginal within the very highest levels of society in a city like Rome. They allied themselves with ambitious ascetics, the most famous of whom in later Christian tradition was Jerome, who was himself both on the make and on the fringes of real power and authority. Together, their combined presence almost immediately and continuously fueled controversy within the established church. Moreover, these women, both virgins and widows, inspired other women who looked to them as models in a way that has been compared to celebrity fan culture today (Schroeder 2017, pp. 59–63). The overall effect was to normalize women's ascetic practice and those writers, like Jerome, who supported it, both at the time and in the Christian tradition afterwards. Because this period is so formative for Christian thought and identity, arguably this occurred at the expense of those at the time who were attempting to defend and define a Christian theology of marriage. Certainly these ascetic debates forever shaped Christian discourses around sexuality.

The first and perhaps the most successful of the ascetic patronesses was Melania the Elder (c. 341–410), one of the *gens Antonia* and, by any estimate, one of the super-rich of her day (see Figure 4.4). Widowed at 21 with three children and already known to be an ascetic, she first used her considerable prestige to launch the political career of her son in Rome. But in 373 or 374, Melania left the city and journeyed with her favorite teacher, Rufinus of Aquileia, to the Holy Land, where she established a religious community on the Mount of Olives. She was also said to have rescued the young ascetical writer Evagrius, in disgrace following a too-close entanglement with an official's wife in Constantinople (Young 2017). According to Palladius, Melania also used to sponsor a group of Egyptian monks, in exile for their Nicene Christianity, by dressing herself as

**Figure 4.4** Melania the Elder. *Source:* Anonymous / Wikimedia Commons / Public domain.

a servant. When an official tried, in effect, to shake down Melania for a bribe by imprisoning her, she responded with a combination of humility, hauteur, and not-so-veiled threat. "I am the daughter of N. . . the widow of N. . ., and the servant of Christ; do not despise the meanness of my appearance. I am capable of raising myself up if I want to; you cannot terrify me in this matter or take what is mine. This I revealed to you so you do not unwittingly incur charges" (Palladius of Aspuna 2015, p. 109). She was immediately released.

Only Evagrius's letters to Melania survive and not hers to him, but what does exist supports the report that Melania was formidably learned. The *Lausiac History* records that, as well as the works of many of the other biblical commentators, she knew around three million lines of Origen – an astonishing figure, indicative both of the strength of Melania's dedication and of Origen's total output, now known only in sadly fragmentary form and in translation (Clark 1983, pp. 164–165; Palladius 2010). It would be Melania's love of the Alexandrian martyr, in part, which polarized the church in the so-called "Origenist controversy," a significant component of which revolved around Origen's notoriously speculative views on gender and the resurrection. For Origen and those teachers who were influenced by him, including Macrina and the Cappadocians, both sex and gender were human constructions which might not last beyond death. The Latin world, however, including Augustine in later decades, argued that biological sex was a component of the physical body and therefore would take part in the resurrection of that body (Brown 2008, p. 384; Krawiec 2017). It is difficult to know how widespread these teachings were or how they were interpreted, particularly in informal conversations between individual women and spiritual directors, but it seems likely that monastic discourses of women "becoming male" through either martyrdom or asceticism featured strongly. When Jerome could not resist sniping against his former friend, Rufinus of Aquileia responded tartly that Jerome had been a devotee of Origen himself in his youth. While quite true, this sent Jerome into a veritable tailspin of invective and self-justification throughout the 390s which, much later, helped to demonize the teachings of Origen in the European west, even though at the time of writing they predated the theological definitions of Nicaea. In the moment, however, safe in Jerusalem and sheltering under Melania's formidable patronage, Rufinus was largely invulnerable to Jerome's attacks, and both he and Jerome knew it all too well (Brown 2012, pp. 260–261, 276–280; Edwards 2015, p. 293).

The story of Jerome and the women who patronized him, and which, by extension, crystallized certain discourses of women's asceticism in the western church, is a story of profound insecurity. Jerome was originally from Stridon, a town so small that it is difficult to locate today, but he had studied with the best rhetoricians in the empire and was a brilliant Ciceronian stylist. His only living was his pen; he had none of Melania's practiced wealth and power, and even his ordination to the priesthood was through a schismatic bishop. Looking for imperial patronage in his early career, Jerome, like Augustine after him, may never have intended to enter the church at all. However, he fell in with the ascetic set in Rome, and with his linguistic talents quickly made himself an authority, especially with Pope Damasus I. One of his first patrons was the widow Marcella (b. 330s, d. 410), who by the 370s had turned her mansion on the Aventine Hill in Rome into a religious community. Her younger sister Asella lived by herself in her Roman townhouse, to whom Jerome wrote an admiring letter describing her way of life. Over the course of an epistolary friendship that spanned some 30 years, only 19 letters of Jerome's survive, most over the course of a single year. What these suggest is that, while Jerome was rhetorically positioning Marcella as a kind of textual alter ego to himself, ultimately he was dependent on Marcella, and not the other way around (Cain 2009, pp. 35–36, 68–98; Cloke 1995, pp. 91–93; Brown 2008, p. 373; Brown 2012, pp. 268–270).

Jerome's friendship with another wealthy widow, Paula, would be both his undoing and his salvation, at least for his literary legacy. Paula (b. 347, d. 404) had been widowed from 381 and had five children, including her daughters Paulina, Blesilla, and Eustochium. Paulina had married the Christian senator Symmachus. Blesilla was already widowed, however, while Eustochium had declared her intention young to make a vow of virginity, and even trained for some time in Marcella's house. It is possible that poor Blesilla felt herself to be in a constant state of ascetic competition with her younger sister which she felt she could never win. Tragically, Blesilla died in 384, and the public outcry against both her known habits and the influence of Jerome himself was such that, after the death of his protector Damasus, Jerome was publicly censured and expelled from Rome in 385. Accompanying him to the Holy Land, despite everything, were Paula and Eustochium. Jerome set himself up as a desert hermit in Bethlehem, although if he was a recluse, he always retained access to friends, including Paula, who had good libraries. All three set about learning Hebrew (Cain 2009, pp. 36–37, 102–114; Brown 2012, pp. 262–272). Jerome's letters to Eustochium regarding the exaltedness of the virgin's vocation became very popular in later centuries, not least because they established the use of the Song of Songs as a component of the spirituality of the religious woman (Jerome 1996).

Paula's daughter-in-law Laeta wrote to Jerome concerning Paula's granddaughter, also called Paula, who would have been very young at that time but was already, like the prophet Samuel, vowed by her family to God. Jerome recommended that the young girl be given forms of educative play – alphabet blocks, in fact – and that she be taught early how to read and write, and how to spin wool. Makeup, elaborate hairstyles, and jewelry should be forbidden, and her parents, nurses, teachers, and friends should keep her from any frivolous habits or exposure to the opposite sex. Given her age, Jerome allowed her to eat meat, but as soon as she was old enough, a vegetarian diet with no alcohol was clearly to be preferred, along with a minimum of trips to the public baths. Her study was to be of scripture (Jerome 1989, Letter 107). Whether chastened by past experience or simply aware of the child's young age, Jerome's advice is fairly moderate – and very much in keeping with more conservative Roman practices, in fact. But it underscores the extent to which raising a daughter to be a practicing ascetic was now an aristocratic family strategy, and one in which Jerome expected everyone to participate.

Jerome's chronic spleen is legendary in the Christian tradition. Less immediately obvious, to pious Christians then and now, is the extent to which Jerome's capacity to pick controversial rhetorical battles kept the subject of women's religious devotion alive in public Latin Christian discourse, discussed by some of the most gifted theologians and rhetoricians of the day at the height of their inventiveness and creativity. As someone living an ostensibly monastic life, Jerome himself was ambivalent, at least publicly, about the extent of his involvement with religious women, complaining plaintively that he would have written for men instead had any been interested. Nevertheless, women and their patronage were without question the foundation of Jerome's largely informal teaching ministry. Unlike Rufinus of Aquileia, he was never a bishop or even a regular priest, despite the cardinal's hat with which he is often depicted in later Christian art. By default, therefore, he described and in some way set as traditional a form of women's asceticism which, because it was financially independent, existed largely separate from the interference of episcopal authority and certainly from the local congregational church.

In Milan, the bishop Ambrose supported both the use of monks in active ministry and women's asceticism, which extended to his public defense of the perpetual virginity of Mary. His own sister Marcellina was a practicing religious woman, and he was profoundly influenced by Athanasius of Alexandria and by the example of the model monk, Anthony, as Augustine would later be. In his 377 work, *On Virgins* or *De virginibus*, like Jerome, Ambrose linked the spiritual life of the Christian virgin both with the expectant love poetry of the Song of Songs and with the discourses of Christian athleticism and martyrdom. Perhaps the most dramatic feat of Ambrose's glittering career was the happy "discovery," in 386, of two brother martyrs, Gervasius and Protasius, as his new church in Milan was under construction. Throughout his career, Ambrose juxtaposed the physical relics of the martyrs with the living relics of the bodies of religious women to create an argument for his own authority within his city (Shuve 2016, pp. 109–137).

Augustine's initial acquaintance with Ambrose was supported and reinforced by his formidable mother, Monica, then a devout widow: "when Ambrose saw me he would burst out in praise of her, telling me how lucky I was to have such a mother" (Augustine 1997, p. 137). Ironically, despite their personal differences, both Ambrose and Jerome seem to have weighed in eloquently in support of religious women, charismatic virgins in particular, partly to compensate for their own, personal insecurities over their own ordinations. Ambrose's own ascent to the bishopric of Milan was famously rushed, while Jerome the outsider remained extremely touchy about his exile from Rome (Hunter 2007, pp. 222–224, 230–242). Fraught and conflicted though this legacy is, however, through the letters and treatises that survive, both Ambrose and Jerome established perhaps the most important and lasting precedent in western Christianity for close, pastoral relationships between male clergy and devout and learned laywomen.

A contemporary of Paula's and Marcella's, but of far greater social status, was Faltonia Betitia Proba (d. 432), who married into the fabled *gens Anicii* of Rome. Jerome, for one, would have loved to have found himself within Proba's social orbit, although she does not seem to have had any kind of reciprocal interest (Brown 2012, p. 313; Hunter 2007, pp. 68–72). Instead, Proba devoted herself to reading and to study, and to the production of an art form particularly distinctive to Late Antiquity: the *cento*. Christian or not, the basis for the education of aristocratic citizens of the Roman Empire remained, for Latin-speakers, the *Aeneid*, and for Greek-speakers, the *Iliad* and the *Odyssey*. The *cento* was an elaborate form of pastiche whereby individual lines from classical epic were recombined to form very different narratives: in Proba's case, retellings of Genesis and the life of Christ made up of lines and half-lines from the *Aeneid*. Despite its frequent dismissal by earlier generations as unoriginal, Proba's *cento* is, first and foremost, an early work of female Christian authorship. But it also represents a historical moment when, like the young Augustine, the educated and literate upper classes discovered Christian scripture. Despite what, to them, felt like a very foreign and often repugnant style, both preachers like Augustine and poets like Proba had to make scripture esthetically and intellectually palatable for themselves and others (Proba 2015; Cooper 2007, pp. 65–68).

This is the world into which the granddaughter and namesake of Melania the Elder, Melania the Younger, was born (c. 385–453; Clark 2021). Inheriting the family's vast fortune, Melania and her young husband, Pinianus, in the wake of losing their two young children, decided to live an ascetic life. First, however, they had to divest themselves of their very considerable possessions in Rome itself. Their mansion in Rome, probably on the Celian Hill, was so lavish that Theodosius's niece Serena, the wife of Stilicho the Vandal general, said that even she could not afford to purchase it (Chin 2017; Clark 2021, pp. 106–109). In later life Melania would utterly refuse such finery, having a kind of allergic reaction when presented with an embroidered gown (Schroeder 2017, p. 52). In 408 or 409, amid the gathering threat of Gothic tribes to the north, Melania and Pinianus left Rome for North Africa and Augustine's birthplace of Thagaste, where one of Melania's estates dwarfed the town that grew up in its shadow (Clark 1993, p. 97). One Sunday in church, Pinianus was very nearly body-snatched into the clergy in the way that Augustine himself had once been in Hippo. Interestingly, it was Melania's quiet refusal, and not Augustine's or even Pinianus's, which seems to have stopped the would-be ordination.

After the sack of Rome in 410, it would be the arrival of a flood of such wealthy, educated, and sometimes pagan refugees from Rome which prompted Augustine to write *The City of God*.

Although Augustine did not need Melania's patronage, he clearly would not have refused it on behalf of his city or his congregation, and certainly he wanted the rhetorical coup of winning such prominent aristocrats to the Catholic cause in North Africa. In the event, Melania and her husband remained in Thagaste until 417, endowing both a men's and a much larger women's religious community (Clark 2021, pp. 131–137). Then they traveled on to the Holy Land, where in the 430s they repaired and further endowed the religious communities once founded by Melania the Elder.

As much as her grandmother amidst the Origenist controversy 20 years before, Augustine worried about some of Melania's other, more overtly Pelagian friends. After all, Pelagius was an itinerant monastic teacher not so very different from Jerome. In fact, between 413 and 414, both men wrote works of advice for the same aristocratic woman, the virgin Demetrias, under the care of her aunt, the widow Juliana, who was herself the daughter-in-law of Proba, while Augustine's 414 treatise, *On the Good of Widowhood*, was also addressed to Juliana and Proba (Drake 2017; Cain 2009, pp. 160–166). Pelagius's own teaching has largely been submerged under the weight of the controversy which followed after his death. His advice to Demetrias, which fortunately survives, is comparatively conventional, but the appeal of his teaching seems to have lain not so much in the content of his teaching as in its exclusive, aristocratic ethos, which drew on Stoic discourses around the proper regulation of the body (Wilkinson 2015, p. 44). Precisely because he was more in step with the class identity of a woman like Proba and her family, Pelagius seems to have been far more successful in Rome than Jerome had been. Certainly some of the vitriol he inspired derived from Jerome's and Augustine's worried reactions to the clout he wielded in the particularly charged and competitive market of spiritual authority in Rome. At the same time, Augustine seems to have waited until Melania had left North Africa for good before he went after Pelagius by name (Cohick and Hughes 2017, p. 214).

## Everyday Saints

In his *Confessions*, through the rich and complex portrayal of his mother, Monica, Augustine created a very different kind of saint from the heroic portrayal of Melania the Elder. Monica's own name seems to be Punic in origin, perhaps better spelled "Monnica," and both she and Augustine were hardly the western Europeans which they are often portrayed as in Christian art (Clark 2015; Brown 2000, p. 21). From a very ordinary social background, Monica seems to have been Christian for all of Augustine's life, in contrast with his pagan father, Patricius, who converted late. With an explosive temper, Patricius was at times abusive, and certainly Augustine has nothing good to say about him. Between mother and son, however, Augustine describes a bond that was intimate to the point of stifling. Famously, when Augustine left for school in Carthage, he compared Monica to Dido weeping on the shore, and he sneaked out so that he would not have to say goodbye to her (Augustine 1997, Bk. V.8). When he became a Manichaean, however, Monica seems to have banned him from the house in Thagaste, and interestingly, it is in these years that Augustine entered into a sexual relationship that would last for the next decade and more of his life. Although Augustine never mentions the name of the woman, usually called his concubine, this woman was almost certainly of much lower social status than Augustine himself. She bore Augustine his only son, Adeodatus.

Ironically, when Augustine got his career-making position as a rhetor in Milan, it was Monica who ended Augustine's relationship, as she prepared to arrange another, more socially advantageous union for him. We never know what happened to this woman, but Augustine describes his own personal devastation. It is possible that Augustine's emotional vulnerability, combined with his newfound respect for Ambrose and the bishop's interpretation of Christian scripture, laid the groundwork for Augustine's subsequent conversion to Christianity. Certainly the society marriage never came together, and Augustine's nervous breakdown before his conversion temporarily destroyed his voice and forced him to leave his position. After so many years of waiting, Monica was overjoyed by Augustine's conversion and accepted their departure; mother and son had by then come to a deep spiritual friendship. In 387, Monica lay ill in the port city of Ostia, and Augustine describes a kind of mystical experience in which, over the course of an ordinary conversation with his mother, the walls of the room seemed to disappear as they talked and they were suspended together in eternity. Monica would die before they could return home, and Augustine vividly describes the numbness of grief which he felt in the immediate wake of her death, so much so that he found himself unable even to weep for her (Augustine 1997, Bk. IX; see Figure 4.5).

Ten years later, Augustine began perhaps his most famous work, *The Confessions*, amidst the unfolding Donatist controversy in North Africa, at the same time when Jerome was ferociously attacking Rufinus in the Origenist controversy. Donatism was itself a North African theological response to Christian martyrdom, whose adherents repudiated all those who had betrayed the scriptures and their fellow Christians to Roman authority. By the time Augustine became a bishop, Donatists constituted perhaps half the North African church (Brown 2000, pp. 207–221). Among many other things, Augustine's *Confessions* represents his exploration of how divine grace gradually works on the unconscious and even actively rebellious soul, the antithesis of what he saw as the Donatists' spiritual perfectionism. By this argument, the persistent and even maddening devotion of his flawed but faithful mother, who by the end of the story has ceased to be Dido-esque even in her son's mind, emerges as one of the most significant conduits of this divine grace. Certainly she is described warmly and lovingly, but Augustine, for all his love of things monastic, uses none of the heroic discourses of the Christian desert with regard to her. As a result, Monica, firmly rooted in her ordinary femininity, is described in vastly different terms from those used to describe Melania the Elder or Macrina the Younger.

**Figure 4.5** The tomb of Monica, Sant'Agostino, Rome. *Source:* Peter1936F / Wikimedia Commons / CC BY-SA 4.0.

In his later years, as the Pelagian controversy grew more and more polarized, Augustine clung to his very personal vision of a church, filled not with rarefied moral agents, but with continuously failing and forgiven sinners: not a monastery, in short, but an ordinary parish (Demacopoulos 2017, pp. 96–105). Augustine's efforts to create a language to describe the ingrained, structural nature of human sinfulness led him to propound what would become in Latin theology the doctrine of original sin. Augustine saw nothing "natural" as sinless or untainted by the willful human desire to dominate others, including the realm of human sexuality. In his search for a vehicle by which original sin was transmitted between parent and child, Augustine chose the disordered power relations of human lust, or concupiscence, a sin to which he admitted extensive personal experience. In the bitterest throes of the Pelagian controversy, in his 424 treatise, *On the Good of Marriage*, Augustine went so far as to say that the procreation of children was the central and only redeeming purpose of Christian marriage. He died only six years later.

These grim reflections were later systematized in western Latin theology in such a way as to place the blame on women, recast as little Eves, for inciting concupiscence – an argument that stands in direct contradiction to the rest of Augustine's thought. Ironically, it is a conclusion far more in keeping with the demonic temptresses of the desert literature than with the reality of Augustine's own, much more rich and complex life experience or even his more generous pastoral instincts. For all his fearsome reputation in the history of Christian attitudes to gender and sexuality, after the Gothic sack of Rome in 410, in which many of the city's religious women were raped, Marcela was beaten, and Melania's fine mansion destroyed, it would be Augustine who would console the victims of sexual violence. What had happened was not their fault, he argued; they could not be blamed for that to which they had not consented, and heaven would treat them no differently (Augustine 2003, Bk. 1, Sections 16–28).

In contrast with the personal detail lavished on Monica in *The Confessions*, Augustine names neither his concubine nor his sister, who joined a religious community in his own diocese. It was for this sister that he composed the rule which bears his name (Augustine 1984). Precisely because it was not a programmatic set of specific directions so much as an open letter which included consistent guiding principles by which the bishop wanted to organize a Christian community, the great strength of the Augustinian Rule has always been its flexibility. Augustine's central emphasis is the mutuality of Christian community, but it is clear that, just as in the letters of Shenoute in Egypt, class distinctions in a monastery remained extremely difficult to eradicate. Gossip, within and without, continued to be a problem, and Augustine himself was clearly experimenting with the degree of distance as a bishop he should keep from women in religious life. In the western church, the Augustinian Rule has traditionally been implemented most often by canons, communities of ordained clergy, and by religious women, for whom its flexibility and open-ended nature has been invaluable, as women's religious communities have adapted and changed in different regional and cultural contexts.

The pilgrimages and patronage of both Melanias in and around Jerusalem set a certain precedent for ascetic women in Rome. It is perhaps in imitation of Melania the Elder that one of Jerome's lesser-known protégés, the twice-married and divorced Fabiola, would travel as a penitent to the Holy Land in 395 (Cain 2009, pp. 172–178). But all of these women were themselves walking in the footsteps, not only of Christ and the disciples, but also of Constantine's mother, Helena, imitating the patterns of patronage of the imperial royal family. Constantine had dedicated the Church of the Resurrection, the ancestor to the Church of the Holy Sepulchre, on Golgotha in 348. An invaluable source in the history of early Christian liturgy is the intrepid Spanish pilgrim Egeria, who traveled east, perhaps from Galicia, most likely between 381 and 384 (*Egeria's Travels* 1999). Egeria is sometimes called an abbess, given that her letter which survives is directed home to her "sisters," often to encourage them that their liturgical practice is in tune with that of Jerusalem. However, such a journey as Egeria made would have taken considerable amounts of both time and money, and it does not seem likely that an abbess could have remained apart from her religious community for so long, or had such resources at her disposal, unless she were to some extent "in the world." On the other hand, her descriptions of Christian liturgy are precise and detailed, particularly concerning the celebration of Holy Week in Jerusalem, which she records with a professional eye. She may well have been a deaconess, although it is impossible to know for certain. In addition to her long stay in Jerusalem, Egeria climbed Mt. Sinai, traveled to Alexandria, and journeyed to Antioch and Constantinople. Along the way, she visited the cells of many monks and hermits, again suggesting the isolation of the desert was, for the dedicated religious tourist, very surmountable and even part of its appeal.

## A Family of Helenas: Theodosian Women

The ascetic women patrons of Rome wielded their greatest degree of influence exactly at a moment when the city itself was becoming strategically marginal. Protecting the northern frontier, the imperial and military presence had shifted north to Milan. In Constantinople, on the other hand, patterns of noble patronage were indelibly shaped by the presence of the emperor Theodosius and the dynasty he created. More than the ancient civic structures of pagan Rome, like a Christian Augustus, Theodosius established his own family and their own personal morality as central to the empire's well-being (Holum 1982). As a consequence, the female members of the Theodosian dynasty were presented with substantial political opportunities, but which depended on the public cultivation of themselves as Christian benefactors. Like Macrina's household monastery, Basil of Caesarea had stressed the need for religious communities to provide poor relief, with a particular commitment to the care of lepers, and this tradition had advanced under the indomitable preaching of John Chrysostom. The emperor Theodosius's first wife, the Spaniard Flacilla, was known for her patronage of hospitals, so much so that, when Theodosius's son Arcadius married a half-Frankish bride, Eudoxia tried to overcome the stigma of her tribal origins by imitating her predecessor (Holum 1982, p. 24; Clark 1993, pp. 68–69).

In 387, Theodosius married his second wife, Galla, who would bear a daughter, Galla Placidia. The little girl was placed in the care of Theodosius's niece and adopted daughter, Serena, and taken to the court of Serena's husband, the Vandal general Stilicho, in Milan in 395. For the next seven years, Galla Placidia grew up in the same world that Augustine had left not long before: a world in which certain non-Roman tribal customs, like the wearing of trousers, were starting to become customary even among the Roman elite (Harlow 2004). Galla Placidia had been taken to Milan to further strengthen the bonds between the imperial family and its military allies in the west; a marriage alliance was proposed between herself and Serena's second son. But in the early fifth century crisis piled upon crisis. Faced with an increasingly united Gothic host, now ably led by a young general, Alaric, Stilicho preemptively decamped from Milan to the city of Ravenna on the marshes of the Adriatic Sea. In Constantinople, the emperor Arcadius died in 408. Sensing Roman weakness and indecision, Alaric and the Goths tried again. This time Stilicho's troops mutinied; later that year Arcadius's successor, his brother Honorius, ordered the mass execution of Stilicho, Serena, and her sons.

In 410, Galla Placidia was 22, and whatever future she had anticipated had been ripped away from her. Taken captive by the Goths during the sack of Rome, she lived with them for three years, eventually marrying Alaric's brother and successor, Athaulf. For the Goths at this time, Galla Placidia's imperial lineage was a tremendous coup, and she would grandly name her first son Theodosius. However, her fortunes quickly changed again when both her husband and her son died in 415. Athaulf's successor was said to have publicly humiliated Galla Placidia by making her walk a circuit of more than 10 miles in front of his chariot. Again left without protectors, Galla Placidia was, however, eventually sent back to Ravenna when the Goths faced famine, and interestingly, she kept a cohort of Gothic soldiers with her in Ravenna. She was again married off, in the same year, this time to the imperial general in Ravenna, with whom she eventually had a son and daughter. Galla Placidia and her new husband, Constantius, were declared co-emperors of the western empire alongside the childless Honorius, her half-brother, until Honorius began to have strange and incestuous designs upon her. In 423, she was banished to Constantinople, the city of her birth, which she had not seen since she was seven years old (Herrin 2020, pp. 23–24).

To this point Galla Placidia's career is already an astonishing instance of how a royal woman could find herself both pawn and participating agent in relations between the Theodosian family and the tribes along the borders of the Roman Empire. It is arguable which group behaved toward her in a more civilized manner. Even more astonishing, however, was the political coup which happened next. When her brother died, Galla Placidia returned to Ravenna, ostensibly to act as regent for her young son. In fact, she would rule the western empire for the next 25 years. Firmly and finally in charge, she took on the full burden of imperial administration and, perhaps not surprisingly given her past history, stubbornly refused to relinquish control even when her son was of age to rule and she ought to have made arrangements for the marriage of her daughter. Herself a Catholic Christian, she nevertheless protected the Arian beliefs of the Goths who continued to live in Ravenna, while her administration laid the foundations of what would be later called the Theodosian Code of Roman law. The gorgeous mosaics of the so-called "Mausoleum of Galla Placidia" in Ravenna were originally intended to be part of a larger church dedicated to the Holy Cross. She included a portrait of herself – perhaps the first time a Roman emperor had placed their image within the church sanctuary – and in general, seems to have created an elaborate program of religious patronage to present herself as the Helena of Ravenna (see Figure 4.6). Galla Placidia was buried in Rome in 450 (Herrin 2020, pp. 34–54).

**Figure 4.6**  The Mausoleum of Galla Placidia, Ravenna. *Source:* Daniele Marzocchi / Wikimedia Commons / CC BY-SA 4.0.

In Constantinople in 399, Theodosius's son Arcadius and his wife Eudoxia had a daughter, Pulcheria. Eudoxia bore a son, also called Theodosius, two years later, before dying as a result of a miscarriage (Mayer 2006). Technically Galla Placidia's great-niece, Pulcheria and she were, in fact, exact contemporaries of one another, although they would not meet again until Galla Placidia's brief exile in 423. Pulcheria was raised by one of the Armenian or Persian eunuchs who staffed the palace, where the memory of her dead mother was still extremely vivid. Perhaps because she was so close to her brother in age, she also received his formidable classical education. During this period, John Chrysostom went into exile as bishop of Constantinople, not least because he had come to disapprove of Pulcheria's mother's use of elaborate court ceremony; when his exile became permanent John would turn his misfortune into an elaborate rhetorical stance, a prophetic persona by which he could appeal to correspondents like the deaconess Olympias (Barry 2019, pp. 92–102). Unlike the ascetic teachers of Rome, who vied with one another, John was in a battle with the imperial court; at stake were the hearts and minds of the devout women of Constantinople, and there are signs that all were becoming more vehement in their theological and political opinions.

In 412, when she had just come of marriageable age by Roman standards, Pulcheria took the startling step of declaring herself the head of the imperial family, and the next year, a consecrated virgin. Unlike Galla Placidia, by declaring herself withdrawn from the marriage market, Pulcheria paradoxically strengthened her claim to be her brother's virtuous guide and guardian. She began to rule as regent for her brother, who partly withdrew from public life and earned a reputation, justified or not, as a clumsy academic recluse. Pulcheria modeled her own piety on the tradition set by her mother Eudoxia, Flacilla, and the empress Helena: her own personal self-regulation justified and supported the exercise of empire, and assisted the smooth progress of its administration. As a consecrated virgin, Pulcheria had, in effect, turned herself into a palace eunuch; publicly devoted to her brother, she could not be accused of furthering the interests of her own children as potential heirs (Tougher 2004). But, like Elizabeth Tudor in the sixteenth century, there was also a strong component of Marian veneration in Pulcheria's Virgin Empress, which emphasized something that had always been a traditional part of women's asceticism in the monastic tradition. In her own virginity Pulcheria emulated how the Virgin became a direct conduit, a relic and an icon, of the Word of God.

The most unfortunate consequence of this aggressive and ambitious political and theological program was that Pulcheria echoed and even furthered the anti-Jewish hostility she shared with John Chrysostom, and which was endemic in the Christian discourse of the day (Jacobs 2004). In 414, Theodosius II passed legislation which forbade the building of new synagogues and permitted the dismantling of old ones, provided it did not disturb the peace (Holum 1982, pp. 98–99). This, of course, was almost impossible for ordinary people to foresee, and in practice the legislation encouraged looting and rioting in cities with historic Jewish communities. When imperial officials attempted to blunt the measures, the outcry from monastic leaders like the Syrian ascetic Simeon Stylites made Theodosius II back down. Although it is easy to exaggerate the degree to which ordinary people understood the finer points of the Christological controversy, where theological debate touched down into popular piety, sectarian urban violence could erupt unexpectedly. The pagan philosopher Hypatia was notoriously trampled to death by a mob of Christians egged on, it is said, by Cyril, bishop of Alexandria.

In 421, a famous ivory, now in Trier, preserved the imperial triumph of the empress Pulcheria with the help of the relics of Stephen the martyr against an attacking Persian force. Next to the church, awaiting the translated relics, Pulcheria holds the long cross of imperial victory (see Figure 4.7). In 415, Pulcheria and Theodosius had consecrated the second church of Hagia Sophia in Constantinople, where she seems to have stood alongside her brother at the high altar, in the

**Figure 4.7** The Trier Adventus Ivory, Trier Cathedral Treasury. *Source:* Chris 73 / Wikimedia Commons / CC BY-SA 3.0. Os repro ex excest quos eum etur aligenist que et quam faccabores debitemquas denissum

Anastasis itself, during the liturgy (Kateusz 2019, pp. 161–163). She was known to donate her own rich silk garments to cover the high altar, and like Galla Placidia, Pulcheria placed her own portrait among the other icons above the altar in the Great Church at Constantinople. It was exactly practices like these that inspired the new bishop of Constantinople, the Antiochene Nestorius, to oust Pulcheria from standing next to her brother, and even to ban her from communion altogether, on Easter Sunday in 428. This was a declaration of war indeed, although Theodosius's initial response seems to have been to try to clear Nestorius from charges of heresy for rejecting *Theotokos*, or *God-bearer*, as an official title of the Virgin Mary. However, by the Council of Ephesus in 431 the battle lines were firmly drawn against Nestorius through a coalition of Pulcheria, Cyril of Alexandria, and popular devotion to the Virgin. In this case, unlike that of John Chrysostom, it was the empress who held the populist position, and it was her brother who backed down.

The Council of Ephesus is sometimes understood to have launched devotion to the Virgin Mary in the history of the church. This is almost certainly an exaggeration; popular devotion to the Virgin had to be of some strength to make it a potent political ally. By the late fourth century, the "Memory of Mary" had already become a feast of the church in Constantinople. Rather, the Council of Ephesus advanced Marian devotion by condoning the widespread incorporation of Marian texts into the liturgy. The *Protoevangelium* of James became a reading in the east, and it was often read in the medieval west even when writers worried over its apocryphal nature. In the fifth century, biblical interpreters in Constantinople began to read Psalm 44, the royal epithalamium sometimes thought to be the marriage of Solomon and the Queen of Sheba, as a Marian allegory. Not surprisingly, it is also often sung during the veiling of a consecrated virgin (Banev 2014). Although it is impossible to date with certainty, it is probably in the sixth century that the Akathist hymn to the Virgin was composed in Constantinople, and it continues to play a central role in Orthodox liturgy today (Maunder 2019, pp. 116–118).

Pulcheria would be displaced, at least temporarily, not by the Persians or even by Archbishop Nestorius but by another woman, Theodosius II's wife Aelia Eudokia. Legendarily beautiful, like Pulcheria she was also highly educated, although from a very different school – Alexandria's great theological rival and Nestorius's home town of Antioch. A pilgrim to Jerusalem with Melania the Younger, Eudokia, not least, was publicly modeling herself as a new Helena, perhaps at Pulcheria's expense. Rivalry between Pulcheria and Eudokia, always intense, in the wake of the Council of Ephesus now became unbearable, and court jokes about imperial threesomes turned sour (Holum 1982, pp. 130–131). One story says that Theodosius laid a trap and gave his wife an apple, who gave it in turn to a court official, who gave it back to the emperor, who had the man executed. Ultimately, Theodosius banned both his sister and his wife from court. Eudokia returned to Palestine and settled among the devout in Jerusalem, in her way living a life not so very different from that of Jerome or of Paula. Like Proba in Rome, she wrote a *cento* which survives, retelling the story of the woman who anointed Jesus's feet. In Greek rather than Latin, many of the lines Eudokia borrows originally belong to the description of Odysseus's old nurse, Eurykleia (Sandnes 2021). Similarly, she wrote paraphrases of Zechariah and Daniel, eight books of commentary on the Octateuch, and a retelling of the martyrdom of Cyprian of Antioch (Cohick and Hughes 2017, pp. 241–252). Pulcheria, meanwhile, entered a religious community in Constantinople.

In 450, Theodosius II was unexpectedly killed in a hunting accident, leaving no heirs. In this fragile moment, Pulcheria left her religious seclusion behind and reentered her public role. She had never attempted to rule alone and in her own right, however, and so, probably to assuage pressing military concerns, the Virgin Empress decided, of all things, to get married. Pulcheria was then over 50, and she entered the marriage on condition that her husband respect her vow of virginity. It was in this urgent spirit of last-minute political reinvention that Pulcheria summoned the Council of Chalcedon in 451. Her motives were undoubtedly mixed, but Chalcedon was also an effort at real theological compromise, helmed by someone who had devoted her entire life to the close relationship between ascetic and liturgical practice and theological language concerning the divine and human nature of Christ. According to tradition, when the council placed its decrees in the tomb of the virgin martyr Euphemia, the saint chose the scroll of what would become the Orthodox formulation of the nature of Christ. True or not, it is a fitting illustration of the power of women's asceticism throughout the duration of the Christological controversy.

Passion spent, Pulcheria died only two years later in 453, and did not live to see the intensity of the division fostered by the Chalcedonian formula, not least among her former friends in the church in Egypt. As with Nicaea, Chalcedonian theology was only fully developed in later centuries, and enforced with particular stringency under the reign of Justinian in the mid-sixth century. Meanwhile, the Coptic church in Egypt, which rejected the Council of Chalcedon, would be instrumental in shaping the growing church in Ethiopia, in particular the strength of its popular Marian devotion. According to tradition, the most senior cleric of Ethiopia, the *abuna*, was an Egyptian monk, but the Ethiopian church maintained links with the church in Syria as well. In 524, the persecution of a group of Ethiopian Christians then in Persian-controlled South Arabia led to the creation of a number of women Christian martyrs, collectively called the Martyrs of Najran, which became popular in both regions – unfortunately featuring the region's numerous Jewish population, instead of the Romans or the Persians, as the women's chief persecutors (Esler 2019; Brock and Harvey 1998, pp. 100–121).

The legacy of Chalcedon created a competitive confessional environment in the Christian Middle East which western Europe would not experience until the Reformation, including multiple distinct groups of Miaphysites, Chalcedonians, and the Nestorian Church of the East. The fine-grained theological discussion of these different churches in Syria, arising primarily out of monastic centers like the great community at Qenneshre, probably passed over the heads of most "simple believers" and, no doubt, most ordinary clergy as well. Nevertheless, in a Middle East which remained predominantly Christian for centuries after the Muslim conquests, whether one addressed the Virgin

Mary as *Theotokos* remained a confessional marker among Christians in Mosul into the fifteenth century (Tannous 2018; Carlson 2018, p. 162). The sixth-century holy woman Shirin from northern Iraq was an ascetic devoted to the recitation of the psalter and the reading of scripture, and acted as a spiritual director to monks, ordinary laywomen, and the Syrian chronicler Sahdona, who writes of her with great affection and real respect (Brock and Harvey 1998, pp. 177–181).

As with the Tudors in the sixteenth century, the direct and unintended consequence of the establishment of the Theodosian dynasty was that, for 25 years and more, both the eastern and western halves of the Roman Empire were ruled by women. The collapse, when it came, occurred not because women's rule made the Roman Empire weak, luxurious, or decadent, but arguably because of the political, administrative, and military instability which preceded their reigns and were precipitated by their deaths, which caused the fracturing of the Roman world-system into isolated regions. Ironically, it seems to have been Galla Placidia's death-grip on the western capital of Ravenna which led her rebellious daughter to propose herself in marriage to Attila the Hun, an alliance which, mercifully, never occurred; another woman was said to have dispatched the great Attila on his wedding night. Inevitably, religious controversy played a role in the weakening of the eastern empire, although it is difficult to prove it was more fatal to the empire's eastern defenses than a century of near-constant war against the Persians would be. In Pulcheria's defense, Justinian and, indeed, no later Byzantine emperor succeeded any more than she had done in resolving the theological questions posed by churches with different languages, liturgies, monastic cultures, and traditions of interpreting scripture. Pulcheria's compromise, although imperfect, remains as part of her religious and political legacy to the Christian tradition.

# References

Andrade, N.J. (2018). *The Journey of Christianity to India in Late Antiquity: Networks and the Movement of Culture*. Cambridge: Cambridge University Press.

Augustine (1984). *The Rule of Saint Augustine: Masculine and Feminine Versions* (trans. R. Canning). London: Darton, Longman, and Todd.

Augustine (1997). *The Confessions* (trans. M. Boulding). New York: New City Press.

Augustine (2003). *City of God*, reprinted ed. (trans. H. Bettensen). London: Penguin.

Banev, K. (2014). "Myriad of names to represent her nobleness": the church and the Virgin Mary in the psalms and hymns of Byzantium. In: *A Celebration of Living Theology* (ed. J.A. Mihoc and L. Aldea), 75–103. London: Bloomsbury.

Barry, J. (2019). *Bishops in Flight: Exile and Displacement in Late Antiquity*. Oakland: University of California Press.

Beshara, A. (2019). *Egyptian Women in the Coptic Orthodox Church of Egypt*. Meadville: Christian Faith Publishing.

Bongie, E.B. (trans.)(2003). *The Life and Regimen of the Blessed and Holy Syncletica by Pseudo-Athanasius*. Eugene: Wipf and Stock.

Brock, S. (2020). Five women martyrs: from Persia to Crete. In: *Garbed in the Body: Embodiment and the Pursuit of Holiness in Late Ancient Christianity* (ed. G. Frank, S.R. Holman and A.S. Jacobs), 221–233. New York: Fordham University Press.

Brock, S. and Harvey, S.A. (1998). *Holy Women of the Syrian Orient*, updated ed. Berkeley: University of California Press.

Brown, P. (1971). The rise and function of the holy man in Late Antiquity. *The Journal of Roman Studies* 61: 80–101.

Brown, P. (2000). *Augustine of Hippo*, 45th anniv. ed. Berkeley: University of California Press.

Brown, P. (2008). *The Body and Society: Men, Women, and Sexual Renunciation in Early Christianity*, rev. ed. New York: Columbia University Press.

Brown, P. (2012). *Through the Eye of a Needle: Wealth, the Fall of Rome, and the Making of Christianity in the West, 350–550 AD*. Princeton: Princeton University Press.

Burrus, V. (2010). *The Sex Lives of Saints: An Erotics of Ancient Hagiography*. Philadelphia: University of Pennsylvania Press.

Cain, A. (2009). *The Letters of Jerome: Asceticism, Biblical Exegesis and the Construction of Christian Authority in Late Antiquity*. Oxford: Oxford University Press.

Carlson, T. (2018). *Christianity in 15th-Century Iraq*. Cambridge: Cambridge University Press.

Chin, C.M. (2017). Apostles and aristocrats. In: *Melania: Early Christianity through the Life of One Family* (ed. C. Michael Chin and T.S. Caroline), 19–33. Oakland: University of California Press.

Clark, E.A. (1983). *Women in the Early Church*. Collegeville: Liturgical Press.

Clark, G. (1993). *Women in Late Antiquity: Pagan and Christian Lifestyles*. Oxford: Clarendon Press.

Clark, G. (2015). *Monica: An Ordinary Saint*. Oxford: Oxford University Press.

Clark, E.A. (2021). *Melania the Younger: From Rome to Jerusalem*. New York: Oxford University Press.

Cloke, G. (1995). *This Female Man of God: Women and Spiritual Power in the Patristic Age, 350–450*. London: Routledge.

Cohick, L.H. and Hughes, A.B. (2017). *Christian Women in the Patristic World*. Grand Rapids: Baker Academic.

Coon, L.L. (1997). *Sacred Fictions: Holy Women and Hagiography in Late Antiquity*. Philadelphia: University of Pennsylvania Press.

Cooper, K. (1996). *The Virgin and the Bride: Idealized Womanhood in Late Antiquity*. Cambridge: Harvard University Press.

Cooper, K. (2007). *The Fall of the Roman Household*. Cambridge: Cambridge University Press.

Curta, F. (2001). *The Making of the Slavs: History and Archaeology of the Lower Danube Region, c. 500–700*. Cambridge: Cambridge University Press.

Curta, F. (ed.) (2005). *Borders, Barriers, and Ethnogenesis: Frontiers in Late Antiquity and the Middle Ages*. Turnhout: Brepols.

Curta, F. (2021). *The Long Sixth Century in Eastern Europe*. Leiden: Brill.

Cyril of Scythopolis (1991). *The Lives of the Monks in Palestine* (trans. R.M. Price). Kalamazoo: Cistercian Publications.

Demacopoulos, G.E. (2017). *Five Models of Spiritual Direction in the Early Church*. Notre Dame: University of Notre Dame Press.

Drake, S. (2017). Friends and heretics. In: *Melania: Early Christianity through the Life of One Family* (ed. C. Michael Chin and C.T. Schroeder), 171–185. Oakland: University of California Press.

Edwards, M. (2015). *Religions of the Constantinian Empire*. Oxford: Oxford University Press.

Egeria's Travels (trans. J. Wilkinson). (1999). 3. Warminster: Aris & Phillips.

Elm, S. (1994). *Virgins of God: The Making of Asceticism in Late Antiquity*. Oxford: Clarendon.

Esler, P.F. (2019). *Ethiopian Christianity: History, Theology, Practice*. Waco: Baylor University Press.

Goffart, W. (2005). *The Narrators of Barbarian History (AD 550–800): Jordanes, Gregory of Tours, Bede, and Paul the Deacon*, reprinted ed. Notre Dame: University of Notre Dame Press.

Harlow, M. (2004). Clothes maketh the man: power dressing and elite masculinity in the later Roman world. In: *Gender in the Early Medieval World* (ed. L. Brubaker and J.M.H. Smith), 300–900. Cambridge: Cambridge University Press.

Harper, K. (2017). *The Fate of Rome: Climate, Disease, and the End of an Empire*. Princeton: Princeton University Press.

Hedstrom, B. and Darlene, L. (2017). *The Monastic Landscape of Late Antique Egypt*. Cambridge: Cambridge University Press.

Herrin, J. (2020). *Ravenna: Capital of Empire, Crucible of Europe*. London: Allen Lane.

Holum, K.G. (1982). *Theodosian Empresses: Women and Imperial Dominion in Late Antiquity*. Berkeley: University of California Press.

Hunter, D. (2007). *Marriage, Celibacy, and Heresy in Ancient Christianity: The Jovinianist Controversy*. Oxford: Oxford University Press.

Jacobs, A.S. (2004). *Remains of the Jews: The Holy Land and Christian Empire in Late Antiquity*. Stanford: Stanford University Press.

Jerome (1989). Letter 107. In: *The Library of the Ante-, Nicene, and Post-Nicene Fathers*, Second series, vol. 6 (trans. W.H. Fremantle), 189–195. Grand Rapids: Eerdmans.

Jerome (1996). To Eustochium (Letter 22). In: *Handmaids of the Lord: Contemporary Descriptions of Feminine Asceticism in the First Six Christian Centuries* (ed. and trans. Joan M. Petersen), 171–217. Kalamazoo: Cistercian Publications.

Kateusz, A. (2019). *Mary and Early Christian Women: Hidden Leadership*. London: Palgrave Macmillan.

Krawiec, R. (2002). *Shenoute and the Women of the White Monastery: Egyptian Monasticism in Late Antiquity*. Oxford: Oxford University Press.

Krawiec, R. (2017). The memory of Melania. In: *Melania: Early Christianity through the Life of One Family* (ed. C. Michael Chin and C.T. Schroeder), 130–147. Oakland: University of California Press.

Madigan, K. and Osiek, C. (ed.) and (trans.)(2005). *Ordained Women in the Early Church: A Documentary History*. Baltimore: Johns Hopkins University Press.

Maunder, C. (ed.) (2019). *The Oxford Handbook of Mary*. Oxford: Oxford University Press.

Mayer, W. (1999). Constantinopolitan women in Chrysostom's circle. *Vigiliae Christianae* 53 (3): 265–288.

Mayer, W. (2006). Doing violence to the image of an empress: the destruction of Eudoxia's reputation. In: *Violence in Late Antiquity: Perceptions and Practices* (ed. H.A. Drake), 205–213. Aldershot: Ashgate.

Miller, P.C. (2005). *Women in Early Christianity: Translations from Greek Texts*. Washington D.C.: Catholic University Press.

Nussbaum, M.C. (1994). *The Therapy of Desire: Theory and Practice in Hellenistic Ethics*. Princeton: Princeton University Press.

Palladius (2010). Life of Melania the Elder. In: *Lives of Roman Christian Women* (ed. and trans. C. White), 49–56. London: Penguin.

Palladius of Aspuna (2015). *The Lausiac History* (trans. J. Wortley). Kalamazoo: Cistercian Publications.

Proba (2015). *Proba the Prophet: The Christian Virgilian Cento of Faltonia Betitia Proba* (ed. S.S. Cullhed). Leiden: Brill.

Sandnes, K.O. (2021). Eudocia's Homeric cento and the woman anointing Jesus: an example of female authority. In: *Patterns of Women's Leadership in Early Christianity* (ed. J.E. Taylor and I.L.E. Ramelli), 211–227. Oxford: Oxford University Press.

Schroeder, C.T. (2017). Exemplary women. In: *Melania: Early Christianity through the Life of One Family* (ed. C. Michael Chin and C.T. Schroeder), 50–66. Oakland: University of California Press.

Shuve, K. (2016). *The Song of Songs and the Fashioning of Identity in Early Latin Christianity*. Oxford: Oxford University Press.

Swan, L. (2001). *The Forgotten Desert Mothers: Sayings, Lives, and Stories of Early Christian Women*. New York: Paulist Press.

Tannous, J. (2018). *The Making of the Medieval Middle East: Religion, Society, and Simple Believers*. Princeton: Princeton University Press.

The Life of St. Mary (trans. N. Constas)(1996). *Holy Women of Byzantium: Ten Saints' Lives in English Translation* (ed. A.-M. Talbot), 1–12. Washington D.C.: Dumbarton Oaks.

The Life of St. Mary of Egypt (trans. M. Kouli)(1996). *Holy Women of Byzantium: Ten Saints' Lives in English Translation* (ed. A.-M. Talbot), 65–93. Washington D.C.: Dumbarton Oaks.

Tougher, S. (2004). Social transformation, gender transformation? The court eunuch, 300–900. In: *Gender in the Early Medieval World, 300–900* (ed. L. Brubaker and J.M.H. Smith), 70–82. Cambridge: Cambridge University Press.

Ward, B. and (trans.)(1975). *The Desert Christian: Sayings of the Desert Fathers*. New York: Macmillan.

Ward, B. (1987). *Harlots of the Desert: A Study of Repentance in Early Monastic Sources*. Kalamazoo: Cistercian Publications.

Watts, E.J. (2015). *The Final Pagan Generation*. Oakland: University of California Press.

Wilkinson, K. (2015). *Women and Modesty in Late Antiquity*. Cambridge: Cambridge University Press.

Williams, R. (2021). *Looking East in Winter: Contemporary Thought and the Eastern Tradition*. London: Bloomsbury.

Young, R.D. (2017). A life in letters. In: *Melania: Early Christianity through the Life of One Family* (ed. C. Michael Chin and C.T. Schroeder), 153–176. Oakland: University of California Press.

# 5

## Bridgeheads in the Early Medieval Kingdoms

Women at the Frontiers, 500–750

In 531, the Frankish king Chlotar I raided the neighboring kingdom of Thuringia, killing its lord, Hermanfred, and many of his household, capturing a small girl. He carried this girl back to his court, where he eventually married her. The girl's name was Radegund, and at the end of her life her friend, the court poet Venantius Fortunatus, wrote an elegiac account of the raid in Radegund's voice: "I, a barbarian woman, cannot do justice to these lamentations nor to the universal mourning, awash with a lake of tears. Everyone had his own cause for grieving, I alone shared them all; that universal grief was a grief that was specific to me. Fortune provided consolation to the men whom the enemy struck down; I alone was left surviving to weep for them all" (Fortunatus 2017, pp. 762–763).

After the death of Galla Placidia, the Roman Empire in the western Mediterranean collapsed. The complex military and economic system of the empire ceased to function, splintering western Europe into smaller, regional territories soon taken over by non-Roman overlords. The most dramatically affected were North Africa and England (Wickham 2005, pp. 87–93, 303–364, 635–644). As Augustine lay dying in 430, the Vandals lay siege to his city, severing North Africa from Sicily and Rome. In 410, the decision to withdraw the legions from England left the island defenseless. It is thought that the frantic British who remained asked Germanic tribes of Angles and Saxons to take the legions' place, but predictably, these soon began to rule in their own right. England was reorganized into a complex patchwork of regional kingdoms, while Wales remained in British hands and the Picts controlled Scotland. The elaborate Roman villas were eventually abandoned, the forts and bathhouses soon thought to be the work of giants. The Angles and Saxons brought their own gods, while Christianity disappeared, along with its books and the craft of writing itself. Writing in the eighth century in the English kingdom of Northumbria, the Venerable Bede could not forgive the British for their apostasy (Campbell 1991; Bede 1999, Bk. I).

After the sack of Rome in 410 that had so appalled Jerome and made Melania the Younger a refugee, the confederation of Goths in Italy split into two factions, sometimes called the Ostrogoths and Visigoths. The Ostrogoths settled in northern Italy, establishing a magnificent court in Galla Placidia's Ravenna under Theoderic the Great (r. 471–526) and his learned daughter Amalasuintha. There, perhaps paradoxically, all things Roman were celebrated and copied, just as they had been when Galla Placidia lived among them. Meanwhile, the Visigoths took control of the old Roman region of Provence, crossed the Pyrenees, and conquered Spain, where they ruled until the Muslim conquest in 711. The rest of Roman Gaul was overrun by other groups, the Burgundians and the Franks, who, like the English, established several regional kingdoms ruled by one interconnected family dynasty, the Merovingians.

*A History of Women in Christianity to 1600*, First Edition. Hannah Matis.
© 2023 John Wiley & Sons Ltd. Published 2023 by John Wiley & Sons Ltd.

The fall of Rome is one of the most debated and value-laden events in world history. Inevitably, the Roman Empire has usually been contrasted with the kingdoms and the people which followed it, either as a fable of civilization destroyed by violent "barbarians," or conversely, in racialized terms, as the infusion of warrior "Germanic" stock into decadent and corrupt Rome (Lopez-Jantzen 2019). In either case, the contrast between Roman and non-Roman is more rhetorical than real, not least because, far from being destroyed, the Roman Empire continued in Constantinople for another thousand years. In the west, different tribes had different agendas and different working relationships with Roman authority: Stilicho was a Vandal, Alaric a Goth. But all of the tribes who came from outside the empire had extensive experience of it, either through living alongside it, through trading with it, or through serving long years in the army. By and large, when possible the early medieval successor-kingdoms sought, not so much to destroy and eradicate their Roman forebears, but to coopt their legacy.

In the short term, from the point of view of an ordinary woman in an ordinary village, not very much about her daily life probably changed after the fall of Rome. When precisely "the fall" had even occurred would have been difficult to pinpoint, or would have seemed to happen in different regions at different times. Overwhelmingly the economy remained agricultural. Without a standing army to support, taxes may well have been lighter, at least in certain places. Urban centers sustained under the empire by state-sponsored long-distance trade suffered massive depopulation, however, with Rome gradually losing three-quarters of its inhabitants. In some areas, the pressure for intensive agriculture seems to have lessened, and with it, some of the desperate need for labor. Women seem to have married later and had fewer children (Wickham 2005, pp. 533–550). Throughout the early Middle Ages, the west, always much more sparsely populated than the great cities of Syria, Egypt, and Asia Minor, simply did not have the people to compete or compare with Constantinople or, in later centuries, with Harun al-Rashid's Baghdad.

## Rome Reunited? Theodora and Justinian

The dream of a reunited Roman Empire persistently remained, however, and for a brief moment under the emperor Justinian, came close to being realized. Justinian was himself a westerner, the nephew of a Latin-speaking general, and a supporter of Chalcedonian orthodoxy. His wife Theodora, by contrast, was the daughter of a bear-keeper at the circus, who in her youth had worked as an actress and, it was whispered, as a stripper. These rumors were gleefully recorded by the historian Procopius in his *Secret History*, and it is difficult to gauge whether they had any basis in fact at all, or were merely sexual slurs from start to finish. Procopius wrote equally poisonous invective against Justinian's general Belisarius, whom he ridicules as a cuckold completely distracted by his wife's infidelity, which he manages to blame on Theodora's bad influence; the *Secret History* is deliberately written as a topsy-turvy depiction of a disordered political life in which women rule (Procopius 2007; Heather 2018, pp. 13–15). Like Augustine's concubine, Theodora had certainly had a previous sexual liaison before Justinian married her, and had borne a daughter. Certainly she was beautiful, like so many of the Byzantine empresses perhaps even chosen with her looks in mind. Theodora proved to be a canny and ruthless political operator, however, and it may well have been her persistent staying power and her influence on Justinian which so annoyed Procopius, who seems to have delighted in portraying both as unnatural rulers. Amidst the Nika riots in 532, Theodora was said to have single-handedly prevented Justinian from abandoning the city. The couple would re-dedicate the present church of Hagia Sophia in the ruins – outdoing, said Justinian, not only Constantine and Helena but Solomon himself. Meanwhile, Theodora became known for her ongoing patronage of

Miaphysite clergy. This may have been a deliberate political compromise worked out by the imperial couple, whereby Justinian supported Chalcedonian orthodoxy publicly, while privately Theodora kept at least some of the Miaphysites loyal to the empire.

In 533, in a brilliant stroke, Justinian's general Belisarius retook North Africa from the Vandals. Amalasuintha's assassination provided the pretext for Belisarius to invade Italy, where he hoped for similar success and the reunification of the empire (Heather 2018, pp. 147–178; Herrin 2020, pp. 89–147). However, fate turned against Justinian and Theodora. The Italian war was disastrous: a long, drawn-out campaign which exhausted the empire's finances, destroyed far more of classical Rome than the Goths had ever done, and exacerbated religious tensions between Catholic Christians and the Arian Goths. The "late antique little ice age" created both extreme cold in Europe and lasting drought in North Africa, hitherto one of the richest regions in the Roman Empire for grain and olive oil. As a result of volcanic eruptions in what is now El Salvador, 536 became known as "the year without summer," which, probably because of extra rainfall, affected rodent populations in Mongolia. In 541 the Justinianic Plague, now known to be bubonic plague, struck the eastern empire, killing somewhere between a third and a half of the population (Harper 2017, pp. 253–255). Even Justinian caught it, though he would be one of the plague's rare survivors.

One of the greatest and yet most perplexing monuments of the reign of Justinian and Theodora is the famous pair of ruler-portraits in mosaic in the church of San Vitale in Ravenna (see Figure 5.1). Placed on either side of the enclosed space of the high altar, emperor and empress are flanked, respectively, by men and women representing both clergy and court, many of whom are depicted in liturgical vestments. Theodora wears imperial purple and the vivid Byzantine crown and jewels that Pulcheria had worn in her defeat over the Persians, and it is she, not Justinian, who is depicted carrying the chalice (Clark 1993, pp. 107–110). One of the ladies in her train is also carrying "the

**Figure 5.1** Theodora and her entourage, the Basilica of San Vitale, Ravenna. *Source:* Hadrian / Flickr / CC BY-SA 2.0.

eucharistic handkerchief," the *mappula* or maniple, often depicted in apse mosaics of the Virgin Mary (Kateusz and Confalonieri 2021, p. 245). Because of her known Miaphysite sympathies, it is not usual to compare Theodora to her predecessor Pulcheria, and yet in her dress and her proximity to the altar in San Vitale, the Theodoran mosaic is clearly placing itself in the "Pulcherian" tradition of imperial women acting liturgically. The church of San Vitale in Ravenna was built by the bishop as a kind of determined religio-political statement that the empire would continue in his diocese, and was modeled in part after a church in Constantinople that Theodora had heavily patronized. The ruler-portraits were put up by the bishop's successor, now the new archbishop of the region, within a very narrow period between 540 and 544 (Herrin 2020, pp. 160–169).

Justinian and Theodora never went to Ravenna themselves, however, and the ruler-portraits may not be actual depictions of court ceremonial. Whether the mosaics reflect what Justinian and Theodora were actually doing, what they were said to be doing, or merely what the bishop thought they might like, depictions of men and women, *orans*, on either side of the altar were understood as a Greek custom. As such, it carried over into places with heavy Greek influence, which at the time included the city of Rome itself. In the city of Pola, not far from Ravenna, an ivory box from around 430 was discovered depicting both men and women around the altar under a ciborium with twisted columns, a depiction of liturgy done in Old St. Peter's (Kateusz and Confalonieri 2021, pp. 233–238). At that time, Pulcheria would have been firmly established in her practice of standing on one side of the high altar, as both empress and consecrated virgin, and it is not difficult to imagine this setting a precedent for other aristocratic and ascetic patronesses of the church.

## *Presbyterae* and Deaconesses in the Early Medieval West

At the same time, in the Latin west, North African Montanist teaching, one aspect of which seems to have been its endorsement of women priests and bishops, continued in Sicily and southern Italy. In 494, Pope Gelasius I complained that women from those regions were serving at the altar (Gelasius 2014, pp. 143–145). Some of the most astonishing depictions of women bishops and teachers in Christian art are the sixth-century paintings of two women, Bitalia and Cerula, in the catacomb of S. Gennaro near Naples. Both figures are *orans*. Cerula is shown in an elaborately decorated stole, and she stands with the gospels, outlined in fire, above each upraised hand, an indication she was probably a teacher and might have been a bishop (see Figure 5.2). One component of the Priscillianist heresy in Spain seems to have been its promotion of women as clergy, although not very much is known about their teaching or practice. Frankish legislation forbids women to serve at the altar with a frequency that suggests the practice continued to occur. It is possible that the graffiti of "Martia presbytera" discovered near Poitiers is Priscillianist, although she could also be simply the wife of a priest (Macy 2016, p. 60; Madigan 2021, pp. 272–277).

On both sides of the empire, the office of the deaconess continued, but it remained far more common in the Greek-speaking world, particularly when churches remained gender-segregated and the deaconess played a role in preparing women for baptism. A mid-sixth-century document from the city of Ravenna describes a local landmark as "the place of the holy deaconesses," *in sanctas diaconissas*. Sergius, who became archbishop of Ravenna in 744, had been married before he took office; his wife "became a deaconess" (Herrin 2020, pp. 213, 341). Far from the urban landscapes and concentrated populations of the east and its environs, however, in the Latin west the deaconess was gradually transformed into the head of a religious community, eventually becoming indistinguishable from an abbess. In the west, without the presence of an established imperial bureaucracy staffing the clergy, monks too were generally much more common, although clerical

**Figure 5.2**   Fresco of Cerula, catacombs of San Gennaro, Naples. *Source:* womendeacons.

celibacy was hardly enforced anywhere so early. Ironically, by strongly encouraging the practice of infant baptism, Augustine may have done more than anyone to undercut the traditional basis for deaconesses' ministry in the western church. Nevertheless, the rite of ordaining a deaconess survives in five early medieval sacramentaries, liturgical books containing rites performed by bishops. Conversely, appointing an abbess of a particular religious community was liturgically equivalent to appointing a priest or a deacon to a particular local church, particularly when many deacons, often called "Levites" in the early medieval church, never went on to the priesthood (Macy 2016; Wijngaards 2021, pp. 200–205). The title, therefore, survived, although what it was meant to convey remained in flux.

## Women in the Early Medieval Archipelago

Even before the Muslim invasions of the seventh century, the eastern and western halves of the Roman Empire drifted apart, exacerbated by linguistic and cultural differences and by religious controversy, which Justinian's efforts only made worse. Over a century of intermittent but exhausting warfare with the Persians sapped Byzantine strength and finances; "the two eyes of the world," Constantinople and Ctesiphon, made complex alliances with smaller regions and tribes along their borders, exacerbating religious and political factionalism. The Armenian and Georgian churches both venerate Shushanik (d. 476), the daughter of Vardan Mamikonian, Armenia's answer to the emperor Constantine, whose heroic death in the battle of Avarayr against the Persians paved the way for the truce permitting Armenian Christians to practice their religion. Shushanik's husband, however, turned Zoroastrian, and ordered his wife to be killed, the act witnessed by her priest and hagiographer, Jacob Tsurtavi (Tsurtaveli 1983).

Meanwhile, the Nestorian Church of the East continued to make converts among the merchants along the Silk Road, most famously the Sogdians. Christians were well established in the Sogdian capital, Samarqand, which became a metropolitanate in the sixth and seventh centuries. A Syriac manuscript from Turfan venerates one of the most famous saints of the region, the monastic founder Baršabbā, alongside two women saints: Shir, perhaps a version of Shirin, and Zarvandokht, who is otherwise unknown. A Christian church was built in Urgut, near Samarqand; elsewhere, caves seem to have served as Sogdian Christian worship spaces, some bearing inscriptions of believers' names in Arabic, Syriac, and Persian. Heading a list of priests and clerics, the ninth-century T'ang-dynasty Luoyang stele commemorates "the deceased mother, the lady of the An family from Bukhara" (Ashurov 2020).

Following hard on the heels of the emperor Heraclius's victorious lightning raid into Persian territory, in which he reclaimed the looted relics of the True Cross, the early Islamic invasions ambushed Persians and Greeks alike. The catastrophic loss of Jerusalem to the Muslims in 637 CE was followed by several sustained sieges of Constantinople. Long years of sheer, dogged survival transformed the late antique inheritance of the Roman Empire into a carefully administered military machine. To his people the Byzantine emperor remained Melchizedek, priest and king, and court and church remained as intertwined as they had been in the days of the empress Pulcheria (Haldon 1990; Dagron 2003; Wickham 2016, pp. 170–185). Travel by water, always the easiest means of transport in this period, became more difficult with the presence of Muslim pirates in the Mediterranean in the seventh century. Meanwhile, the Byzantine Empire became known for its navy. Some travel to the Holy Land and to Constantinople continued even in the depths of the seventh century, but in this period the entire orientation of the western empire shifted north after the Muslim invasions. The North and Irish Seas did not divide so much as unite the insular world in a giant archipelago stretching north to Iceland and Scandinavia. The coastal and island monasteries founded at this time may seem exotic and remote to contemporary Christians, but at the time they were interconnected in a wider web of water traffic along which things, people, and ideas continued to move (Cunliffe 2001; McCormick 2001; Pye 2014, pp. 27–68).

The eventual re-conversion of the English to Christianity was supposedly inspired when Pope Gregory the Great (r. 590–604) chanced upon English children in the slave market in Rome and remarked, "Non Angli sed angeli!" "Not Angles, angels!" (Bede 1999, Bk. I.23–36, Bk. II.1). It is a reminder that at least one slave market continued to exist in Rome at the end of the sixth century, and that captives from as far away as Britain could end up there. In ensuing centuries, it has been argued that the chief export western Europe had to offer the more advanced Islamic world was, in fact, slaves from eastern Europe – the word slave derives from "Slav" – although firm data is understandably difficult to come by. Within the old Roman Empire, former Roman *latifundia*, the great senators' estates worked by hundreds of slaves, passed into the hands of the new warrior aristocracy. *Servus*, or slave, eventually became "serf": unfree tenant labor formed the underpinnings of the early medieval economy, now largely invisible to us. However, this was no longer the unified "slave society" of Roman Late Antiquity, but a multitude of interlocking "societies with slaves": a diversity of practices around unfree labor, in fact, existed in the early medieval world. Often, women seem to have remained "slaves" as domestic labor in private households, while men became "serfs" with particular agricultural obligations, although unfree women also seem to have worked making textiles in workshops on the old grand estates (McCormick 2001, pp. 792–797; Harper 2011, pp. 497–509; Rio 2017, pp. 141–143, 161–162). Becoming unfree as a prisoner of war remained a significant risk. Meanwhile, for elite and royal families, the taking of hostages was a customary guarantee of political loyalty, and could become a kind of enforced political and cultural education for young men. For aristocratic women, however, captivity led often enough to arranged marriage. Regardless, exile and captivity in all its forms, and the threat of them when outside one's own kin group, was a constant in early medieval society.

Violence, particularly among the nobility and by the nobility against the peasantry, was a terrible if customary part of early medieval life, particularly in remote and unprotected areas. Violence against women we may assume to be even more common. Women in religious communities were not immune, particularly if they traveled. Marriage by capture had a certain precedent in Germanic law codes, and when marriage itself remained very hazily defined, abduction and rape were common (Bitel 2002, pp. 154–199; Nelson and Rio 2013). Common-law marriage was the norm in most cases, but a diversity of marriage practices existed throughout early medieval Europe. Pre-Christian Ireland possessed a massive body of oral laws used to calculate the delicate balance of social status within marriage, and designated multiple grades of union – as many as eight or nine – according to the socio-economic status of both the woman and the man and the amount of property they each brought to the marriage (Bitel 1996; Charles-Edwards 2000).

The Frankish aristocracy and, certainly, Merovingian kings designated a particular queen or primary wife, but it is difficult to say that monogamy was the order of the day. Early medieval queens managed the royal household and, by extension, the royal treasury, in an age when wealth was very often portable, courts were itinerant, and the expectation on the part of guests was of lavish hospitality and royal largesse. Later stories, such as the English epic *Beowulf*, describe the ideal role of a great lord's wife as a "peace-weaver," smoothing over potentially violent quarrels and acting as the generous, hospitable face of royal power (Enright 1988; *Beowulf* 2020, lns. 612–641, 1160–1232). Conversely, however, the queen could be blamed for unpopular policies much more easily than her royal husband and, rightly or wrongly, was often accused of sowing dissension in the shadows.

Beyond managing her children, dependents, and animals, women's work centered around the household manufacture of cloth: flax for linen, but predominantly wool. Carding, dying, spinning, weaving, knitting, and sewing were all essential skills and components of women's labor, and were also the default means by which a women's religious community could supplement its income. Many aristocratic women in particular practiced tablet weaving, which created bands of complex and delicate embroidery. Although medieval textiles do not survive well in the archeological record, some of these woven embroideries have survived as embellishments on ecclesiastical vestments or even as parts of reliquaries. The so-called "Belt of Ailbecunda" preserves the name of the ninth-century woman who made it, alongside her invocation of the name of Christ; it was later turned into a belt which held a small reliquary (Garver 2009, pp. 224–268; Coatsworth and Owen-Crocker 2018, pp. 313–316). Other women sent cloaks to confessors or holy men like St. Cuthbert of Farne, the seventh-century English saint. On his death, the famous hermit's body was wrapped in Byzantine silk, perhaps the garment mentioned in the saint's life, or *vita*, as an abbess's gift (Bede 1998, Section 37; Coatsworth and Owen-Crocker 2018, pp. 327–332, 429–430). Constantinople had smuggled the secrets of silk-making out of China in the reign of Justinian and was the source of fine silk until the high Middle Ages. In the rest of Europe, most people could not afford silk, of course, or would have seen it only in religious vestments or in the garments of royalty. When women could not serve behind the altar, however, they did make or fashion the fine cloth that covered the altar and its precious relics; they clothed the bodies of their clergy and adorned the shrines of their saints.

## A Golden Age for Women?

In the early medieval west a woman was inescapably defined, for good or ill, by her family and her kin group, who would protect her and support her in old age, if she lived so long, and in whose status she participated (Rosenthal 1990). In the Frankish world, women were understood to have a responsibility to maintain the memory of their family, an extension of their role as the keepers of the household. Frankish women's monasticism was deeply connected to the practice of commemoration of the founders and benefactors of individual houses. Religious women in this period often composed the lives of the royal women who founded their communities, and in later years would sometimes circulate confraternity books among other monastic houses and to their patrons and benefactors in the world. In this way, by extension, the commemoration of the dead could lead certain women within a religious community toward the keeping of annals and to the writing of history.

In England, women seem to have enjoyed more rights than they would after the Norman Conquest in 1066 and for centuries after (Stafford 1997; Bitel 2002, pp. 66–94). The prominent roles that women played in religious houses in England in this period are indeed striking, but throughout the insular world it is important to recognize that they were an expression not so much of support for women's rights or status in and of themselves, as of the amount of power at certain women's command by virtue of their family and social connections. Without a professional class or an entrenched bureaucracy in royal courts, royal and aristocratic women could take advantage of opportunities to wield significant power, often when they acted as regents for young sons. In pre-Christian regions such as Ireland, this has sometimes been portrayed as a golden age of women's liberty before the introduction of Christianity brought with it insidious ideas of women's inferiority. But caution is advisable: the powerful and vengeful Queen Medb of the *Táin*, the great Irish epic poem, was an idealization to the poet at the time as much as she is to the modern reader now (*The Táin* 1985, pp. 52–72, 102–110, 168–172, 250–251). Many accounts of "pagan" folklore are, at best, creative Christian retellings or reinventions by monks and clerics of an already long-vanished past.

For better or for worse, in the early Middle Ages, Christianity remained inextricably intertwined with the legacy of Rome. In many places, in a time of great change, that continuity which remained with the older, Roman world lay in the church, with the episcopate in particular becoming the refuge of the old Roman aristocracy. In Spain and Italy, the Goths retained their Arian beliefs into the sixth century, creating tensions with local Catholic believers. In the seventh century, the Lombards in northern Italy were Chalcedonian but repudiated Justinian's Three Chapters, the controversial condemnation of three Nestorian theologians issued in 543. In the complex world of the successor kingdoms, with their shifting attitudes toward Rome and the church, queens were ideally placed to act as bridgeheads, sheltering missionaries and patronizing a new wave of monastic foundations.

## Women and Early Medieval Monasticism

Monasteries in the early medieval West fulfilled a complex set of interlocking roles within society. In a climate colder than the caves of Egypt, shelter was harder to come by, and cenobitic or community monasticism was prevalent. Monasteries were profoundly local institutions, products of, and responsive to, individual acts of patronage. No formal orders yet existed or would exist, arguably, until the twelfth century. The Rule of St. Benedict only began to attract adherents in this period, and did not become any kind of standard of monastic life until the Carolingian Reform in the ninth century. In fact, the first manuscript of the Benedictine Rule that survives is English, dating to around 700 (Benedict 1971–1972; Breay and Story 2018, pp. 100–101). The absolute rule of the abbot or abbess, a legacy of eastern monasticism, created a mechanism by which a good deal of everyday practice could be worked out on a case-by-case basis within each community. Many monastic "rules" were, in fact, largely oral teaching, while some male and female religious were only selectively literate. Chant was local, as were the scripts developed in individual monastic workshops, the *scriptoria*. A great deal of scriptural knowledge, the psalter in particular, was memorized.

Perhaps the most profound consequence of the fall of Rome in the west was the extinction of the Roman educational system, and with it, the gradual disappearance of any sort of cultural glue that united a class of professional, literate, interconnected people (Ward-Perkins 2005; Brown 2013, pp. 232–247). Rome's legal caste, the rhetors, which had produced so many early Christian theologians, was now gone. In its place, monasteries of both men and women copied scripture and the great theologians and, at the same time, preserved classical texts on medicine, philosophy, rhetoric, and the natural world. The rhythms of monastic life to some extent transcended linguistic and cultural boundaries and permitted charismatic monks like the Irish *peregrini*, bent on pilgrimage as a form of ascetic renunciation, periodically to enliven the landscape of continental Europe. This was the great age of the monk-missionary (Wood 2001).

Monasteries were endowed to pray for the welfare of the kingdoms in which they were founded, to bring about divine favor through their own holiness of life, and to pray for the souls of their founders and benefactors. Many were built around the divine power concentrated in holy relics, the sacred bodies of the saints, and in the living bodies of monks and religious women. Particular holiness was attributed to virgins, understood to be living relics imbued with divine power (Brown 1981). There was a fashion in this period for uncorrupt saints, whose bodies did not decay after they were buried initially, and were discovered when translated, or moved, to a new and finer resting place. Perhaps originally inspired by cases of bodies buried in an anaerobic environment, such as a peat bog, monasteries may well have gently engineered the preservation of their future saints in the hopes of attracting pilgrimage traffic and gifts to their native house. Monasteries recorded miracles and circulated the lives, or *vitae*, of their most famous saints; particular monastic houses stole relics from one another and championed local saints' cults in a way at times reminiscent of modern sports teams (Geary 1978).

Like the biblical Hannah giving her son Samuel to the Levitical priesthood, early medieval families sometimes placed children, often very young children, in the care of monastic houses. They were educated but did not have to take final vows until much later, in the case of the young women, later than many aristocratic marriages (De Jong 1996). Women's houses made safe places for young women to stay, sometimes only for a time before their families pulled them out again to form marriage alliances. Monasteries were often places of political exile and could even function as prisons at need. They were also places to which widows could retire, donating what property remained to them in exchange for security. For all these reasons, a women's monastery always contained within it a certain number of women who were not present in the community entirely by their own choice, alongside other women who may well have found in the community an escape from sexual violence, unhappy or transitory marriages, and the dangers of childbirth. Monastic life offered literacy and access to books, the music and the rhythms of the daily office, a certain amount of female companionship, regular if vegetarian meals, and an order to the day.

This is not to discount the real and sincere piety of these religious communities. Inevitably, a women's monastery in this period was porous to interference from the outside world, reliant upon the local bishop's household to supply a priest to celebrate Mass, as well as to hear confession. However, abbesses in this period often heard the confessions of their own nuns and sometimes even veiled them personally. Within their own communities, religious women in the Frankish world seem to have read the gospel, preached, and served at the altar in some capacity (Muschiol 1994, pp. 94–100, 219–263; Wemple 1981, p. 160). At the same time, for those houses in particular with significant numbers of aristocratic women, many of whom expected no change in the lifestyle they had known outside the monastery and brought clothes, furniture, and servants into retirement with them, monastic rigor was probably impossible to enforce. This apparent laxity gave reformers ample opportunity to discredit women's houses as dens of impropriety and iniquity. But in a community in which the patrimony of one wealthy woman supported the lives of everyone else in the house, an abbess might well have felt she had to be tactful for the continued survival of everyone. Because of the lack of standardized rules and the ambiguities attached to women in religious life, as well as the amount of control families continued to exert over their female members, it is inaccurate and anachronistic to refer to women religious as "nuns" in this period; certainly it is difficult to see the clear distinction between nuns and canonesses which emerged in later centuries (Foot 2009). Many monastic sources refer to "virgins and widows" or simply to "virgins" categorically. The rules in use by women's communities in the early Middle Ages vary, therefore, in ascetic rigor and in practice, and were likely to vary enormously from house to house.

Other than Augustine's Rule, one of the most important rules developed specifically for women's houses was that of Caesarius of Arles (r. 503–543; de Vogüé 1985; Caesarius of Arles 1988). One of the bishops formed by the famously rigorous monastic school on the island of Lérins off the coast of France, Caesarius authorized the building of a monastery within the city walls of Arles for an already existing community of women, in which his sister, Caesaria, was abbess. The house was initially built at some distance from the city, but after it was attacked in 507, it was rebuilt inside the city for the protection of both the women and the children within the community. Their solitude was enforced by a policy of strict enclosure, the hallmark of Caesarius's Rule. The women wore undyed and unembellished woolen habits, slept in a common dormitory, supported themselves through textile work, and tellingly, also copied manuscripts. Caesarius granted to his community the right to appoint their own abbess from within the community, although he continued to tinker with his Rule for the rest of his life. It is thought that around two hundred women lived in the monastery at the time of his death, although, by all accounts, his ideal of unvarnished simplicity did not long outlive him (Klingshern 2004; Tilley 2018; Coatsworth and Owen-Crocker 2018, pp. 321–326).

Caesarius was living in the shadow of one of the greatest monastic reformers of the era: St. Martin, whose shrine at Tours became one of the great pilgrimage destinations in early medieval Europe. Martin's *vita* by Sulpicius Severus portrays him as an awe-inspiring blend of Elijah with John the Baptist: a social outsider and miracle-worker, a fearless evangelist with power over demons (Stancliffe 1983). The patron saint of Paris, Genovefa or Geneviève, clearly also intended to place herself within this same tradition. Likely from an extremely aristocratic family, and despite her lack of any official title, Genovefa essentially acted as the bishop of the city of Paris (Bitel 2009). From the small village of Nanterre, a childhood encounter with another early saint of the Frankish church, Germanus of Auxerre, left her determined to vow her life to God. But Genovefa hardly chose to seclude herself. Living in Paris during the invasion of Attila the Hun in 451, Genovefa led a prayer vigil with a group of the city's matrons in the baptistery on the Île de la Cité, oblivious to death threats from within and the enemy without. The author of her *vita* compared her both to Judith and to Esther. When the siege was over, Genovefa revealed a vision of the true resting place of St. Denis in a disued Roman cemetery outside the city walls, championing the construction of a basilica on the site. Genovefa's own shrine and basilica, as well as her *vita*, were later commissioned by the Burgundian queen of the Franks, Clothild (see Figure 5.3). Clothild would be instrumental in the conversion of her husband, Clovis, the first Frankish king to be baptized into Nicene Christianity. Both Clovis and Clothild were buried in Genovefa's church.

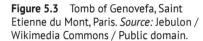

**Figure 5.3** Tomb of Genovefa, Saint Etienne du Mont, Paris. *Source:* Jebulon / Wikimedia Commons / Public domain.

## Women and Insular Christianity

Meanwhile, at the beginning of the fifth century, a young British teenager, perhaps from near Carlisle, was captured by Irish pirates and taken back to Ireland as a slave (Morris 2021, pp. 148–149). The boy was named Patrick, and Ireland, if not unknown, was in many ways a very different world from the one he had left. Beyond the boundaries of the Roman Empire, Ireland was entirely rural, its language was forbiddingly complex, and its society was divided into regional family and kin networks. It was also an entirely oral culture, although that did not prevent it from having an immensely complex legal system.

Patrick was a slave in Ireland for a number of years, long enough to learn the language, before he was able to escape on a boat bound for Britain. He then studied in Francia, where he became ordained. Without consulting his superiors in the Frankish church, Patrick then proceeded to return to Ireland as its self-appointed apostle and prophet. The date of Patrick's mission is debated, most likely occurring in the middle of the fifth century (Charles-Edwards 2000, pp. 182–240). By then there were almost certainly other Christians in Ireland, mostly likely British slaves captured like Patrick or their descendants. Twenty years before, Palladius had become the first bishop sent to the island, an appointment that would not have occurred if some population of Christians were not already there. Patrick's mission owes at least something to these Christians whose names have been lost. Certainly, Patrick's own message relied on the conversion to the monastic life of a number of aristocratic women, and on the gifts and support of others.

One of these early converts, or so the story goes, was a young woman by the name of Brigid. Daughter of a druid and his slave, Brigid was baptized young and decided to consecrate herself to the religious life. There is a certain amount of debate over whether Brigid was a historical person who later acquired some of the attributes of a pre-Christian fertility goddess, or if she was an instance of a local pagan cult that was later baptized into Christianity (Kissane 2017). Her main monastic center at Kildare was sacked multiple times over the course of the Middle Ages, and the beginnings of her hagiography are written a century after her death, so there is no way to be certain either way. The earliest version of her life, by the monk Cogitosus, describes her first miracles occurring some distance from Kildare and centering around the presence of the saint's physical body, which is an argument for a real historical woman behind the legend (Cogitosus 1849; Connolly and Picard 1987; Esposito 1912; Connolly 1989). The ninth-century Irish version of her life, the *Bethu Brigte*, describes how an excited cleric accidentally consecrated her as a bishop, an ordination which was then ratified by the appearance of a pillar of fire from heaven (Macy 2016, p. 54). As well as the fluctuating status of bishops in early Ireland, this story probably also reflects the pretensions of Brigid's house at Kildare, which became a thriving community of both monks and nuns, rivaling in influence Patrick's own foundation in Armagh. While clearly eccentric, the tale of Brigid's ordination would hardly have made sense if it were inherently impossible, and Brigid became the most renowned saint in Leinster, the "Mary of the Gael." Known outside of Ireland as St. Bride, her cult spread to Wales and from there to the continent, where she was known as the patron saint of women in childbirth.

Ireland developed its own, distinctive form of Christianity in the early Middle Ages, over-whelmingly monastic in tone and temperament. Because writing came to Ireland only with Christianity, as with the pre-Colombian Americas, much of what is known about pre-Christian Ireland derives entirely from later Christian, and usually monastic, sources. Without pre-existing cities, monasteries formed the kernels around which later urban development would form. Bishops in Ireland derived their influence from particular kin groups and thus seem to have varied a great deal in status and political power. As would also be the case in England in later centuries, bishops did not form a separate, competitive hierarchy within the church. Instead, they existed in symbiotic relationship with, often living in, the monasteries. These could form federations, links of mother- and daughter-houses that could extend over large areas (Hughes 1980; Sharpe 1992; Etchingham 1999). The most famous of these would be Columba's island monastery at Iona, which, much later, founded a daughter-house at Kells. At the time, Iona was not remote at all, but formed an extension of growing Irish influence into western Scotland. It was a monk from Iona, Aidan, who was one of the first missionary bishops of the English kingdom of Northumbria. In 697, at the Synod of Birr, Columba promulgated one of the earliest measures intended to protect non-combatants from war. Called the Cáin Adomnáin, or "Law of the Innocents," Columba's measure forbade violence by warriors against women, children, and clergy (Adomnán of Iona 1995, pp. 51–52).

The few women saints of early Ireland who are known, without exception, practiced the harsh asceticism characteristic of insular monasticism. In the seventh century, Moninne, later called Darerca, said to be from one of the greatest clans in Ulster, founded the monastic house at Killeevy (Ó Cróinín 2005, p. 218). Perhaps the best-loved woman saint in early Ireland after Brigid is Íte of Killeedy (d. 570) from County Limerick, who despite her asceticism lived to a great age. Attributed to her is a vision of Jesus as an infant, with a lyric which, while deeply poignant, also says some-thing about the grades of status with which the church in Ireland remained entangled and their implications for wet-nursing and fostering: "It is little Jesus who is nursed by me in my little her-mitage. Though a cleric have great wealth, it is all deceitful save Jesukin. The nursing done by me in my house is no nursing of a base churl: Jesus with Heaven's inhabitants is against my heart every night" (Murphy 1998, pp. 26–29; see Figure 5.4). When the forbidding ascetic Samthann (d. 739) was asked in what posture one should pray, she responded tartly, "One must pray in all positions" (Plummer 1968, vol. 2, p. 259).

**Figure 5.4** Madonna and Child, the Book of Kells, TCD MS 58, Dublin. *Source:* Digitized Medieval Manuscripts Blog.

## Gregory the Great's Correspondents

The most influential figure of the period, and perhaps of the early Middle Ages entirely, was Pope Gregory the Great (r. 590–604; Straw 2016). Born to an aristocratic Roman family which had already produced one bishop of Rome, Gregory grew up in the family mansion on the Caelian Hill, which like Macrina he would later convert to a monastery. In Gregory's younger years, he spent several years as an ambassador to Constantinople. While there, he made several influential social connections and seems to have served as a kind of spiritual director among Latin-speaking aristocrats in the capital. On his return to Rome he had planned simply to live as a monk; when told of his election to the papacy in 590 his reaction, famously, was to refuse to emerge from his rooms. However, emerge he eventually did, and despite chronic illness and the invasion of a new people group, the Lombards, into northern Italy, Gregory reshaped the role of the church in the city of Rome and the nature of western Christendom itself. Cut off from help from Constantinople, Gregory restructured church finances and church estates, primarily in Sicily, so as to provide a steady stream of income to support the poor of the city of Rome. In so doing, Gregory took up the civic responsibility once shouldered, at least in part, by the old Roman state. He could not have foreseen that it was a civic and political role the papacy would continue to occupy in the city for centuries to come, and that the power of Constantinople would never return. Left dependent on his own resources, Gregory began to use monks in official positions within church government, which ensured that these parallel ecclesiastical vocations would be much more entangled in the west than in eastern Christianity (Demacopoulos 2017, pp. 144–163). In particular, the monk-bishop, while not solely a Gregorian invention, became associated with his legacy. Likewise, "Gregorian chant," while not invented by the man himself, certainly developed with Gregory's patronage and encouragement. His biblical interpretation, as well as other works such as *The Pastoral Rule*, was foundational throughout the medieval tradition, not least as one of the principal mediators of the thought of Augustine of Hippo.

It was the reputation of Gregory which helped to popularize the *Rule of St. Benedict* as a necessary corrective to the more flamboyant experiments in asceticism that were prevalent in Italy at the time. According to legend, Benedict had a sister, Scholastica, who was also committed to the monastic life; they are buried together in his principal foundation in Monte Cassino (Stouck 1999, pp. 167–203). The historicity of both sister and brother has been questioned by modern scholars, while Monte Cassino was almost completely destroyed by Allied bombing in World War II. However, the place of Scholastica within the Benedictine tradition, like that of Augustine's sister, points to the ongoing importance of the Benedictine Rule for communities of women. Until St. Clare in the thirteenth century, if a women's community was to be "regular" – in other words, if it was to live formally under a monastic rule – then its two principal choices were the Augustinian Rule for canonesses and the Benedictine Rule for nuns.

In the letters of Gregory the Great which have survived, one continuous strategy of the pope's that emerges is Gregory's distinctive cultivation of diplomatic relationships with prominent royal and aristocratic women, sometimes using women as messengers. Throughout his pontificate, Gregory sent letters to a Roman aristocrat by the name of Rusticiana, who may well have been the granddaughter of the writer Boethius (Cooper 2007, pp. 84–85). Gregory encouraged Rusticiana on her visit to the Holy Land, and teased her that she couldn't wait to cut short her arduous but improving stint in the Sinai desert for the delights of Constantinople. But he also received significant sums of money from her and from the empress Constantina to use for the ransom of captives taken by the Lombards (Gregory the Great 2004, 1.2.24, 1.4.44, 2.5.38, 2.8.22). In another instance, he used some of their donations to buy bedclothes for three thousand religious women in Rome during a very cold winter, an index both of the empress's generosity and of the significant presence of religious women in the city. In another letter to Constantina, Gregory describes taxation in Corsica and Sardinia that was so severe parents were being forced to sell their children into slavery (Gregory the Great 2004, 2.7.23, 2.5.38). He writes two letters to a noblewoman named Clementina because she clearly has some influence over a local episcopal election. Gregory adopts as wards of the church two small girls, Barbara and Antonina, whose father had once been a monk in Palermo, and in one charming letter thanks them for the cloaks they have sent to him (Gregory the Great 2004, 2.9.86, 3.11.23, 3.11.59).

Gregory wrote to three early medieval queens over the course of his pontificate: the Merovingian queen Brunhild, the Lombard queen Theodelinda, and the English queen Bertha of Kent. Both Theodelinda and Bertha were Catholics while their husbands were not, and it is clear that Gregory viewed them as necessary allies and pathways toward the future conversion of their husbands and their kingdoms. A queen who maintained her Catholic belief might support a priest or three within her household. In 597, Gregory sent a missionary bishop, Augustine (not to be confused with the bishop of Hippo), to Bertha and her husband Aethelberht of Kent in Canterbury. There, to his surprise, Augustine discovered the surviving church of St. Martin, built of Roman stonework, where the queen worshipped. Dating from before the legions left, it is the oldest parish church in England (*St. Martin's Church* 1950). Augustine wrote a notorious letter back to Gregory with an elaborate list of questions regarding women's purity and whether they could take the Eucharist during menstruation or after childbirth. The earnest but rather panicked tone of the letter suggests that the stressed missionary was unsure how to manage the specific application of biblical texts to his messy local reality. Gregory's response was, as ever, pastoral, reminding Augustine that it was the state of the women's hearts that really mattered (Bede 1999, Bk. I.27).

## Queens of the Franks

In the poem with which this chapter began, Radegund speaks simultaneously as the orphaned girl, the queen she became, and the enclosed abbess, now free to remember her old grief at the murder of her family. If the poem represents anything of Radegund's own emotions – and Fortunatus would hardly have written it for her to read if it did not – it is suggestive of how grief and trauma could habitually shadow the lives of early medieval women, and may partly explain the choices Radegund made and the ascetic nature of her piety. Not surprisingly, the marriage to her captor, Chlothar, was not a resounding success. The queen kept herself as distant from her husband as she could, but frequently got up in the middle of the night to pray and perform self-flagellations. She collected relics of the saints, and it was at this time that her brother, in exile in Constantinople, sent her relics of the True Cross. Her religious observances became so intrusive that Chlothar complained he had married someone already vowed to God, and when he ordered the death of her brother, Radegund left him and was consecrated into the religious life.

At the same time, Radegund was also ordained a deaconess, and went on to found the Abbey of the Holy Cross in Poitiers. When the local bishop refused to bless the new community, Radegund ignored him, adopting the Rule of Caesarius with its rule of strict enclosure, appointing one of her own religious women as abbess, and placing the abbey under the direct protection of the king. Radegund's own piety was dramatically physical in ways that may be repugnant to modern tastes, but she outlived her former husband by more than 25 years, dying in 587 (see Figure 5.5). Venantius Fortunatus, better known today for the great Christian hymn in honor of the Holy

**Figure 5.5** *The Life of St. Radegund*, Bibliothèque municipale de Poitiers, MS 250(136). *Source:* Unknown author / Wikimedia Commons / Public domain.

Cross, *Pange lingua*, or, "Sing, my tongue, of the glorious battle," composed the first version of her *vita* (Fortunatus 1885, pp. 364–377; Stouck 1999, pp. 205–217).

Twenty years later, the abbess commissioned a second version of Radegund's life from a woman, Baudonivia, from within the saint's own community to commemorate the legacy of this "second Helena" (Baudonivia 1885, pp. 377–395; Coates 1998). Since Radegund's death, the Abbey of the Holy Cross had not had an easy time of it. The bishop and historian Gregory of Tours recounts how the same bishop of Poitiers, who had refused even to countenance providing pastoral care to the community, had again neglected the women. Meanwhile, two members of the community, Clothild and Basina, both of royal descent, protested both against their standard of living and against their abbess, claiming they were being forced to live like servants while she entertained lay visitors in style. Clothild and some others came to seek Gregory's advice at Tours, worn-out, hungry, and desperate, and determined to seek a royal audience. The fragile community, meanwhile, was splintering, with some women leaving the religious life altogether to seek marriage. Finding themselves excommunicated by the local episcopacy, Clothild, Basina, and others barricaded themselves into a church in Poitiers, formed a mob, and attempted a violent coup against the abbess. This state of affairs lasted, Gregory notes tartly, until they ran out of winter fuel, and at a formal tribunal the miscreants were suspended from the Eucharist and sent to do penance. Gregory's niece was the prioress at the abbey, and therefore was a well-informed but biased witness. Whatever the rights and wrongs of the case, the revolt at Poitiers is a case study of everything that could so easily go wrong in a small community of religious women (Gregory of Tours 1977, Bk. VI.29, IX.39–43).

One of the most complex and fascinating of Pope Gregory's correspondents was the formidable Merovingian queen Brunhild. A native of Visigothic Spain, she and her sister Galswinth were married to brother Frankish kings, Sigibert and Chilperic. Chilperic would order Galswinth's murder, and when Sigibert died as well, Brunhild was left a foreigner with no connections or protection of her own. Chilperic took away her son and married Brunhild to his own son, Merovech. Chilperic himself died soon after, it was rumored, murdered at Brunhild's instigation, and the queen promptly took political control, acting through her son, Childebert. When he died in 596, Brunhild continued to act as regent for her two grandsons. The queen had a firm hand on the court at this point, and seems to have blocked or opposed any legitimate marriages and political alliances her grandsons might have contracted when they came of age (Wood 1994, pp. 126–136; Charles-Edwards 2000, pp. 344–390).

Gregory's letters to Brunhild in this period are extremely polite (Gregory the Great 2004, 2.6.58, 2.6.60, 2.8.4, 2.9.213–214, 3.11.46–48, 3.13.5). The queen put significant pressure on him to ratify the nomination of her favorite churchman, Syagrius the bishop of Autun, and it was Syagrius, among others, who would consecrate Augustine bishop en route to England in 597. In response to further requests from the queen, and in gratitude for Syagrius's contributions to the English mission, Gregory granted the bishop a pallium, an important mark of office. Beyond this exchange of favors, he also sent Brunhild a manuscript which he says that she requested, and he enlisted her, or tried to, in his efforts to curb simony in the church. This may well have been a lost cause, even for Gregory the Great, if control of the offices of the church was one of the means by which the queen maintained her grip on power at court.

It was at this moment that Brunhild attempted to enlist the charisma of the Irish monastic exile and teacher Columbanus, requesting that he bless her great-grandsons born to a concubine. Columbanus blanched, however, and at the queen's displeasure he ultimately abandoned his new monastic foundation at Luxeuil to found another in northern Italy, at Bobbio. In subsequent hagiography Brunhild is depicted as the Jezebel to Columbanus's Prophet Elijah. But this portrayal masks the more general resistance the Irishman also encountered from the native Gaulish episcopal establishment, who used the diplomatic fracas with Brunhild to protest the alternate Irish observance of Easter (Bullough 1997). Columbanus's protégé, the religious woman Burgundofara, in 617 founded the important Frankish double monastery at Faremoutiers.

When Brunhild was finally overthrown at the death of her grandsons, the invading Chlothar II made the old queen the scapegoat for the murderous palace politics she had survived for so long. Bound with ropes, she was torn apart by wild horses. However, the dramatic role-call of Merovingian royal deaths by violence masks, to some extent, their steady, controlled administration of lands and estates, which amassed a vast amount of wealth for the ruling dynasty (Wood 1994, pp. 203–220; Wickham 2005, pp. 102–115). No serious rival to the throne had yet emerged from the aristocracy, and paradoxically, this meant that Merovingian kings had some freedom in contracting marriage alliances, particularly if these were not expected to last long. In the 640s, Balthild, an English slave in the household of the king's chief official, was chosen as a bride by Clovis II. On his death, however, Balthild served as regent for her son for upwards of seven years. Two of her sons would become king, in fact, and the queen became as active a leader in the Frankish church as Brunhild had been, perhaps even more so. Balthild appointed bishops, endowed monastic foundations, and donated relics. Her support of monasticism in the church may represent the kind of infusion of authenticity Gregory the Great thought the Frankish church was in dire need of, and in this light, her support of the shrine of a reformer like Martin of Tours may be a kind of statement (Wood 1994, pp. 197–202). Her most famous religious community, however, was at Chelles, where the queen retired when she was finally edged out of the court in 664. Chelles became one of the finest women's houses in Francia, and a woman from her own community would compose Balthild's *vita* (*Vita Sanctae Balthildis* 1885, pp. 475–508; see Figure 5.6). Before women's religious communities existed in England, Chelles, and other houses like it, would be where English women learned the religious life. Through them, the Benedictine Rule came to England.

**Figure 5.6** The chemise of Balthild, Musée Alfred Bonno, Chelles. *Source:* The University of Iowa Libraries.

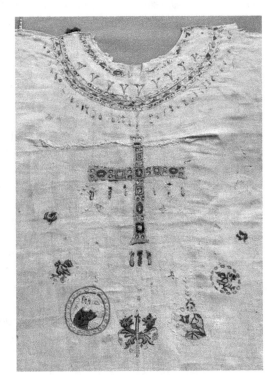

## The Abbesses of *The Ecclesiastical History of the English People*

Besides Cuthbert of Farne, the other English saint for whom the Venerable Bede shows particular devotion is Etheldreda, also called Aethelthryth or Audrey (Bede 1999, Bk. IV.17). The daughter of the king of East Anglia, Etheldreda preserved her chastity through two marriages, much to the exasperation of her husband Ecgfrith, the king of Northumbria. When she was finally given permission to enter the monastic life, she joined the religious community at Coldingham, now on the Scottish border, before returning south again to become the abbess of Ely in the East Anglian fens. Bede records Etheldreda's simple lifestyle and her habitual prayer from matins until dawn, and he claims that she predicted an attack of plague on the community. Dying from a tumor on her neck, the saint wryly reflected on her youthful love of jewelry, and was buried in a simple wooden coffin. When her sister, who succeeded her as abbess, brought from Grantchester a fine stone (and presumably Roman) coffin in which to bury her instead, the community discovered that Etheldreda's body, whether through personal holiness or the preservative qualities of the Ely fens, had not decayed. Also found incorrupt and later stolen back to Ely is another sister of hers, Wihtburh or Withburga of Dereham. In all, some four of her sisters joined the religious life, becoming abbesses in communities on both sides of the English Channel (Blanton 2007; Sneesby 2010, pp. 19–63). Alongside the queen's stubborn determination to preserve her virginity, therefore, Etheldreda's story is one of sisterhood in vocation and of dynastic family politics.

Also standing at the nexus of family interest and personal vocation is the formidable Hild. Bede tells us that her life was divided into two equal parts: the first 33 years in "secular habit" and the second 33 years in the religious life. What Hild did before joining a religious community is not known. Intending to travel to Chelles, she was persuaded instead by Aidan, the Irish bishop of Northumbria, to come home and found a monastery there. With Aidan's support, Hild seems to have founded, passed through, or administered a sequence of women's religious houses in Northumbria: Hartlepool, Tadcaster, and finally, Whitby (Bede 1999, Bk. IV.21; Inman 2019). A grave-marker of a woman named Berchtgyd survives from Hild's house at Hartlepool, her name written in half-uncial script (Breay and Story 2018, p. 121). Although Bede speaks very favorably of Hild, it is possible that his concern to present her as an enclosed royal saint like Etheldreda led him to underestimate how significant she was in the Christianization of Northumbria (Foot 2020). Hild's monastery at Whitby was home to both male and female religious, serving as a school for clergy and a string of future bishops, whom she trained personally. Another reason for Bede's reticence may be the close association of Hild with Aidan, and therefore, her role in the so-called "Easter Controversy," which was eventually resolved at the Council of Whitby in 664. Aidan was dead by then, and it is no accident that the debates over whether the Irish or Roman calculation of Easter were correct occurred at Hild's own community, even if it was the king who ultimately presided over the council. The Council of Whitby decided in favor of the Roman observance of Easter, but many of Northumbria's clergy, which included the young Cuthbert, were formed by the Irish presence in the region, and by Hild's legacy as a scholar and a teacher.

After Rome's fall in the west, the church maintained its presence in society through the network of monasteries now scattered across Europe. The early medieval successor-kingdoms would repurpose Rome's political and cultural legacy in many different ways, just as they set its artistic treasures in new and unexpected frames. In the hundred and fifty years between Augustine and Gregory the Great, the world of the western Roman Empire had irrevocably changed (Markus 1990). As with Patrick's mission to Ireland, Christianity both preserved and reached beyond the cradle of Roman civilization in which it had grown up. Women were pivotal in this transformation. Even when extremely vulnerable, women became essential bridgeheads between late Roman Christianity and the new early medieval kingdoms. Through intercession, devotion, and internecine family politics, women were vitally important in the spread of monasticism to the new kingdoms, while the monasteries they founded operated as missionary outposts. Where the great theologians were copied, the complex discourse about sex and gender in the late Roman world was superimposed on new landscapes and on different class systems and kinship networks. Certain women, however, found opportunities by virtue of their family connections, and sometimes by sheer force of will, to wield great influence over the church. The early Middle Ages, then, represent a transitional but transformational era for women in the church.

# References

Adomnán of Iona (1995). *Life of St. Columba* (ed. R. Sharpe). London: Penguin.

Ashurov, B. (2020). Religions and religious space in Sogdian culture: a view from archaeological and written sources. *Sino-Platonic Papers* 306.

Baudonivia (1885). Vita Radegundis. In: *MGH SS Rer. Merov. 2* (ed. B. Krusch). Hanover: Hahn.

Bede (trans. J.F. Webb)(1998). *The Age of Bede*, rev. ed. London: Penguin.

Bede (1999). *The Ecclesiastical History of the English People*, reprinted ed. (ed. J. McClure and R. Collins). Oxford: Oxford University Press.

Benedict (1971–1972). The Rule of St. Benedict (ed. Adalbert de Vogüé). *Sources Chrétiennes* 181–182. Paris: Éditions du Cerf.

Beowulf (trans. M.D. Headley) (2020). New York: Farrar, Straus and Giroux.

Bitel, L. (1996). *Land of Women: Tales of Sex and Gender in Early Ireland*. Ithaca: Cornell University Press.

Bitel, L. (2002). *Women in Early Medieval Europe, 400–1100*. Cambridge: Cambridge University Press.

Bitel, L. (2009). *Landscape with Two Saints: How Genovefa of Paris and Brigit of Kildare Built Christianity in Barbarian Europe*. Oxford: Oxford University Press.

Blanton, V. (2007). *Signs of Devotion: The Cult of St. Æthelthryth in Medieval England, 695–1615*. University Park: Pennsylvania State University Press.

Breay, C. and Story, J. (ed.) (2018). *Anglo-Saxon Kingdoms: Art, Word, War*. London: British Library.

Brown, P. (1981). *The Cult of the Saints: Its Rise and Function in Latin Christianity*. Chicago: University of Chicago Press.

Brown, P. (2013). *The Rise of Western Christendom: Triumph and Diversity, 200–1000*, 10th anniv. rev. ed. Oxford: Wiley Blackwell.

Bullough, D. (1997). The career of Columbanus. In: *Columbanus: Studies on the Latin Writings* (ed. M. Lapidge), 1–28. Ashgate: Boydell Press.

Caesarius of Arles (1988). The Rule of Caesarius of Arles (ed. A. de Vogüé and J. Courreau). *Sources Chrétiennes* 345. Paris: Éditions du Cerf.

Campbell, J. (ed.) (1991). *The Anglo-Saxons*. London: Penguin.

Charles-Edwards, T. (2000). *Early Christian Ireland*. Cambridge: Cambridge University Press.

Clark, G. (1993). *Women in Late Antiquity: Pagan and Christian Lifestyles*. Oxford: Clarendon Press.

Coates, S. (1998). Regendering Radegund? Fortunatus, Baudonivia, and the problem of female sanctity in Merovingian Gaul. *Studies in Church History* 34: 37–50.

Coatsworth, E. and Owen-Crocker, G.R. (2018). *Clothing the Past: Surviving Garments from Early Medieval to Early Modern Western Europe*. Leiden: Brill.

Cogitosus (1849). Sanctae Brigidae virginis vita. In: *Patrologia Latina 72* (ed. J.P. Migne), cols. 775–790.

Connolly, S. (1989). *Vita Primae Sanctae Brigidae*: background and historical value. *The Journal of the Royal Society of Antiquaries of Ireland* 119: 5–49.

Connolly, S. and Picard, J.M. (1987). Cogitosus's life of St. Brigid: content and value. *The Journal of the Royal Society of Antiquaries of Ireland* 117: 5–27.

Cooper, K. (2007). *The Fall of the Roman Household*. Cambridge: Cambridge University Press.

Cunliffe, B. (2001). *Facing the Ocean: The Atlantic and its Peoples*. Oxford: Oxford University Press.

Dagron, G. (2003). *Emperor and Priest: The Imperial Office in Byzantium* (trans. J. Birrell). Cambridge: Cambridge University Press.

De Jong, M. (1996). *In Samuel's Image: Child Oblation in the Early Medieval West*. Leiden: Brill.

De Vogüé, A. (1985). *Les règles monastiques anciennes (400–700). Typologies des sources du moyen âge occidental 46*. Turnhout: Brepols.

Demacopoulos, G.E. (2017). *Five Models of Spiritual Direction in the Early Church*. Notre Dame: University of Notre Dame Press.

Enright, M. (1988). Lady with a mead-cup: ritual, group cohesion, and hierarchy in the Germanic Warband. *Frühmittelalterliche Studien* 22: 170–203.

Esposito, M. (1912). On the earliest life of St. Brigid of Kildare. *Proceedings of the Royal Irish Academy* 30 (C): 307–326.

Etchingham, C. (1999). *Church Organisation in Ireland, AD 650–1000*. Maynooth: Laigin Publications.

Foot, S. (2009). *Monastic Life in Anglo-Saxon England c. 600–900*. Cambridge: Cambridge University Press.

Foot, S. (2020). Bede's abbesses. In: *Women Intellectuals and Leaders in the Middle Ages* (ed. K. Kerby-Fulton, K.A.-M. Bugyis and J. Van Engen), 261–275. Woodbridge: D.S. Brewer.

Fortunatus, V. (1885). *De vita Sanctae Radegundis libri duo* (ed. Bruno Krusch) *MGH SS Rer. Merov. 2*. Hanover: Hahn.

Fortunatus, V. (trans. and ed. M. Roberts)(2017). *Poems*. Dumbarton Oaks Medieval Library 46. Cambridge: Harvard University Press.

Garver, V. (2009). *Women and Aristocratic Culture in the Carolingian World*. Ithaca: Cornell University Press.

Geary, P.J. (1978). *First Sacra: Thefts of Relics in the Central Middle Ages*. Princeton: Princeton University Press.

Gelasius, I. (2014). *The Letters of Gelasius I (492–496)*. (trans. B. Neil and P. Allen). Turnhout: Brepols.

Gregory of Tours (1977). *The History of the Franks*, reprinted ed. (trans. L. Thorpe). London: Penguin.

Gregory the Great (2004). *The Letters of Gregory the Great* (trans. J.R.C. Martyn), vol. 3. Toronto: PIMS.

Haldon, J.F. (1990). *Byzantium in the Seventh Century: The Transformation of a Culture*. Cambridge: Cambridge University Press.

Harper, K. (2011). *Slavery in the Late Roman World, AD 275–425*. Cambridge: Cambridge University Press.

Harper, K. (2017). *The Fate of Rome: Climate, Disease, and the End of an Empire*. Princeton: Princeton University Press.

Heather, P. (2018). *Rome Resurgent: War and Empire in the Age of Justinian*. New York: Oxford University Press.

Herrin, J. (2020). *Ravenna: Capital of Empire, Crucible of Europe*. London: Allen Lane.

Hughes, K. (1980). *The Church in Early Irish Society*. London: Methuen and Co.

Inman, A.E. (2019). *Hild of Whitby and the Ministry of Women in the Anglo-Saxon World*. Lanham: Lexington Books and Fortress Academic.

Kateusz, A. and Confalonieri, L.B. (2021). Women church leaders in and around fifth-century Rome. In: *Patterns of Women's Leadership in Early Christianity* (ed. J.E. Taylor and I.L.E. Ramelli), 228–260. Oxford: Oxford University Press.

Kissane, N. (2017). *St. Brigid of Kildare: Life, Legend, and Cult*. Dublin: Four Courts Press.

Klingshern, W.E. (2004). *Caesarius of Arles: The Making of Christian Community in Late Antique Gaul*. Cambridge: Cambridge University Press.

Lopez-Jantzen, N. (2019). Between empires: race and ethnicity in the early Middle Ages. *Literature Compass* 16: (9–10).

Macy, G. (2016). *The Hidden History of Women's Ordination: Female Clergy in the Medieval West*. Oxford: Oxford University Press.

Madigan, K. (2021). The meaning of *presbytera* in Byzantine and early medieval Christianity. In: *Patterns of Women's Leadership in Early Christianity* (ed. J.E. Taylor and I.L.E. Ramelli), 261–289. Oxford: Oxford University Press.

Markus, R.A. (1990). *The End of Ancient Christianity*. Cambridge: Cambridge University Press.

McCormick, M. (2001). *Origins of the European Economy: Communications and Commerce, AD 300–900*. Cambridge: Cambridge University Press.

Morris, R. (2021). *Evensong: People, Discoveries, and Reflections on the Church in England*. London: Wiedenfeld and Nicolson.

Murphy, G. (ed.) and (trans.)(1998). *Early Irish Lyrics*. Dublin: Four Courts Press.

Muschiol, G. (1994). Famula Dei: Zur Liturgie in merowingischen Frauenklöstern. In: *Beiträge zur Geschichte des alten Mönchtums und des Benediktinertum*, vol. 41. Munster: Aschendorff.

Nelson, J.L. and Rio, A. (2013). Women and laws in early medieval Europe. In: *The Oxford Handbook of Women and Gender in Medieval Europe* (ed. J. Bennett and R.M. Karras), 103–117. Oxford: Oxford University Press.

Ó Cróinín, D. (ed.) (2005). *A New History of Ireland. Volume One: Prehistoric and Early Ireland*. Oxford: Oxford University Press.

Plummer, C. (1968). *Lives of Irish Saints*. Oxford: Oxford University Press 1e, 1922.

Procopius (2007). *The Secret History*, rev. ed. (trans. G.A. Williamson and P. Sarris). London: Penguin.

Pye, M. (2014). *The Edge of the World: A Cultural History of the North Sea and the Transformation of Europe*. New York: Pegasus.

Rio, A. (2017). *Slavery After Rome, 500–1100*. Cambridge: Cambridge University Press.

Rosenthal, J.T. (1990). Anglo-Saxon attitudes: men's sources, women's history. In: *Medieval Women and the Sources of Medieval History* (ed. J.T. Rosenthal), 259–284. Athens: University of Georgia Press.

Sharpe, R. (1992). Churches and communities in early medieval Ireland: towards a pastoral model. In: *Pastoral Care Before the Parish* (ed. J. Blair and R. Sharpe), 81–109. Leicester: Leicester University Press.

Sneesby, N. (2010). *Etheldreda: Princess, Queen, Abbess and Saint*. Ely: Fern House.

St. Martin's Church (1950). *Canterbury: An Illustrated Guide*. Canterbury: Stevens and Sons.

Stafford, P. (1997). *Queen Emma and Queen Edith: Queenship and Women's Power in Eleventh-Century England*. Oxford: Blackwell.

Stancliffe, C. (1983). *St Martin and His Hagiographer: History and Miracle in Sulpicius Severus*. Oxford: Clarendon Press.

Stouck, M.-A. (1999). *Medieval Saints: A Reader*. Toronto: Broadview Press.

Straw, C. (2016). *Gregory the Great*, reprinted ed. London: Routledge.

The Táin (trans. T. Kinsella)(1985). From the Irish). *Táin Bó Cúailnge*. Mountrath: The Dolmen Press.

Tilley, M. (2018). Caesarius's *Rule* for unruly nuns: permitted and prohibited textiles in the monastery of St. John. *Early Medieval Europe* 26: 83–89.

Tsurtaveli, I. (1983). *Muchenichestvo Shushaniki, or The Martyrdom of Shushanik*. Tbilisi: Khelovneba.

Vita Sanctae Balthildis (1885). *MGH SS Rer. Merov. 2* (ed. B. Krusch). Hanover: Hahn.

Ward-Perkins, B. (2005). *The Fall of Rome and the End of Civilisation*. Oxford: Oxford University Press.

Wemple, S.F. (1981). *Women in Frankish Society: Marriage and the Cloister, 500 to 900*. Philadelphia: University of Pennsylvania Press.

Wickham, C. (2005). *Framing the Early Middle Ages: Europe and the Mediterranean, 400–800*. Oxford: Oxford University Press.

Wickham, C. (2016). *Medieval Europe*. New Haven: Yale University Press.

Wijngaards, J. (2021). Women deacons in ancient Christian communities. In: *Patterns of Women's Leadership in Early Christianity* (ed. J.E. Taylor and I.L.E. Ramelli), 195–210. Oxford: Oxford University Press.

Wood, I. (1994). *The Merovingian Kingdoms, 450–751*. Abingdon: Routledge.

Wood, I. (2001). *The Missionary Life: Saints and the Evangelisation of Europe, 400–1050*. New York: Longman.

# 6

# Charlemagne's Daughters

Women, Empire, and Reform, 750–1050

In 732, an English girl wrote a letter to her kinsman. She reminded him of his connection to her mother, Aebbe, and his friendship with her father, Dynne, and she enclosed some halting Latin verse she had written. From now on, she asked, "I would like to regard you as my brother." The young girl's name was Leoba; her kinsman, Wynfrith, originally from the kingdom of Wessex, became known as Boniface, "apostle to the Germans" and founder of the great monastery at Fulda on the Saxon frontier. Boniface was attacked and killed by pagan Frisians in 754. Fulda preserves the copy of the book of biblical commentary Boniface held up to defend himself in his final moments, dramatically slashed and torn. Now called the Ragyndrudis Codex, it had been the gift of a woman (McKitterick 1989, p. 259; see Figure 6.1).

Behind the heroic endeavors of the great missionary-saint lay an elaborate network of relationships connecting England to the continent (Levison 1956; Story 2002). Known for his Latin learning, Boniface maintained a voluminous correspondence with English monasteries who supported and furthered his work abroad. Education and mission were not distinct activities for Boniface and his followers, just as pastoral care happened within a predominantly monastic context. A striking number of Boniface's correspondents were women, many of them highly connected and very learned indeed. Two rare eighth-century veils survive which have been historically attributed to the Anglo-Saxon sisters Harlindis and Relindis, who founded the women's community at Aldeneik, now in Belgium. Friends with both Boniface and Willibrord, they were known for their skills in textile work (Coatsworth and Owen-Crocker 2018, pp. 341–344). Another English religious woman, who traveled to the monastery at Heidenheim in Bavaria to support Boniface's mission, wrote her name in an elaborate cipher between two English saints' lives she had just copied: "I, a Saxon nun named Hugeberc, composed this" (Wellesley 2021, pp. 222–225).

Twelve years before Leoba's first letter, the abbess Eadburga, also known as Bugga, had sent Boniface a very welcome parcel of books, money, and an altar cloth. Eadburga was the pupil of the great Kentish saint Mildrith and her successor as abbess of the women's community at Minster-in-Thanet. Throughout the 730s, Eadburga repeatedly sent books to Boniface, who had by then been made archbishop of Germany by the pope, although he did not have a fixed see until 746. Boniface, in the thick of strategies to convince new converts of the importance of scripture and the written word, commissioned Eadburga for a copy of the letters of St. Peter, embellished in gold leaf. He sent her the gold, interestingly, suggesting that the abbess's community either made books themselves or could commission fine craftsmanship more easily than Boniface himself could do. Eadburga soon got the itch to travel herself, however, and discussed plans with Boniface to go on pilgrimage from Kent to Rome, just as a mutual acquaintance, "their sister Wihtburga," had done. From a later letter of Boniface's, we know Eadburga went (Boniface 1976, letters 6, 7, 19, 77, and 85).

*A History of Women in Christianity to 1600*, First Edition. Hannah Matis.
© 2023 John Wiley & Sons Ltd. Published 2023 by John Wiley & Sons Ltd.

**Figure 6.1** The Ragyndrudis Codex (*Codex Bonifatius II*), Fulda. *Source:* Unknown author / Wikimedia Commons / Public domain.

Eadburga also corresponded with Aldhelm, the Irish-educated bishop of Sherbourne and flamboyant Latin stylist, and she may have been Leoba's teacher for a time (Foot 2001, vol. 1, p. 24). Certainly Leoba began to learn her Latin from the equally formidable Tetta, abbess of Wimbourne in Wessex, where Leoba had grown up. Leoba's *vita* describes a vivid dream she had at Wimbourne at this time: she pulled a purple thread from her mouth, which did not break but which she laboriously gathered into a ball. An older woman in the community prophesied that the thread signified Leoba's wise council in both word and deed, and in the event, it was a fair assessment of a life marked by moderation, self-control, and the seemingly endless practice of reading, remembering, and teaching. While Leoba herself may be extraordinary, her accomplishments were made possible by the learned ecclesiastical culture cultivated by English abbesses in the early Middle Ages.

In 735, Boniface asked that Leoba join him in Germany, where she became the abbess of the new women's community at Tauberbischofsheim. Her *vita* records one of the tensest moments in Leoba's time as abbess: an unmarried woman in the village bore a child and left the body by the abbey pond, saying that the baby had been one of the sister's. With the town in uproar, Leoba gathered the women in the chapel, where they recited the entirety of the psalter with their arms outstretched, and then repeatedly processed around the abbey grounds carrying a crucifix aloft, until the woman broke down and confessed (Rudolph of Fulda 1887). Leoba's response was a masterful exercise in both piety and public theater, but it also illustrates the seriousness of the accusation and the vulnerability of a women's religious community to sexual rumor.

In the event, Leoba's career at Tauberbischofsheim was long and her influence profound. Her hagiographer noted that she read and interpreted both testaments, the church fathers, councils, and ecclesiastical law. While the community clearly had access to books, this knowledge was also conveyed verbally and by memory. This does not mean it was imprecise: it was said, when her younger sisters read Leoba to sleep with scripture, they deliberately made mistakes, only to have the saint correct them. Like Hild of Whitby, Leoba trained the next generation of abbesses in Germany, from whose testimonies her life was compiled. While she was said to have avoided the royal court if she could help it, she became friends with Hildegard, the much younger queen of Charlemagne, and in her later life she participated in many convent visitations (Lifshitz 2014, pp. 16–28; Nelson 1996, pp. 199–222). When she died in 779, she was buried with Boniface in the abbey church at Fulda, honoring an old request of his. The Fulda monks, however, seem to have become less and less comfortable with Leoba's presence as the years went by, translating her relics twice to keep her an increasingly safe distance from her adoptive brother (*Vita Leobae* 1887).

## The Rise of the Carolingians

If the fifth and sixth centuries represent the extension of Christianity beyond the boundaries of the Roman Empire, the seventh and eighth centuries saw the return to continental Europe of insular missionaries who would rejuvenate the church. Boniface, Leoba, and their followers infused English and Irish learning and scribal practice into the native Frankish church, as well as their profound respect for the authority of the pope in Rome. But the eighth century also saw the meteoric rise of one family, the Carolingians, named after Charles Martel, the mayor of the palace of the Frankish Merovingians and patron of Boniface and Leoba. The close alliance between the English missionaries, Charles Martel's son Pepin, his grandson Charlemagne, and the papacy would foster the creation of the institutional structures of Christendom in Europe, and even the birth of Europe itself as many would now understand it (Noble 2015). Women were instrumental in the ongoing Christianization of Europe and the rise of the Carolingian family, but the very ordering and institutionalization of the church attempted by the Carolingian and Gregorian reform movements, and the increasing importance of the Eucharist, made women's participation in the church more difficult. The presence of women, so essential in the early years of reform, became for later generations a disorderly or polluting presence that needed to be cleansed from God's house, and against which reformers defined themselves, camouflaging their own innovations as the reassertion of ancient tradition (Scheck 2008, pp. 27–52).

In 732, Charles Martel, or "Charles the Hammer," won his title defeating a force of raiding Muslims at the battle of Poitiers, also called the battle of Tours, the northernmost point reached by the armies which swept across North Africa and into Spain and France in the century after the Prophet Muhammad's death. The actual military significance of the battle of Poitiers has been much debated by historians, and may have been no more than a skirmish (Fouracre 2013). The legend of his grandson, Charles the Great, or Charlemagne, was later enshrined in the epic poem *The Song of Roland*, depicting the king as a patriarchal proto-crusader possessed of fabled longevity and potent divine favor. The historical Roland, however, was killed not by Muslims but by Basque raiders in a botched retreat from Spain. In reality, the ascendancy of the Carolingian dynasty was far less inevitable than later crusaders' history made it sound: far more fragile, and just as dependent on interconnected networks of relationship and consensus as on raw military aggression (Gabriele 2011). More than Charles Martel's victory at Poitiers, Carolingian success rested on the creation of new political strategies: their successful administration of monasteries by lay supporters, and a sequence of extremely advantageous marriage alliances, which left the mayors of the palace in control of a vast number of estates in what is now France and Germany (Wood 2004). After Charles Martel's son Pepin, nicknamed "Pepin the Short," suppressed any potential rivals from within his own family, he felt strong enough to challenge the remaining Merovingian kings and to take the kingship for himself.

In 749, Pepin wrote a very famous letter to the pope in Rome, asking whether it was fitting for someone to rule who had only the appearance of authority and no actual power (*Royal Frankish Annals* 1970, p. 39; Noble 1984, pp. 67–94). The question was, of course, diplomatic code, asking for the complex and mutually beneficial alliance which the papacy then struck up with Pepin. The papacy countenanced and supported the Carolingian usurpation of the Merovingian throne, in exchange for which the Carolingian rulers provided much-needed military support for the papal territories in Italy. Although the popes ostensibly continued to owe their political allegiance to the Roman emperors in Constantinople, in practice it was becoming clear that no Greek military aid would be forthcoming.

Meanwhile, Rome had become a thriving and prosperous center for Christian pilgrimage, drawing the likes of Abbess Eadburga to the graves of the early Christian martyrs. The biographies of the popes in this period record an ambitious pattern of gift-giving and the lavish refurbishment of the martyrs' churches in Rome, which can still be observed today (*The Book of Pontiffs* 2000; Thunø 2015; Maskarinec 2018). The jewel-box-like chapel of San Zeno in the church of S. Prassede, the virgin martyr, was built by Pope Paschal II as part of a massive building program throughout Rome, intended perhaps as a place for his mother Theodora's body to rest. A mosaic on the wall of the San Zeno chapel depicts her with the title *Theodora episcopa*. In an effort to cover up this rather awkward inscription, a door has subsequently been knocked into the wall of the chapel, but the mosaic and its inscription remain (see Figure 6.2). The title may simply reflect Theodora's being the mother of the bishop of Rome; however, the early medieval title may also signify Theodora's administration of church property, by then something of a going concern (Macy 2016, pp. 53–58). The papacy was becoming an increasingly free and independent agent, although the city of Rome remained prone to factional violence and its territory vulnerable to invasions from the ambitious Lombard kingdom in northern Italy. Eminently practical though the alliance with Pepin was,

**Figure 6.2** Mosaic from the chapel of San Zeno, S. Prassede, Rome. *Source:* Sixtus / Wikimedia Commons / CC BY-SA 3.0

therefore, it did represent an innovation which displaced the old charisma of the Merovingians in favor of a family that, on the surface of it, had no such traditional glamour. In 754, Pope Zachary anointed not only Pepin but his wife Bertrada, the first time in western Europe that a queen was so singled out, and their young son, Charles.

## Charlemagne and the World of the Carolingian Court

Charles the Great, or Charlemagne, (r. 768–814) amassed the largest empire in the early medieval west since the fall of Rome. Physically powerful and militarily able, he spent virtually the entirety of his early reign on horseback, conquering the Lombard kingdom in northern Italy, attempting an unsuccessful invasion of Muslim Spain, launching a series of raids against the Saxons on his eastern frontier, and conquering the Avars to the southeast. The plunder from this last conquest was immense, and was said to have subsidized the construction of the great palace at Aachen. In all, Charlemagne reigned for nearly 50 years, a remarkable span for his time and essential in developing lasting Carolingian political and dynastic strategies for rule.

At Aachen, Charlemagne's court attracted some of the most gifted intellectuals from across Europe, most famously Alcuin of York, the Northumbrian poet, liturgist, and biblical scholar, who saw himself as a teacher in the tradition of the Venerable Bede. The Carolingian Reform which flourished in these decades combined the talents of émigré English, Spanish, Italian, and Irish scholars with the native Frankish clergy. Charlemagne's circle sought to standardize religious practice in Carolingian lands based on Roman liturgical precedent and Roman textual models, while Alcuin and the Spaniard Theodulf of Orléans sought to copy and circulate the Vulgate text of the bible (Bullough 2004, pp. 371–391). The fruit of this religious and cultural fusion of talent was felt throughout the church, even down to the creation of a distinctive script, Caroline or Carolingian minuscule, which has become the basis for most printed text today.

One of Alcuin's most notable correspondents was Charlemagne's sister, Gisela (Scheck 2008, pp. 53–71). Born in 757 after her parents' anointing, her baptismal shawl was sent to the pope in Rome. It was not immediately apparent that she should join the religious life, but after two proposed marriages fell through, Gisela became the abbess of Balthild's community at Chelles. In 799, she is described at the meeting of her brother and Pope Leo:

> . . . in shimmering white, accompanied by the band of virgins she gleams along with the golden offspring. Covered in a mallow-colored cloak she shines, her supple veil of purple has a reddish glow. Voice, face, hair shimmer with radiating light . . . Her hand appears to be made from silver, her golden brow flashes, and the light of her eyes conquers the great Phoebus (*Karolus Magnus et Leo Papa* 1966; trans. Garver 2009, p. 21; Scheck 2008, p. 42).

Gisela, in short, had become a living reliquary, her body a vessel of divine power and sign of the favor granted to the Carolingian family (Mayr-Harting 2007; Nelson 1995). At Chelles, Gisela oversaw a scriptorium which produced liturgical books for export to many of the great monastic houses of the realm, underscoring the connection between the Carolingian Reform and correct liturgical practice based on Roman models. It is believed that the Gelasian Sacramentary, the second oldest liturgical manuscript in the west, was made at Chelles. In addition, certain women's houses with close connections to the Carolingian family, among them Chelles and St. Mary's at Soissons, began compiling historical annals, essential to modern historians' understanding of the period (Nelson 1996, pp. 191–195). In this way, Carolingian women's monasticism preserved the intimate and traditional connection between women's prayer and intercession and women's commemoration and memorialization of the family.

By the 790s, Charlemagne's court circle were becoming disturbed by the confused reports that were emerging from Constantinople of what is now referred to as the iconoclastic controversy. Early imperial efforts to suppress the veneration of particular images of the saints in worship had been followed by a palace coup and their whole-hearted embrace by "iconodule" monks under the leadership of the empress Irene. A marriage alliance had once been floated between Irene and Charlemagne, who also considered marrying his daughter Rotrud to Irene's son, Constantine VI. But since then relations had cooled. By 794 and the Council of Frankfurt, Charlemagne's court circle had begun to view itself as a kind of Nicaea reborn under the leadership of a second Constantine. They defined themselves against what they viewed as the Greek perversion of empire under the rule of a woman, spawning drunken swerves in the church's teaching around images in worship (Noble 2009). The Franks were relying on second-hand, garbled translations of events in Constantinople, of which the pope at least was well aware. In fact, Charlemagne's queen Fastrada appears to have played a highly influential role at Frankfurt before her death later in the year. That she was not remembered kindly by Theodulf of Orléans, perhaps Charlemagne's preeminent biblical scholar, may reflect the extent to which misogyny generally had now become a chief component of the aggressive and ambitious Carolingian political ideology of the late 790s (Nelson 2019, pp. 302–306). On Christmas Day 800, these plans came to fruition, as Charlemagne was crowned emperor in the west by the pope in Rome.

Alcuin and the rest of Charlemagne's court believed sincerely that faithful, purified Christian observance would ensure divine favor for the new Israel, the Franks. Where possible, they attempted to impose baptism and to promote basic Christian catechesis (Phelan 2014; Mayr-Harting 2002). Carolingian legislation took the form of royal admonition mixed with biblical exhortation. These were not impersonal instruments of bureaucratic government, therefore, but tools to generate consensus and unity, however fragile, between the king, his clergy, and aristocratic magnates, all of whom were expected to model praiseworthy conduct for their dependents, clients, and followers (*Admonitio generalis* 2004, pp. 69–78). It is not surprising, then, that religious and even monastic models of conduct were enjoined upon and adopted by laypeople.

One of the most powerful personal documents to survive from the period is the *Handbook for William* of Dhuoda, the wife of Bernard, the Duke of Septimania and royal chamberlain. William was Dhuoda's son, and she wrote her handbook for him to carry as he was sent off to court in a bid to ensure his father's loyalty. Despite the fact that she seems largely to have administered her husband's territories in his absence, Dhuoda's *Handbook* is not a political manual or advice on estate management so much as an extraordinary blend of maternal affection, etiquette guide, and devotional text (see Figure 6.3). Scholars have wondered whether the teenage William really engaged in his mother's exhaustive prescribed round of daily prayers. However, it seems clear that it was important for him to *look* as if he did. Dhuoda's *Handbook* is indicative of the extent to which moral expectations fostered in the Carolingian Reform gradually filtered down and out to society through the court (Dhuoda 1991; Airlie 1990).

Perhaps the most significant development imposed by the Carolingian Reform was its encouragement and gradual imposition of monogamous marriage within Frankish society (Wemple 1981, pp. 75–123). This may have made a religious vocation a less attractive alternative to some women than it had been under the Merovingians, but not necessarily so, and it is not clear that these boundaries were so very sharply drawn in early medieval society. When girls did take formal vows, the ceremony in this period imitated many of the conventions of secular marriage, such as the ring and the veil. Women's religious communities remained intimately connected with local society and with local families: girls might well be educated in a religious community before marrying, and, years later, return with their dower when they became widows (Nelson 1995; Schilp 1998). In contrast with the aggressive, flamboyant charisma of many Merovingian female saints and queens, Carolingian women's saints' lives suggest broad social expectations of a more inward-looking, domestic femininity which they shared with their married sisters (Smith 1995; Garver 2009, pp. 122–169). After an early life effectively managing a large estate in Saxony, the saint Liutberga became a recluse living in a cave, where she continued to teach young women how to spin (*Vita Liutbergae* 1937). And even while the church's encouragement of marriage protected many laywomen, they remained marginalized from the general assemblies where so much Frankish court politics took place. Moreover, the more widespread ideals and expectations surrounding domestic, monogamous marriage became, the more it made possible barbed political attacks on prominent women's chastity, particularly on that of the queen.

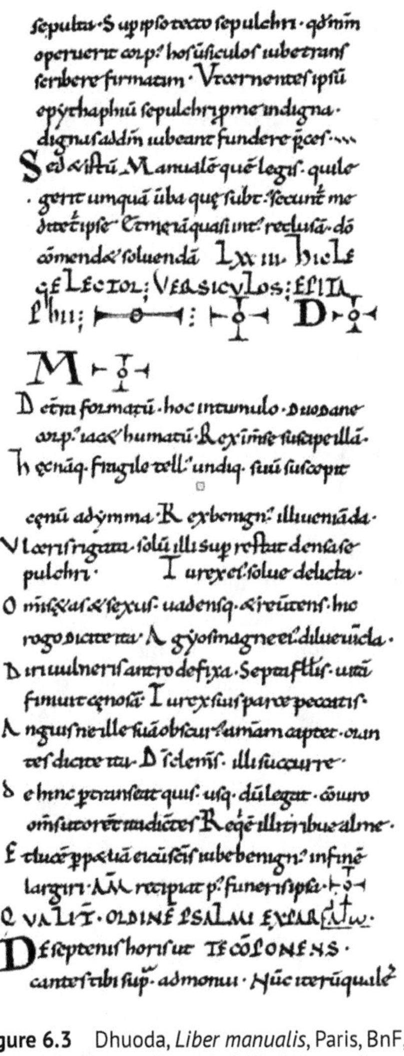

One person who never could be brought to adopt the church's strictures on his sexual behavior was Charlemagne himself. Having sent away his first wife, a Lombard princess, on the eve of conquering her father's kingdom, Charlemagne had a series of queens – Hildegard, Fastrada, and Liutgard – as well as a string of unnamed concubines, fathering some 19 children in all. The case of his last queen, Liutgard, demonstrates how fluid the terminology remained around marriage, at least when it concerned the king and the court. Liutgard appears to have been accepted on a sort of trial basis after Fastrada's death in 794, gradually accumulating more of the titles and dignities of her position before her death in 800. For the next 14 years, Charlemagne had no official queen, and it has been argued that his seven daughters acted as a kind of "collective queen" in Liutgard's place, taking over the management of the often itinerant household (Nelson 1993, 2002, 2019, pp. 377–380). A court poet, Angilbert, describes with great enthusiasm the beauty of the princesses, particularly the poetic discrimination of Charlemagne's daughter, Bertha (Angilbert 1881). Despite the fact that Angilbert eventually had some four children with Bertha, one of whom would become the historian Nithard, Charlemagne's biographer Einhard records that the king did not allow any of them to marry (Einhard 2009, Bk. III, Section 19).

**Figure 6.3** Dhuoda, *Liber manualis*, Paris, BnF, ms. 12293. *Source:* Dhuoda 843 / Wikimedia Commons / Public domain.

Einhard cites Charlemagne's great affection for his daughters as the reason for his unwillingness to part with any of them. Fundamentally, however, the king's concerns were political and dynastic: formal marriage now conveyed legitimacy, and the Franks continued to practice the division of an estate between the sons of a family. Charlemagne had once forced his younger brother into a monastery before becoming king himself, and wanted no sons-in-law to marry into the Carolingian family and produce rival heirs. In the end, only Hildegard's son Louis, later called Louis the Pious, was Charlemagne's recognized successor, inheriting an undivided kingdom. But it is clear that Charlemagne's sexual behavior did not make everyone comfortable – in a court in which he was routinely compared to the biblical David, the story of Bathsheba naturally suggested itself – and after his death one brave woman at least had the nerve to describe a vision in which the old king was tormented in hell for immorality (Dutton 1994, pp. 67–69). One of Louis's first actions as king was to turn out his sisters from the palace at Aachen, citing their improper behavior, but it is also an indication of their political importance (The Astronomer 2009; Nithard 1970, p. 130; Dutton 1994, pp. 58–60).

## King Solomon's Wives

In contrast with his father, who famously could barely write, Louis the Pious grew up within the culture of the Carolingian Reform and was far more intimately steeped in its aims. Since his youth as a prince in Aquitaine and the Spanish marches, Louis had been a patron of the Spanish monk Witiza, now known as Benedict of Aniane. Carolingian legislation had long sought to impose clear distinctions between a monastic and a canonical life, but Benedict aimed to reform monasticism within Carolingian lands along strictly Benedictine lines, and in particular to implement its ideals of stability, manual labor, and the separation of the genders (Williams 2012). Of particular concern were those double monasteries which still survived, but more generally, the reformers targeted the intimate involvement of prominent monastic communities with lay local society. As we have seen, an abbess like Leoba traveled a great deal, perhaps even more than her hagiographer wanted to admit. In 817, the Council of Aachen imposed a raft of measures, including the promulgation of the Benedictine Rule and the *Institutio sanctimonialium*, which for women's communities mandated strict enclosure and more stringent standards concerning private property.

In the long run, it has been argued that the legislation at Aachen eroded the appeal of, and economic basis for, women's monasticism in early medieval society (Wemple 1981, pp. 165–188; Schulenberg 1984). However, this is perhaps to give the reformers more credit for practical effectiveness than they deserve. Behind the aggressive rhetoric, the reformers had no firm strategy to enforce the measures passed at Aachen other than through the cooperation and consent of local society. It seems that the decisions made at the council were not widely copied and may not even have been immediately known or enforced beyond Benedict's immediate circle of supporters (Vanderputten 2018, pp. 13–28). Many monastic houses, such as the great foundation of Corbie on the Somme, which supported at least one literate women's community, paid lip service to the Benedictine Rule while recording exceptions to it in its customary, or house rules. Early medieval monastic reform was not a unified or consistent movement imposed from above but an endless process of adaptation, in which local houses had enormous powers of passive resistance, or actively selected which aspects of the Rule they would adopt (Bodarwé 2011). Women's communities were vital nodes of social networking, essential for the commemoration and memorialization of family groups. Certain women's houses, such as San Salvatore in Brescia and Remiremont in the Vosges, preserve their memorial "books of life," or *libri vitae*, spiritual address books in which women recorded the names of their donors and benefactors and for whom the sisters interceded in their daily prayers. In this way, even if they were enclosed – and San Salvatore in particular, which was on a pilgrimage route to Rome, fought hard not to be – women's houses were part of a web of social connection, prayer, and patronage. Regional aristocracies, meanwhile, did not particularly want to hand over these communities to the control of royal appointees if they could help it. As a result, a patchwork of enclosed women's foundations continued to exist alongside surviving houses of semi-enclosed canonesses; on the continent, only by the turn of the millennium does the Latin noun *sanctimonialis* signify a nun living according to the Benedictine Rule.

Louis the Pious, meanwhile, had troubles of his own. Unlike his father, he had multiple adult heirs who all expected to inherit something, and in place of his father's conquests, Louis was increasingly on the defensive from Viking and Slavic raids. After the death of his wife Irmengard in 818, Louis had married a second time. Later stories tell of a Byzantine-style bride show in which the new queen, Judith, was chosen for her beauty. This may be a biblical allusion to Esther, to whom Judith was compared by court poets alongside her formidable namesake; however, to link Judith with exotic Byzantine custom may also have been a later, subtle ploy to discredit her (De Jong 2004; Joye 2012). For Judith had a son, provocatively and ambitiously named Charles. Later, and perhaps erroneously, nicknamed "Charles the Bald," his father's need to create an inheritance for his third legitimate son disrupted the always fragile and carefully calibrated networks of clients, food renders, and military support in the empire. Louis's furious son Lothar accused Judith of committing adultery with Bernard of Septimania, Dhuoda's husband, and the resulting polarization of court opinion ultimately plunged the kingdom into civil war.

Louis's very desire to foster religious reform and to abide by the dictates of the church was, in this way, a powerful political strategy, but one that could be turned against him. In 822, Louis was cornered into performing public penance, in the style of the Roman emperor Theodosius before Ambrose, for the botched blinding and death of his nephew, Bernard of Italy (De Jong 2009). Both Louis and Judith were forced for a time into monastic retirement, before the king emerged triumphant and was able to wrest control of the empire from his sons. The final division of the kingdom split the empire between Lothar, Louis "the German" in the east, and Charles the Bald, who inherited west Francia.

Lothar's kingdom, later called Lotharingia or Lorraine, included the Carolingian palace at Aachen but otherwise extended, with apparent disregard for geographic coherence or military defensibility, across the Alps and down into Italy. Lothar's son, Lothar II, married a German noblewoman, Theutberga. When the couple could not conceive, Lothar attempted to divorce Theutberga for his mistress, Waldrada. Lothar's efforts to annul the marriage included wild and graphic accusations of Theutberga having a sexual relationship with her brother and aborting the resulting child (Hincmar 2017). The pope, Nicholas I, refused to countenance these charges or Lothar's remarriage to Waldrada, the first time a pope had attempted to arbitrate in a Carolingian succession crisis. How Theutberga felt about having to reconcile with a husband who had shamed her so grotesquely is, unfortunately, lost to history. The mysterious Lothair Crystal, an elaborately carved quartz gem now in the British Museum, depicts a series of scenes of the biblical Susannah, unjustly accused of sexual misconduct. Although little is known about where or when the intaglio was made, it may have been commissioned either by Lothar himself in an attempt at penitence, or by one of his bishops in an effort to shame him into it. Regardless of who commissioned the Lothair Crystal, any portrayal of the trial of Susannah necessarily reflected the *cause célèbre* of its day (Flint 1995; MacGregor 2010, pp. 339–344; see Figure 6.4).

Lothar's lack of heir unfortunately coincided with the linguistic and cultural drift beginning to separate the kingdom of Charles the Bald in the west from that of his older brother, Louis the German. Paradoxically, the prosperous heartland of Charlemagne's empire, from the Low Countries along the Rhine down to the Swiss border, now became the most ill-defined and most fought-over border zone in European history. Political and religious complexity, even chaos, however, also created opportunities for women. The lack of centralized political and religious

**Figure 6.4** The Lothair Crystal, the British Museum. *Source:* World History Archive / Alamy Stock Photo.

authority, the wealth of the area, easy transport and communication, and its early urbanization combined with the powerful legacy of early medieval women's monasticism to create a kind of cradle for a variety of experiments in women's spirituality and women's religious communities that flourished in later centuries. In the short term, however, the pressure of repeated Viking raids exacerbated the breakup of Charlemagne's fragile empire into the more regional kingdoms of his descendants. It is in the tenth century rather than the ninth that many women's houses on the continent shrink or fail, while many of the historical annals simply cease in this period.

## Women and the Benedictine Reform in England

In England under Danish invasion, many women seem to have sought the religious life on land privately owned by their families, leaving little trace in the historical record. A recent archeological discovery suggests that Cynethryth, the wife of King Offa widowed in 796, established a religious community strategically located on the border of her husband's kingdom, now Cookham in Berkshire, the parish church of the twentieth-century English artist Stanley Spencer. The Benedictine community of St. Mary's in Winchester, founded, according to tradition, by Alfred the Great's wife Ealhswith, was commonly called the Nunnaminster. A ninth-century manuscript, now known as the Book of Nunnaminster, survives and remained at Winchester, where it was in use for another century (Wellesley 2021, pp. 165–168; see Figure 6.5). A compilation of a variety of texts centered around the body of Christ, it may have been the work of a woman, and included not only extracts from the gospels but also texts on the communion of saints, the sacraments, and a series of "Christ Prayers" centered on different parts of his body.

**Figure 6.5**  The Book of Nunnaminster, London, Harley MS 2965. *Source:* Dsmdgold / Wikimedia Commons / Public domain.

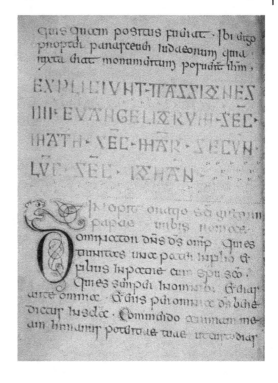

The result is a charm-like quality reminiscent of "St. Patrick's Breastplate," and like many insular prayers, contains a strong numerological component:

> O my unique, nearest mercy, redeemer God, you who flawlessly kept the seven charisma of the Holy Spirit and the eight Beatitudes always enclosed in your breast, I give thanks, and entreating I beg you, Highest God, loosen my breast from the eight greatest vices and from the contagion of all sins purify my body and soul, you who, pure and shining, shone with all the virtues, Lord Jesus Christ, Amen (*Book of Nunnaminster* 2019, p. 89).

To some extent, Alfred's reforms echoed aspects of the earlier Carolingian Reform under Charlemagne, including the circulation of Gregory the Great's *Pastoral Rule*, translated into Old English. Alfred's sister, Aethelswith, made a pilgrimage to Rome, where her name appears in the *liber vitae* of San Salvatore at Brescia, while Alfred's formidable daughter, Aethelflaed, "the Lady of the Mercians," corresponded with Dunstan, the archbishop of Canterbury (Atherton 2017).

Benedictine Reform in England drew on the legislation passed a century before at the Council of Aachen, but as on the continent, monastic reform took time, and just as on the continent, perfect implementation of the Benedictine ideal proved impossible (Scheck 2008, pp. 73–96). There continued to be a mix of cloistered or enclosed nuns, "mycena" in Old English, living alongside semi-enclosed, secular "vowesses," confusingly called "nunnan." Many of these women were widows, who might have inherited property from either of their parents as well as their husbands. Reforming clergy like Dunstan waged a continuous and often unsuccessful battle to keep these women simply from setting up religious communities in their own homes, and it is perhaps with this aim in mind that Bishop Aethelwold of Winchester made a bilingual version of the Benedictine Rule intended specifically for women's communities (Foot 2001, pp. 104–144). However, Aethelwold would also consecrate Edith, daughter of the English king Edgar, as abbess not only of the women's community at Wilton, but also of the important women's community of Barking in Essex and the Nunnaminster in Winchester, a measure hardly in keeping with Benedictine practice. Indeed, Edith seems to have had little practically to do with the governance of either Barking or the Nunnaminster. As Abbess of Wilton, Edith would embroider a linen alb with an elaborate yoke of gold, pearls, and gems. Combining simplicity and wealth, the authority of her office with the humility enjoined upon Christian leaders, the alb smacks of both vestment and relic, and is unmistakably meant for public display, within the community and beyond (Bugyis 2019, pp. 90–95).

## The Triumph of Orthodoxy: Women Saints in Byzantium

Sanctity in Constantinople in this period, for both women and men, is inextricably associated with the progression of the iconoclastic controversy, and the religious and political polarization it inspired. It remains extremely difficult to reconstruct the nature of Byzantine iconoclasm, partly because all evidence is scarce, but also because any texts in favor of the iconoclastic position have been almost entirely obliterated or submerged behind the hagiographies of the pro-icon, or iconodule, party (Brubaker and Haldon 2011). In Constantinople itself, the most obvious and prominent heroines are the empresses Irene and Theodora (r. 829–842), the latter married to an iconoclast emperor. As regent for her son, however, she oversaw the Triumph of Orthodoxy in 843, in which iconoclasm was finally banned (Herrin 2001; see Figure 6.6). On the icon of the Triumph itself, along with the empress Theodora there is one female saint, Theodosia, the most famous of a group of women who had been executed under the iconoclast Emperor Leo III. It was attested, in the letters of Theodore of Stoudios, among others, that women represented the strongest supporters of icon veneration and practice throughout the iconoclastic controversy, although their names are not at all well represented in the subsequent hagiography; like English recusant Catholics in the sixteenth century, women brought food and support to iconodule monks and clerics in prison and represented an unofficial network which kept the cause alive in the face of imperial resistance (Talbot and Kazhdan 2001).

In later Byzantine hagiography, empresses continued to model their public piety on the example of Helena, Flacilla, and Pulcheria, acting as charitable benefactors who founded hospitals and women's religious communities. Even Theodora, of Theodora and Justinian, was said to have founded a community for reformed prostitutes, an ironic gesture given the nature of the rumors that circulated around her sexual past. Theophano (d. 897), the wife of Leo VI, became particularly well-known for this kind of charitable philanthropy, which would influence later empresses like Theodora of Arta, wife of Constantine Doukas, in the thirteenth century (Talbot 2001). It seems to have been mostly widows who entered religious communities in the Byzantine world, and those who patronized them clearly understood their social utility.

The ninth and tenth centuries saw a series of women ascetic saints who had been orphaned by the Muslim annexation of Crete and subsequent raids in the Aegean. After her family were killed, Theoktiste of Lesbos became a hermit on the island of Paros, dressing like a man in the tradition of the Egyptian desert. A traveler encountered her by chance and was stunned to see that "she had the shape of a woman but the appearance of a superhuman being." Theoktiste requested that he bring back and leave for her the Eucharist, which she had not received for years (*Life of Theoktiste of Lesbos* 1996). The ninth-century life of Theodora of Thessalonike describes her as another orphan and refugee. When her husband and children died, she entered a religious community, where the superior of the community was her last remaining relative, Anna. Toward the end of her life, Anna fell and broke her hip and was said to go mad, perhaps showing signs of dementia;

**Figure 6.6**   Icon of the Triumph of Orthodoxy, the British Museum. *Source:* The Trustees of the British Museum.

Theodora nursed her throughout. When Theodora herself died, her body was said to give off a miraculous and holy oil (*Life of Theodora of Thessalonike* 1996). Called a *myroblytos* saint, it was a fashion that occasionally appeared in western European hagiography in frontier regions, such as that of the thirteenth-century saint Elizabeth of Hungary.

In the late ninth and early tenth century, a new model of Byzantine women's hagiography emerged which anticipated, in some ways, models of sanctity for women in the late European Middle Ages: that of the ordinary, married woman saint (Talbot 2001). In life, these women, such as Mary the Younger, also called Mary of Bizye, and Thomaïs of Lesbos, showed no extraordinary signs of sanctity. When miracles occurred after their deaths, however, their male hagiographers sought to explain why this might be the case, despite what, to them, seemed unprepossessing makings for sanctity. "Although she was a woman, although she was married and bore children, nothing hindered her in any way from finding favor with God" (*Life of Mary the Younger* 1996). Thomaïs was described as an unusually public and devout church-goer, who venerated the icon of the Virgin, the Hodegetria, in particular (*Life of Thomaïs of Lesbos* 1996). In both cases, the answer given by these hagiographers to explain such posthumous miracle-working was that, in life, both these women practiced charity and endured domestic abuse patiently. Mary of Bizye was literally beaten to death by her husband; in effect, these women saints were martyred by their spouses.

## Ottonian Queens

In 856, Charlemagne's grandson, Charles the Bald, had married his daughter, named Judith after his mother, to the English king Aethelwulf of Wessex, the father of Alfred the Great. Despite her youth, Judith was both anointed and crowned queen by the bishop of Rheims, only the second time this ceremony had occurred, after Charlemagne's mother, Bertrada. There was to be no mistaking who was doing whom a diplomatic favor. Fifty years later, however, the tables had turned. The Carolingian dynasty had flickered out, and the new power in German-speaking lands was Henry the Fowler, later called Henry I. The English king Æthelstan sent two of his sisters abroad, with Edith becoming the wife of Henry's young son, Otto I, in 930 (Foot 2011, pp. 44–52).

The Ottonian dynasty was distinguished by a series of extremely powerful and visible queens: Henry's wife Matilda (or Mechthild), her daughter Gerberga, the English Edith, Otto's second wife Adelheid, and the Byzantine princess Theophanu, married to Otto II. In comparison with their Carolingian forebears the difference is palpable, and it has been argued that it was precisely the comparative instability and insecurity of the new Ottonian kings that made strong and active queens a dynastic necessity (Maclean 2017, p. 21). Many of these women were royal in their own right, bringing large dowries with them and endowed in turn in keeping with their status. They were, in short, what distinguished their husbands from the rest of the German nobility. This narrative had its flaws, of course. Matilda was actually Henry's second wife, after his first scandalous alliance with a woman who had actually been in a religious community when he married her. It is debatable whether Adelheid, Otto I's second wife, was actually queen of Italy by virtue of her first marriage. Theophanu was a much less important princess than the *porphyrogenita*, or emperor's daughter, for whom Otto had originally bargained. That these infelicities were later smoothed over and the women's status was, if anything, retroactively inflated is an argument for just how important queenship had become in the tenth century.

The Ottonian court was itinerant, and therefore did not possess a fixed geographical center so much as a network of estates and monasteries held in relationship, like an electrical circuit, powered by hierarchical, symbolic ideology inspired in part by the example of the Byzantine court (Mayr-Harting 2007, pp. 57–58). Liturgy which exalted Mary as Queen of Heaven mirrored the highly visible role of the queen in the court; it was in this period that the great hymn *Salve Regina* was composed at the monastery of Reichenau. The queen was routinely addressed as the leader of female religious in her realm, as if she were an abbess. Matilda's favorite royal foundation at Quedlinburg had no abbess, in fact, while she was in retirement there after her son's marriage to Edith, and treated her as its leader even though she never took formal vows (Jestice 2018, p. 142). Gerberga worked closely with her brother, Bruno, the archbishop of Cologne, both as regent for her son and to patronize Benedictine Reform in west Francia; she was addressed as "mother of monks and leader (*dux*) of holy virgins." A silk banner with depictions of the saints, discovered wrapped around relics in the cathedral treasury in Cologne, declares "Gerberga made me" in gold embroidery, and was probably given to Bruno by the queen (MacLean 2017, pp. 84–86; Rubenstein 2019, p. 36). She sponsored a life of the Merovingian queen Chlotild, Clovis's wife, while a life of Matilda likened the queen to Radegund. Adelheid, who corresponded with the abbots of Cluny, was later declared a saint.

It is this religious landscape, in which queens were so intimately involved with religious foundations that, in effect, they were treated as members of the community and hailed as saints, which produced one of the most extraordinary writers of the tenth century: Hrotsvitha of Gandersheim in Saxony. Hrotsvitha is perhaps most famous for her series of plays modeled on the work of Terence, in which she pointedly tackles the Roman author's misogyny (Scheck 2008, pp. 143–165). These demonstrate the extent to which the Carolingian Renaissance had fostered the study of classical antiquity through the copying of ancient texts, and suggests the number and quality of books to which Hrotsvitha had access at Gandersheim. But she also turned her hand to writing history, in the tradition of the anonymous annalists: if some of these were women, as historians now believe, it was not such a difficult conceptual leap for Hrotsvitha to make. As with her refashioning of Terentian comedy, Hrotsvitha's *Deeds of Otto*, the title notwithstanding, is actually a celebration of royal women (Nelson 1996, pp. 187–191; Scheck 2008, pp. 121–141). Perhaps the most dramatic and unique story in the collection describes the escape of the newly widowed Adelheid from the clutches of the evil villain Berengar of Italy. Hrotsvitha describes Adelheid digging a secret tunnel from her prison with her maid and a priest, fleeing her pursuers, hiding in caves and grain fields, until she reached the rescuing arms of Otto I (Hrotsvitha of Gandersheim 2001). Written in the late 960s and dedicated to her own abbess and Adelheid's son, Otto II, Hrotsvitha's work is a kind of family history, both commemoration and intercession, which linked Gandersheim seamlessly to the world of the Ottonian court.

That Queen Matilda never took formal vows in Quedlinburg meant that there was nothing to stop her re-emerging from retirement when circumstances required it: she was a figure on the Ottonian political scene until her death in 968, more than 30 years after the death of her husband. A similar coalition of empresses was on display during the most acute crisis the dynasty faced: the death in 983 of the 28-year-old Otto II in Rome. Otto left behind a three-year-old son, Otto III, and his mother, the Byzantine princess Theophanu. Theophanu had arrived at court as a girl with a trousseau of Byzantine silks and possibly a Greek and Latin interlinear psalter to help her learn the language; her marriage documents were preserved almost by accident at Gandersheim (McKitterick 1993; Herrin 1995; Muthesius 2004, pp. 8–9; Jestice 2018, p. 74). Although an outsider in theory, Theophanu had actually spent almost as many years at the Ottonian court as in Constantinople, and when Otto died, she had been crowned queen for nearly a decade. With rebellion threatening, Theophanu, acting as regent for her son, her mother-in-law the empress Adelheid, and Adelheid's daughter Matilda, the abbess of Quedlinburg, acted in concert to forestall potential uprising and to solidify political support for the child-king (Thietmar 2001, Bk. 4, Section 8; Engels 1995). Theophanu reigned for the rest of the decade, ostensibly in her son's name, but in 990, a year before her death, she issued charter documents in which she styled herself *Theophanius imperator*, using terms both imperial and male (Ciggaar 1995). It was during Theophanu's reign that the Golden Madonna of Essen was commissioned, possibly by the abbess of the women's community at Essen, a granddaughter of Otto I and Edith, or possibly by Theophanu herself. One of the oldest sculptures of the Madonna, and one of the oldest statues to survive outside of Italy, the Madonna of Essen is a carved wooden figure with mosaic eyes, covered entirely in gold leaf, clearly influenced by Byzantine depictions of the Virgin (Lafontaine-Dosogne 1995; Westermann-Angerhausen 1995; see Figure 6.7).

**Figure 6.7** The Golden Madonna of Essen, Essen Cathedral Treasury. *Source:* Arnoldius / Wikimedia Commons / CC BY-SA 2.5.

## Women and the Gregorian Reform

During Theophanu's lifetime, her exotic background was, if anything, an asset. Fifty years later, however, the rhetoric of reform had shifted again. In the eleventh century, a series of popes, most notably Gregory VII, advocated for the primacy and status of the papacy as the moral arbiter of Christendom, and his rightful control over ecclesiastical appointments in the empire. The claims of the Gregorian Reform collided with the fragile Ottonian political network that the German emperors had inherited, creating the rolling disasters of the investiture controversy (Robinson 1990, pp. 398–441). The ambitions of the papacy and its reforming cardinals would also lead to lasting schism with the patriarch of Constantinople in 1053.

Of all the regional differences that had developed between the eastern and western churches over the centuries, perhaps the most immediately obvious was the acceptance of clerical marriage in the east. In the west, many clergy had married as well, and priesthood was often an inherited, family profession, reflecting as much as anything the sheer poverty of many priests in remote parishes (Karras 2012, pp. 115–164; Barrow 2015, pp. 135–147). However, the reforms at Aachen and the Gregorian Reform sought to impose more formal rules on cathedral clergy, such as the rule for canons by Chrodegang of Metz, and in particular, to promulgate clerical celibacy. This reflects the increasing prominence of the Eucharist in early medieval devotion by the eleventh century, when Europe had been largely Christianized, adult baptisms were less frequent, and memorial masses had become one of the most significant ways to honor the dead. Celibate priests were seen as more ritually pure, and therefore as a desirable, if not always achievable, ideal. When combined with the politics of the investiture controversy, however, which centered on whether the pope or the emperor should have the right to appoint bishops, Gregorian Reform clergy had a potent weapon with which to attack the imperial prince-bishops of the empire and their ambiguous, layered, improvisational approach to rule.

Collateral damage in this battle royale was the reputation and memory of powerful women, particularly if already suspiciously Greek in origin. The eleventh century saw a kind of retroactive *damnatio memoriae* of the empress Theophanu, with the Italian reformer Peter Damian reporting an ongoing affair with a Greek scholar at court, John Philagathos (Peter Damian 1880, col. 253A). The reforming popes also turned on their own history of the previous century, in which Roman ecclesiastical offices were thoroughly intertwined with secular titles, and in which aristocratic descent and inheritance patterns were often reckoned through the female line. The Roman aristocrat Teofilatto and his wife Teodora, who dominated early tenth-century Roman politics, were succeeded by their daughter, Marozia, who effectively ruled Rome between 925 and 932 and was later known as the mistress of both Pope Sergius III and his successor, John X (Liutprand of Cremona 2007, Sections 47–48; Wickham 2015, pp. 189–211).

Most poignant of all is the case of Matilda of Tuscany (1046–1115). The daughter of Beatrice and Boniface II, the Duke of Tuscany, after her father died her mother married again and made a match between Matilda and her new husband's son, Godfrey the Hunchback. The marriage did not prosper, and the couple soon separated. Matilda's mother and her husband both died in 1076, leaving her an important political player in imperial–papal relations. For much of her life, Matilda had been cultivated and even groomed as a papal ally by Gregory VII, who simultaneously praised her spiritual attainments while refusing to allow her to enter a monastery, as so many of her female relatives had done. It was at Matilda's palace at Canossa that the pope famously received the penitent and excommunicated Emperor Henry IV in 1077 (Cowdrey 1996, pp. 296–302; Madigan 2017, pp. 139–143). In these years, Matilda's court circle in Florence produced biblical commentaries which likened Matilda allegorically to the ideal wife of Proverbs 31 and even to the Bride of the

Song of Songs (Robinson 1983). In imperial circles, however, it was frequently whispered that Matilda was the pope's mistress (Nash 2017; Miller 2014, p. 172; 2020).

The church in early medieval society relied on the contributions of women. In the age of the missionary saints, women both supported monastic pioneers and, as in the case of Leoba and her sisters, traveled themselves to spread the reach of the church. Women's monasticism flourished in Frankish lands precisely insofar as the institution was flexible and adaptable in local society. Religious women made vestments and altar cloths and copied manuscripts, taking part in the huge Carolingian endeavor to preserve ancient learning, propagate correct liturgy, and teach the bible and its interpretation. Women's communities educated children, particularly girls of aristocratic family, who often returned to take formal vows when they became widows. This continuity of experience and the presence of these widows in the religious life ensured that few early medieval religious communities could be punitively strict. Conversely, however, many aristocratic women seem to have pursued private devotions that were not so very different from women who took formal vows. The deep Frankish association between a woman's management of the household and her role as preserver of family memory led naturally to a monastic spirituality focused on the commemoration and prayer for the souls of their family members and benefactors. In literate communities, this might lead, moreover, to an interest in keeping annals and the writing of history. For all these reasons, therefore, women's monasticism never could flourish in splendid isolation, but thrived as part of a broader web of social connection. However, that very connectedness could make women vulnerable to charges of worldliness or of sexual misconduct. As under the Ottonians, powerful queens could potentially capitalize on moments of political disorder and transformation. The subsequent rhetoric of reform, however, then turned on the contributions of women to the church and on the presence of women's political authority, authorizing the legitimacy of reformers' innovations while painting a lurid picture of the corrupting power of women's influence. These exaggerations betray the essential fragility both of religious reform and of political unity in the early medieval world: behind the aging Charlemagne was a palace full of daughters.

# References

Admonitio generalis (trans. P.E. Dutton)(2004). *Carolingian Civilization: A Reader*, 69–78. Toronto: Broadview Press.

Airlie, S. (1990). Bonds of power and bonds of association in the court circle of Louis the Pious. In: *Charlemagne's Heir: New Perspectives on the Reign of Louis the Pious (814–40)* (ed. P. Godman and R. Collins), 191–204. Oxford: Clarendon Press.

Angilbert (1881). To Charlemagne and his entourage. In: *Angilberti Carmina. Monumenta Germaniae Historica Poetae*, vol. *1* (ed. E. Dümmler), 360–363. Berlin: Weidmann.

Atherton, M. (2017). *The Making of England: A New History of the Anglo-Saxon World*. London: IB Tauris.

Barrow, J. (2015). *The Clergy in the Medieval World: Secular Clerics, Their Families and Careers in North-Western Europe, c. 800–c.1200*. Cambridge: Cambridge University Press.

Bodarwé, K. (2011). Eine Männerregel für Frauen: Die Adaption der Benediktsregel im 9. und 10. Jahrhundert. In: *Female vita religiosa between Late Antiquity and the High Middle Ages* (ed. G. Melville and A. Müller), 235–272. Vienna: Lit Verlag.

Boniface (ed.) (1976). *The Letters of St. Boniface* (ed. and trans. E. Emerton). New York: W.W. Norton and Co.

Brubaker, L. and Haldon, J. (2011). *Byzantium in the Iconoclast Era, c. 680–850: A History*. Cambridge: Cambridge University Press.

Bugyis, K.A.-M. (2019). *The Care of Nuns: The Ministries of Benedictine Women in England during the Central Middle Ages*. Oxford: Oxford University Press.

Bullough, D. (2004). *Alcuin: Achievement and Reputation*. Leiden: Brill.

Ciggaar, K. (1995). Theophano: an empress reconsidered. In: *The Empress Theophano: Byzantium and the West at the Turn of the First Millennium* (ed. A. Davids), 49–63. Cambridge: Cambridge University Press.

Coatsworth, E. and Owen-Crocker, G.R. (2018). *Clothing the Past: Surviving Garments from Early Medieval to Early Modern Western Europe*. Leiden: Brill.

Cowdrey, H.E.J. (1996). *Pope Gregory VII: 1073–85*. Oxford: Clarendon Press.

De Jong, M. (2009). *The Penitential State: Authority and Atonement in the Reign of Louis the Pious, 814–840*. Cambridge: Cambridge University Press.

De Jong, M. (2004). Bride shows revisited: praise, slander, and exegesis in the reign of the empress Judith. In: *Gender in the Early Medieval World, 300–900* (ed. L. Brubaker and J.M.H. Smith), 257–277. Cambridge: Cambridge University Press.

Dhuoda (1991). *Handbook for William: A Carolingian Woman's Counsel for Her Son* (trans. C. Neel). Washington D.C.: Catholic University Press.

Dutton, P.E. (1994). *The Politics of Dreaming in the Carolingian Empire*. Lincoln: Nebraska University Press.

Einhard (2009). *Charlemagne and Louis the Pious: Lives by Einhard, Notker, Ermoldus, Thegan, and the Astronomer* (trans. T.F.X. Noble). Philadelphia: University of Pennsylvania Press.

Engels, O. (1995). Theophano, the western empress from the east. In: *The Empress Theophano: Byzantium and the West at the Turn of the First Millennium* (ed. A. Davids), 28–48. Cambridge: Cambridge University Press.

Flint, V.I.J. (1995). Susanna and the Lothair Crystal: a liturgical perspective. *Early Medieval Europe* 4 (1): 61–86.

Foot, S. (2001). *Veiled Women: The Disappearance of Nuns from Anglo-Saxon England*, vol. 2. Aldershot: Ashgate.

Foot, S. (2011). *Æthelstan: The First King of England*. New Haven: Yale University Press.

Fouracre, P. (2013). *The Age of Charles Martel*. London: Routledge.

Gabriele, M. (2011). *An Empire of Memory: The Legend of Charlemagne, the Franks, and Jerusalem before the First Crusade*. Oxford: Oxford University Press.

Garver, V. (2009). *Women and Aristocratic Culture in the Carolingian World*. Ithaca: Cornell University Press.

Herrin, J. (1995). Theophano: considerations on the education of a Byzantine princess. In: *The Empress Theophano: Byzantium and the West at the Turn of the First Millennium* (ed. A. Davids), 64–85. Cambridge: Cambridge University Press.

Herrin, J. (2001). *Women in Purple: Rulers of Medieval Byzantium*. Princeton: Princeton University Press.

Hincmar of Rheims (2017). *The Divorce of King Lothar and Queen Theutberga: Hincmar of Rheims's De divortio* (trans. R. Stone and C. West). Manchester: Manchester University Press.

Hrotsvitha of Gandersheim (2001). Gesta Ottonis. In: *Opera omnia* (ed. W. Berschin), 276–305. Saur: Monachii et Lipsiae.

Jestice, P. (2018). *Imperial Ladies of the Ottonian Dynasty*. London: Palgrave Macmillan.

Joye, S. (2012). Carolingian rulers and marriage in the age of Louis the Pious and his sons. In: *Gender and Historiography: Studies in the Early Middle Ages in Honour of Pauline Stafford* (ed. J. Nelson, S. Reynolds and S.M. Johns), 101–114. London: University of London Press and the Institute of Historical Research.

Beumann, H., Brunhölzl, F., and Wilkelmann, W. (ed.) (1966). *Karolus Magnus et Leo Papa: Ein Paderborner Epos vom Jahre 799*. Paderborn: Schöningh.

Karras, R.M. (2012). *Unmarriages: Women, Men, and Sexual Unions in the Middle Ages*. Philadelphia: University of Pennsylvania Press.

Lafontaine-Dosogne, J. (1995). The art of Byzantium and its relation to Germany in the time of the empress Theophano. In: *The Empress Theophano: Byzantium and the West at the Turn of the First Millennium* (ed. A. Davids), 211–230. Cambridge: Cambridge University Press.

Levison, W. (1956). *England and the Continent in the Eighth Century*. Oxford: Clarendon Press.

Lifshitz, F. (2014). *Religious Women in Early Carolingian Francia: A Study of Manuscript Transmission*. New York: Fordham University Press.

Liutprand of Cremona (2007). Retribution II. In: *The Complete Works of Liudprand of Cremona* (trans. P. Squatriti), 71–107. Washington D.C: Catholic University Press.

MacGregor, N. (2010). *A History of the World in 100 Objects*. Allen Lane: Penguin.

MacLean, S. (2017). *Ottonian Queenship*. Oxford: Oxford University Press.

Macy, G. (2016). *The Hidden History of Women's Ordination: Female Clergy in the Medieval West*. Oxford: Oxford University Press.

Madigan, K. (2017). *Medieval Christianity: A New History*. New Haven: Yale University Press.

Maskarinec, M. (2018). *City of Saints: Rebuilding Rome in the Early Middle Ages*. Philadelphia: University of Pennsylvania Press.

Mayr-Harting, H. (2002). Charlemagne's religion. In: *Am Vorabend der Kaiser Krönung: Das Epos "Karolus Magnus et Leo papa," und der Papstbesuch in Paderborn 799* (ed. P. Gorman, J. Jarnut and P. Johanek), 113–124. Berlin: Akademie Verlag.

Mayr-Harting, H. (2007). *Church and Cosmos in Early Ottonian Germany: The View from Cologne*. Oxford: Oxford University Press.

McKitterick, R. (1989). *"The Literacy of the Laity." The Carolingians and the Written Word*. Cambridge: Cambridge University Press.

McKitterick, R. (1993). Ottonian intellectual culture and the role of Theophano. *Early Medieval Europe* 2: 53–74.

Miller, M. (2014). *Clothing the Clergy: Virtue and Power in Medieval Europe, c. 800–1200*. Ithaca: Cornell University Press.

Miller, M. (2020). Women donors and ecclesiastical reform: evidence from Camaldoli and Vallombrosa, c. 1000–1150. In: *Women Intellectuals and Leaders in the Middle Ages* (ed. K. Kerby-Fulton, K.A.-M. Bugyis and J. Van Engen), 343–357. Woodbridge: D.S. Brewer.

Muthesius, A. (2004). *Studies in Silk in Byzantium*. London: Pindar Press.

Nash, P. (2017). *Empress Adelheid and the Countess Matilda: Medieval Female Rulership and the Foundations of European Society*. London: Palgrave Macmillan.

Nelson, J. (1993). Women at the court of Charlemagne: a case of monstrous regiment? In: *Medieval Queenship* (ed. J.C. Parsons), 43–62. New York: St. Martin's Press.

Nelson, J. (1995). The wary widow. In: *Property and Power in Early Medieval Europe* (ed. W. Davies and P. Fouracre), 82–113. Cambridge: Cambridge University Press.

Nelson, J. (1996). *The Frankish World, 750–900*. London: Hambledon Press.

Nelson, J. (2002). Charlemagne: *pater optimus?* In: *Am Vorabend der Kaiser Krönung: Das Epos "Karolus Magnus et Leo papa," und der Papstbesuch in Paderborn 799* (ed. P. Gorman, J. Jarnut and P. Johanek), 269–281. Berlin: Akademie Verlag.

Nelson, J. (2019). *King and Emperor: A New Life of Charlemagne*. London: Allen Lane.

Nithard (1970). *Histories*. In: *Carolingian Chronicles* (trans. B.W. Scholz with B. Rogers), 127–174. Ann Arbor: University of Michigan Press.

Noble, T.F.X. (1984). *The Republic of St. Peter: The Birth of the Papal State*, 680–725. Philadelphia: University of Pennsylvania Press.

Noble, T.F.X. (2009). *Images, Iconoclasm, and the Carolingians*. Philadelphia: University of Pennsylvania Press.

Noble, T.F.X. (2015). Carolingian religion. *Church History* 84 (2): 287–307.

Peter Damian (ed. J.P. Migne)(1880). *Patrologia Latina*, 155. Paris: J.P. Migne.

Phelan, O. (2014). *The Formation of Christian Europe: The Carolingians, Baptism, and the Imperium Christianum*. Oxford: Oxford University Press.

Robinson, I.S. (1983). "Political allegory" in the biblical exegesis of Bruno of Segni. *Récherche de théologie ancienne et médiévale* 50: 69–98.

Robinson, I.S. (1990). *The Papacy, 1073–1198: Continuity and Innovation*. Cambridge: Cambridge University Press.

Rubenstein, J. (2019). *Nebuchadnezzar's Dream: The Crusades, Apocalyptic Prophecy, and the End of History*. Oxford: Oxford University Press.

Rudolph of Fulda (1887). *Vita Leobae abbatissae Biscofesheimensis*. In: *Monumenta Germaniae Historica Scriptores*, vol. 15.1 (ed. G. Waitz), 121–131. Hanover: Hahn.

Scheck, H. (2008). *Reform and Resistance: Formations of Female Subjectivity in Early Medieval Ecclesiastical Culture*. Albany: State University of New York Press.

Schilp, T. (1998). *Norm und Wirklichkeit religiöser Frauengemeinschaften im Frühmittelalter: die Institutio sanctimonialium Aquisgranensis des Jahres 816 und die Problematik der Verfassung von Frauenkommunitäten*. Göttingen: Vandenhoeck and Ruprecht.

Schulenberg, J.T. (1984). Strict active enclosure and its effects on the female monastic experience, ca. 500–1100. In: *Medieval Religious Women*, vol. 2 (ed. J.A. Nichols and L. Shank), I.51–I.86. Kalamazoo: Cistercian Publications.

Smith, J.M.H. (1995). The problem of female sanctity in Carolingian Europe. *Past and Present* 146 (1): 3–37.

Story, J. (2002). *Anglo-Saxon England and Carolingian Francia, c. 750–870*. Aldershot: Ashgate.

Talbot, A.-M. (2001). Byzantine women, saints' lives, and social welfare. In: *Women and Religious Life in Byzantium*, 105–122. Variorum: Ashgate.

Talbot, A.-M. and Kazhdan, A.P. (2001). Women and iconoclasm. In: *Women and Religious Life in Byzantium*, 391–408. Ashgate: Variorum.

The Astronomer (2009). *Charlemagne and Louis the Pious: Lives by Einhard, Notker, Ermoldus, Thegan, and the Astronomer* (trans. T.F.X. Noble). Philadelphia: University of Pennsylvania Press.

The Book of Nunnaminster (2019). *A Benedictine Reader, 530–1630* (ed. H. Feiss, R.E.P. OSB and M. O'Brian), 78–93. Athens, OH: Cistercian Publications.

*The Book of Pontiffs (Liber pontificalis): The Ancient Biographies of the First Ninety Roman Bishops to AD 715* (trans. R. Davis) (2000). Liverpool: Liverpool University Press.

The Life of Mary the Younger (trans. A.E. Laiou)(1996). *Holy Women of Byzantium: Ten Saints' Lives in English Translation* (ed. A.-M. Talbot), 239–289. Washington D.C: Dumbarton Oaks.

The Life of Theodora of Thessalonike (trans. A.-M. Talbot)(1996). *Holy Women of Byzantium: Ten Saints' Lives in English Translation* (ed. A.-M. Talbot), 159–237. Washington D.C: Dumbarton Oaks.

The Life of Theoktiste of Lesbos (trans. A.C. Hero)(1996). *Holy Women of Byzantium: Ten Saints' Lives in English Translation* (ed. A.-M. Talbot), 95–116. Washington D.C: Dumbarton Oaks.

The Life of Thomaïs of Lesbos (trans. P. Halsall)(1996). *Holy Women of Byzantium: Ten Saints' Lives in English Translation* (ed. A.-M. Talbot), 291–322. Washington D.C: Dumbarton Oaks.

The Royal Frankish Annals (1970). *Carolingian Chronicles* (trans. B.W. Scholz with B. Rogers), 35–126. Ann Arbor: University of Michigan Press.

Thietmar (trans. D. Warner)(2001). *Ottonian Germany: The Chronicon of Thietmar of Merseburg.* Manchester: Manchester University Press.

Thunø, E. (2015). *The Apse Mosaic in Early Medieval Rome: Time, Network, and Repetition.* Cambridge: Cambridge University Press.

Vanderputten, S. (2018). *Dark Age Nunneries: The Ambiguous Identity of Female Monasticism, 800–1050.* Ithaca: Cornell University Press.

Vita Leobae abbatissae Biscofesheimensis (ed. G. Waitz) (1887). *Monumenta Germaniae Historica Scriptores* 15.1, 121–131. Hanover: Hahn.

Vita Liutbergae virginis (ed.) (ed. O. Menzel)(1937). *Monumenta Germaniae Historica Deutsches Mittelalter Kritische Studientexte*, 3e. Leipzig: Verlag Karl W. Hiersemann.

Wellesley, M. (2021). *Hidden Hands: The Lives of Manuscripts and Their Makers.* London: Riverrun.

Wemple, S.F. (1981). *Women in Frankish Society: Marriage and the Cloister, 500 to 900.* Philadelphia: University of Pennsylvania Press.

Westermann-Angerhausen, H. (1995). *"Did Theophano Leave Her Mark on the Ottonian Sumptuary Arts?" The Empress Theophano: Byzantium and the West at the Turn of the First Millennium* (ed. A. Davids), 244–264. Cambridge: Cambridge University Press.

Wickham, C. (2015). *Rome: Stability and Crisis of a City, 900–1150.* Oxford: Oxford University Press.

Williams, J.B. (2012). Working for reform: acedia, Benedict of Aniane, and the transformation of working culture in Carolingian monasticism. In: *Sin in Medieval and Early Modern Culture: The Tradition of the Seven Deadly Sins* (ed. R.G. Newhauser and S.J. Richard). York: York Medieval Press.

Wood, I. (2004). Genealogy defined by women: the case of the Pippinids. In: *Gender in the Early Medieval World* (ed. L. Brubaker and J.M.H. Smith), 300–900. Cambridge: Cambridge University Press.

# 7

## New Learning, Old Problems

Women and the Reformations of the Twelfth Century, 1050–1200

In 1096, a princess gazed in astonishment at the barbarian horde converging on her city. The princess was Anna Comnena, daughter of the Byzantine emperor Alexius Comnenus, and the barbarian horde was a desperate crowd of ordinary people caught up in the apocalyptic rhetoric of the First Crusade. In Anna's eyes the Franks were aggressive, disorganized, and unstable. Her father was wary of "their readiness to approach anything with violence," because "they were known to be always immoderately covetous of anything they strove after and to break very easily, for any reason whatsoever, treaties which they had made" (Anna Comnena 2009, Bk. 10, Section 5). This was Anna's first encounter with western civilization, recalled decades later and colored by her family's subsequent experiences with the Franks. In another century, they would destroy her world.

The twelfth century is such a formative period for the identity of western Europe that it is sometimes difficult to remember that, until the crusader sack of Constantinople in 1204, Byzantium was the preeminent world power in the region. There was still no city anywhere in Europe like Constantinople, and the religious and cultural influence of Byzantium spread north, east, and west through the alliance of missionary clergy with aristocratic women (Obolensky 1971). In 955, Princess Olga of Kyiv was baptized a Christian, taking the name of Elena (Hussey 1986, pp. 98–101, 117). Serving as regent for her son, she led a particularly murderous campaign against a neighboring tribe, the Drevlians, in which she slaughtered their leaders and burned their capital. However, Olga's grandson grew up to become the saint and king Vladimir the Great, who married a Byzantine princess and sister of the emperor, Anna Porphyrogenita, and brought Christianity to the Kievan Rus (Bartlett 2020, pp. 13–14). Likewise, in 966, the Bohemian princess Dobrawa led her Polish husband, Mieszko, to baptism (Berend 2006, p. 181). In 965, Princess Mlada, the niece of Wenceslas of Bohemia, was sent on a diplomatic mission to Rome to be baptized and to establish an independent Latin bishopric in Prague, which suggests that she already knew some Latin (Thomas 2013). For centuries to come, Byzantine influence would remain strong in Bohemia and Hungary, alongside that of the western church. In 1185, Margaret of Hungary's first marriage was to the Byzantine ruler Isaac Angelus II in Thessalonica, when she was christened Maria and entered the eastern church. When she married again, this time to the Frank Boniface of Montferrat after the Fourth Crusade, she had to reconvert to the Catholic faith (Hussey 1986, p. 190).

Anna Comnena was born a century earlier in Constantinople in 1083, the eldest of nine children. Her father, Alexius Comnenus, had only become emperor two years before, after decades of religious factionalism and the recent, simmering annexation of Armenia. Religious refugees from the region, the Bogomils and the Paulicians, traveled westwards, serving in the army, and may even have included the emperor's mother, the formidable Anna Dalassena (Hussey 1986, pp. 160–161). Married at 15, Anna Comnena would have two daughters and four sons, before becoming

*A History of Women in Christianity to 1600*, First Edition. Hannah Matis.
© 2023 John Wiley & Sons Ltd. Published 2023 by John Wiley & Sons Ltd.

widowed in her thirties. Her mother, Irene, bequeathed to her the control of a monastery, where she studied and wrote until her death in 1153.

In her lifetime, Anna would witness both the First and the Second Crusade, and her chronicle, the *Alexiad*, charts events at court from her insider's perspective. She was formidably educated in the classical Greek writers that inspired her own work, as well as in mathematics, philosophy, and the sciences. Anna Comnena commissioned commentaries on Aristotle, when that philosopher's thought was only beginning to be rediscovered in the west through the work of Jewish translators in Spain. In her funeral panegyric, she was described as a phoenix, a marvelous mythical creature of both genders and neither. However, gender inescapably shaped both Anna's work as a historian and also how that historical work was received in later centuries. Like Hrotsvitha of Gandersheim, Anna Comnena was writing family history, which by definition could not be anonymous. But historical writing in the Thucydidean tradition was supposed to include eyewitness accounts and verbatim reportage. How could Anna include such material without undermining perceptions of her own moral character as a loyal daughter and good wife, and therefore, her own credibility along the way? Alongside her careful defense of her father, therefore, Anna chose to demonstrate, even to perform, her femininity in rhetorically elevated passages in the *Alexiad*, which later writers and historians, ironically, have often dismissed as hysterical products of thwarted ambition (Neville 2016).

The case of Anna Comnena illustrates the extent to which, precisely insofar as a woman lives in a mature, sophisticated society, she may find herself trapped by the complexity of that society's discourses and expectations surrounding gender and religion. Throughout the twelfth century in western Europe, more rigid inheritance patterns, the rediscovery of Roman law, the founding of the medieval universities, and a dramatic increase in the production and use of written documents contributed to a more ordered society than had existed since before the fall of Rome. The twelfth century has been called both a renaissance and a reformation before the early modern period. Precisely insofar as western Europe became conscious of its own identity, however, it became a "persecuting society" which defined itself against Jews within Europe, and Muslims and Greeks it encountered abroad (Southern 1953; Haskins 1955; Constable 1996; Moore 2007). Although these factors circumscribed the roles, status, and inheritance rights of women in society in many ways, the very inflexibility of these structures could sometimes be coopted by women. As always, a royal family's dynastic claims could indirectly create opportunities for its female members. Direct lineage and primogeniture often excluded women from inheriting land alongside their brothers, but it also made possible female regencies and some spectacular cases of female royal succession.

## Women and the Crusades

Ironically, the Crusades themselves created many of these opportunities. In the Christian *Reconquista* of Spain, the refugee wife of the Muslim ruler of Seville, known to history and legend as Zaida, became mistress to Alfonso VI of León and Castile. Baptized Isabel, Zaida married Alfonso and bore him a son, Sancho. When he died in battle, it would be Alfonso's daughter, Urraca, who became Queen of Castile (Bartlett 2020, pp. 17–18). Meanwhile, the unexpected success of the First Crusade led to the establishment of the Kingdom of Jerusalem under Baldwin. Called Outremer or "over the sea," the crusader kingdom was chronically fragile, gradually eroded externally by the successful Muslim counterattack led by Saladin, and internally by Frankish infighting. Greek Christians were both influential and deeply mistrusted. When Baldwin died, he was succeeded by his cousin, also named Baldwin, who had married an Armenian princess,

Morphia, in one of the more unexpected romances of the crusading era. Their daughter, Melisende, was confirmed as ruler of Jerusalem in 1131, after bearing her first son to the Frankish noble Fulk of Anjou. Much less happy in her marriage than her parents, Melisende was accused by Fulk of having an affair with her cousin, who fled to Egypt and was then assassinated, it was rumored, on Fulk's orders. The Melisende Psalter, which Fulk commissioned in remorse, was made by Syrian and Armenian artisans from the scriptorium of the Church of the Holy Sepulchre, and demonstrates the cultural fusion that could occasionally occur amidst the turmoil of the kingdom (Montefiore 2011, pp. 221–223; Tranovich 2011; see Figure 7.1). With a precedent established for female succession, the kingdom of Jerusalem would see four queens in all, including two sisters, Jeanne and Marguerite of Constantinople, who ruled the ever-shrinking kingdom for the whole of the thirteenth century (Jordan 2006).

More generally, the widespread nature of crusading fervor, as well as disease and the military catastrophes of the Crusades themselves, left numbers of aristocratic women in control of their husbands' estates for protracted periods, even longer if they were managing lands in the name of a young son. Married in their early teens, many of these women were widowed by their mid-twenties. Some remarried a second or even a third time over the course of their lives, but many others chose to remain unmarried, particularly if they were financially independent as they were. It is these women who were perhaps most influential amidst the explosion of religious experimentation in the twelfth century, providing financial support, social connections, and

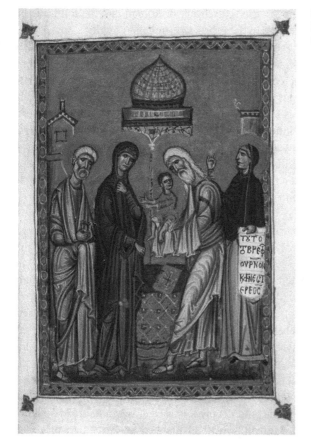

**Figure 7.1**  The Melisende Psalter, British Library, Egerton MS 1139. *Source:* Psalter of Queen Melisende / flickr / Public domain.

administrative skills in supporting often vulnerable religious communities of women. Throughout, the old imperative for an aristocratic woman to remember and to memorialize her family existed in parallel with the ongoing injunction for her menfolk to go on crusade, perhaps never to return (Paul 2012, pp. 165–170).

These women were the lucky ones. For many more, the Crusades brought disruption, impoverishment, trauma, and danger. A cavalcade of women would be taken prisoner after the disastrous battle of Heraclea in 1101, including Corba, a woman from Fulk's Anjou already widowed once by crusade and taken to the Holy Land by her second husband, who abandoned her (Rubenstein 2019, pp. 84–85). One of the most extraordinary survivors of the period is Margaret of Beverly, also called Margaret of Jerusalem, born in Outremer around 1150 to pilgrim parents but raised in Yorkshire. When her brother joined Thomas Becket in the monastic life at Froidmont in France, Margaret journeyed east, where she fought with the crusaders in 1187 in the defense of Jerusalem, only to be enslaved when the city fell to Saladin. Bought and freed in Tyre by a fellow Christian, she would be recaptured and released once more, whereupon Margaret then begged her way down the Levant coast with only a psalter to her name. Her pilgrim journeys continued: from Acre to Santiago de Compostella in northern Spain to Rome to France. Like her brother, she joined a Cistercian community as a lay sister and, her journeys finally done, lived there for 18 years until her death in 1214 (Lester 2011, pp. 147–149; Michaud 1841, VI, pp. 59–60).

## Clerical Identity and Lay Enthusiasm

In the eleventh century, the Gregorian Reform had sought to wrest control of the church's property and prestige from the Ottonians' successors and from the lay aristocracy. The reformers' rhetoric around clerical celibacy, particularly vitriolic attacks on married or "Nicolaitan" clergy, led to the collective forgetting of generations of married priests, and as collateral damage, generations of priests' wives (Karras 2012, pp. 116–122). But the rediscovery of Roman law in northern Italy also led to a fundamental shift in the church's understanding of what defined and constituted ordination itself. The early medieval understanding had pragmatically recognized as ordained the offices of abbesses, deaconesses, and even the occasional *episcopa*, as well as the mixed status of a crowned and anointed queen. By contrast, the Gregorian Reform narrowly defined ordination in connection with the priesthood, and priesthood exclusively in terms of a priest's appointment to a particular church and the priest's celebration of the Eucharist. The rhetorical arms race of the investiture controversy necessitated that church reformers reinvent clerical masculinity in such a way as to outshine that of secular lords, but this had knock-on effects on how the clergy would view the political role of queens and powerful laywomen (Macy 2016; Miller 2003; Johns 2003, pp. 13–29).

As the discipline and discourses of canon law took shape, it systematized this revolution in ecclesiastical attitudes to ordination. Over the course of the twelfth century, this would be further reinforced by the creation of the medieval universities in Bologna, Paris, and Oxford, and the widespread adoption by both church and state of documentary evidence over oral tradition. From the twelfth century onwards, exponentially greater numbers of documents survive (Clanchy 2013). Much of the religious history of the twelfth century can be understood as the negotiation between, on the one hand, the church's codification and occasional reinvention of its own traditions, and on the other, a tremendous popular groundswell in religious devotion, the desire of ordinary people to live an authentic apostolic life modeled on that Christ in the gospels, as well as a more general response to the pressures and anxieties of a society in transition. What has often been understood as an explosion of heresies in this period can be seen, from another perspective, as groups of sincerely devout lay people who found themselves left behind by new theological terminology and new religious practice (Grundmann 1995; Van Engen 1986).

Women were the most obvious of these groups: unable to enter the new universities, often, although not always, untaught in the new Aristotelian philosophical terminology and the scholastic method. Precisely insofar as monks, clergy, and laypeople desired to live a life modeled on that of Christ in the New Testament, however, many felt the imperative to find a place for women within their ministry as Christ had done. How that was to be accomplished without imperiling vows of chastity was a more complex problem, leading to some of the most creative experimentation in modes of monastic life in this period. What was undeniable, and what had to be reckoned with by everyone, however, was the women's enthusiasm.

## The Empress and the Anglo-Normans

In the wake of the Norman Conquest in 1066, the Anglo-Norman ruling class launched itself into the eradication of the older English wooden churches and houses of ordained canons, and their replacement by stone churches, Romanesque cathedrals, and communities of Benedictine monks. Perhaps paradoxically, these monks then embarked on collecting the saints' lives of the English they had ousted. Goscelin of Saint-Bertin collected *legendae* of early English female saints, including Edith of Wilton and the saintly abbesses of Barking. The highly dramatic saga of Saint Osyth described how the English princess, like Etheldreda, avoided her marriage to an East Anglian king by veiling herself and founding her own religious community. When Osyth was beheaded by the Danes her body carried her own head into her church, placed it on the high altar, and then sat down facing east, composing her hands in prayer. Another early medieval saint retold for a later audience was Frideswide, the patron saint of Oxford, around whose monastery the town had later developed. Her twelfth-century life describes how she was supposed to have hidden in Binsey Wood to avoid another royal suitor, struck blind when he pressed his advances (Baker 1911; Blair 1988). She was associated with a sacred spring at Binsey, like the Welsh martyr Winifred, whose cult at Holywell the Benedictines of Shrewsbury promoted at this time (see Figure 7.2). The Benedictine abbot Geoffrey of Burton-upon-Trent popularized the life of Modwenna, a sixth-century Irish pilgrim saint who was, in legend, the teacher of Brigid of Kildare, and who became the patron saint of English hospitals (Bartlett 2010, p. 176).

Of course, there were still live English princesses with a reputation for sanctity. Edith, the daughter of Earl Godwine and the wife of King Edward the Confessor, outlived him in retirement in Winchester and was buried in Westminster Abbey (Stafford 1997, pp. 255–279). The English princess Margaret, now called Margaret of Scotland, was born in Hungary in exile and fled north after the Norman Conquest, where she married Malcolm III of Scotland. She corresponded with Lanfranc, a future archbishop of Canterbury, and generally attempted to bring the Scottish church into closer relationship with Roman practice. She set her serving women to making vestments, and patronized pilgrimage to the church at St. Andrews, where, in another century, the cathedral would be built. She established Dumferline in place of Iona as the Scottish royal burial place, although she also restored the abbey at Iona (Bartlett 2003, 2020, pp. 163, 257). Her daughter Edith inherited her mother's sense of vocation, and may have wanted to enter the religious community at Wilton, which had been Queen Edith's favorite foundation. Instead she was married to Henry I, son of William the Conqueror, after an inquest determined that she had not taken formal vows. Thereafter she was known as Matilda or Maud.

**Figure 7.2**  St. Winefride's Well, Holywell. *Source:* Author photo.

Her daughter, born in 1102, was also called Matilda, and engaged as a child to the German emperor Henry V. Crowned at the age of eight, the empress Matilda was effectively raised at the imperial court. Her husband would inherit the lands of Matilda of Tuscany and the couple was crowned again in Rome in the Ottonian imperial tradition. In 1125, however, when Matilda was only 23, catastrophe struck with the death of Henry. Returning to England was not so much a homecoming for the empress as traveling to a completely foreign country. Matilda would have had to re-learn the language – French at this time – as well as the different, and much less formal customs and culture of the English court. After King Henry's son drowned in the White Ship Disaster, Matilda was his only heir, her claim aided by the contemporary political precedents of Urraca of Spain and Melisende of Jerusalem. Over Matilda's protests a marriage was arranged between herself and Melisende's son-in-law, Geoffrey Plantagenet, then only 13 years old. King Henry died six weeks later.

Matilda's marriage to Geoffrey was a disaster even by the standards of the day, but she was able to give birth to her son, Henry II, at the then-geriatric age of 31. Matilda's two pregnancies nearly killed her, however, and while she was recovering, Stephen of Blois, the son of William the Conqueror's formidable daughter Adela, claimed the throne as Stephen I. Both Stephen and Matilda, therefore, traced their claim through the female line. Matilda, however, found herself in the doubly humiliating position of having to fight for a position without a name: having been crowned empress twice, she was not interested in inheriting the throne of England either through her teenage husband or through her infant son, and she never attempted to be a conventional "queen" of England.

That title is usually given to Stephen's wife, also called Matilda. When the empress held London and seemed on the verge of success, Queen Matilda was able to raise an army and drive her from the city and then from a siege at Oxford in 1142, where the empress dramatically escaped from the castle over the frozen moat and in the snow. In the ensuing period of civil war, sometimes called

The Anarchy, the empress gained a reputation for haughtiness that is probably undeserved and almost certainly gendered. Her mistake but also her lasting political legacy, it has been argued, was her effort to claim the crown in her own right (Hanley 2019). Ironically, when Stephen and Queen Matilda had no male heir, "Henry FitzEmpress" was able to make good Matilda's claim in a way that she could not, remaining in monastic retirement in Normandy while Henry II was formally adopted by Stephen. It is perhaps the final insult that her dynasty takes its name from her husband.

Just as a sequence of powerful Ottonian queens had encouraged the development of devotion to Mary Queen of Heaven, the visible political presence of these noble women fostered and inspired devotion to Mary by the Franks. The connection is particularly obvious in the case of Anselm, Archbishop of Canterbury. Born in northern Italy, Anselm was a monk at Bec in Normandy until he was made archbishop in 1093. Anselm was a regular correspondent with the devout Adela of Blois, as well as Countess Ida of Boulogne, Eulalia the abbess of Shaftesbury, and Matilda of Tuscany, to whom he sent his passionate prayers to Christ and to the Virgin Mary before his death in 1109 (Morrow 2005). The year before, Queen Edith-Matilda founded Holy Trinity Priory in Aldgate in London, a house of Augustinian canons, which became one of the wealthiest religious houses in England. Its first prior was one of Anselm's protégés (Schofield and Lea 2005, pp. 143–149). In 1061, the noblewoman Richeldis de Faverches had a vision in which she was enjoined to build a copy of the house in Nazareth where Gabriel had visited Mary. In the twelfth century, a monastic community was created, and in another century Walsingham in East Anglia had become one of the most popular pilgrimage sites in England (Waller 2011, pp. 1–37; Morrison 2000, pp. 10–42).

Anselm was an early exponent of devotion to "Jesus as Mother," employing feminine imagery drawn from the gospels to describe Christ. His three prayers to the Virgin, which he revised obsessively toward the end of his life, represent a new emotional directness and an emphasis on the humanity of both Christ and the Virgin that is one of the distinctive sea-changes in devotion in the twelfth century (Southern 1969, pp. 219–257; Bynum 1982; Power 2001; Fulton 2002; Ward 2018, pp. 101–126). To see Christ and Mary not only as king and queen of heaven but also as a human mother and son marked a shift in theological emphasis that was new ground in the Christian west. The foremost theologian of the Cistercian Order, Bernard of Clairvaux, was also an eloquent and passionate promoter of this new, often chivalric devotion to the Virgin, "our Lady" (Warner 1976, pp. 129–131). In place of the traditional, Greek-inspired image of Mary as *Theotokos*, in which the Virgin and Child are depicted formally seated and enthroned, western artists now often portrayed Mary in free-standing sculpture, holding the infant Christ (Gold 1985, pp. 43–75).

Anselm's correspondents represented a generation of Anglo-Norman noble women, comfortable on either side of the Channel, who introduced monasticism from the continent into England. Many, like Queen Matilda, had found themselves in de facto positions of lordship, particularly when their husbands left on crusade – in the case of Adela of Blois, twice. Others felt the financial pinch of supporting the crusading effort. For all the stridency of the reformers' rhetoric against powerful women, in practice political reality was more pragmatic and complex. The older understanding, in which women exercised office in the absence, or as an extension, of men still lingered in the secular world (Stafford 1997). Women could and did act as signatories on their husbands' charters and on their own, particularly as widows, and many did see their own role endowing and supporting religious communities of women as an extension of their own motherhood. These communities in turn had powerful links not only to a geographical place but also to a particular social set of benefactors, for whom they were an extension of their families' collective memory.

This religious networking appears to have been, if anything, even more active and important during the Anarchy, and it may be that these communities were supporting women in distressed

**Figure 7.3**  Godstow Abbey, Oxford. *Source:* Charlie / Flickr / CC BY-SA 2.0.

circumstances (Elkins 1988, pp. 61–62). But it could also be that these aristocratic women were intervening where groups of women already existed in religious life, in some cases helping communities to become financially self-sufficient or to administer their scanty resources. The formidable widow turned abbess Edith would both found and endow the religious community at Godstow, near Frideswide's Binsey and Oxford (see Figure 7.3). Most famous in later years for housing Henry II's mistress, Rosamund Clifford, Godstow's dedication was attended by both Stephen and Queen Matilda (Burton 1994, p. 92). Abbess Edith's personal seal survives, one of the few that do for royal or aristocratic women, and its distinct design shows Edith prostrate between a victorious Virgin Mary and a penitent John the Baptist (Bugyis 2019, pp. 237–239). For all her ostensible humility, Edith, it seems, wanted no one to forget who her protectors were.

## Sunday Daughters

More often, isolated individuals seem to have lived in loose and undefined affiliation with formal male monastic foundations, particularly if these contained a supportive abbot or bishop who could act as a spiritual director. These individual women could reside in anchorholds, small cells built off or contained within the nave of a parish church, and recluses could sometimes live together. Over time, these informal arrangements could be formalized, the anchorholds sometimes endowed with an allowance, the recluses sometimes forming the nucleus of a women's community. The half-Danish, half-Lotharingian recluse Eve of Wilton entered the monastic life herself at seven years old, but did not stay; she would be enclosed, 15 years later, across the channel in Angers in France. A correspondent with Goscelin of St.-Berlin, Eve apparently lived to the ripe old age of 70, much beloved by both men and women in her community. Burchwine, the sister of the sailor-turned-hermit Godric of Finchale, lived as a recluse and was buried with the Benedictine community at Durham Cathedral (Elkins 1988, pp. 21–24, 39).

The most vivid account of a twelfth-century woman's progress in religious life, however, is undoubtedly the saint's life of Christina of Markyate (*The Life of Christina of Markyate* 2009). Born around 1096 to a merchant family in East Anglia, the name of her father, Auti, is Danish, while her aunt, Aelfgifu, was the long-standing mistress of the mercurial Norman bishop of Durham, Ranulf Flambard. The life records considerable pressure on Christina, and even an attempted rape, by Ranulf, who intended her as her aunt's successor. When she refused to comply, her family arranged a marriage with Beorhtred, a local noble boy. Christina's life captures a moment in time when the medieval church's definitions of what made a marriage were themselves in transition: did a vow alone make a marriage, or did the union have to be consummated (Karras 2012, pp. 45–49; D'Avray 2005, pp. 171–179; Madigan 2017, pp. 315–318)? Christina maintained that she had already vowed her virginity to Christ, but her ambitious family bullied her and encouraged their village to do the same. One imagines what would have happened if Elizabeth Bennet had suddenly declared a religious vocation – and in particular, whether her mother would have understood. In Christina's case, her family pressured Beorhtred to consummate the marriage by force. When the rape failed, they turned to a local prior to dissuade her. Beaten and stripped by her parents, Christina dressed herself as a man and fled to the recluse Aelfwynn. She would share another cell secretly with the hermit Roger for four years, the two avoiding one another assiduously in the tiny space, Christina enduring cold, heat, nosebleeds, and not being able to go to the bathroom for hours rather than returning to her birth family. Poignantly, to Roger she was "myn sunendæge dohter," "my Sunday daughter."

Absolved of her marriage by the archbishop of York, Christina found herself briefly in another male recluse's cell, where, rather disarmingly, the two developed a raging mutual crush. The archbishop had wanted to send her abroad like Eve of Wilton, but Christina was determined to remain in England. In later life, her closest relationship was with Geoffrey, abbot of the Benedictine abbey at St. Albans. Initially ambivalent and hesitant about the woman living, so to speak, on his doorstep, Geoffrey became Christina's strongest supporter. It is then and only then, after years of living as an ascetic, that Christina took any kind of formal vows, clearly living in association with, but physically separate from, the monks. Her sister Margaret joined her there, as well as other women who were part of the monastery's extended community. The life describes an Emmaus-like miracle in which Christina and her sister, like Mary and Martha, welcome a pilgrim who then vanishes. The day before Christmas Eve, the ill Christina had a vision of her pilgrim Christ as he truly is, standing in the midst of the monks' choir: young, beautiful, and spangled with dew, "the fairest of the children of men" (*Life of Christina of Markyate* 2009, pp. 83–86).

In this way, a woman is described as proclaiming the presence of the risen Christ to a group of men and to the community of women who would later crystallize around her charismatic presence. The Saint Albans Psalter, which was given to Christina personally by Abbot Geoffrey, contains an illuminated patch added later to the manuscript which depicts Mary Magdalene preaching to the apostles in the guise of Christina and the monks (Geddes 2005; see Figure 7.4). In Christina's lifetime, popular devotion would flower around the Magdalene, her shrine at Vézelay in France becoming increasingly important in this period. The "apostle to the apostles," Mary Magdalene represented another model from the gospels for women's devotion to follow, particularly if, unlike Christina, they had sexual experience. The author of Christina's life predominantly saw her in the tradition of Cecilia the virgin martyr, but the sheer quantity of personal information and vivid detail that the life contains attests to the work's intimate connection to those who remembered Christina, some of them women. It may well have been written by Abbot Geoffrey's nephew, based

**Figure 7.4** The St. Albans Psalter, Dombibliothek, Hildesheim Cathedral. *Source:* Unknown author / Wikimedia Commons / Public domain.

on a book which Christina's sister probably compiled, kept by the nuns of Christina's community at Markyate (Kerby-Fulton 2009, p. 14; Bugyis 2019, pp. 28–30).

In the case of either Eve or Christina, it is difficult to say that these women had joined a religious order in any formal way that church authorities would have recognized. In fact, their ambiguous status allowed their mode of life to shift and change over time. What is also clear is the active support and admiration that these women were receiving from particular men within the church. The clerical misogyny, then, found in reformers' texts must be placed in tension with other discourses within monasticism, such as Christ's own personal example, Jerome and his correspondent-patronesses, and traditional brother–sister pairs such as Augustine and his sister and Benedict and Scholastica. Within reforming circles, certain individuals felt the impulse to center their ministry around women, particularly their own sisters and kinsfolk. The nuns' priest, although not an imposing or dramatic figure, was probably much more common throughout the medieval world than later sources admit (Venarde 1997; Griffiths 2018).

Nevertheless, women's religious communities throughout Europe remained much more financially vulnerable and institutionally unaffiliated – and therefore unprotected and less attractive for donations – than their male counterparts. As both the papal curia and medieval courts increasingly formalized their use of written documents, women's communities needed but did not always possess enough Latin literacy to keep abreast of predatory legal battles. Some, such as Radegund's priory of the Holy Cross, were able to maintain their status by appealing to the pope against the reformers who sought to place their houses under direct episcopal oversight (Edwards 2019). The preeminent Benedictine foundation in Europe, Cluny in southern France, created only one priory for women in 1055, at Marcigny. Adela of Blois stayed there for some 16 years, as did Queen Matilda, and Cluny's great abbot, Peter the Venerable, placed his mother and niece there. Marcigny's necrology, kept in its early years by a woman, recorded some ten thousand names, indicative of the vast reach of its social connections (Thompson 1991, pp. 84–85; Vanderputten 2013).

Adela of Blois also patronized the founder of the Cistercian order, Robert of Molesme. The most famous and successful of the twelfth-century experiments in monasticism, the Cistercians swiftly found themselves surrounded by numerous communities of women who had adopted their way of life or received spiritual care without in any way being formally integrated into the highly sophisticated structure of the order. Certain individuals wrote treatises devoted to the spiritual care of women, one such, by Aelred of Rievaulx in Yorkshire, being dedicated to his own sister (Aelred of Rievaulx 1971). A few houses in France had particular early links to the Order – Jully, Tart, and Coiroux – and two houses would be founded in Acre and Tripoli in Outremer, the crusader kingdom centered on Jerusalem. Meanwhile, the daughter of Eleanor of Aquitaine, Eleanor of England, with her husband Alfonso VIII of Castile, would establish the extremely grand Cistercian convent at Las Huelgas in Burgos in 1187 (Burton and Kerr 2011, pp. 25, 27, 51; Berman 2018, pp. 6–10). In comparison with the explosion of Cistercian men's houses across Europe, however, these were few indeed and, ironically, usually far more aristocratic than the men supposed to provide them with pastoral care. Sometimes portrayed as reluctant to shoulder the burden of women who might dilute their reforming zeal, the Cistercian order would wait to recognize most of its women's communities as formally part of the order until the next century.

Meanwhile, the papacy issued a series of mandates to integrate these women and their ilk into some kind of ordered monastic life. Whereas in early medieval women's communities abbesses frequently heard confession, now even enclosed women's communities had to admit male priests at regular intervals. Whether a women's community could appoint its own confessors, a particularly coveted privilege, or whether they were dependent on a bishop's appointment or an unenthusiastic but nearby men's house, soon became an ongoing bone of contention. Insofar as many orders enforced a physical barrier such as a wall or screen between priests and religious women, they could sometimes find themselves cut off from any visual participation in the Eucharist at all.

## Nuns and Priests: Men and Women Together

In German-speaking lands between 1080 and 1150, a circle of Benedictine, Cluniac, and Augustinian houses oriented around Hirsau would make the spiritual care of women and the foundation of dual-gender houses a particular and distinctive priority. In some houses the genders were strictly segregated but still followed the same rhythms of daily life. In others, such as the aristocratic monastery at Admont, book production became a central part of their vocation. To maintain their strict enclosure, this necessitated the women having their own scriptorium where they copied patristic texts, as well as the homilies delivered to the women's community (Hotchin 2001; Beach 2004). Admont preserved the manuscript of Anselm's *Prayers and Meditations* that he sent to Matilda of Tuscany, and most famously, the manuscript containing the thoroughly bawdy vernacular poetry set to music in the early twentieth century by Carl Orff, the *Carmina Burana*. An Austrian woman known only as Ava Inclusa (d. 1127) is the first known poetess in German (Olsen 2005; Mulder-Bakker 2010, p. 323). More sedately, the Hirsau circle was behind the creation of the *Speculum virginum*, or *Manual for Virgins*, which describes a dialogue between a young woman, Theodora ("lover of God"), and her spiritual director, Peregrinus ("pilgrim"). The work became one of the most important textual models for this kind of spiritual relationship, and enabled and legitimated further experimentation (Mews 2001).

Gilbert of Sempringham would found an order combining nuns and ordained canons between 1131 and 1154 in the north of England. A pupil of one of Christina of Markyate's supporters, Gilbert had wanted to integrate his women's communities into the Cistercian order. When the Cistercians refused to admit them, however, he added Augustinian canons to his order to provide the women with pastoral care. Lurid scandal threatened, however, when a young nun at Watton Priory was found pregnant by one of the canons. Keeping the girl in chains, the nuns brought her runaway lover before her and made the girl castrate him, shoving the still-bleeding body parts into her mouth. According to Aelred of Rievaulx, the girl was saved from utter humiliation, however, when her pregnancy miraculously disappeared and her shackles vanished. Clearly both shocked and titillated by the drama, Aelred was hardly an unbiased commentator. The story encapsulates, even for someone who supported Gilbert, the lurking threat posed by women to men in religious life. If the story is even partly true, it also shows the often brutal methods of self-policing to which women had to resort to maintain their legitimacy when their religious status remained provisional. As a result of the contretemps at Watton, Gilbert's vision for monastic life was deemed increasingly suspect by ecclesiastical authorities (Elkins 1988, pp. 81–84, 106–111).

On the continent, Norbert of Xanten founded a house of canons in Prémontré in Laon in 1120. Papally approved in 1126, the Premonstratensians, like the Gilbertines, initially contained populations of both women and ordained men, although the women far outnumbered the men. The women worked making textiles and occasionally produced manuscripts, as well as carrying out the manual labor of laundry and cooking. They appear to have very intentionally modeled their spirituality on the biblical Martha and Mary, blending the active and the contemplative lives. The Premonstratensians became wildly popular, particularly in Germany, where the order may have had as many as ten thousand members in the twelfth century (Beach 2004, pp. 28–29). An early Premonstratensian, Ricwera, ran a hospital, a vocation which became central to the women's houses in the next century. Perhaps for this reason, belated efforts after Norbert's death to impose any kind of segregation of the genders in Premonstratensian houses proved impossible to enforce (Thompson 1991, pp. 138–139).

In France, the reformer Robert of Arbrissel seemed to have developed close pastoral relationships with women with the ulterior motive of testing the strength of his own personal commitment to chastity. Be that as it may, he was just wise enough to appoint two highly capable widows to act as the heads of his new order at Fontevraud, Petronilla de Chémilly and Hersende. It would be these women who spearheaded the campaign for Robert of Arbrissel's canonization, not least because of the honor it would bring to the house (Venarde 2013). The Fontevraudines became known for their strict adherence to silence. They founded several daughter-houses in England, attracting the particular patronage of Henry II and Eleanor of Aquitaine. After their tempestuous marriage and Eleanor's almost 16 years of imprisonment, Henry died suddenly and was buried at Fontevraud in 1189. Eleanor eventually also retired to Fontevraud as a canoness before she died in 1204, finally perhaps, in silence, having the last word.

In addition, numerous women also joined the Hospitallers' new foundations, or other reformed orders such as the Arrouaisians, an order of Augustinian canonesses with carefully segregated male canons. They were formed in response to the Second Lateran Council's critique of lax canonesses, but in practice individual women's houses sometimes changed their observance as political circumstance required. For example, the Arrouaisians became a favorite choice for women's communities in the shifting world of Ireland after the Plantagenet invasion, and the overall impression is of a fluid and experimental situation (Hall 2003, pp. 67–70). Although women's orders attempted to adopt distinctive combinations of dress, in practice, the various permutations and combinations of dress, often involving undyed and black wool, must have been fairly interchangeable.

## The World of the Cloister: Herrad and Hildegard

Jerome had once complained to his detractors that he *would* have worked with men rather than women if any men were actually interested. Similarly, some women were able to coopt the very language of reform from the reformers: if men were uninvolved or incapable of reform, the argument went, women had a legitimate Christian responsibility to step in, even if it made them unconventional (Kerby-Fulton 2005, p. 34). That is the tactic adopted by the Augustinian canoness Herrad of Hohenbourg, in a reminder that experimentation in religious education and reform was not the exclusive purview of the new orders. Hohenbourg was in Alsace, one of those houses affiliated with the Hirsau reform which had adopted the Augustinian Rule around 1153 in the wake of the critiques of the Second Lateran Council. It had subsequently enjoyed imperial patronage, and like Admont, supported a women's scriptorium with access, through other reformed houses in its circle, to the latest learning coming out of the medieval universities.

The central problem from Herrad's point of view was the quality of pastoral care that the Hohenbourg women were receiving. In response, Herrad replaced the Benedictine chaplains usually sent to the community by founding two houses of male canons to support Hohenbourg, and within her own scriptorium, to create a magnificent manuscript, the *Hortus Deliciarum*, or *The Garden of Delights*. While the manuscript was destroyed in 1870 in the Franco-Prussian War, modern copies of its text and illuminations survive, revealing Herrad's formidable program of theological education (see Figure 7.5). In compiling the work, Herrad compared herself to "a little bee" collecting nectar from many flowers. *The Garden of Delights* is, in effect, a one-manuscript curriculum, containing extracts from the very latest Paris thinkers, as well as the current papal policy on excommunication. It is so very contemporary with its sources, in fact, that scholars date the manuscript by the works it contains. *The Garden of Delights* also contains more traditional, "monastic" texts, as well as Byzantine material and Herrad's own acrostic poems (Joyner 2016, pp. 41–68). Most striking to a modern audience are the rich and complex illuminations, which demonstrate the extent to which nearly all medieval teaching relied on the visual, often as tools for training the memory (Carruthers 1998).

Poised between university and reforming monastic circles, the manuscript is one woman's work intended for other women's learning, yet concedes absolutely nothing in tone, content, or level of Latin literacy. In fact, if the women of Hohenbourg worked their way through Herrad's *The Garden of Delights*, arguably they would be better educated than any chaplain who might realistically have been sent to provide them with pastoral care (Griffiths 2007). Herrad's strategy, therefore, to ease the dependency of women religious on male clergy was the in-house religious education of women, combined with her efforts for Hohenbourg to build some sort of independent institutional relationship with their own houses of priests. The manuscript was never copied, and it is difficult to know how well her strategy ultimately worked, but certainly Herrad's was not an isolated or unique attempt.

Working within many of the same constraints was the visionary genius Hildegard of Bingen. Born in 1098 to aristocratic parents, she was "tithed" to the religious life at the house at Disibodenberg on the Rhine under the care of a devout and ascetic recluse, Jutta. Like Christina of

**Figure 7.5** Herrad of Hohenburg, *Hortus deliciarum*, Engelhardt reconstruction. *Source:* Herrad of Landsberg / Wikimedia Commons / Public domain.

Markyate, Jutta lived alongside the monastic house and attracted more women to the religious life around her (Kerby-Fulton 2010). The relationship between Jutta and Hildegard seems to have been intimate but complex. Hildegard later acknowledged that she disapproved of Jutta's physical asceticism, and it is perhaps significant that she only spoke of her visions, which she said she had had from childhood, after Jutta's death. Hildegard herself became head of the female community at Disibodenberg in 1138, and it was only from this position of authority that she felt able to begin to dictate descriptions and interpretations of what she had seen. Taking these down in writing was her confessor and loyal supporter, the monk and priest Volmar.

Perhaps the most famous image of Hildegard is the portrait of her as the so-called "Sibyl of the Rhine," dictating to Volmar peering in from the next room, while the Holy Spirit's tongues of fire reach down to wrap around her head (Hildegard of Bingen 2001b, p. 26; see Figure 7.6). In 1146, she wrote to Bernard of Clairvaux, then the most respected theologian in Christendom, asking for advice about whether to make her visions widely known. She said that the Holy Spirit had long taught her the meaning of Scripture, and she felt a burning, prophetic compulsion to speak (Hildegard of Bingen 2001a, pp. 3–5). The persona of the seer made all Hildegard's subsequent achievements possible: throughout the rest of her career, Hildegard was surrounded by the aura of one who was specially chosen and therefore able to do strange and gifted works. Marked and licensed by her unique gift, she claimed she had received papal approval, although proof is difficult to find. She was the only woman of her time to preach publicly, arguably the first musical composer in the modern sense of the word, the inventor of her own language, an herbalist, doctor, poet, and dramatist, and she oversaw the making of the vivid illuminations that accompany her visions (Newman 1998).

Like Herrad, Hildegard was also a monastic reformer who was able to coopt the rhetoric of monastic reform for her own ends. It was because of the present corruption of the church, she argued, that a mere woman had been called to speak. In 1150, she began the grueling task of constructing a new and independent monastic foundation in the forest at Rupertsberg, despite an ongoing feud with the monks at Disibodenberg. Hildegard as abbess would cultivate a thicket of relationships with German aristocratic families from whom her nuns were predominantly selected. An altar frontal survives from Rupertsberg which depicts in embroidery not only Hildegard, but also 10 members of her community, as well as illustrious spiritual forbears like the English abbess Hild and the Ottonian queen Adelheid (Griffiths 2018, pp. 188–194). Placing themselves on the

**Figure 7.6** Hildegard of Bingen, Rupertsberg Codex of the *Liber Scivias. Source:* Unknown author / Wikimedia Commons / Public domain.

altar, albeit in textile form, there are definite echoes here of the Last Supper. To have been a nun with Hildegard as abbess – and there were as many as 50 nuns at Rupertsberg, as well as lay sisters – was to participate in a spiritual program every bit as rigorous as Herrad's. These nuns were the first singers of Hildegard's complex music, their abilities surely inspiring and shaping Hildegard's compositions, and they participated, sometimes in costume, in her poetic dramas. Hildegard had a particularly close relationship with one young nun, Richardis von Stade, and was personally devastated when Richardis's family removed her from Hildegard's charge to head up her own monastic foundation.

In 1158, Hildegard began the first of four preaching tours, in which she spoke against the decadence of the established church and the heretical group which would become known as the Cathars. In Hildegard's thought, unstoppable force met immovable object: her relentless creativity pushed against her own rigidly ordered, hierarchical theology and cosmology. Far from being spontaneous or emotional effusions, many of her visions take the form of diagrams. However one may understand Hildegard's visions, her inspiration was not a form of divine dictation, but a set of powerful and even debilitating experiences. She clearly suffered from migraines and from chronic illness, perhaps stress-induced. Hildegard's task was to fit these experiences into already established, familiar patterns of orthodox teaching; in other words, she could only be so creative before herself becoming heretical. Moreover, she did not have only herself to think about: the fate of her infant foundation at Rupertsberg and the lives of all her nuns would have hung dangerously in the balance had there ever been any real questions about her orthodoxy (Newman 1997). Hildegard had to continue to present herself as "unlearned," someone who could never presume to teach anyone outside the walls of Rupertsberg. Once her reputation as a seer was established, however, she could not very well stop writing, either.

From 1138, Hildegard's first major work, *Scivias*, or *Know the Ways*, took the next 10 years to write: it was not completed until 1151. The *Liber vitae meritorum*, or the *Book of the Rewards of Life*, she wrote between 1158 and 1163. In 1163, she spoke about a vision so powerful that it would take another decade, until 1174, to compose her gospel homilies and the *Liber divinorum operum*, or *The Book of Divine Works* (Hildegard of Bingen 1996). She died five years later, in 1179. The actual process of Hildegard's writing was ruminative, the slow and patient working-out, at great personal cost, of the things she had seen. In contrast with Anna Comnena the historian, Hildegard was a theologian who could never directly admit to being one as such, in part because her self-presentation centered around being a bastion of traditional monastic learning. Paradoxically, Hildegard is representative of the intellectual curiosity and confidence of the "Twelfth-Century Renaissance," and yet she was shut outside of the venues where many of these questions were being asked. In her own works Hildegard was notoriously obfuscatory about her sources, and yet she clearly had access to some texts, even if only via correspondents and oral knowledge acquired through the divine office (Kienzle 2009; Carlevaris 2001). This need not discredit Hildegard's reputation as a mystic. Given what was at stake, she would have been a fool if she had not been very careful indeed about what she circulated under her name.

Over the course of the twelfth century, the Gregorian redefinition of ordination exclusively around the priesthood was countered by the increasing importance of the female visionary, with her direct and unmediated access to God and the saints. In Germany, Hildegard's younger contemporary Elisabeth of Schönau seems to have modeled her own visionary career on the Sibyl of the Rhine. When asked to test the true identity of human remains unearthed in Cologne, Elisabeth answered that the Holy Spirit had indeed reassured her that these were the relics of St. Ursula and her ten thousand martyred virgins. Like Hildegard, Elisabeth became the head of her own monastic community, and like Hildegard she preached against the Cathars while denouncing the moral failures of the episcopacy (Clark 2010). Even while many of these visionary women were held up as models by the church to counter the asceticism of heretical groups, the potential threat that the visionary posed can be seen in the ambivalent reputation of even so stunning a figure as Hildegard. Despite receiving papal approval during her lifetime, Hildegard's later canonization was extremely controversial. Insofar as she mesmerized the twelfth-century church, she set the pattern for later women to become visionaries and reformers themselves, but she also became a byword for those who sought to restrict women's visionary expression. To the inquisition in the later Middle Ages, to display too much interest in the works of Hildegard was a damning warning sign (Kerby-Fulton 2006, p. 203).

## Héloïse and Abelard

Sometime around 1116 in Paris, the brilliant and contrarian Breton scholar Abelard maneuvered his way into teaching and then seducing the equally brilliant and strong-minded Héloïse. The daughter, perhaps, of a crusader who had died abroad, Héloïse had grown up in the Benedictine women's community at Argenteuil outside of Paris, before coming to live with her uncle Fulbert, a canon in the city. Although often portrayed as a teenager, Héloïse was probably in her early twenties and Abelard in his mid-thirties when their relationship began. Héloïse's reputation for learning was what had drawn Abelard to her in the first place, and he aggressively pursued her. Far from being his puppet or his intellectual creation, however, Héloïse was a different kind of scholar from Abelard, steeped not in philosophy and theology but in Latin classical authors – she clearly read satire – and in poetry. While her uncle remained oblivious, the passionate affair continued under his nose, but the lovers were eventually discovered and separated. When Héloïse found she was pregnant, she, at least, was overjoyed. Abelard helped Héloïse escape to his sister's home until she could have her son, whom, with characteristic élan, she christened Astralabe. Héloïse may well have composed the song of the pregnant woman in the *Carmina Burana*, although it is impossible to prove (Mews 2010; Newman 1995, pp. 46–75). Abelard insisted that they marry, to the active dismay of Héloïse, who was convinced that a wife and child would derail his academic career. Héloïse remained secretly at Argenteuil, where the couple met at night, snatching clandestine encounters in the refectory. And then catastrophe struck: Fulbert and his household sought revenge by ambushing and castrating Abelard. Knowing conventional married life was now impossible for him, Abelard told Héloïse to remain at Argenteuil, where she seems to have taken monastic vows in a state of numb despair. Backed by the Cluniac abbot Peter the Venerable, she seems to have been made prioress at Argenteuil by 1123, but she would not hear from Abelard again for nearly a decade.

Gradually regaining his intellectual confidence, Abelard began again to cut a swathe through the universities and cathedral schools of Europe, ending in his condemnation for heresy in 1121 and his retirement to monastic life in Brittany. After Abbot Suger of Paris closed down the community at Argenteuil, citing misconduct, in 1129 Abelard moved Héloïse and her nuns to a new experiment in monasticism, the oratory of the Paraclete, where they saw one another for the first time in 10 years. Like Gilbert of Sempringham and Norbert of Xanten, Abelard was now known for his active support of women in the religious life. A voice pushing back against the clerical marginalization of women religious, Abelard would in later life defend abbesses as the historical continuation of the ancient order of deaconesses (Abelard and Héloïse 2003, pp. 116–117; Macy 2016, pp. 93–96). Like Gilbert, he encountered hostility and suspicion as a result.

Abelard's *History of My Calamities* was written in 1132 in an effort at self-defense, in which he detailed, among other things, his past affair with Héloïse. Someone gave Héloïse the book; she seems to have had little or no warning of what it contained. In response, she wrote Abelard a scorching, heart-breaking letter, revealing the depth of her long-standing despair and sexual frustration. She felt betrayed by a husband who, perhaps to assuage his own guilt, had assumed she had more of a vocation than she did and implied that she had ever cared a scrap for her own social respectability:

> It was not any sense of vocation which brought me as a young girl to accept the austerities of the cloister, but your bidding alone, and if I deserve no gratitude from you, you may judge for yourself how my labors are in vain. I can expect no reward for this from God, for it is certain that I have done nothing as yet for love of him. When you hurried towards God I followed you, indeed, I went first to take the veil – perhaps you were thinking of how Lot's wife turned back when you made me put on the religious habit and take my vows before you gave yourself to God. Your lack of trust in me over this one thing, I confess, overwhelmed me with grief and shame. I would have had no hesitation, God knows, in following you or going ahead at your bidding to the flames of Hell. My heart was not in me but with you, and now, even more, if it is not with you it is nowhere; truly, without you it cannot exist (Abelard and Héloïse 2003, pp. 51–54).

In cautious response, perhaps trying to help Héloïse understand her present position as part of an honorable tradition, Abelard wrote what might be called an early attempt at the history of women in Christianity, beginning with Old Testament *exempla* and culminating with the women who were witnesses to the resurrection (Abelard and Héloïse 2003, pp. 54–62).

Whether Abelard's response immediately effected any sort of change in Héloïse's heart, over time she began to engage with religious life in a slightly more heartened spirit. In a later letter, she requested his advice for adapting the Benedictine Rule specifically for communities of women, from the vantage point of 14 years' experience. She pointed out, for example, that the Benedictine Rule took no account of women's menstruation when it dictated appropriate garments, and she wanted to reorder their liturgy so that priests and deacons were not entering the community in the small hours to read the gospel during the night office. She noted how Benedict himself was a pragmatist who regarded his own rule "as no more than a basis for virtuous living" (Abelard and Héloïse 2003, pp. 93–111).

While most of Héloïse's suggestions were rhetorically couched as accommodating the "weaker sex," in fact her criticisms were equally applicable to both genders in the monastic life, aiming to bring rule in line with actual practice. She noted that her women were not doing manual labor – neither were most Cistercian choir-monks by then – and she thought it foolish that new nuns were asked to make a life-long vow after only a year-long novitiate and three readings of the Rule. "Would that our religion could rise to this height – to carry out the Gospel, not to go beyond it, lest we attempt to be more than Christians!" (Abelard and Héloïse 2003, p. 98). Clearly her sense of irony had not deserted her, which she directed most pointedly at reformers' chronic propensity to over-promise and under-deliver: "It should be sufficient for our infirmity, and indeed, a high tribute to it, if we live continently and without possessions, wholly occupied by the service of God, and in doing so equal the leaders of the Church themselves in our way of life or religious laymen or even those who are called Canons Regular and profess themselves especially to follow the apostolic life," tartly remarked the canon's niece. "[A]s things are, they all hurry almost equally indiscriminately to enter monastic life: they are received without proper discipline and live with even less, they profess a Rule they do not know and are equally ready to despise it and set up as law the customs they prefer" (Abelard and Héloïse 2003, p. 100). In the event, like so many women in this period, Héloïse would outlive her former husband by some 20 years. Abelard was buried at the oratory of the Paraclete, and she remained quietly but firmly loyal to his memory and to his vision of monastic life, even in the teeth of disapproval from Abelard's bête noir, Bernard of Clairvaux. Like Petronilla de Chémilly, it was Héloïse who managed the practicalities of their legacy, and the order of the Paraclete would have six daughter-houses by the time she died in 1164 (see Figure 7.7).

The twelfth century witnessed an explosion in the numbers of women eager to participate in the new forms of religious life and to live a life modeled on that of Christ and his disciples. While this has sometimes been explained as simple population surplus, women left over after men had departed on the Crusades, this is a highly reductionistic explanation for a complex phenomenon – and, moreover, one which takes no real account of the women's own religious motivations. As always, there must have been women like Héloïse who found themselves in monastic life after grief and loss, but that hardly explains the multiplicity of new forms of life that were invented over the course of the century. Nor does it address the clear enthusiasm felt, at least within some circles, for regulated interaction and engagement between the sexes within a monastic context, rather than their complete separation. The same popular enthusiasm unleashed in the Crusades ensured that not all these experiments in monasticism would involve only aristocrats: in fact, the provisional, improvisational quality of religious life led by women recluses like Christina of Markyate

**Figure 7.7** The grave of Abelard and Héloïse, Père-Lachaise, Paris. *Source:* Pierre-Yves Beaudouin / Wikimedia Commons / CC BY-SA 3.0.

and her community meant there were fewer financial bars to women's participation. With the support of aristocratic women, these small women's houses clung to life, although they remained vulnerable, not least from efforts at regulation within the church. As the threat of heresy loomed larger over the institutional church, women both preached against heresy and found themselves the target of clerical suspicions, cut off from the more systematic, scholastic Latin theology emerging from the medieval universities. Ultimately there was nothing for it: women would have to speak in their own words.

# References

Abelard and Héloïse (2003). *The Letters of Abelard and Heloise* (trans. B. Radice). London: Penguin. First edition, 1974.

Aelred of Rielvaux (1971). *De institutis inclusarum*. In: *Opera omnia* (ed. A. Hoste and C.H. Talbot), 636–682. *Corpus Christianorum Continuatio Medievalis 1* (ed. C.H. Talbot). Turnhout: Brepols.

Baker, A. (1911). An Anglo-French life of St. Osith. *The Modern Language Review* 6: 476ff.

Bartlett, R. (ed. and trans.) (2003). *The Miracles of Saint Æbbe of Coldingham and Saint Margaret of Scotland*. Oxford: Clarendon.

Bartlett, A.C. (2010). Holy women in the British Isles: a survey. In: *Medieval Holy Women in the Christian Tradition c. 1100–1500* (ed. A. Minnis and R. Voaden), 165–193. Turnhout: Brepols.

Bartlett, R. (2020). *Blood Royal: Dynastic Politics in Medieval Europe*. Cambridge: Cambridge University Press.

Beach, A. (2004). *Women as Scribes: Book Production and Monastic Reform in Twelfth-Century Bavaria*. Cambridge: Cambridge University Press.

Berend, N. (2006). The expansion of Latin Christendom. In: *The Central Middle Ages, 950–1320* (ed. D. Power), 178–207. Oxford: Oxford University Press.

Berman, C.H. (2018). *The White Nuns: Cistercian Abbeys for Women in Medieval France*. Philadelphia: University of Pennsylvania Press.

Blair, J. (1988). *Saint Frideswide, Patron of Oxford: The Earliest Texts*. Oxford: The Perpetua Press.

Bugyis, K.A.-M. (2019). *The Care of Nuns: The Ministries of Benedictine Women in England during the Central Middle Ages*. Oxford: Oxford University Press.

Burton, J. (1994). *Monastic and Religious Orders in Britain, 1000–1300*. Cambridge: Cambridge University Press.

Burton, J. and Kerr, J. (2011). *The Cistercians in the Middle Ages*. Woodbridge: Boydell Press.

Bynum, C.W. (1982). *Jesus as Mother: Studies in the Spirituality of the High Middle Ages*. Berkeley: University of California Press.

Bynum, C.W. (1987). *Holy Feast and Holy Fast: The Religious Significance of Food to Medieval Women*. Berkeley: University of California Press.

Carlevaris, A. (2001). Ildegarda e la patristica. In: *"Im Angesicht Gottes such der Mensch sich selbst": Hildegard von Bingen (1098–1179)* (ed. R. Berndt), 65–80. Berlin: Akademie Verlag.

Carruthers, M. (1998). *The Craft of Thought: Meditation, Rhetoric, and the Making of Images, 400–1200*. Cambridge: Cambridge University Press.

Clanchy, M.T. (2013). *From Memory to Written Record: England, 1066–1307*, 3e. Chichester: Wiley-Blackwell.

Clark, A.L. (2010). Elisabeth of Schönau. In: *Medieval Holy Women in the Christian Tradition c. 1100–1500* (ed. A. Minnis and R. Voaden), 371–391. Turnhout: Brepols.

Comnena, A. (2009). *The Alexiad*, rev. ed. (trans. E.R.A. Sewter). London: Penguin.

Constable, G. (1996). *The Reformation of the Twelfth Century*. Cambridge: Cambridge University Press.

D'Avray, D.L. (2005). *Medieval Marriage: Symbolism and Society*. Oxford: Clarendon Press.

Edwards, J. (2019). *Superior Women: Medieval Female Authority in Poitiers' Abbey of Sainte-Croix*. Oxford: Oxford University Press.

Elkins, S.K. (1988). *Holy Women of Twelfth-Century England*. Chapel Hill: University of North Carolina Press.

Fulton, R. (2002). *From Judgement to Passion: Devotion to Christ and the Virgin Mary, 800–1200*. New York: Columbia University Press.

Geddes, J. (2005). The St. Albans psalter: the abbot and the anchoress. In: *Christina of Markyate: A Twelfth-Century Holy Woman* (ed. S. Fanous and H. Leyser), 197–216. London: Routledge.

Gold, P.S. (1985). *The Lady and the Virgin: Image, Attitude and Experience in 12th-Century France*. Chicago: University of Chicago Press.

Griffiths, F. (2007). *The Garden of Delights: Reform and Renaissance for Women in the Twelfth Century*. Philadelphia: University of Pennsylvania Press.

Griffiths, F. (2018). *Nuns' Priests' Tales: Men and Salvation in Medieval Women's Monastic Life*. Philadelphia: University of Pennsylvania Press.

Grundmann, H. (1995). *Religious Movements in the Middle Ages: The Historical Links between Heresy, the Medicant Orders, and the Women's Religious Movement in the Twelfth and Thirteenth Century*. London: University of Notre Dame Press.

Hall, D. (2003). *Women and the Church in Medieval Ireland, c. 1140–1540*. Dublin: Four Courts Press.

Hanley, C. (2019). *Matilda: Empress, Queen, Warrior*. New Haven: Yale University Press.

Haskins, C.H. (1955). *The Renaissance of the Twelfth Century*. Cambridge: Harvard University Press.

Hildegard of Bingen (1996). *Liber divinorum operum*. In: *Corpus Christianorum Continuatio Medievalis 92* (ed. P. Dronke). Turnhout: Brepols.

Hildegard of Bingen (2001a). *Hildegard of Bingen: Selected Writings* (trans. M. Atherton). London: Penguin.

Hildegard of Bingen (2001b). *Illuminations of Hildegard of Bingen: Text by Hildegard of Bingen with Commentary by Matthew Fox*. London: Penguin.

Hotchin, J. (2001). Female religious life and the *cura monialium* in Hirsau monasticism. In: *Listen, Daughter: The Speculum Virginum and the Formation of Religious Women in the Middle Ages* (ed. C.J. Mews), 59–83. London: Palgrave.

Hussey, J.M. (1986). *The Orthodox Church in the Byzantine Empire*. Oxford: Oxford University Press.

Johns, S. (2003). *Noblewomen, Aristocracy, and Power in the Twelfth-Century Anglo-Norman Realm*. Manchester: Manchester University Press.

Jordan, E.L. (2006). *Women, Power, and Religious Patronage in the Middle Ages*. New York: Palgrave Macmillan.

Joyner, D. (2016). *Painting the Hortus Deliciarum: Medieval Women, Wisdom, and Time*. University Park, PA: Pennsylvania State University Press.

Karras, R.M. (2012). *Unmarriages: Women, Men, and Sexual Unions in the Middle Ages*. Philadelphia: University of Pennsylvania Press.

Kerby-Fulton, K. (2005). When women preached: an introduction to female homiletics, sacramental and liturgical roles in the later Middle Ages. In: *Voices in Dialogue: Reading Women in the Middle Ages* (ed. L. Olsen and K. Kerby-Fulton), 31–55. Notre Dame: University of Notre Dame Press.

Kerby-Fulton, K. (2006). *Books under Suspicion: Censorship and Tolerance of Revelatory Writing in Late Medieval England*. Notre Dame: University of Notre Dame Press.

Kerby-Fulton, K. (2009). Skepticism, agnosticism, and belief: the spectrum of attitudes toward vision in late medieval England. In: *Women and the Divine in Literature before 1700: Essays in Memory of Margaret Louis* (ed. K. Kerby-Fulton). Victoria: ELS Éditions.

Kerby-Fulton, K. (2010). Hildegard of Bingen. In: *Medieval Holy Women in the Christian Tradition c. 1100–1500* (ed. A. Minnis and R. Voaden), 343–369. Turnhout: Brepols.

Kienzle, B.M. (2009). *Hildegard of Bingen and Her Gospel Homilies: Speaking New Mysteries*. Turnhout: Brepols.

Lester, A.E. (2011). *Creating Cistercian Nuns: The Women's Religious Movement and its Reform in 13th-Century Champagne*. Ithaca: Cornell University Press.

Macy, G. (2016). *The Hidden History of Women's Ordination: Female Clergy in the Medieval West*. Oxford: Oxford University Press.

Madigan, K. (2017). *Medieval Christianity: A New History*. New Haven: Yale University Press.

Mews, C. (2001). Virginity, theology, and pedagogy in the *Speculum Virginum*. In: *Listen, Daughter: The Speculum Virginum and the Formation of Religious Women in the Middle Ages* (ed. C.J. Mews), 15–40. London: Palgrave.

Mews, C. (2010). Héloïse. In: *Medieval Holy Women in the Christian Tradition c. 1100–1500* (ed. A. Minnis and R. Voaden), 267–281. Turnhout: Brepols.

Michaud, J. (1841). *L'Histoire des croisades*, vol. 6. Paris: Furne et cie.

Miller, M. (2003). Masculinity, reform, and clerical culture: narratives of episcopal holiness in the Gregorian era. *Church History* 72: 25–52.

Montefiore, S.S. (2011). *Jerusalem: The Biography*. London: Weidenfeld and Nicolson.

Moore, R.I. (2007). *The Formation of a Persecuting Society*, 2e. Oxford: Blackwell.

Morrison, S.S. (2000). *Women Pilgrims in Late Medieval England*. London: Routledge.

Morrow, M.J. (2005). Sharing texts: Anselmian prayers, a nunnery's psalter, and the role of friendship. In: *Voices in Dialogue: Reading Women in the Middle Ages* (ed. L. Olsen and K. Kerby-Fulton), 97–113. Notre Dame: University of Notre Dame Press.

Mulder-Bakker, A.B. (2010). Holy women in the German territories: a survey. In: *Medieval Holy Women in the Christian Tradition c. 1100–1500* (ed. A. Minnis and R. Voaden), 313–341. Turnhout: Brepols.

Neville, L. (2016). *Anna Komnene: The Life and Work of a Medieval Historian*. Oxford: Oxford University Press.

Newman, B. (1995). *From Virile Woman to WomanChrist*. Philadelphia: University of Pennsylvania Press.

Newman, B. (1997). *Sister of Wisdom: St. Hildegard's Theology of the Feminine*. Berkeley: University of California Press First edition, 1987.

Newman, B. (1998). *Voice of the Living Light: Hildegard of Bingen and Her World*. Berkeley: University of California Press.

Obolensky, D. (1971). *The Byzantine Commonwealth: Eastern Europe, 400–1453*. London: Weidenfeld and Nicolson.

Olsen, L. (2005). Reading, writing, and relationships in dialogue. In: *Voices in Dialogue: Reading Women in the Middle Ages* (ed. L. Olsen and K. Kerby-Fulton), 1–31. Notre Dame: University of Notre Dame Press.

Paul, N.L. (2012). *To Follow in Their Footsteps: The Crusades and Family Memory in the High Middle Ages*. Ithaca: Cornell University Press.

Power, K. (2001). From ecclesiology to Mariology. In: *Listen, Daughter: The Speculum Virginum and the Formation of Religious Women in the Middle Ages* (ed. C.J. Mews), 85–110. London: Palgrave.

Rubenstein, J. (2019). *Nebuchadnezzar's Dream: The Crusades, Apocalyptic Prophecy, and the End of History*. Oxford: Oxford University Press.

Schofield, J. and Lea, R. (2005). *Holy Trinity Priory, Aldgate, City of London: An Archaeological Reconstruction and History*. London: Museum of London Archaeology Service.

Southern, R.W. (1969). *The Making of the Middle Ages*. New Haven: Yale University Press.

Stafford, P. (1997). *Queen Emma and Queen Edith: Queenship and Women's Power in Eleventh-Century England*. Oxford: Blackwell.

*The Life of Christina of Markyate* (trans. C.H. Talbot; ed. and rev. S. Fanous and H. Leyser) (2009). Oxford: Oxford University Press.

Thomas, A. (2013). Between court and cloister: royal patronage and nuns' literacy in medieval east-central Europe. In: *Nuns' Literacies in Medieval Europe: The Hull Dialogue* (ed. V. Blanton, V. O'Mara and P. Stoop), 207–221. Turnhout: Brepols.

Thompson, S. (1991). *Women Religious: The Founding of English Nunneries after the Norman Conquest*. Oxford: Clarendon Press.

Tranovich, M. (2011). *Melisende of Jerusalem: The World of a Forgotten Crusader Queen*. London: East and West Publishing.

Van Engen, J. (1986). The "crisis of coenobitism" reconsidered: Benedictine monasticism in the years 1050–1150. *Speculum* 61: 269–304.

Vanderputten, S. (2013). Female monasticism, ecclesiastical reform, and regional politics: the northern archdiocese of Reims, ca. 1060–1120. *French Historical Studies* 36 (3): 363–383.

Venarde, B.L. (1997). *Women's Monasticism and Medieval Society: Nunneries in France and England, 890–1215*. Ithaca: Cornell University Press.

Venarde, B.L. (2013). Making history at Fontevraud: abbess Petronius de Chemillé and practical literacy. In: *Nuns' Literacies in Medieval Europe: The Hull Dialogue* (ed. V. Blanton, V. O'Mara and P. Stoop), 19–31. Turnhout: Brepols.

Waller, G. (2011). *Walsingham and the English Imagination*. Farnham: Ashgate.

Ward, B. (2018). *Give Love and Receive the Kingdom*. Brewster: Paraclete Press.

Warner, M. (1976). *Alone of All Her Sex: The Myth and Cult of the Virgin Mary*. London: Picador.

# 8

# Clare and Company

The Social Mystics, 1200–1300

In 1230, Clare of Assisi went on a hunger strike against the papacy. Tensions had been escalating for some time between Clare and Cardinal Hugolino, now the newly elected Pope Gregory IX. Twenty-five years before, in 1204, Francis had had a vision in the ruined church of San Damiano, in which Christ spoke from the great icon-cross hanging in the nave and commanded him to "Rebuild my church" (Bonaventure 1978, pp. 191–198). Francis had belatedly realized that perhaps it was not only San Damiano that Christ had meant, but from 1211 the church, as well as its hospice, became the home of Clare and a growing community of religious women. Clare and her community generally ate only one meal a day, taken from the broken bread they begged in the town, and clung to Francis's model of radical poverty. In the wake of Francis's death in 1226, Clare had wrung from the papacy the so-called "Privilege of Poverty," a document kept and pointedly treasured at San Damiano (Gregory 2006; Mueller 2010, pp. 65–89). A reluctant Gregory IX, however, sought to enclose the community, first by seeking to endow San Damiano with property, which Clare refused, and then by sending to the women friar questors, men appointed to do the women's begging for them. When Gregory declared that any other friars, such as the women's confessors, would require papal permission to enter the community, Clare sent the friar questors away. If the women were to be shut away, they would not eat (Mooney 2016, pp. 73–87).

It is often difficult to distinguish Clare from the overwhelming memory of Francis. Like Héloïse, however, Clare lived almost 30 years beyond the death of her former mentor, defiantly protective of his memory and of the particular, radical model of life he had bequeathed to his followers, in the face of popes who wanted nothing more than for Clare to run a conventional women's house. More broadly, the battle of wills between Clare and Gregory IX illustrates what was at stake for many religious women in the thirteenth century: their increasingly urban orientation, their bent toward practical charity, and their ministry to, and self-identification with, the poor. This necessitated a certain degree of being "in the world," which placed women's communities in tension with ecclesiastical authorities' determination to set about their regulation, order, and control – usually their enclosure and the renunciation of all ties outside. If religious women negotiated these efforts successfully, they also continued to require productive pastoral support from men's orders. In the end, what remained most concretely within the women's field of agency was their own bodies: unlike Héloïse or Hildegard of Bingen, Clare's religious devotion is inseparable from her habitual fasting and extreme physical asceticism, as uncomfortable to modern audiences as it probably was to the likes of Pope Gregory. For medieval religious women, however, physical asceticism often represented, as well as a form of self-control, a form of self-sacrificial love modeled on that of Christ, a feeding of others with one's body and blood (Bynum 1987, pp. 260–276; Mantel 2004).

*A History of Women in Christianity to 1600*, First Edition. Hannah Matis.
© 2023 John Wiley & Sons Ltd. Published 2023 by John Wiley & Sons Ltd.

## The Boom-Time and the Poor

For the rest of the Middle Ages, feeding others would be a matter of urgent concern. The twelfth century had been a period of unusually good weather and bountiful harvests. Agricultural innovations, not least by monastic orders like the Cistercians, improved breeding stock, drainage, and water management, and made more systematic use of marginal lands. Bequests to monastic orders also consolidated property which could be let again to peasant tenants. The population of western Europe began to increase dramatically, pushing relentlessly against the capacity of the land to feed everyone. Legislation by the church around sex and marriage, such as that enacted by the Fourth Lateran Council in 1215, emerged from a historical context in which the peasant population was in the process of tripling in size (Wickham 2016, p. 121).

Women were necessarily caught in the midst of these intersecting pressures: the physical toll of successive pregnancies, bearing and feeding children who might not survive to adulthood, laying out the dead. Women were also disproportionately affected by two of the major technological advances of the thirteenth century: the introduction of the spinning wheel and the mechanized horizontal loom to western Europe, making cloth manufacture radically more efficient. Over the course of the thirteenth century, the textile industry ballooned, particularly in the cities of northern Italy and the old Lotharingia, the Low Countries, supplied with enormous quantities of English wool. Women overwhelmingly formed the bulk of the unskilled labor required to prepare and spin the wool. For the rest of the Middle Ages, young women too poor to be readily marriageable, later called "spinsters," might travel to work in these newly urbanizing areas. Some inevitably turned to prostitution to supplement their wages; later medieval terminology regularly conflates "single woman" with "prostitute." Women weavers were nearly always married, not least because of the money required to buy a loom (Bennett et al. 1989; Karras 1996; 2004; St. Clair 2019, pp. 115–133).

For the first time in European history, wealth was generated that did not directly derive from agriculture and owed less to the complex pyramid of feudal obligations that still obtained in rural society. In the twelfth century, particularly after the death of Matilda of Tuscany in 1115, the political structures formed which established the communes of Pisa and Genoa (Mazzaoui 1981; Johnstone 2002, pp. 34–35; Wickham 2015, pp. 67–71). In the thirteenth century, the Mediterranean trade, not to say piracy, of Pisa and Genoa established their status as important trading partners with the Islamic world, even as Saladin closed in around the crusader fortress at Acre. Slavery continued on a small scale in both directions: captured Europeans were sold primarily in North Africa, and some Africans, like Shakespeare's Othello, were brought back to Italy. Indirectly, everyone benefited from the peace, if not the wars, of Ghengis Khan (d. 1227) and the enormous empire he and his successors created across Central Asia. In the middle of the thirteenth century, a Flemish Franciscan, William of Rubruck, traveled across the central Asian steppe to begin a mission to the Mongols; Kublai Khan's sister, it was rumored, had become a Christian. William discovered that Christianity had arrived centuries before – although in a different language, and in a different form from the faith he knew. In his travelogue, he describes how, according to the rite of the Church of the East, an important Mongol lady, Lady Cotota, kissed icons, lit incense, censed the priests, and was censed herself, before what may have been her baptism (William of Rubruck 2017).

Meanwhile, Pisans and Florentines sold saffron grown in Tuscany to the Mamluks in Egypt, and imported alum from Turkey necessary as a fixative for the dying of textiles. Textiles made in Italy and the Low Countries were sold not only in Europe but also across the Islamic world, netting enormous profits. In 1252, Florence minted the florin, the first gold coin made in Europe since the fall of Rome (Abu-Lughod 1989; Abulafia 2011). The Venetians had bankrolled the Fourth Crusade that sacked Constantinople in 1204, and triumphantly carried off its treasures westwards. At the end of the century, perhaps as Acre finally fell to the Muslims, in a similar act of religious and cultural piracy, the Angelos family seem to have transported, respectively, a stone house from Palestine and a miracle-working icon from Trsat in Croatia, and constructed the shrine of Mary's house at Loreto, which became a significant late medieval pilgrimage destination.

Assisi became an independent commune in 1202. The icon-cross hanging in the church of San Damiano, like those in many churches in Umbria, reflected the immense popularity of Greek devotional objects in Italy at this time. Francis's father was a cloth merchant, and "Francesco," whose very nickname evoked his father's trading connections, grew up in a state of comparative luxury which he would later deplore. In an effort to control the vehemence of Francis's conversion, Pietro di Bernardone would take his son to court before the bishop in Assisi. Famously, Francis returned his clothes to his father in the courtroom and walked out naked (Bonaventure 1978). It is no coincidence that, in a society obsessed with cloth and its monetary value, Francis modeled himself on a stripped and naked Christ, and that Francis and Clare's devotion would often center on the crèche and its vulnerable Christ Child (Dzon 2017, pp. 63–76).

Of noble background herself, Clare refused to let any of her family, even her sisters, buy her out of her dowry. Although she would not make use of it herself, she was determined to repurpose it directly for the use of the poor (Mooney 2016, p. 28). In the early years of the community, Clare seems to have supported herself at San Damiano by making vestments and altar linens, alongside the work of the hospice. On Francis's death in 1226, the desperately shabby tunic he had been wearing, still kept as a relic in Assisi today, was gently patched by her own hands with fabric taken from Clare's own cloak (Miller 2014, p. 141; Coatsworth and Owen-Crocker 2018, pp. 171–174; see Figure 8.1). As it developed, the Franciscan order represented a potent critique of a mercantile society under pressure and a response to the urban problems created by rapid social change, but it also inevitably built on – and built with – the profits accrued by that mercantile society. A century after the death of a man who did not want his order to own property, there would be a Franciscan church in every major Italian town.

The urbanizing of these regions brought together not only people but texts. This did not mean that everyone could necessarily read in the modern sense, and certainly not that everyone could

**Figure 8.1** Tunic attributed to Francis of Assisi, Assisi. *Source:* REUTERS / Alamy Images.

both read and write, but beyond functional familiarity with documents, thirteenth-century society increasingly formed "textual communities" defined by their orientation around particular works and genres of works (Stock 1983; Bell 1995, pp. 59–60). In a community of religious women, but also in a workshop of women spinning, one person might read to the room at large. Furthermore, if the same works or kinds of works were being read in lay and religious communities, distinctions between the two groups had the potential to blur. As scholastic theology developed as a discipline within the universities, women had some access to Latin literacy but very little to formal theological training. Vernacular romance, by contrast, soared in popularity among laypeople, aided by the patronage of Eleanor of Aquitaine and the talents of women like Marie de France. Francis pledged his loyalty to Lady Poverty in chivalric terms. By the end of the thirteenth century, not only Dante Alighieri but also many religious women were developing the conventions of chivalric romance, called *fin'amor* or, later, *fine amour*, to formulate their own theology, devotion, and spirituality in the vernacular. As the church turned against the religious experimentation of the twelfth century, however, literacy and the use of documents also became the means by which the church could record and police religious dissent.

## The Perfect and the Inquisition

Not far from the heartlands of the Provençal troubadours, other kinds of religious teachers began to appear in the politically decentralized regions of southern France, Piedmont, and into the towns and communes of northern Italy. Formidably ascetic, these teachers, mostly men but including a few women as well, ate neither meat, eggs, nor cheese, refused to swear oaths, venerated neither the cross nor the saints, and gave up all sexual activity. Called "the perfect," only the men preached, although the women's asceticism naturally commanded deep respect, and they lived mendicant lives not so different, at least on the surface, from that of Francis. They completely eschewed the institutional church, offering their own forms of the sacraments to their followers. To greet a perfect was itself a blessing, and they adapted their own form of the Lord's Prayer for their followers to say. The dying were encouraged to take the *consolamentum*, in which lay people embarked on the practices of the perfect, and sometimes the grim *endura*, in which they neither ate nor drank, to purge evil from their bodies in their last moments (Wakefield and Evans 1991; Lambert 2002, pp. 115–157).

Behind these various devotions was a form of dualism that divided the world into spiritual good and material evil, the realms of a good god and a bad god – a world, in fact, without the Christian doctrine of the Incarnation. Where these teachings came from, and if that is even the right question to ask, continues to divide scholars. "Cathar" and "Catharism" is a later coinage from Germany, and is never a name that the perfect called themselves. Some Bogomil refugees from Byzantine Bulgaria do seem to have traveled west to southern France, perhaps on Italian trade routes. Others have located aspects of Cathar teaching in the distinctive Provençal language and culture, or seen it as a response to the wealth and aristocratic dominance of the institutional church in the area (Ladurie 1979; Pegg 2006; Biller 2010; Madigan 2017, pp. 174–210).

The preaching of Hildegard of Bingen and Elizabeth of Schönau notwithstanding, by the mid-twelfth century Cathar teachings had spread throughout southern France, dominating entire villages, reaching into northern Italy and the cities of Germany. Traveling through southern France with the king of Castile, the young Spanish priest Dominic Guzman was shocked by the hold Catharism seemed to have over the region. In 1184, the papacy issued *Ad abolendam*, the bull authorizing independent papal representatives to visit these areas and to seek out the roots of dissent. In so doing, the papacy created the office, if not the institution, of the inquisition

(Kieckhefer 1995; Arnold 2001). When one legate was murdered in 1208, Innocent III called the Albigensian Crusade, in which, for the next 20 years, northern French knights sporadically went heresy-hunting in what was, to them, a foreign country. In 1209, the knights indiscriminately slaughtered every inhabitant of the town of Béziers, Cathar and Catholic (Pegg 2008).

In 1215, Innocent III, perhaps one of the papacy's most gifted administrators, called the Fourth Lateran Council (Duffy 2002, pp. 144–151; Madigan 2017, pp. 214, 249, 310–311, 357–358). The culmination of medieval canon law to that point and the authoritative statement of medieval church teaching on the sacraments, the council sought to respond more constructively to the pastoral vacuum the Cathars were clearly filling in many places in Christendom. The Fourth Lateran Council defined the medieval doctrine of transubstantiation, further raising the status of the Eucharist in parish life. From the thirteenth century, the elevation of the host as the climax of the eucharistic service became customary, with laypeople looking on even if they did not receive. Parish priests were now required to hear confession of everyone in their charge at least once a year, and all marriages were now to be blessed by a priest in church. The council defined the doctrine of purgatory, firming up the connection in devotional practice between purgatory and penance and laying the foundation for the late medieval use of indulgences. Notoriously, the Fourth Lateran Council required that Jews be designated publicly by a yellow star on their clothing, while convicted heretics were marked by a yellow cross. It recognized the ministry of Francis of Assisi and Dominic, while discouraging the creation of any more new orders. Finally, it declared heretical the vivid apocalyptic teachings of the Italian cleric Joachim of Fiore on the coming Age of the Holy Spirit.

From the point of view of a Provençal woman, however, these neat distinctions and boundaries may have been much less clear. After the Albigensian Crusade the Cathar perfect continued to wander, relying on networks of clandestine and outwardly conformist supporters, and even if they taught, they did not always preach Cathar teachings openly. Other heretical groups traveled as well, and in many of the same regions. The Waldensians similarly did not venerate the cross or the saints, declared – probably in reaction to the Council's definition of purgatory – that unbaptized infants were sinless, rejected the Council's definition of transubstantiation, forbade all killing and sexual activity, and encouraged both men and women to preach and to practice poverty. They would survive in the Swiss Alps until the Reformation (Audisio 1999). A century after Francis's death, the spiritual Franciscans, who rejected their order's decision to own property on a collective, if not individual, basis, and were deeply influenced by the apocalyptic prophecies of Joachim of Fiore, were also declared heretical. Alongside the "friends" of the Waldensians appeared large numbers of third-order Franciscans: laypeople who adopted some Franciscan practices and supported the friars, while not taking formal vows themselves. Many, even most, of these were women. In fact, a spectrum of religious belief and practice existed by the end of the thirteenth century, only some of which was openly heretical. Long after the Albigensian Crusade, Cathars continued to live alongside Catholics as far south as the papal stronghold of Orvieto, 80 miles from Rome (Lansing 1998; Snyder 2006). In 1328, in the heart of Cathar country in Carcassonne, a woman named Na Prous Boneta, a third-order Franciscan and supporter of the *spirituali*, was burned at the stake for claiming to be the vessel for the incarnation of the Holy Spirit (Burr 2001, pp. 230–237, 315–346).

Paradoxically, virtually all that survives of Cathar belief today is what was indirectly recorded in inquisitorial records. Both Franciscans and Dominicans, but the Dominicans in particular, seemed to have adopted the office of inquisition as a kind of intellectual and spiritual vocation, even as they became integral to the theological faculties of all the medieval universities in Europe. From the perspective of a university-trained theologian steeped in Augustine of Hippo, Catharism was obviously a form of Manichaeanism reborn. But Manichaeanism was described much more eloquently and comprehensively by Augustine than by any Provençal villager. Over time, inquisitors trained in the scholastic method systematized lists of questions to ask those under suspicion, often on subtle theological points. The revival of Roman law in the previous century helped to make acceptable the use of torture in interrogation, although often the mere threat of it must have been enough. The social stress on the person under inquisition was extreme, particularly if the person was placed in isolation or otherwise confined before interrogation. People did not often run away outright, but they did try to lie or implicate their neighbors, and often they were attempting to recall conversations and incidents that had taken place years before, or with people who had since died. Leading questions, torture, outright lies, the vagaries of memory, and lack of basic Christian education in the vernacular all combined in such a way that in a very real sense the inquisition often helped to systematize, even to create, the very heresy it hunted.

## Embracing Poverty

Of course, none of this was clear at the time, least of all to the inquisitors. In 1230, Clare of Assisi was facing off against a highly confident, monarchical papacy determined to eradicate heresy root and branch, not least by channeling the tremendous energy of the friars and their potentially dangerous female followers into recognizably orthodox and respectable channels. It is an indication of Clare's own strength of will, however, and of the amount of support she had within Assisi and beyond, that she was able to make her point. Ultimately Gregory backed down, outlining more practical legislation for the Franciscans to provide the women of San Damiano with pastoral care. The Privilege of Poverty became, for the San Damiano community, a hard-won locus of their own identity as Franciscans – an identity that they owed, not to the order or even really to Francis, but to Clare (Gennaro 1996; see Figure 8.2).

**Figure 8.2** Fresco of Clare and her companions, church of San Damiano, Assisi. *Source:* Gunnar Bach Pedersen / Wikimedia Commons / Public domain.

Clare herself, meanwhile, began a correspondence with Agnes of Prague, the youngest daughter of the king of Bohemia. Three letters have survived that were written by Clare between 1234 and 1238. As well as offering precious evidence of Clare's own voice and the extent of her Latin education, this seems to have been a conscious attempt on Clare's part to outflank the papacy by creating independent channels of communication between the two women (Mueller 2006). Upon the Franciscans' arrival in Prague in 1233, Agnes had founded two Franciscan communities of women, one connected to a hospital. Very quickly, she found herself balancing her own intentions, Gregory's pressure to enclose the women completely, and the conflicting rules and regulations by which she was trying to live. By contrast, Clare offered both clarity and challenge. Her letters describe poverty as a path to contemplation, even divinization, drawing on the language of the Song of Songs. She encouraged Agnes to "be mindful, like a second Rachel, of your founding purpose, always seeing your beginning." Taking the pregnant Virgin as a model, she encouraged Agnes to "place your mind in the mirror of eternity; place your soul in the splendor of glory; place your heart in the figure of the divine substance; and, through contemplation, transform your entire being into the image of the Divine One himself" (Clare of Assisi 2006).

This passionate, even mystical embrace of poverty was downright regal in its language, and it suggests why both Gregory and his successor, Innocent IV, found it so difficult to administer female Franciscan communities into meek acceptance of property and enclosure. Amidst a fractured and fractious order, however, many male Franciscans saw women as the Achilles heel by which the papacy could potentially dilute their founder's zeal. When Innocent legislated that they, like the Dominicans, should be pastorally responsible for women's houses, many Franciscans, such as the author of *The Little Flowers of St. Francis*, Ugolino di Monte Santa Maria, responded by retelling stories of their founder which scrupulously separated him from women and from Clare in particular. Paradoxically, Innocent's parting gift to Clare on her deathbed in 1253 was the so-called "Forma vitae," a document describing her as the abbess of San Damiano and deliberately mingling her voice with that of Francis: a monastic rule for a woman who had, throughout her life, resolutely refused both rule and rank (Clare of Assisi 2006; Knox 2008, pp. 57–86; Mooney 2016, pp. 170–192).

In 1281 in Milan, a woman named Guglielma died who claimed to be Agnes of Prague's sister. If true, she had been married and had at least one child, but she had entered the Cistercian house of Chiaravalle, at least for a time. When she emerged, like Na Prous Boneta, Guglielma was reported to be the female incarnation of the Holy Spirit. In this role she seems to have celebrated Mass and to have attracted a certain aristocratic following in the city. While this was certainly extraordinary, Milan was rife with Joachimite apocalyptic prophecy and had a history of home-grown religious dissent going back two hundred years. Guglielma dressed as a member of a religious order, the Umiliati, who were similar to third-order Franciscans; she may not have seemed quite so strange in context as she appears now. She certainly attracted at least a few supporters, including a noblewoman, Maifreda, who on Guglielma's death declared herself to be her successor, calling herself "the Papessa" and celebrating Mass. She was burned at the stake in 1300 (Newman 1995, pp. 182–223; 2010).

## The Confessor and the Religious Woman

Not surprisingly, Guglielma and Maifreda lacked what was becoming the *sine qua non* of female spirituality in the thirteenth century: a male confessor. The twelfth century had seen many such partnerships evolve between religious women and their male supporters, even a particular religious energy unleashed by reforming monastic life in order to include women. The church after the Fourth Lateran Council, however, sought order and clarity, and was most accepting of clearly defined and demarcated forms of religious life. Particularly if they did not wish to affiliate themselves with an existing monastic order, religious women needed the institutional protection offered by a male confessor if they were to avoid the suspicion of the inquisition. Religious devotion, particularly fervent forms of devotion to the Eucharist that would become more powerful as the century progressed, required the intimate involvement of a confessor. When most laypeople received the Eucharist once or twice a year, many religious women made a point of receiving the host multiple times a year, even every day in extraordinary cases.

Male confessors represented access not only to the sacraments, but also, in many cases, to literacy and learning. With a few exceptions, virtually every hagiography of a religious woman in this period was written by her confessor or by another cleric closely connected to him. A religious woman often developed her own theological ideas in concert with, and sometimes in despite of, her university-trained confessor, often moving back and forth between Latin and the vernacular. As with the early days of the monastic movement, a learned confessor sometimes delighted in the "unlearned" wisdom of his female charge, or saw in it signs of the woman's visionary status or special proximity to God, and emphasized the contrast with himself in his saint's life for rhetorical purposes (Coakley 2006). Particularly if the woman was a visionary, it was always safer to be "unlearned," whether or not it was true. In modern terms, the confessor acted in many ways as the woman's public relations representative. In most cases, where a saint's life is the only historical evidence that survives, it is difficult or impossible to see the religious woman apart from the confessor's hagiographical "frame." Hagiography is itself a self-referential and dogmatic genre, and confessors often described holy women in terms of already existing models and fashions of sanctity, or the women preemptively and self-consciously adopted these practices themselves. Increasingly, sanctity and canonization was a documented process centrally regulated by the papal curia, not a matter of local or popular acclaim as it had been in the past, and it was a process in which women's piety was often treated with suspicion. From the thirteenth century, it seems to have become much more difficult for women to get canonized at all: Margaret of England (d. 1192), another pilgrim saint with connections to the Cistercian order, would be the last female English saint until after the Reformation.

The confessor, then, potentially wielded an immense amount of power over the women in his charge. In some cases this became extremely manipulative, and it is hard to avoid suspecting a significant sexual component sometimes existed as well. One of the most horrifying woman–confessor relationships in the entire Middle Ages was that of Agnes of Prague's cousin, Elizabeth of Hungary, and her confessor, the inquisitor Conrad of Marburg. Like Agnes, Elizabeth became a third-order Franciscan who opened a hospital on her husband's death. Conrad obtained a promise of Elizabeth's complete obedience and her refusal to marry again, against the intentions of her family; he isolated her from her children and frequently beat her. Elizabeth died in 1231 at the age of only 24, perhaps as a result of her extreme fasting (see Figure 8.3). Her body was said to emit a miraculous oil, a trait of some Byzantine saints. Canonized only four years later, she was the exception that proved the rule of the clerical mistrust of potential women saints: her royal status and her submissive relationship with Conrad combined to pave the way (Elliott 2004, pp. 85–116). Not all religious women were this desperately abject, of course, and in negotiating such a complex relationship over the course of years or even decades, many women were perfectly capable of managing and even manipulating their confessors in their turn.

More positively, the thirteenth century would see the integration of the friars into already existing networks of women's religious houses. In some of these cases, the women religious could be said to have seniority, while the friars were adapting to an environment far from their roots in urban Italy. England, for example, was still overwhelmingly rural, and when a woman could not join a traditional order, she tended to become an anchoress in the tradition of Christina of Markyate: enclosed but hardly alone, often attached to a parish church, under some form of episcopal oversight, and usually with the support of her local community, financial and otherwise. The ratio of women to men who became anchorites reached four to one in the thirteenth century. Anchoresses often received royal and aristocratic support, particularly benefiting from Henry II's penitential stance after the murder of Thomas à Becket. His grandson Henry III was a friend of Loretta the Countess of Leicester, who appears to have been an anchorite for 45 years, between 1219 and 1265 (Warren 1985, pp. 18, 147, 166–167).

Between 1200 and 1230, a set of texts were written and incorporated into a larger body of work now collectively known as *Ancrene Wisse*, or "A Guide for Anchoresses." Written in the English of the West Midlands, with the occasional Norse and Welsh word thrown in, the work appears to have been written for three sisters, perhaps associated with Limebrook Priory on the modern Welsh border, perhaps by a Dominican, perhaps by the Augustinian canons at Wigmore Abbey (Savage and Watson 1991, pp. 12–15; Wellesley 2021, pp. 229–234). The work outlines the women's devotional regimen and then turns to practical pastoral council, much of which focuses on the dangers of gossip and distraction. Envisioning a cell with two curtained windows, one by which the religious woman could see the high altar in church, the other the "parlor" window to the outside world, the author counsels, "Love your windows as little as you possibly can" (Savage and Watson 1991, p. 66; Jones 2019). Legally

**Figure 8.3** Elizabeth of Hungary, altarpiece by Pietro Nelli, Bonnefantenmuseum, Maastricht. *Source:* Ophelia2 / Wikimedia Commons / Public domain.

dead though she may have been, this suggests a certain amount of foot traffic to and from the parish church past the anchorite's cell, and that she was only separated from her local community in certain, particular ways. When the Franciscans arrived at nearby Hereford in 1224, they seem to have adopted *Ancrene Wisse* themselves for use as confessors, spreading the use of the text.

## Women and the Cistercians

For women Cistercians, the thirteenth century saw the institutional regulation of women's houses in the order, but also, by default, their official recognition by the Cistercian general chapter. From 1213, women could not enter Cistercian houses without contributing financially to their upkeep, while any future Cistercian nunneries were to be enclosed and required the permission of the chapter (Burton and Kerr 2011, pp. 51–52). Nevertheless, the order continued to grow through the first half of the century, particularly in France, which, like England, was more rural than the Low Countries and Italy. In fact, women's houses may have been more popular than men's foundations in the thirteenth century (Berman 2018, p. ix). From 1228, women's communities in the Cistercian order had a simple but distinctive woolen habit – an undyed cowl with a black veil. They were to be visited annually by a member of the order. In 1244, a visitation revealed that, at the extremely aristocratic convent at Las Huelgas, its abbesses were blessing, preaching homilies, and hearing confession – a regular occurrence in a previous age, but now suspect practice to the papacy. From 1250, the papacy required that abbots should conduct these visitations; some Cistercian abbesses also took up the task, claiming to be better representatives of the women's interests. Several of the great heiresses of France, such as Isabella of Chartres, her daughter Matilda of Amboise, and Matilda "the Great" of Courtenay, were all conspicuous monastic benefactors, particularly of women Cistercians (Burton and Kerr 2011, p. 95; Berman 2018, pp. 18–30, 73–99). This culture of religious donation was, if anything, strongly encouraged by fragile French kings in the first half of the twelfth century as a means by which to check the encroaching territorial ambitions of their barons.

It could not have hurt the Cistercians that the most powerful woman of her day was a particularly generous patroness of the order. Blanche of Castile (d. 1252) was the daughter of Alfonso VIII of Castile and Eleanor of England and the granddaughter of Eleanor of Aquitaine (Grant 2016). Blanche was personally chosen by her ailing grandmother as the guarantee of peace between England and France, according to legend because Eleanor thought her sister Urraca too difficult a name for the French court to pronounce. "Blanche" was something of a misnomer for a woman who certainly was not blonde and who seems to have spoken Castilian with her household throughout her life. Married in 1200 at the age of 12, she and Louis VIII grew up in the court and in the shadow of Louis' father, Philip Augustus. Philip's relationship with the church was often tempestuous. The Henry VIII of his day, for reasons that still remain obscure Philip rejected his queen, Ingeborg of Denmark, for his chosen wife, Agnes of Meran, whom he sought for 10 unsuccessful years to legitimate. Meanwhile, Blanche's own marriage with Louis was a happy one, and predominantly in the years while Philip remained king, she bore at least 12 children.

In 1223 Philip died, and both Louis and Blanche were anointed and crowned king and queen. In the next year, as her husband besieged the city of La Rochelle, Blanche organized a penitential procession in which she, her niece Berengaria, and Queen Ingeborg walked from the cathedral at Notre Dame to the Cistercian women's community at St. Antoine-des-Champs: a bravura display of public theater, rewarded when her husband succeeded in capturing the city. Only two years later, in 1226, Louis would die on crusade in the south of France, leaving Blanche as regent for their surviving eldest son, Louis IX. Louis IX trusted his mother to rule for much of his life, leaving Blanche as regent when he went on crusade in 1248 (Grant 2016, pp. 133–145). She died in 1252, having lived for 50 years at the center of the French court, for nearly 30 of those years as a ruling queen.

Throughout her long career, Blanche was known for her particular patronage of Spanish clergy. She had something of a special relationship with the Dominicans, for example, who founded their house of St. Jacques in Paris at that time. In 1229, ironically to protect church property from a Carnival riot in which two people were killed, Blanche escalated a confrontation with the university in Paris which saw many of the masters leave the city temporarily. Pope Gregory IX eventually sided with the Paris masters and matters were resolved, but in the meantime the Dominicans seem to have stepped into the vacuum created by their absence. In her lifetime, Blanche and Louis patronized the making of three lavishly illustrated "moralized bibles," a particular style of biblical interpretation then popular in Paris in the wake of the Fourth Lateran Council. She had made at least two psalters, the Leiden Psalter and the so-called "Blanche Psalter," pointing to her level of Latin education and perhaps to her interest in the exegesis and Islamic and Jewish science of her homeland. The opening illumination in the Blanche Psalter depicts three astronomers with an astrolabe, referring to texts in Arabic. Although both Philip and Louis IX are usually known for their intolerance toward the Jews in France at this time, in 1240 Blanche sat as judge in a strange "trial of the Talmud," which seems to have been instigated by the suspicions of Gregory IX. Interestingly, however, this trial took place in a royal court with Blanche in the role normally occupied by the king, and all charges against the Talmud were dismissed (Grant 2016, pp. 127–129, 304).

At the same time as her continued patronage of the Dominicans, Blanche, the daughter of the founders of Las Huelgas, founded and endowed three new Cistercian women's communities in France, one of which she named in honor of Mary, Queen of Heaven, in direct imitation of the Spanish Cistercians (Grant 2016, pp. 215–218). This is all the more striking because Blanche had come to France as a bride with no inherited property in the country to donate: over time, she gifted the rents and tithes of particular cities placed within her control to monastic communities, gradually building up their endowment, which the nuns then further developed and consolidated (Berman 2018, pp. 100–149). In the case of one house, Blanche overrode her husband's wishes in order to found it. In the case of her favorite foundation, Mabuisson, she built a house of her own on the grounds and placed her enormous copper tomb in the middle of the nuns' choir. In 1244, to general consternation, she appears to have foisted herself and her considerable entourage upon the Cistercian General Chapter. Blanche played a significant role in the negotiations leading up to the acquisition of the relic of the Crown of Thorns from the Venetians. With her son Louis, she sponsored the construction of Sainte-Chapelle, in whose famous stained glass the Castilian crest is ubiquitous. Sainte-Chapelle's distinctive shape may have been inspired by that of the martyrs' chapel, the Cámara Santa, in Oviedo (Cohen 2015, pp. 120–121). The ceremonial procession by which the relic was installed in Sainte-Chapelle followed the same itinerary of the queens' 1224 penitential progress, but in reverse. A yellow castle on a red ground, Blanche's crest can also be seen in the north rose window of Chartres Cathedral, which she commissioned (see Figure 8.4).

Blanche of Castile's long career combined monastic patronage with the support of the clergy, particularly through the French court, and support of the university in Paris. Exquisite manuscripts, churches, and monastic foundations proclaimed the special piety but also the cultural preeminence of the French court. Both Blanche's son and daughter would be declared saints: Louis IX (d. 1270), the only French king to be canonized, and Isabelle de France (d. 1270), who declared her vocation after two potential royal marriages collapsed. In contrast with their mother, both Louis and Isabelle affiliated themselves with the Franciscans, a sign of the order's meteoric rise in popularity over the course of the thirteenth century. Like Agnes of Prague, Isabelle founded a Franciscan women's house, devoting herself to care of the poor, while Louis IX popularized belief in "the king's touch" to cure certain skin diseases (Coatsworth and Owen-Crocker 2018, pp. 175–178, 241–244; Field 2020). Royal women like Agnes, her sister Anne in Silesia, Elizabeth of Hungary, and the Polish princesses Salome (d. 1268) and Cunigunda (d. 1292), used Franciscan devotion in public ritual and private practice. In these cases, Franciscan poverty and the glamour of royalty were combined and mutually reinforcing, rather than mutually exclusive, categories.

The twelfth century had seen two new Marian feasts added to the church calendar: the Visitation and the Immaculate Conception of the Virgin. In Rome, the twelfth-century apse mosaic of the great church of Santa Maria in Trastevere depicted Christ crowning the Virgin,

**Figure 8.4** The north rose window of Chartres Cathedral. *Source:* Andreas F. Borchert / Wikimedia Commons / CC BY-SA 3.0.

addressing her in language from the Song of Songs. Two hundred years later, the first Franciscan pope, Nicholas IV (r. 1288–1292) remodeled the apse mosaic of Santa Maria Maggiore also to depict the Coronation of the Virgin. This theme became immensely popular in European devotional art in this period, with the Virgin over time looking less regal and more the young and humble girl (Gold 1985, pp. 43–75). Depictions of the Coronation of the Virgin sometimes placed Mary between Christ and the Father in a quasi-Trinitarian arrangement which emphasized the longstanding historical association between the Virgin and the Holy Spirit. Later devotional art sometimes depicted two Trinitarian groupings, one with the Father, Son, and the individual (female) soul, another with the Virgin's mother Anne, Mary herself, and the Christ Child (Hamburger 1997, pp. 148–150; see Figure 8.5). Women like Guglielma of Milan and Na Prous Boneta, who had no access to the debates raging in the universities between the Franciscans and Dominicans over the Immaculate Conception, may have been influenced instead in their beliefs by devotional art (Newman 1995, pp. 182–223). From this period onwards, Marian images, some of which were said to perform miracles, became an extremely common feature of medieval urban life: not only in churches but in manuscripts, paintings, frescoes, statues, and ceramics in the city streets (Rubin 2009; Russakoff 2019).

## Beguines and Penitents

Faced with such royal paragons of virtue, what was an ordinary woman to do? As the traditional orders firmed up their entrance requirements and were increasingly dominated by the aristocracy, a new kind of women's religious life emerged in the diocese of Liège in the Low Countries: the beguines. Where the name comes from remains extremely obscure. Sometimes attributed to a woman, Begga, or to the hermit Lambert le Bègue, "beguine" could also derive from the undyed wool that the women wore, or from a vernacular word for "muttering," a popular swipe at the women's practice of private prayer (Van Engen 2005, p. 21). They were known by a variety of names: *filles-Dieu, pinzochere, bizoke, bona femina, humiliatae, conversae.* Beguines could be any age, from young women to elderly widows, and lived in many different kinds of community: individual houses with only a few other women, groups of houses together in certain designated quarters of the city, or, at the height of the movement from 1230, massive, purpose-built "court beguinages," which con-

**Figure 8.5** The Virgin and Christ with St. Anne, Archbishopric Museum, Olomouc Museum of Art. *Source:* Zde / Wikimedia Commons / CC BY-SA 4.0.

tained thousands of women (see Figure 8.6). The beguines did not require the entry fees of a conventional monastic house, opening the lifestyle to a broader range of women. The wealthier among them could keep private property without surrendering it permanently to the church. Rather than with any kind of landed endowment, many beguines supported themselves doing textile work: preparing wool, spinning, or later, making the lace for which the Low Countries became renowned. Since only married women and widows were legal adults with the power to open or to run businesses, they were necessarily important for the continuance of a movement so closely connected to commerce. At the same time, young women could enter beguine households and leave them to marry without making or breaking formal vows.

The beguines combined practical charity, a lay identity with an ambiguous institutional status, and an often visionary spirituality, usually focused on the Eucharist and the sufferings of Christ. Many proudly invoked the tradition of the biblical Martha, alongside the contemplative Mary. In fact, the union of the active and contemplative lives seems to have been a large part of their appeal, as it had been for the Premonstratensians a century before. Sometimes called a "women's movement," the beguines had no internal organization and were hardly coordinated among themselves, varying locally by region, vernacular language, and diocese, from the Low Countries to the cities on the Rhine (Simons 2001, p. 112). Beguine life and spirituality coexisted with, and sometimes blended into, other existing forms of women's religious life: Poor Clares, third-order Franciscans and Dominicans, Augustinians, Premonstratensians, and Cistercians, even traditional Benedictines. Beguines could draw their confessors from any order where they found support. Conversely, in a region like Champagne on the edge of the Low Countries, where the counts had sponsored famously lucrative fairs in the mid-thirteenth century, Cistercian women's

**Figure 8.6** The beguinage at Bruges. *Source:* FAO Forestry / Flickr / CC BY-SA 2.0.

foundations mimicked beguine communities. The nuns ran leper hospitals, houses for reformed prostitutes, and *domus Dei*, with urban rents making up virtually all of their income (Lester 2011).

There is no question that the beguines were a response to many of the same socio-economic conditions affecting the Cistercians and the Poor Clares: an urban context, the need for practical charity for uprooted and desperate peasants, the fact of prostitution, the omnipresence of the textile industry. The beguines also benefited from the lack of centralized religious and political oversight in the Low Countries, which, combined with massive population growth, had helped to encourage the textile industry in the first place. Whether beguines were supported or suppressed often depended on the personal inclinations of individual bishops, the bishops' own relationships with the papacy and the friars, and a host of other factors. Like Clare, virtually all of these women practiced extreme forms of fasting, paired with ecstatic visions and sensations around seeing and receiving the Eucharist which very few men report, least of all the clergy. Many beguines describe extremely personal and conversational visions with Christ himself or with Mary and the saints, in which the beguine often nursed or bathed an infant Christ. Also significant was the growing popular importance of the doctrine of purgatory after the Fourth Lateran Council. Beguine visionary spirituality, asceticism, and intercession for the souls in purgatory drew on the ancient monastic tradition of women as the keepers of family memory, as well as their traditional role in laying out and burying the dead (Newman 1995, pp. 108–138). Many beguines nursed lepers and outcasts and practiced other forms of penitential asceticism, firm in the conviction that their actions released souls from purgatory.

Three lives of the earliest beguines were vividly popularized by Jacques de Vitry, the crusading bishop of Acre, who became a cardinal. The peasant Alpaïs of Cudot (d. 1211) was said to have lived for 40 years only on the eucharistic host. Jacques had a particularly close relationship with Marie d'Oignies (d. 1213), who became a kind of spiritual director for him. In many ways Marie was an archetypical beguine, if such a thing can be said to exist, and it has been argued that Jacques deliberately used her as a model to guide the early beguine movement into safer and more orthodox waters (Neel 1989). A widow with children, she kept her family property but gave up her life of comfort to beg and to nurse the indigent. Eating very little, she described a taste and scent of honey when she received the Eucharist, and, though she was unlearned, she asked Jacques probing questions about the assumption of the Virgin Mary into heaven (McNamara 1993, p. 12; Coakley 2006, pp. 68–88). Yvette or Juetta of Huy (d. 1228) ended her life in a Cistercian habit, but for most of her life lived as a unaffiliated beguine, "always busy like an industrious businesswoman profitably multiplying the accumulated talents" (Jacques de Vitry 2011; Lester 2011, pp. 117–119; Berman 2018, p. 217). An early vocation was thwarted by marriage, and Yvette, poignantly or chillingly, was described as praying for her husband's death. Widowed at 18, she raised her two sons for five more years before she could live as an enclosed woman attached to Huy's house for lepers. Both sons would become Cistercian abbots. Otherwise, Yvette's life is strikingly critical of the regular clergy she encountered, her visions informing her of their sexual peccadilloes, even while she fretted over the rumors one bullying priest spread about her.

The life of Christina Mirabilis, or Christina "the Astonishing" (d. 1228), by Thomas of Cantimpré describes the life of a poor beguine from Sint-Truiden in Flanders in the highly colored terms of the early Christian desert. Wandering and desperate, Christina was said to have sustained herself on milk from her own miraculously lactating breasts. Imprisoned by her friends for supposed insanity, she again lactated, this time with oil. A recluse for nine years, she died and was miraculously resurrected twice. The first time, her body flew up into the rafters of the church, before the saint recounted her spiritual journey through purgatory (King 1987; Brown 2008; Thomas of Cantimpré 2008). Like Yvette, Ida of Leuven (d. after 1231) ended in the Cistercian community at Roosendaal in Flanders after a life spent in the world. Like Christina, locked up by her family for insanity, Ida rebelled against her tight-fisted merchant father by fasting and working to give charity to the poor. Said to receive the stigmata, she had a vision in which she nursed from Christ's breast and from the wound in his side, and was said to change beer into wine. Lutgard of Aywières (d. 1246) was also said to levitate, and undertook three seven-year fasts in her efforts to identify with Christ on the cross and to free souls in purgatory. Partly through the instigation of her neighbor Christina, Lutgard deliberately transferred herself into a French Cistercian community where she would understand no one and have no status, and where, in the last decade of her life, she also went blind (Thomas of Cantimpré 2008).

Juliana of Mont-Cornillon (d. 1259) was an orphan raised on a dairy farm turned leper house, where she tended cows. She may have had some French and Latin instruction there, as well as musical training, and from the beginning was passionately devoted to the observance of the feasts of the church. In a vision, she saw the moon not quite at the full, which she was told by Christ was the present church's calendar. According to her *vita*, after some 20 years in prayer about this vision, Juliana developed both the text and the chant of a new feast of the church to make the calendar complete, in conversation with her confessor, John of Lausanne, and another beguine, Isabelle of Huy. Made prioress of her community, Juliana was the principal casualty of an internecine administrative squabble and an embezzling prior. Taking refuge for a time with another anchoress, Eve of St. Martin, for much of the rest of her life Juliana would wander from monastic community to monastic community. On her death, her companions had a vision in which Juliana was seen to assist Christ with the eucharistic chalice, giving communion to the angels and the saints. Although she did not live to see it, her feast, supported by the lobbying of

Eve of St. Martin, would be eventually received into the church's calendar in 1317 as the festival of Corpus Christi (Rubin 1991, pp. 169–177, 181–196; Newman 2011).

Beatrice of Nazareth (d. 1268) was a Cistercian nun who had been committed to the beguines as a child of seven to learn to read. She joined a Cistercian house founded by her father at 16, became prioress of the community, and died at 68, despite the extreme penitent asceticism attributed to her. Beatrice's treatise, called the *Seven Steps* or *Seven Manners of Love*, was written in Middle Dutch, perhaps the first document written in the first person in the language, and is reminiscent of other beguine authors who envisioned the soul embarking on a sequence of spiritual progressions toward God, first gaining virtues and then rising beyond them (Scheepsma 2004; Van Engen 2020, p. 157). Elizabeth of Spalbeek (fl. 1246–1304) ended her life at the Cistercian house at Herkenrode in Liège with a Cistercian confessor. One of the first people known to receive the stigmata after Francis of Assisi, part of her spiritual discipline was the physical reenactment of the crucifixion of Christ (Brown 2008, pp. 27–50, 191–218).

The only female writer produced by the Carthusians, an order of austere hermits who modeled their lives on the desert fathers, was Margaret of Oignt (d. 1310), who entered the house at Poleteins in her early twenties. She wrote two treatises, her *Mirror* in Latin, and her *Page of Meditations* in the vernacular, and both show affinities with beguine concerns. The *Page of Meditations* describes Christ as a tradesman out to purchase souls, the beautiful savior who "seemed to be a leper." In the tradition of Ambrose of Canterbury, Margaret describes the Passion as a kind of birth, and asks Christ, "Are you not my mother and more than my mother?" In her *Mirror*, she begins by describing Christ holding a book held closed with two clasps, respectively called "God is marvelous in his saints" and "God will be everything to everyone" (Margaret of Oignt 1990).

One of the reasons it is difficult to consider the beguines a "movement" is that many beguines could not seem to find their place within established religious life, even religious life as defined by communities of other beguines. Very quickly, some women who wrote in the vernacular became critical of the beguine commitment to labor, practical charity, and by-rote devotions, several asserting the greater sovereignty of the soul brought to nothing who leaves even the virtues behind. To the inquisition this was teetering on the verge of antinomian heterodoxy, and several of the women writers among the beguines either joined a more conventional order or were forced to as a result of a heretical inquiry. Some women came to accept that the attitude of the heart mattered more than feats of asceticism, or saw even their extreme fasting as ultimately centered on themselves. For others, whatever additional suffering they sought must be understood against a backdrop of successive pregnancies, chronic pain, and untreated mental and physical illness. Beguine vernacular theology attempted to reconcile existing human suffering with the will of a God who is Love, leading several to question the church's traditional teachings on divine judgment and hell. Certainly much beguine writing is mystical; as with Clare of Assisi, abjection, solitude, and suffering existed alongside, or was itself seen as the path to the exaltation and glorification, even the deification, of the soul.

One of the most original of all beguine authors was the poet Hadewijch (fl. 1240s). Despite the fact that she seems to have had some Latin education, she deliberately chose to write in her native Dutch. Beyond her writings, very little about Hadewijch is known, except that she seems to have been evicted from her beguinage and quite possibly charged with heresy. Her poems employ but invert the conventions of courtly love, often describing God and Christ as the willful Lady Love and herself as the masculine lover, in torment and in exile over Love's whims. The poems themselves are contrafacts, which like the "hymnal metre" of Emily Dickinson, were designed to be set to already existing tunes and perhaps sung in small and intimate groups (Fraeters 2014). As much as the more famous Dominican theologian Eckhart or the Dutch mystic Ruusbroec, who was influenced by her, Hadewijch's poems use paradox to evoke spiritual dereliction and a profound sense of the absence of God. The more one reaches to touch Christ, "he is always untouched," even while love grows in the believer like a pregnancy, and, like Jacob, one wrestles with God (Hadewijch 1980, pp. 52–53, 70–74, 221–223, 344–350). The climax of one poem proclaims, "Hell should be the highest name of Love." Elsewhere, she is more wryly resigned to her fate: "although I have no fish,/ I do not want any frog;/ or any elderberries either,/ instead of a bunch of grapes:/ Although I have no love, I do not want anything else,/ whether Love is gracious to me or hostile" (Hadewijch 1980, pp. 333–335, 352–358). Hadewijch both saw God in suffering and sought union with God through suffering; her visions describe a Christ who demands that she not merely become God with God, but remain as one with him in his humanity (Hadewijch 1980, pp. 263–271, 280–282, 302–305).

Around the same time that Beatrice of Nazareth was writing the *Seven Steps*, Mechthild of Magdeburg was composing the collection of texts now known as *The Flowing Light of the Godhead*. Unlike Beatrice's work, *The Flowing Light* was a completely original work in the vernacular with no Latin exemplar. Ironically, the only complete version of the book that survives is the Latin translation made by the Dominicans at Halle under the supervision of Mechthild's confessor, alongside a precious earlier translation of excerpts from Mechthild's original by Henry of Nördlingen (Poor 2004). *The Flowing Light* is a startlingly creative work, also drawing on the language of courtly love and the poetry of the Song of Songs, its style slipping between prose and rhyming poetry. Mechthild describes the human soul as an extension of the overflowing Trinity: "When God could no longer contain Himself, he created the soul and, in His immense love, gave Himself to her as His own." In the presence of God, "in this utter blindness she sees most clearly; in this pure clarity she is both dead and living." These experiences do not last long, however, and as with Hadewijch, the soul is often left bereft.

Mechthild combines vivid, if conventional, devotion to the Virgin Mary and the saints with descriptions of the souls in purgatory, and with fierce critiques of empty or misdirected devotion. While she is loyal to the Dominicans, like Yvette of Huy there are both strong anticlerical and apophatic elements in Mechthild's thought. Like Mary Magdalene in the true desert, the penitent soul "should love nothingness; you should flee somethingness; you should stand alone" (Mechthild of Magdeburg 1998, p. 55). She insists that she wrote her book at Christ's behest, although she was warned that it would be burned. In 1274, the Council of Lyon initiated an inquisitorial investigation into the teachings of certain beguines, and it is possible that this was the moment when Mechthild, at the age of 60, joined the reformed Benedictine community at Helfta, where she remained until her death. She did not appear to be particularly happy or comfortable there, and indeed, may have felt outclassed and uneducated in comparison with the nuns, but she doggedly remained, accepting humility at the last.

The abbess of the community was another Mechthild, called Mechthild of Hackeborn, who had arrived at Helfta at the age of seven. Under her guidance, the literate women at Helfta collectively popularized devotion to the sacred heart of Christ through the works of visionary writers who, unlike the beguines, managed to remain firmly orthodox (Mechthild of Hackeborn 2017; Newman 2020). Mechthild's own collection of visions, her *Book of Special Grace*, describes her entering Christ's heart like a grand house, within which is "a little cottage built of cedar wood," the human soul enclosed within the heart of God. In another vision, she saw her soul "in the form of a little rabbit, asleep in the Lord's lap with open eyes" (Mechthild of Hackeborn 2017, pp. 76–79, 158–159). Like Juliana of Cornillon, Mechthild was also musically and liturgically gifted; at the moment of her death, her community described Christ, "that Cantor above all cantors," singing "a melody for his nightingale" (Mechthild of Hackeborn 2017, pp. 234–235). Perhaps because of the

**Figure 8.7** Gertrude the Great, nineteenth-century Mexican retablo, El Paso Museum of Art. *Source:* Anonymous, Mexican painter/ Wikimedia Commons / Public domain.

intimate fusion of visionary and liturgical spirituality, her book was tremendously successful. Even more influential, however, was the younger nun, her friend Gertrude the Great (1256–1302), the highly educated writer of the Latin treatises *The Herald of God's Loving-Kindness*, her *Spiritual Exercises*, and *The Divine Heart*. Like many beguines, she was said to receive the imprint of Christ's five wounds. Like Mechthild, Gertrude's visions were profoundly centered on the music and liturgy of the office, and her work influenced Teresa of Avila, among others (Shank 1987; Barratt and Stoudt 2010; see Figure 8.7).

Beyond the Low Countries, women who became Franciscan tertiaries had family backgrounds and patterns of piety very similar to the beguines, particularly in Italy. Like the beguines, Douceline of Digne (d. 1274) fasted and went into ecstasies at receiving the Eucharist. With her brother, who was a Franciscan friar, Douceline seems to have shared in the spiritual Franciscan taste for Joachimite prophecy, and they founded a network of houses which brought the beguinage to the south of France. Douceline's life was written by her house's prioress, Felipa de Porcellata, from their house in Marseilles, a city which already was a major center of devotion for the cult of the penitent Mary Magdalene (Blumenfeld-Kosinski 2010, pp. 245–246). In the heart of Rome, the aristocrat Margherita Colonna (d. 1280) fasted, cut her hair, and wore a hair shirt and a habit resembling that of the Poor Clares without being a member of the order. Like Clare, she took the proceeds of her dowry and gave them directly to the poor. She placed herself in domestic service to another woman, Altruda, and gradually gathered a community around her. Her life is one of the few written by a layman – her brother, in fact – with a later version written by one of her followers, only known as Stefania. It is clear that they and perhaps Margherita herself modeled her piety on Isabelle de France, whose Rule for Franciscan Sisters the community adopted in 1285, as well as the newly canonized Elizabeth of Hungary (Giovanni Colonna and Stefania 2017). Less aristocratic was the case of Margaret of Cortona (d. 1297), a former midwife who was a local lord's

**Figure 8.8**  Angela of Foligno. *Source:* XVIIth century print / Wikimedia Commons / Public domain.

mistress for nine years, bearing him a son. Penitent in later life, Margaret also took Mary Magdalene for her model, and was reputed to have said that she wanted to die of starvation in order to feed the poor. She became a Franciscan tertiary with a piety almost frantically centered on the daily reception of the Eucharist (Coakley 2006, pp. 130–148).

One of the most complex of the Italian penitents was the visionary Angela of Foligno (c. 1248–1309), formally canonized in 2013 (see Figure 8.8). Married with children and by all accounts comparatively wealthy, after the deaths of her husband, her children, and her mother from disease, Angela, nicknamed "Lella," became a Franciscan tertiary in her forties. In many ways her life and spirituality parallel the beguines', such as her particular concern for lepers and her many moments of ecstatic contemplation. She lived with a female companion, known only as "M" (Angela of Foligno 1993, pp. 23, 190–191). Like Ida of Leuven, Angela had a vision in which she drank from the side of Christ, as well as a powerful and poignant vision of herself kissing the dead Christ in his sepulcher on Holy Saturday, pressing her cheek tenderly to his. Her occasional violent weeping and shouting bears some similarities to that of Margery Kempe a century later. Angela's cousin and confessor, the Franciscan Arnaldo, transcribed her *Book of the Experience of the True Faithful* out of Umbrian into Latin, claiming he did not add or omit anything she said. Another scribe, known as Brother A., did the same for her *Book* or *Memorial of Divine Consolation*, and in both cases, Angela seems to have exercised a good deal of editorial control over what was written (Angela of Foligno 1993, p. 179).

Like Margherita Colonna in Rome or Catherine of Siena with the Dominicans, Angela gradually gathered a community around her, particularly of Franciscans; she seems to have met and counseled the spiritual Franciscan Ubertino da Casale, although she otherwise avoided open contact with the often heretical movement (Coakley 2006, pp. 111–129). Angela's pilgrimage to Assisi in 1291 formed the culmination of a series of mystical experiences in which the Trinity came to dwell in her soul. But after this climax, like Hadewijch, she alternated between moments of ecstatic understanding and profound periods of dryness, silence, and the absence of God; in a metaphor worthy of Hadewijch, from her dryness Angela described God's presence moving back and forth from her like a sickle (Angela of Foligno 1993, pp. 139–144, 172–184). She described her soul attacked by demons undermining the virtues of her soul, which she likened to a man hanged who cannot die; but then the pressure lifted and she saw God in the darkness: "I then lost the love which was mine and was made nonlove" (Angela of Foligno 1993, pp. 196–202). Her later visions are full of the language of divine "darkness," of the presence of God in all things and all places, even in evil, and of the soul's annihilation in God.

The thirteenth century would see the continuation of the groundswell of women's enthusiasm for religious life which had begun in the twelfth century. Responding to the ongoing presence of popular heresy and religious dissent, however, the papacy sought to regulate women's religious life according to the sacramental system established at the Fourth Lateran Council through the combined efforts of university-trained confessors and, on occasion, the inquisition. However, women's religious life remained persistently amorphous, not least because of the pressures of family life and the nature of a woman's lifecycle. The women best able to live "conventionally" in religious life as nuns were usually more aristocratic by birth, although convents for women often became desperately poor over time. Many women's communities, although not all, were naturally closer to population centers in any case, and in the thirteenth century, very obvious and pressing pastoral needs were emerging in the cities alongside new ways of making a living. The Franciscans were one response to these new socio-economic conditions, but with branches of their order teetering on the verge of heterodoxy themselves, the friars balked at too-close and too-risky affiliations with women. Meanwhile, inspired by Francis's example, many women who for a variety of reasons might not ever be accepted into a convent, along with others who did not even desire to be fully enclosed, wanted to participate in urban religious life all the same.

Ultimately, Clare of Assisi and others like her worked out their own solutions largely on their own, negotiating the inquisition, papal intervention and regulation, and the role of their confessors. On the one hand, it is important to stress the diversity of both women and methods that resulted: even labels like "third-order Franciscans" and "beguines" and "penitents" conceal a dizzying array of individual stories, choices, visions, practices, and regional identities. In addition, a certain amount of retroactive tidying of this complex history has occurred by monastic orders belatedly recognizing in their institutional history the sanctity of women who were only loosely affiliated, if that, with the orders at the time. On the other hand, similarities and continuities do exist within women's piety in the thirteenth century, from the Poor Clares to the beguines, to the French and Iberian Cistercians, to the Italian penitents and the Polish and Hungarian Franciscans. The same kinds of issues were being addressed, particularly the need for practical charity and women's concern for lepers and the poor. Women returned to the same devotional touchstones – the Eucharist and the humanity of Christ, devotion to the Blessed Virgin Mary and the penitent Mary Magdalene – and the same practices of fasting, visionary spirituality, and eucharistic ecstasies. Against this shared religious landscape, however, in which both Christ's humanity and the presence of suffering loomed large, women worked out their salvation in their own words.

## References

Abulafia, D. (2011). *The Great Sea: A Human History of the Mediterranean*. Oxford: Oxford University Press.

Abu-Lughod, J.L. (1989). *Before European Hegemony: The World System A.D. 1250–1350*. New York: Oxford University Press.

Angela of Foligno (1993). *Angela of Foligno: The Complete Works*. Introduction by Romana Guarnieri (trans. P. Lachance, OFM). New York: Paulist Press.

Arnold, J. (2001). *Inquisition and Power: Catharism and the Confessing Subject in Medieval Languedoc*. Philadelphia: University of Pennsylvania Press.

Audisio, G. (1999). *The Waldensian Dissent: Persecution and Survival, c. 1170–1570* (trans. C. Davison). Cambridge: Cambridge University Press.

Barratt, A. and Stoudt, D.L. (2010). Gertrude the Great of Helfta. In: *Medieval Holy Women in the Christian Tradition c. 1100–1500* (ed. A. Minnis and R. Voaden), 453–473. Turnhout: Brepols.

Bell, D.N. (1995). *What Nuns Read: Books and Libraries in Medieval English Nunneries*. Kalamazoo: Cistercian Publications.

Bennett, J., Clarke, E.A., O'Barr, J.F. et al. (ed.) (1989). *Sisters and Workers in the Middle Ages*. Chicago: University of Chicago Press.

Berman, C.H. (2018). *The White Nuns: Cistercian Abbeys for Women in Medieval France*. Philadelphia: University of Pennsylvania Press.

Biller, P. (2010). Women and dissent. In: *Medieval Holy Women in the Christian Tradition c. 1100–1500* (ed. A. Minnis and R. Voaden), 133–162. Turnhout: Brepols.

Blumenfeld-Kosinski, R. (2010). Holy women in France: a survey. In: *Medieval Holy Women in the Christian Tradition c. 1100–1500* (ed. A. Minnis and R. Voaden), 241–265. Turnhout: Brepols.

Bonaventure (1978). *Life of St. Francis* (trans. E. Cousins). New York: Paulist Press.

Brown, J.N. (2008). *Three Women of Liège: A Critical Edition and Commentary on the Middle English Lives of Elizabeth of Spalbeek, Christina Mirabilis, and Marie d'Oignies*. Turnhout: Brepols.

Burr, D. (2001). *The Spiritual Franciscans: From Protest to Persecution in the Century after Saint Francis*. University Park: University of Pennsylvania Press.

Burton, J. and Kerr, J. (2011). *The Cistercians in the Middle Ages*. Woodbridge: Boydell Press.

Bynum, C.W. (1987). *Holy Feast and Holy Fast: The Religious Significance of Food to Medieval Women*. Berkeley: University of California Press.

Clare of Assisi (2006). "Clare: her writings in translation" and her *Forma vitae*. In: *A Companion to Clare of Assisi: Life, Writings, and Spirituality* (trans. J. Mueller), 261–285. Leiden: Brill.

Coakley, J. (2006). *Women, Men, and Spiritual Power: Female Saints and Their Male Collaborators*. New York: Columbia University Press.

Coatsworth, E. and Owen-Crocker, G.R. (2018). *Clothing the Past: Surviving Garments from Early Medieval to Early Modern Western Europe*. Leiden: Brill.

Cohen, M. (2015). *The Sainte-Chapelle and the Construction of Sacral Monarchy: Royal Architecture in Thirteenth-Century Paris*. New York: Cambridge University Press.

Colonna, G. and Stefania (2017). *Visions of Sainthood in Medieval Rome: The Lives of Margherita Colonna by Giovanni Colonna and Stefania*(trans. L. Field; ed. L. Knox and S.L. Field). Notre Dame: University of Notre Dame Press.

Duffy, E. (2002). *Saints and Sinners: A History of the Popes*, 2e. New Haven: Yale Nota Bene.

Dzon, M. (2017). *The Quest for the Christ Child in the Later Middle Ages*. Philadelphia: University of Pennsylvania Press.

Elliott, D. (2004). *Proving Women: Female Spirituality and Inquisitional Culture in the Later Middle Ages*. Princeton: Princeton University Press.

Field, S. (2020). Agnes of Harcourt as intellectual: new evidence for the composition and circulation of the *Vie d'Isabelle de France*. In: *Women Intellectuals and Leaders in the Middle Ages* (ed. K. Kerby-Fulton, K.A.-M. Bugyis and J. Van Engen), 79–95. Woodbridge: D.S. Brewer.

Fraeters, V. (2014). Hadewijch of Brabant and the beguine movement. In: *A Companion to Mysticism and Devotion in Northern Germany in the Late Middle Ages* (ed. E. Andersen, H. Lähnemann and A. Simon), 49–71. Leiden: Brill.

Gennaro, C. (1996). Clare, Agnes, and their earliest followers: from the Poor ladies of San Damiano to the Poor Clares. In: *Women and Religion in Medieval and Renaissance Italy* (trans. M.J. Schneider) (ed. D. Bornstein and R. Rusconi), 39–55. Chicago: University of Chicago Press.

Gold, P.S. (1985). *The Lady and the Virgin: Image, Attitude and Experience in 12th-Century France.* Chicago: University of Chicago Press.

Grant, L. (2016). *Blanche of Castile: Queen of France.* New Haven: Yale University Press.

Gregory IX (2006). Sicut manifestum est (17 September 1228). In: *The Lady: Clare of Assisi, Early Documents*, rev. ed. (trans. R.J. Armstrong), 86–88. New York: New City Press.

Hadewijch (1980). *Hadewijch: The Complete Works* (trans. C. Hart). New York: Paulist Press.

Hamburger, J. (1997). *Nuns as Artists: The Visual Culture of a Medieval Convent.* Berkeley: University of California Press.

de Jacques, V. (2011). Yvette of Huy. In: *Living Saints of the Thirteenth Century* (trans. J.A. McNamara; ed. A.B. Mulder-Bakker), 71–139. Turnhout: Brepols.

Johnstone, P. (2002). *High Fashion in the Church: The Place of Church Vestments in the History of Art from the Ninth to the Nineteenth Century.* Leeds: Mandy.

Jones, E.A. (2019). *Hermits and Anchorites in England, 1200–1550.* Manchester: Manchester University Press.

Karras, R.M. (1996). *Common Women: Prostitution and Sexuality in Medieval England.* New York: Oxford University Press.

Karras, R.M. (2004). "This skill in a woman is by no means to be despised": weaving and the gender division of labor in the Middle Ages. In: *Medieval Fabrications: Dress, Textiles, Cloth Work, and Other Cultural Imaginings* (ed. E.J. Burns), 89–104. London: Palgrave Macmillan.

Kieckhefer, R. (1995). The office of inquisition and medieval heresy. *Journal of Ecclesiastical History* 46 (1): 36–61.

King, M.H. (1987). The sacramental witness of Christina *Mirabilis:* the mystical growth of a fool for Christ's sake. In: *Peace Weavers: Medieval Religious Women*, vol. 2 (ed. J.A. Nichols and L.T. Shank), II.145–II.164. Kalamazoo: Cistercian Publications.

Knox, L.S. (2008). *Creating Clare of Assisi: Female Franciscan Identities in Later Medieval Italy.* Leiden: Brill.

Ladurie, E.L.R. (1979). *Montaillou: The Promised Land of Error* (trans. R. Bray). New York: Vintage.

Lambert, M. (2002). *Medieval Heresy: Popular Movements from the Gregorian Reform to the Reformation*, 3e. Oxford: Blackwell.

Lansing, C. (1998). *Power and Purity: Cathar Heresy in Medieval Italy.* New York: Oxford University Press.

Lester, A.E. (2011). *Creating Cistercian Nuns: The Women's Religious Movement and its Reform in 13th-Century Champagne.* Ithaca: Cornell University Press.

Madigan, K. (2017). *Medieval Christianity: A New History.* New Haven: Yale University Press.

Mantel, H. (2004). Some girls want out. *London Review of Books* 26: 5.

Margaret of Oingt (1990). *The Writings of Margaret of Oingt: Medieval Prioress and Mystic (d. 1310)* (ed. R. Blumenfeld-Kosinski). New York: Columbia University Press.

Mazzaoui, M.F. (1981). *The Italian Cotton Industry in the Later Middle Ages, 1100–1600.* Cambridge: Cambridge University Press.

McNamara, J.A. (1993). The rhetoric of orthodoxy: clerical authority and female innovation in the struggle with heresy. In: *Maps of Flesh and Light: The Religious Experience of Medieval Women Mystics* (ed. U. Wiethaus), 9–27. Syracuse: Syracuse University Press.

Mechthild of Hackeborn (2017). *The Book of Special Grace* (trans. B. Newman). New York: Paulist Press.

Mechthild of Magdeburg (1998). *The Flowing Light of the Godhead* (trans. F. Tobin). New York: Paulist Press.

Miller, M. (2014). *Clothing the Clergy: Virtue and Power in Medieval Europe, c. 800–1200*. Ithaca: Cornell University Press.

Mooney, C.M. (2016). *Clare of Assisi and the Thirteenth-Century Church: Religious Women, Rules, and Resistance*. Philadelphia: University of Pennsylvania Press.

Mueller, J. (2006). *The Privilege of Poverty: Clare of Assisi, Agnes of Prague, and the Struggle for a Franciscan Rule for Women*. Philadelphia: University of Pennsylvania Press.

Mueller, J. (2010). The politics of "infants' milk": Clare of Assisi and the privilege of poverty. In: *A Companion to Claire of Assisi: Life, Writings, and Spirituality*, 65–89. Leiden: Brill.

Neel, C. (1989). The origins of the beguines. In: *Sisters and Workers in the Middle Ages* (ed. J. Bennett, E.A. Clarke, J.F. O'Barr, et al.), 240–260. Chicago: University of Chicago Press.

Newman, B. (1995). *From Virile Woman to WomanChrist*. Philadelphia: University of Pennsylvania Press.

Newman, B. (2010). Agnes of Prague and Guglielma of Milan. In: *Medieval Holy Women in the Christian Tradition c. 1100–1500* (ed. A. Minnis and R. Voaden), 557–579. Turnhout: Brepols.

Newman, B. (2011). The life of Juliana of Cornillon. In: *Living Saints of the Thirteenth Century* (ed. A.B. Mulder-Bakker), 181–302. Turnhout: Brepols.

Newman, B. (2020). Mechthild of Magdeburg at Helfta: a study in literary influence. In: *Women Intellectuals and Leaders in the Middle Ages* (ed. K. Kerby-Fulton, K.A.-M. Bugyis and J. Van Engen), 383–395. Woodbridge: D.S. Brewer.

Pegg, M. (2006). Heresy, good men, and nomenclature. In: *Heresy and the Persecuting Society in the Middle Ages: Essays on the Work of R. I. Moore* (ed. M. Frassetto), 227–239. Leiden: Brill.

Pegg, M. (2008). *A Most Holy War: The Albigensian Crusade and the Battle for Christendom*. Oxford: Oxford University Press.

Poor, S. (2004). *Mechthild of Magdeburg and Her Book: Gender and the Making of Textual Authority*. Philadelphia: University of Pennsylvania Press.

Rubin, M. (1991). *Corpus Christi: The Eucharist in Late Medieval Culture*. Cambridge: Cambridge University Press.

Rubin, M. (2009). *Mother of God: A History of the Virgin Mary*. New Haven: Yale University Press.

Russakoff, A. (2019). *Imagining the Miraculous: Miraculous Images of the Virgin Mary in French Illuminated Manuscripts, ca. 1250–1450*. Toronto: PIMS.

Savage, A. and Watson, N. (ed.) (1991). *Anchoritic Spirituality: Ancrene Wisse and Associated Works*. Mahwah: Paulist Press.

Scheepsma, W. (2004). Beatrice of Nazareth: the first woman author of mystical texts. In: *Seeing and Knowing: Women and Learning in Medieval Europe* (ed. A.B. Mulder-Bakker), 49–66. Turnhout: Brepols.

Shank, L.T. (1987). The God of my life: St. Gertrude, a monastic woman. In: *Peace Weavers: Medieval Religious Women*, vol. 2 (ed. J.A. Nichols and L.T. Shank). Kalamazoo: Cistercian Publications II.239–273.

Simons, W. (2001). *Cities of Ladies: Beguine Communities in the Medieval Low Countries, 1200–1565*. Philadelphia: University of Pennsylvania Press.

Snyder, S.T. (2006). Cathars, confraternities, and civic religion: the blurry boundary between heresy and orthodoxy. In: *Heresy and the Persecuting Society in the Middle Ages: Essays on the Work of R.I. Moore* (ed. M. Frassetto), 241–251. Leiden: Brill.

St. Clair, K. (2019). *The Golden Thread: How Fabric Changed History*. New York: Liveright Publishing Corporation.

Stock, B. (1983). *The Implications of Literacy: Written Language and Models of Interpretation in the Eleventh and Twelfth Century*. Princeton: Princeton University Press.

Thomas of Cantimpré (2008). *Thomas of Cantimpré: The Collected Saints' Lives* (trans. M.H. King and B. Newman; ed. B. Newman). Turnhout: Brepols.

Van Engen, J. (2005). *Sisters and Brothers of the Common Life: The Devotio Moderna and the World of the Late Middle Ages*. Philadelphia: University of Pennsylvania Press.

Van Engen, J. (2020). A woman author? The Middle Dutch dialogue between a "good-willed layperson" and "Meister Eckhart". In: *Women Intellectuals and Leaders in the Middle Ages* (ed. K. Kerby-Fulton, K.A.-M. Bugyis and J. Van Engen), 155–168. Woodbridge: D.S. Brewer.

Wakefield, W.L. and Evans, A.P. (ed.) (1991). *Heresies of the High Middle Ages*, 3e. New York: Columbia University Press.

Warren, A.K. (1985). *Anchorites and Their Patrons in Medieval England*. Berkeley: University of California Press.

Wellesley, M. (2021). *Hidden Hands: The Lives of Manuscripts and Their Makers*. London: Riverrun.

Wickham, C. (2015). *Sleepwalking into a New World: The Emergence of Italian City Communes in the Twelfth Century*. Princeton: Princeton University Press.

Wickham, C. (2016). *Medieval Europe*. New Haven: Yale University Press.

William of Rubruck (2017). *The Mission of Friar William of Rubruck: His Journey to the Court of the Great Khan Mongke, 1253–55* (ed. P. Jackson). London: Routledge.

# 9

# The Political Visionary, 1300–1500

In 1310, in the Place de la Grève in Paris, Marguerite Porete was burned at the stake as a heretic. She had spent the previous two years under house arrest in the city, refusing to testify and thereby incriminate herself before the inquisition. She had seen her book, *The Mirror of Simple Souls*, sometimes called the first mystical text written in French, burned in front of her (Marguerite Porete 1986; 1999). Three years before, the French king Philip IV, sometimes called Philip the Fair, in order to avoid repaying the loans he owed to the Knights Templar, had turned on the wealthy order, accusing it of heresy and of imprisoning and torturing its members. Philip's actions were transparently self-interested – when the king later died young it was said to be divine punishment for what he had done to the Templars – and so Marguerite's execution has to be understood in the context of an ambitious and aggressive king determined to prove himself on the right side of orthodoxy. Dying alongside her was the young man Guiard de Cressonessart, the self-christened "Angel of Philadelphia," who had declared himself her supporter and emissary. It is not clear what, if any, real connection he had to the determinedly solitary Marguerite one encounters in the *Mirror of Simple Souls*.

We know very little about Marguerite Porete except that she was from Hainault, a region whose trading connections and culture would have a profound influence, not least, on the fourteenth-century English court (Warner 2019; Turner 2019). She was French-speaking, she was either aristocratic or keen to present herself as such, she was familiar with the conventions of courtly love in the vernacular, and she had some contact with communities of beguines, if only enough vehemently to reject their piety centered on the Eucharist and on the practice of active charity (Van Engen 2013). While Marguerite's thought was certainly radical, it was not unrecognizably so when compared to some of the more pointed sayings of Hadewijch or Mechthild of Magdeburg, who were themselves marked by something of Marguerite's inward-turning mysticism and institutional iconoclasm.

Whether she was a member of a community or their greatest critic, the year after Marguerite's execution, Pope Clement V and the Council of Vienne made a blanket pronouncement against the beguines. The 1317 papal decree *Cum de quibusdam mulieribus* condemned the beguines explicitly for swearing no oaths of obedience, for wearing a habit while not being under a rule, and for retaining personal property. It recommended that these hypocritical aspects of the beguine way of life be eradicated from the church. Another Clementine decree coming out of the Council of Vienne, *Ad nostrum*, named certain teachings as suspect that point directly to Marguerite's complex and difficult work, particularly her description of the "soul brought to nothing" who has left behind, not only spiritual vices, but also the virtues as well (Marguerite Porete 1999, pp. 17–20; Marin 2010; Piron 2013). The public association of Marguerite with a young man she may not have

*A History of Women in Christianity to 1600*, First Edition. Hannah Matis.
© 2023 John Wiley & Sons Ltd. Published 2023 by John Wiley & Sons Ltd.

known, much less influenced, suggested more reach and organization to Marguerite's teachings than probably existed. Ironically, in the act of publishing its neat list of suspect teachings, it was the Council of Vienne which may well have systematized, publicized, and thus paradoxically created what would later be called the heresy of the Free Spirit (Lerner 1972; Simons 2001, pp. 132–135).

Meanwhile, the Dominican friar Eckhart visited the house of St. Jacques in Paris, where he met one of the inquisitors appointed to vet Marguerite's orthodoxy. As a consequence, Eckhart may well have read *The Mirror of Simple Souls* himself. Whether or not he was directly influenced by Marguerite, however, Meister Eckhart's vernacular sermons were often very pointedly directed at the beguines at home in his congregation in Cologne, as in one sermon which playfully privileges Martha over Mary as a spiritually superior role model, deliberately flouting a thousand years of Christian commonplace (Eckhart 1981, pp. 177–181; Van Engen 2020). Eckhart died before he could be formally declared a heretic by the papacy, and he remains an impish and formidably difficult figure to categorize even today, writing in both Latin and the vernacular, bringing together the spirituality and the mindset of the beguines with the rigor and clarity of scholastic philosophy.

After Marguerite's death, her book was smuggled out of Paris and copied by the Carthusians, its true author forgotten until the twentieth century. Eckhart likewise remains beloved in the Christian mystical tradition to this day. If, therefore, Marguerite was not monumentally different from the broader ecology of the beguine tradition, and her book by itself even considered useful reading by the most notoriously austere of the monastic orders, this suggests that she was ultimately burned as a heretic because, as a solitary woman, she did not have the protection of a confessor or a monastic order behind her at a time when church and state were vying for moral supremacy, most particularly within the city of Paris. The European religious and political landscape generally was less tolerant of the institutional ambiguity hitherto so much a part of beguine identity, while the lurid stories that circulated around the heresy of the Free Spirit increasingly made beguine mysticism sound excessive and dangerous.

Strictly speaking, a great deal of the shape and content of women's piety in the late Middle Ages can be understood in broad continuity with what had come before. As monumental a figure as Catherine of Siena took up the rudiments of a penitent religious life already well established in Italian cities and towns by the fourteenth century, only formally affiliating herself with the Dominican order after she had lived a religious life in her family home for quite some time. What distinguishes Catherine from Franciscan penitents like Angela of Foligno or Margaret of Cortona, however, is that she was overtly political and even nationalistic, at least in her public advocacy for the Sienese, in a way that seems new for the time (Wickham 2016, p. 208). Catherine seems to have had an instinct for how to play what could become a very dangerous game, and certainly she could don a mask of determined naïveté to protect herself in the midst of it. For other women, however, from Marguerite Porete to Joan of Arc, distinctions between religious and political prophecy soon blurred, and visionary simplicity was not enough to prevent them from becoming pawns in a game they could not control (Watt 1997).

## The Late Middle Ages: Crisis and Transformation

For western Europe, the fourteenth century was a time of intense disruption, crisis, and downturn, after the booming two centuries that had come before. Acknowledging that it was a "calamitous" time has led many historians to describe this period as the "autumn of the Middle Ages," marked by the macabre and by decadent and esoteric philosophy (Tuchman 1978; Huizinga 2016; Elliott 2010, p. 30). More recently, scientific data has underscored the interconnected nature of the multiple crises faced by the medieval world (Campbell 2016; McNeill 1976). The sharp drop in the temperature of the European climate in the early years of the century led to widespread crop failure, alongside outbreaks of sheep and cattle disease, culminating in the Great Famine between 1315 and 1322. Meanwhile, the bubonic plague, now thought to have originated in Xinjiang, traveled across the Mongol-controlled Russian steppe to the Black Sea, where Genoa and Venice had turned to trade after the fall of Acre in 1291, amidst an already fragile and faltering economy. The Black Death arrived in 1348, killing between a third and a half of the population of Europe, its presence continuing to linger and re-emerge unexpectedly in subsequent decades. Entire towns vanished or were severely depopulated for more than a century after the plague's arrival, while the piety and spirituality of those who survived understandably were marked by the trauma they had experienced (see Figure 9.1). Once it arrived, there was virtually nothing that anyone could do either to prevent the spread of the plague, or to stop its progress in the infected; with no place of safety, and no traditional solutions which worked, for many it must have felt like the end of the world, while others wondered what had brought such a calamity upon them. Late medieval society reflected these deep stresses and, in some cases, gradually realigned in new directions. Certainly, the arrival of the Black Death and its aftereffects should not be seen either to represent some kind of failure of moral fiber on the part of late medieval civilization generally, or to make inevitable the particular shape of the Reformation and the early modern world.

For the late medieval church, the single event most destructive to its reputation was the Great Schism, which lasted nearly four decades from 1378 to 1417. And yet, while Philip the Fair's abduction of Pope Boniface VIII and the uprooting of the papal court to southern France could be said to be neither party's finest hour, certainly from the perspective of the time the Avignon papacy was not inevitably doomed from the beginning (Falkeid 2017; Rollo-Koster 2015). In many ways Avignon was a more efficient organization from a bureaucratic perspective, with the advantage that it could start from scratch, away from Roman aristocratic politics and an occasionally malarial climate. However, the widespread perception of the papacy as the creature of the French crown destroyed any possibility of it being viewed with neutrality. As a result, both the French crown and the papacy arguably became more sensitive to doctrinal and political threat, further exacerbated by the politics of the Hundred Years' War during the Schism proper. Regardless, when it was customary for the inquisition to hand over obdurate heretics to the arm of the state for corporal punishment, the more closely the inquisition and the crown worked together, the less likely justice was to be restorative and the more likely it was to be violent.

Particularly in late medieval cities dominated by guilds and factions, medieval state power, as in the sumptuary laws which governed fashion and conspicuous consumption, aimed to show people their place and keep them in it. By 1400, for example, the huge increase in urban prostitution had been regulated, it was hoped, through the creation of public brothels (Karras 1996, pp. 35–43; Mazzi 2020, pp. 23–29). And yet, precisely because late medieval cities were complex hives of activity humming with the forces of international trade and travel, social order and control became a much more difficult task realistically to achieve. It is unfortunate but not very surprising, then,

**Figure 9.1** Danse Macabre, Holy Trinity Church, Hrastovlje. *Source:* John of Kastav / Wikimedia Commons / Public domain.

that state-sanctioned violence became a more visible part of medieval urban life, with the increased cooperation of the inquisition. Outbreaks of violence against Jews in German-speaking lands, often as a result of blood libel fantasies in which Jews were thought to torture Christian children or desecrate the eucharistic host, were particularly numerous at the turn of the century, and in later years, tended to occur in connection with the new feast of Corpus Christi, instituted in 1317. These later riots were generally condoned by the crown and the inquisition, which also employed torture more frequently in connection with blood libel rumors. Particularly in the reign of Isabella of Castile, Spain's turn to increasingly vehement anti-Jewish measures would be driven by the head of the Spanish Inquisition, Torquemada. Medieval witchcraft accusations, which emerge in Germany and the Swiss cantons at this time, must be understood as reflective of an ambitious inquisition working closely with state power desiring to impose order on this restless urban context. After the Black Death, the city of Nuremberg, unlike many of its more alpine neighbors, did not have witchcraft accusations, but it did have a pogrom (Stokes 2011). Local religious and political context was determinative.

## A Climate of Suspicion

Likewise, what this increasingly ambitious alliance of church and inquisition meant for women's religious communities was a healthy helping of suspicion but also of opportunity, if they could carefully negotiate the ambiguities present in church legislation with local religious leaders. In 1289, the Franciscan pope Nicholas IV had inadvertently "created" an order of women penitents through a bull which, though it did not formally tie the mendicant orders to their pastoral care in any formal way, did present beguine communities in the Low Countries with enough ratification that the measure could be used as an institutional shield from suspicion (More 2018, pp. 36–62). A manuscript from the turn of the century records a dialogue, in French, between a Dominican and a beguine which affirms their differences and even suggests the superiority of beguine identity (Simons 2001, p. 131). This was then followed a decade later by Boniface VIII's attack on the authority of abbesses in his bull, *Periculoso*. However, the edict was incoherent enough in its terms that it was ultimately very difficult for bishops to know how to enforce it, and was paradoxically ineffective in many places, not least in the Low Countries.

The Council of Vienne darkened the climate of opinion yet again, but as with previous legislation, whether or not it was enforced depended largely on how individual bishops discriminated between "good" and "bad" communities of beguines and religious women. Circles of convents calling themselves "Friends of God" formed in the 1350s along the Rhine, circulating not only beguine literature but the mystical writings of the Dutch Jan Ruusbroec, the German John Tauler, and the ever-present Eckhart. Ruusbroec had certainly read some of the works of Hadewijch at least, but he was very explicit in his condemnation of Marguerite Porete and the Free Spirits, perhaps precisely because, at moments, he could sound very similar to them. Ultimately Ruusbroec faced suspicions surrounding his orthodoxy and was pressured to retire to the community at Groenendaal as a canon in 1343. In practice, beguine communities in the Low Countries continued to increase in membership until the Black Death, which was far more effective in practice as a brake to the movement than papal legislation had been.

By the time the population of Europe had recovered sufficiently to support women's religious communities again, it has been argued that a rolling "crisis of conversion" had gathered momentum in the 1370s and continued for the next 50 years (Van Engen 2005, pp. 18, 32–40). It is possible that the crises of the fourteenth century and the chronic uncertainty of life helped to foster personal and private devotion and an appetite for regular self-examination – something the individual could, in a sense, control – in the face of impending heavenly judgment and the pains of purgatory. By and large, these were ordinary people with no great appetite for mystical experience, yet with a deep desire to engage with their faith nonetheless, who were seeking for ways and means even as the clerical hierarchy was distracted by the politics of the Schism. Certain extraordinary women visionaries remained compelling to the church throughout this period, even though they were often treated with suspicion while they were alive and regularly tested, either by the inquisition or simply by rival clerics they encountered. Safely dead, many of these women were embraced as authentic, sometimes with almost bewildering speed. In fact, since many of these women visionaries spoke against the Schism in one way or another, clergy were concerned to reassert their authority against the charismatic power of these luminaries after the Council of Constance resolved the Schism in 1418 (Coakley 2006, p. 209). Jean Gerson, the chancellor of the University of Paris and the best known of the conciliarists, was famously ambivalent about women visionaries, supporting Angela of Foligno and Joan of Arc but not Bridget of Sweden, according to his influential practice of the discernment of spirits (Anderson 2006).

## Devotion in the Vernacular

In the meantime, most late medieval piety remained firmly focused on vernacular devotional literature and prayer structured by the canonical hours of monastic devotion.

The psalter remained at the heart of all late medieval lay devotion, and was the essential primer for literacy generally. Most laypeople concentrated their devotion on internal groupings of psalms that could be easily memorized over time, such as the seven penitential psalms. In the thirteenth century, elite women such as Blanche of Castile had commissioned luxury manuscripts and Latin bibles from the bookmakers of Paris, who clustered around the cathedral of Notre Dame and the church of Saint-Séverin, near the present-day Sorbonne. Around 1250, these and other bookmakers began to experiment with what would become the medieval "book of hours," a highly flexible compendium of texts that usually included some combination of the Little Office of the Virgin, the Hours of the Cross, the penitential psalms, the gradual psalms or the "psalms of ascents," the litany of the saints, the office of the dead, collections of other intercessions, hymns, and nearly always, calendars and images suitable for meditative devotion. Books of hours became something of an industry in Paris, a "medieval bestseller" and the most widely circulated and produced book of the late Middle Ages (Wieck 1997; Duffy 2006; Reinburg 2012, pp. 20–22). From the fourteenth century, French became the official language of Philip the Fair's crown and chancery, and books of hours throughout Europe increasingly were compiled in the vernacular. These were far more accessible to laywomen, and as such, were immensely popular (see Figure 9.2). Collections of familiar, illustrated texts often served as the gateway to women's literacy, and circulated in huge numbers as gifts and bequests to patrons, clients, friends, family, and monastic foundations. The illuminations themselves could serve as inspiration for nuns' painting or even tapestry made in religious communities, although, precisely because these were often very ordinary and perishable in quality, they have not usually survived except by historical accident (Mecham 2014).

Likewise, when the archbishop of Genoa, Jacobus de Voragine, compiled his collection of saints' lives in the mid-thirteenth century, *The Golden Legend* promptly rocketed to similar levels of universal popularity. Translated into the vernacular, copied, and later printed in huge numbers, *The Golden Legend* reintroduced saints like Margaret of Antioch and Catherine of Alexandria into the bloodstream of late medieval piety, not least as personal names for girls

**Figure 9.2** Book of Hours of Simon de Varie, Koninklijke Bibliotheek. *Source:* Koninklijke Bibliotheek / Wikimedia Commons / Public domain.

(John Capgrave 2011). But it also included a life of the Virgin Mary, and particularly when used in tandem with the books of hours, made Marian piety so ubiquitous and potent a force in the late Middle Ages (Rubin 2009, p. 192). In the Low Countries, the rosary, with its associated prayers that could be said alongside the offices or illuminations in a book of hours, developed from this rich and complex vernacular devotional environment. Late medieval rosary beads were often used in women's religious communities and could depict intricate miniature scenes carved out of boxwood, the so-called "prayer nuts" (Winston-Allen 1997; Hamburger 1997, p. 68; Winder 2020, p. 124; see Figure 9.3). Catherine of Bologna (d. 1463) combined a humanist education with her religious vocation, becoming an Augustinian and then a Poor Clare. Among her voluminous works is the *Rosarium*, a poem on the rosary (Matter 2010). In the circles of the *devotio moderna* in the Low Countries, also called the Sisters and Brothers of the Common Life, men's houses supported themselves through copying books, while the women's communities largely worked in preparing wool, spinning, and textiles. Even in the women's communities, however, individual women often kept personal scrapbooks or *rapiaria*, miscellaneous collections of devotional sayings, prayers, and sometimes of the searching personal reflection and self-examination so central to the ethos of the Modern-Day Devout.

With lay literacy at a high in western Europe, it says something for the commitment of ordinary laypeople to their faith that, overwhelmingly, the books most copied and circulated were vernacular devotional literature. So much was copied, in fact – at least half of all books copied in England, for example, and three quarters of vernacular German and Dutch prose – that one can argue for the general saturation of the market prior to the printing press, which then only reinvigorated

**Figure 9.3** Prayer nut, Kunsthistorisches Museum, Vienna. *Source:* Vassil / Wikimedia Commons / Public domain.

demand immediately prior to the Reformation (Van Engen 2005, p. 77). In combination with the flexibility and personalized nature of the books of hours, for example, this suggests that a high degree of individual agency was possible and, indeed, sought after by many women readers. Women were reading but also writing with increasing frequency, for both personal and commercial reasons. The Teutsche Schulen taught as many as half of the urban children of Bavaria to read and write by 1400 (Mulder-Bakker 2010, p. 315). The mighty Fugger banking dynasty rose to prominence in the fourteenth century through the business acumen of the widows of the family, while a busy fifteenth-century aristocrat like Margaret Paston wrote frequently to her absent husband, sometimes with a secretary, sometimes without, and on paper rather than expensive parchment (Wickham 2016, pp. 191–192; *The Paston Letters* 2008; Bell 1995, p. 16). When both her father and her husband died in 1380, Christine de Pizan (d. 1430) became a copyist in Paris and then a writer, in 1405 publishing *The Book of the City of Ladies*, her apologia in defense of women's capacity for moral action. Her last published work would be a defense of Joan of Arc.

In counterpoint with the enthusiasm for devotional literature existed a strong vein of anticlerical discourse, of which Chaucer's Pardoner or Boccacio's disreputable friars are only the most famous examples. In England, the followers of John Wyclif were nicknamed "Lollards" for their practice of private prayer. Many of Wyclif's teachings represented an attack on the special prerogatives of the clergy, not least his promotion of vernacular scripture and, indeed, of celibacy. For this reason, Lollards were treated as radicals and anarchists by religious and political authorities. But these attitudes were widely shared, and as with earlier heretical groups, a particularly pious laywoman like Margery Kempe knew she could find herself easily confused with a Lollard. In England, the Constitutions of Arundel, published between 1407 and 1409, represented a form of censorship targeting preaching and scripture in the vernacular in an effort to suppress the Lollards. However, the measure was ultimately ineffective precisely because it was too clumsy actually to find the Lollard needle in the general devotional haystack. Certainly, it had no effect in private religious houses or their immediate circles of lay followers, and may have been intended to guide rather than inhibit vernacular popular devotion (Kerby-Fulton 2006, pp. 260, 278). After the Constitutions, would-be church reformers often turned instead to the writing of vernacular hagiography, hoping to teach rather than to deter, and the result is a surprising number of depictions of "ordinary" lay-people trying to live holy lives amidst complicated and challenging family dynamics. This element of religious soap opera, always latent in the hagiography of women saints in particular, appears to have been very appealing to readers in the fifteenth century and perhaps aimed to target lay women readers (Winstead 2020).

The two centuries between 1300 and 1500 embrace the transition from the medieval to the early modern world. They have often acted as foils to one another, the disasters and the "decadence" of the late medieval world in contradistinction to the "rebirth" or the rational inquiry of the early modern. Any such controlling distinctions blur or disappear, however, the closer one comes to the historical individual whose lifespan extended across neat lines of historical periodization. Exact contemporaries are frequently assigned to "medieval" or "early modern" historiographical narra-tives, respectively, based on anachronistic, contemporary criteria. Groups such as the Lollards or the *devotio moderna* are often viewed as "pre-reformers," without locating these groups within their own time, thereby underscoring the seeming inevitability of the Reformation (Oberman 1967; Somerset and Kerby-Fulton 2005). As a result, "pre-reformation" narratives stress certain aspects of these groups' identity at the expense of others which do not fit the "Reformation" paradigm, such as the Lollards' encouragement of lay celibacy or the Modern-Day Devout's use of liturgical prayer. The increasing power of monarch and crown, the use of the vernacular alongside a growing sense of national identity, and a rising middle class with international connections and mercantile business values are characteristic across the period, as is the occurrence of a social phenomenon like witch-hunting. The popularity of devotional literature can be understood as allied with, rather than distinctive from, mercantile values, salving the guilt of a new group of *nouveau riche* and act-ing as a kind of self-help or self-improvement literature. Flashes of the "interiority" and "individu-alism" usually thought characteristic of the Reformation can be seen throughout the fourteenth and fifteenth centuries, although the one does not necessarily follow from the other (Bryan 2008). Even such hallowed moments as Luther's conversion experience and his description of justifica-tion by faith can be understood as the transformation of ideas common in earlier, medieval wom-en's mysticism, transmitted to the early modern world via the likes of Ruusbroec and the German mystic Tauler.

Likewise, the German Heinrich Suso (1295–1366) had close friendships with other women reli-gious, and indeed, seems to have found his particular vocation as a nuns' priest. What makes Suso distinctive, in fact, is precisely how many ways he seems to mirror women's spirituality rather than men's, particularly in his use of the language of bridal mysticism, his devotion to Mary as "the rose without thorn," and his experience of eucharistic miracles (Bynum 1987, pp. 102–105). There is some debate about whether his life, often called the first German autobiography, was in fact written by Suso himself or by the nun Elspeth Stagel (Williams-Krapp 2004). Her life in turn was written by Johannes Meyer, another nuns' priest and the great chronicler of Observant Dominican reform in women's communities in Germany. His history of reform is, at the same time, a sister-book, describing such unforgettable personalities as Elisabeth Meringer (d. 1422), who "did not like noise" and who, after her death, appeared in a vision to the nun who had inherited Elisabeth's bedstead and had the temerity to erect a private altar. "I decorated this bedstead with great poverty and you have erected such a construction with clutter," the apparition declared, and knocked over the altar. Clara of Ostren was one of the original 13 founders of her community, who for the 50 years of her career taught her nuns to sing. The chronicle records her allegorical interpretation of the solfeggio scale, which for sheer inventiveness rivals *The Sound of Music* (Jones 2019).

Margaret Ebner (d. 1351), a Dominican nun in the community of Maria Medingen northeast of Augsburg, was another figure who brought beguine spirituality into a safer and more conventional context. She had entered the convent as a child, but like Julian of Norwich, mortal illness in her twenties and an encounter with one of the "Friends of God" left a profound spiritual mark upon her. She seems to have been deeply ill for much of the rest of her life, in fact, her illness perhaps compounded by fasting and asceticism, which combined to isolate her often from her community. In her thought, the soul does not leave the virtues behind, but the concepts of "Silence" and "Binding Silence" are central, along with such common beguine devotions as nursing the infant Christ. From 1332, Margaret's spiritual director was Henry of Nördlingen, who sent her Mechthild of Magdeburg's work in its German translation in 1345. Margaret's community venerated her enough for her to be buried in the chapter room itself, and after her death her book, *Revelations*, was translated into Latin as part of the unsuccessful push for her canonization (Koch 2010; Schmidt 1993). She would be beatified in 1979.

## The Angelic Speech of Bridget of Sweden

Far more widely known, and the only woman canonized in the fourteenth century, was the charismatic and controversial figure of Bridget of Sweden (1303–1373). Born Birgitta Birgersdotter, she was a noblewoman who married the queen's councillor, Ulf Godmarsson. She seems to have been accustomed to a royal court circle small enough that a single assertive personality could make a significant impact. As well as receiving a high level of musical training, Bridget managed her husband's estates, bore him eight children, and went with him on pilgrimage to Santiago de Compostella in northern Spain in 1341. On this journey she would have seen some of the most famous Christian shrines in Europe, including Mary Magdalene's cult center at Vézelay. When she was widowed, Bridget became a third-order Franciscan, and then launched upon her prophetic career with the same degree of managerial authority she had employed in her earlier life. She founded the double religious community at Vadstena, the first "Bridgettine" house, which encouraged its nuns to pursue poverty, with the significant exception of acquiring and copying books, particularly their own liturgical books (Hedlund 2013; Coatsworth and Owen-Crocker 2018, pp. 45–48).

Like Hildegard, Bridget set her visions to liturgical music. In place of the more usual excerpts of devotional writings, she meant the community to recite her *Sermo angelicus* at matins (Zieman 2005). Bridget described over seven hundred visions, some of which she had had as a child and many, she said, received directly from Christ. She had a particularly intimate devotion to the Virgin Mary, with whom she bathed and swaddled the infant Christ, and whom, she argued, was "co-crucified" with Christ (Dzon 2017, pp. 186–245). To Christ himself Bridget was "my bride and my channel," mediating his authority and calling in particular for a return of the papacy from Avignon to Rome, where she went on pilgrimage when she left Sweden in 1349. Her confessors, particularly Alfonso of Jaén, helped to edit and publish her visionary corpus, and it was perhaps a desire to check their work that prompted a then middle-aged Bridget to take up Latin (Voaden 1999, pp. 74–94). Her calls to resolve the Schism had made her political, not to mention her support of the English claim to the French throne during the Hundred Years War. When she died, she was under simultaneous review both for sainthood and by the inquisition.

In England, however, Bridget was adopted as a star supporter of the Lancastrian dynasty. Still sensitive about Henry Bolingbroke's usurpation of the crown from Richard II, in 1415, the young Henry V founded a double house of Bridgettine sisters and priests at Syon Abbey. Syon was virtually around the corner from the Carthusians at Sheen Priory, itself founded the year before on a former royal manor of King Richard's. Women at Syon outnumbered men in the community by more than two to one, some 60 women to 25 men, and from the beginning, Syon Abbey was meant to be a prominent royal institution. Henry VI continued his father's patronage, and Syon's chapel was even larger than its near-contemporary, the famous chapel at King's College, Cambridge.

Syon had the budget, therefore, to support the finest library in a women's community in late medieval England. One third of all surviving books traced to English women's communities come from Syon, which actively promoted the use of the vernacular, again, in a spirit of Lancastrian patriotism and as a discouragement to Lollardy (Schirmer 2005). It was there that Catherine of Siena's *Dialogue* would be translated into English as *The Orchard of Syon*, her thought in somewhat muted form (Despres 1996; see Figure 9.4). Many of Syon's books were copied by the sisters themselves: Anne Charles, Swedish by birth, is the first named women scribe, present from the abbey's founding. In the sixteenth century there are several recorded nuns and scribes, many of them humanist-educated: Katherine Wey (d. 1509), Elizabeth Woodford (d. 1523), Agnes Wriothesley (d. 1529), and Mary Nevel (d. 1557/8) (O'Mara 2013; Bainbridge 2010). Its prioresses were often noble, such as Matilda Newton, who had been a nun at Barking before Syon's founding. Matilda would hold on grimly to Bridget's original vision of the abbess's maternal authority over her community in the teeth of papal efforts to take it away from her (Warren 1985, p. 178; Warren 2001, pp. 3–29; Ellis 1996). Anne de la Pole (d. 1501) was the seventh prioress and granddaughter of Cecily, Duchess of York, who left her books to her. In the sixteenth century, the noble, educated sisters Dorothy, Susan, and Eleanor Fettyplace all found their home in Syon, one as a widowed vowess of the house and two as nuns (Erler 2002, pp. 85–99).

Bridget was hugely influential as a model of sanctity to late medieval women, partly because she was the only new female saint in the fourteenth century, but also because, as non-royal, a mother, and a widow, she was someone with whom laywomen could easily identify. Despite the fact that, by any standards, she was not a terribly accurate seer, others would try to imitate her distinctive mix of the prophetic and the political. There is the bizarre case of Marie Robine (d. 1399), who became a papal representative of the Avignon papacy to the French king Charles VI, only to turn on the pope she had once served as the result of a vision (Blumenfeld-Kosinski 2010, p. 252). Bridget's visions were translated into German in the city of Lübeck, where they inspired Dorothy of Montau (d. 1394), and where they would later be printed and circulated by the cities of the Hanseatic League. Dorothy was a Prussian laywoman, married with nine children to a probably abusive husband, who accused her of begging for the poor rather than doing housework. On his death in 1390, she threw herself fully into extreme fasting, as well as the physical enactment of the crucifixion. Accused of Free Spirit heresy, she quickly found herself a confessor, the dean of the

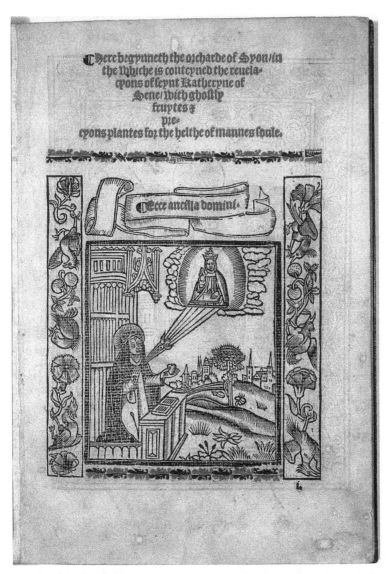

**Figure 9.4**   Catherine of Siena's Orchard of Syon, published by Wynken de Worde, 1519. *Source:* Wellcome Collection / Wikimedia Commons / CC BY 4.0.

cathedral, John Marienwerder, and was fully enclosed there. She modeled herself on the maternal piety of Bridget, including an experience of mystical pregnancy. While her initial canonization bid failed in 1404, she would become the patroness of the Teutonic Knights and a kind of patron saint of Prussia. She was canonized in 1976 (Stargardt 2010; Suerbaum 2014).

## The Political Visionary: From Catherine of Siena to Joan of Arc

Less obviously, Bridget was a model for the completely original personality of Catherine of Siena (1347–1380). Born Caterina di Giacomo di Benincasa, she was said to be the twenty-fourth child of her mother, called Lapa. In fact, Catherine was one of a set of twins; Lapa kept Catherine to breast-feed personally, while her twin was given to a wet nurse and did not survive. In later life Catherine would use a very tender image of Christ as wet nurse, taking medication that the child cannot bear directly. One wonders, however, what the psychological toll of the loss, even in infancy, of a twin might have been, compounded by further deaths in her family from the plague (Catherine of Siena 1989, p. 52). Certainly the relationship with Lapa was intense but not comfortable for either mother or child, with Catherine her mother's favorite but, as a consequence, given little room to breathe. In the succinct summation of Sigrid Undset, "Lapa loved her immeasurably and understood her not at all" (2009, p. 7).

Of the large extended family, Catherine was most close with her elder sister, Bonaventura, who encouraged Catherine to put on more feminine clothes and was something of a moderating influence on the girl's emerging asceticism. But Bonaventura died in childbirth just as Catherine was entering puberty, an unfortunate juxtaposition of circumstances that had the opposite effect of what Bonaventura had perhaps intended (Bynum 1987, p. 167). Catherine cut her hair and shut herself away, refusing to sleep or eat or tend to her illness until she was commanded by her confessor to eat at the family table. She insisted on serving the family as a maid, however, and lived for the next several years in a cupboard under the stairs as a kind of in-house anchorite, where she learned to read. This period seems to have lasted for quite some time, and it may have been unease over Catherine's unaffiliated state which later prompted her Dominican confessor to backdate when she took the habit of a Dominican penitent, a *mantellata* (More 2018, pp. 75–77).

In 1373, Catherine inherited her confessor, Alfonso of Jaén, immediately after he had compiled Bridget of Sweden's canonization dossier. In the next year she met the Dominican who would become her foster son, Raymond of Capua, prior of Santa Maria sopra Minerva in Rome, who himself had known John Marienwerder in Prague. Like Angela of Foligno, Catherine had at that time gathered a circle of clergy around her, with whom she talked and to whom she gave advice. In the midst of these years she described a series of powerful spiritual experiences, initiations into the suffering of Christ, which she described as her "mystical espousal" and her "mystical death," and in which she received invisible stigmata. In 1377, she became politically active when she interceded to lift the papal interdict over Siena. Perhaps again modeling herself on Bridget, she founded a women's religious community but she never stayed there, and in the next year she threw herself into writing what would become *The Dialogue*.

What was meant by Catherine miraculously learning to write – the physical act or whether she was granted *auctoritas* to dictate her teachings – is unclear (Mooney 2013; Luongo 2020). Regardless, like Dante she spoke or wrote in her native Tuscan, and her writing style reflects her conversational, oral milieu: looping back again and again to certain governing metaphors, rather than marching through a linear, progressive structure. Like Dante, while she could not but be aware of the newly canonized Aquinas, the influence of Augustine's thought on *The Dialogue* is also palpable (Catherine of Siena 1989, pp. 56, 102). Perhaps her most famous image is that of Christ the living bridge extending over a great river, the only means by which the Christian can cross: because Christ took embodied form, the body for Catherine becomes the way and the path (Warren 2010, pp. 30, 37). Real tension, and at best fruitful counterpoise, exists in Catherine's thought between the freedom and burning desire of the soul for God, whom Catherine frequently likens to a great sea, and the body's own limitations. The soul only increases in desire the closer the soul gets to God, but the soul sees only through the instrument of the body. Catherine frequently returns to the image of a tree planted within certain bounds within which it must stay: "stay his, then, within self-knowledge, and don't be caught outside yourselves" (Catherine of Siena 1989, p. 125).

It is perhaps not surprising that Catherine's own body bore the brunt of so much focused energy and passion. Sometimes called "the social mystic," the active and contemplative aspects of Catherine's life, as with many beguines, blur and blend together. The author of some 385 letters,

**Figure 9.5** The grave of Catherine of Siena, S. Maria sopra Minerva, Rome. *Source:* Peter1936F / Wikimedia Commons / CC BY-SA 4.0.

Catherine frequently proclaimed her own servant status – something every pope since Gregory the Great had done – as well as that she was writing in the blood of Christ himself. With devastating simplicity, Catherine would intercede with Gregory XI and, on his death, his successor Urban VI for the papacy to return to Rome. Unlike Bridget, she would succeed. She moved to a house in Rome near Raymond's church of Santa Maria sopra Minerva, but made herself walk to St. Peter's every day, despite the fact that she was starting to become extremely weak. Her mother, who had traveled to Rome with her, would die at that time. Soon after, Catherine stopped eating altogether, and died in 1380 at the age of only 33 (see Figure 9.5).

Within Catherine's Dominican *famiglia* she was much beloved. However, beyond that charmed circle others within the church may well have looked at her askance. Her diplomatic coup with Urban VI may have been overshadowed by the aftermath of the Schism which erupted after his death. Certainly, her title now as a doctor of the church conceals that sainthood was not necessarily a foregone conclusion for Catherine of Siena. Ironically, rather than the Dominicans, it appears to have been the lay nobility of Siena who walked the canonization process through under the auspices of Pope Pius II, himself Sienese. But even Pius seems to be rather embarrassed by Catherine, moderating all descriptions of her eucharistic enthusiasms, her invisible stigmata, her asceticism, and her visions. Later, such things would even be censured (Krafft 2013).

The ambivalent status of the woman political visionary in the late Middle Ages is perhaps most apparent in the brief but astonishing life of Jeanne d'Arc, or Joan of Arc (Hobbins 2005). Most stories of Joan's appearance at the French court, and indeed of her entire career, are highly colored dramas which focus on the legitimacy, or lack thereof, of her visions. In fact, Joan had a great deal more in common with someone like Catherine of Siena, another young woman without the protection of noble birth, than one might initially suppose. Born in Domrémy, Joan (or Jeanne) left her parents to work at an inn in Neufchâteau in Lorraine. The clientele were largely soldiers, and the women, like so many unprotected and uprooted working girls, felt the pressures of prostitution. Joan confessed that she learned to ride horses at that time. It is not difficult to imagine that she also discovered the men's clothing which, at her trial, she said her voices had commanded her to wear. At her trial she identified her voices as the angel Michael and the saints Catherine (of Alexandria) and Margaret; she had heard them since she was 13, she said, and they only spoke in French. When Joan appeared at the French court in March of 1429, it was not unaccustomed to the presence of women visionaries: there had been the case of Marie Robine, and later, Jeanne Marie de Maillé (d. 1414). A series of Dominican women acted as resident court prophetess to various Italian city-states from the late fifteenth century: Osanna Andreasi and Stefania Quinzana in Mantua, and Lucia Brocadelli in Ferrara (Matter 2010; More 2018, p. 142; Herzig 2007). There was no denying Joan's effectiveness. By May of 1429, she had broken the siege at Orléans. Ennobled by Charles VI, she had a household of retainers, horses and armor, and her own banner, which she particularly loved. In her relationships with her followers, she claimed she knew whom God loved or hated, and like Catherine of Siena she had a particular trick of signing her letters, referring to a silver ring that she wore.

Joan was captured in May of 1430, however, and turned over to the Duke of Burgundy, who supported the English claim to the throne. When she learned of this, she tried to jump from the tower where she was held prisoner. Denying the charge of attempted suicide, she dryly remarked, "God helps those who help themselves." In truth, Joan faced death no matter what happened next, and while her trial for heresy has frequently been regarded as a sham, to get her to recant may actually have been the one way potentially of saving her life (Hobbins 2005, p. 19). Joan is actually one of the first people in history to be accused of witchcraft, in this case by the English king Henry VI, precisely because the English did not want her to be seen as a prisoner of war (Wickham 2016, pp. 190–191). Denied the sacraments and threatened with torture, Joan tried unsuccessfully to appeal to the pope, and then recanted in desperation. But on May 28, she had returned to her men's clothes and recanted her recantation; tried for relapse, on May 30, 1431, she went to the stake. By 1456, the verdict had been overturned by the papacy, although she was not canonized until 1920 in the wake of the sufferings of the French people in World War I, a political saint until the end.

In the fifteenth century, Catherine of Siena, like Clare of Assisi, would be retroactively fitted into a new narrative of "observant" reform. Both Franciscans and Dominicans attempted to formalize the status of women historically associated with them, particularly their "third orders," and to impose a "regular" monastic status on these women which was readily comprehensible in contemporary canon law. Instrumental in the Dominican Order was Catherine of Siena's protégé, Raymond of Capua, so much so that he is sometimes considered a second founder of the order. One side effect of this administrative and legal housecleaning was the virtual creation of "nuns" out of the messy reality of the beguines and penitents of earlier centuries. It was in 1430 that the body of Augustine's mother, Monica, would be moved from Ostia and placed in the church of San Agostino in Rome, arriving with a cautionary tale in which the Virgin appeared to Monica, enjoining her to take the veil (More 2018, p. 106). Even the most historically flexible of monastic orders now felt it needed to be clear.

## From Weeping to Preaching: Magdalene Spirituality

Ironically, however, the woman most associated with the Observant movement herself demonstrates how difficult it was to impose on women the kind of institutional clarity both reformers and canon lawyers most desired. Colette of Corbie (1381–1447) was an orphan who, as a child, was said to fast or give her food away, and who never menstruated, perhaps as a result of prolonged near-starvation. One of her strangest visions is of the flesh of the Christ Child cut into small pieces on a platter by the sins of humanity, which grieved her deeply long after the vision itself; it is difficult to know whether the imagery of such food was meant to inspire hunger or disgust (Bynum 1987,

p. 67). She lived as a beguine, a Benedictine, a third-order Franciscan, an anchoress, and finally settled as a Poor Clare, founding 20 foundations and reforming 20 more (Blumenfeld-Kosinski 2010; Blumenfeld-Kosinski 2020). She received the Eucharist daily, bore stigmata, and went into visionary ecstasies. Like the beguines and Clare herself, Colette seemed to have a particular impulse to care for lepers and those with skin diseases. In later life she did not seem to have wanted her nuns to follow in her footsteps and encouraged them to eat. More for her wandering vocation and desire for reform rather than for any kind of sexual past, Colette and her confessor, Peter of Vaux, modeled her piety on that of Mary Magdalene, whose apostolate of weeping, fasting, and preaching also inspired Catherine of Siena (Arnold 2018, p. 27).

The power of the Magdalene, in fact, and her deep association with beguine or penitent spirituality, rather acted to interrupt the neat Observant narrative. Columba of Rieti (d. 1501), who fasted herself to death at a pitifully young age, and the widow turned Augustinian Rita of Cascia (d. 1456/7), the so-called "patron saint of lost causes," both refused to choose a religious life of easy enclosure. In the heart of Rome, the aristocrat and visionary Francesca Ponziani, later called Francesca Romana (1384–1440), began a religious community of women who did not take formal vows and had a special license from the pope to live without enclosure in order to serve the poor, running a hospital and ministry to lepers (Scanlan 2018). Buried near the high altar in the church of Santa Maria Nova next to the Colosseum, she is beloved of Roman cab drivers even today. Catherine of Genoa (1447–1510), caught in an unhappy and abusive marriage, found new direction after a mid-life conversion, seamlessly combining profound mystical and visionary experience with opening a hospital. "My only me," she declared, "is God" (1979).

Perhaps the woman most notorious for her weeping in the late Middle Ages is the Norwich laywoman Margery Kempe (b. 1373). The daughter of John Brunham, a burgess of King's Lynn, Margery would marry another burgess, John Kempe, and have some 14 children. Norwich at that time was at its most economically vibrant, intimately connected with the wool export trade to the Low Countries and to the cities of the German Hanse, and Margery describes her love of fine clothes, as well as her ventures into brewing and a certain desire to impress the neighbors (Kempe 2001; Goodman 2010). But a complicated fifteenth pregnancy was followed by deep postpartum depression, complicated still further by a fraught experience of private confession which left Margery in utter despair. In the midst of this, Margery had a vision of Christ, who impressed on her her spiritual status as his beloved, and after this personal experience of conversion Margery embarked upon a visionary career which seems to have been modeled at least in part on Bridget of Sweden and the Magdalene. Margery interspersed her loud weeping with frequent visions of the Virgin and the Christ Child and intimate and loving conversations with Christ. Dressing herself in white, she bargained with her husband and eventually bought her way out of their sexual relationship. She would travel on pilgrimage to Jerusalem, as well as around the major shrines of East Anglia, anxious wherever she went to find the approval of the clergymen and confessors with whom she conversed. In practice, however, Margery frequently disregarded their advice and stubbornly found her own way in religion, although she knew she alienated many.

Margery's book, said to be the first autobiography in English, was composed in the 1430s, and illustrates just how difficult it was for a woman without consistent religious sponsorship, even a woman of substantial means, to initiate the recording of a visionary tale that might potentially come under suspicion. The first version of her text was taken down by an Englishman who had lived a long time in Germany and perhaps was not accustomed to English scribal practice, the second by a very nervous priest with poor eyesight, who put Margery off for years and then complained he could barely read the first version. Both scribes found themselves up against Margery's considerable strong-mindedness in how she wanted her story to be told (Watson 2005). In a version of her life printed in the sixteenth century, Wynken de Worde also appears to have been embarrassed by many aspects of her story, and managed to turn the irrepressible Margery into a much more conventional anchorite (Voaden 1999, pp. 147–148).

One of the people Margery met with on her peregrinations was, at least at first blush, exactly the kind of quiet recluse of which de Worde was thinking. But in many ways, Julian of Norwich is not entirely the woman that she appears. Julian is the name of the (male) patron saint of the small Norwich church where she was enclosed; what her given name was is unknown. As a young woman in her twenties, she became so ill she was given last rites. As the crucifix was held over her bed, it was as if the body of Christ on the cross came alive and, like Margery, she had a profound conviction of the abiding love of God. Julian records a series of visions from that time, although they are not described as ongoing in the same way as Margery's. Instead, the short and the long text of her *Revelations of Divine Love* are separated by a decade of thought and meditation on these past experiences. While it is usually assumed the Short Text was composed shortly after her enclosure in 1373 and the Long Text in the 1390s, it is entirely possible that even the Short Text was written later in the 1380s, and the Long Text later still (Watson 1998).

Both texts of the *Revelations* are highly deliberate creations, just possibly submitted as part of a process of routine episcopal oversight. They are extended meditations on the love of God, the redemption of the soul, and the existence of sin and suffering. In many ways her *Revelations* are theology or devotional literature – Passion meditation, to be specific – couched in a visionary frame. Her authorial persona is as crystalline as Catherine of Siena's, even though Julian tells us virtually nothing about herself (Bryan 2008, pp. 145–149). Her language, such as her famous image of the created world, which she describes as small and contained as a hazelnut held in the hand of God, or her use of maternal imagery when applied to God and Christ, manages to be striking and unexpected while remaining within the strict boundaries of orthodoxy. When she might have been tempted to pronounce categorically, for example, upon the eventual universal redemption of all humanity, she simply says what she does not "see" (Julian of Norwich 2015, p. 23).

Precisely because of the profound control of Julian's writing, it is very easy to imagine her in isolation, tranquilly concluding that "all things shall be well." In fact, then as now, her anchorite's cell at St. Julian's was not far from the river and the Norwich docks (see Figure 9.6). She lived next door to a house of Augustinian canons whose protégé was part of Catherine of Siena's entourage, and she must have spent a considerable portion of her time visiting with clergy and other devout laypeople like Margery (Warren 2010, p. 23). Wealthy as it was, Norwich supported a large number of anchorites and hermits: nearly a fifth of Norwich wills from after the Black Death to the Reformation record bequests by merchants to named individuals, including Julian (Warren 1985, p. 223). Margery de Nerford and Katherine Manne were both Norwich anchoresses with Lollard family connections who were nevertheless supported by the town and had Carthusian spiritual directors. A wealthy laywoman, Margaret Purdans, stayed active in society for the nearly 45 years of her widowhood, moving easily between women's religious houses, hospitals, and devout laywomen living in community (Erler 2002, pp. 48–51, 68–84, 100–105).

Beyond Norwich proper, Elizabeth de Burgh, Lady of Clare (d. 1360) and her friend Mary of St. Pol, Countess of Pembroke (d. 1377) founded Clare and Pembroke Colleges in Cambridge as communities of learned clergy. Chaucer's granddaughter, Alice de la Pole, the Countess of Sussex (d. 1475), was buried in a beautiful alabaster tomb – the only transi tomb in England for a woman which survives – in the parish church in Ewelme in Oxfordshire, next to the almshouse she had founded. The dense fabric of late medieval social and religious connections penetrated everywhere, even to those, like the anchorites, ostensibly declared legally dead.

**Figure 9.6** On-site recreation of the anchorite's cell, St. Julian's Church, Norwich. *Source:* echinkle22 / Wikimedia Commons / CC BY-SA 4.0.

## Sisters in a Common Life

The conflicted late medieval attitude to women's visionary experience, as well as the need to conform to a more clearly enclosed and "regular" religious status, can be clearly seen across the history of the Sisters of the Common Life, the women of the *devotio moderna*. The "sister-books" kept by beguine communities in both the German cities and the Low Countries, which stop around the time of the plague, were in some cases later copied by other religious women in the fifteenth century. A woman like Christine Ebner (d. 1356), a contemporary of Suso and Elisabeth Stagel, can write of "graces" and "seeings," but the later books record a deliberate turn away from beguine mysticism under inquisitorial pressure. The Sisters' communities, which appear in numbers in the Low Countries from the 1380s, emphasized instead constancy in prayer, daily self-examination, confession, and the occasional burst of spiritual "sweetness," as recorded by the canoness Salome Sticken (1369–1449; Van Engen 1988, pp. 49, 176–186). Tellingly, the head of the Sisters' community was called the "Martha." Their reading of devotional literature, and particularly their use of the psalter in the vernacular, led to another burst of inquisitorial zeal in 1397 in Utrecht, which led in turn to the Sisters' reinvention of themselves as tertiaries in 1401, the "Sisters of Penance who live a common life." It was entirely possible to live in such a community without profound religious convictions, however. Sister Stijne (d. 1445) remarked, with dry realism, that there were three kinds of people in a community of Sisters: those "taken on" by the Lord, placed there by their parents, those "nailed to the Lord" by poverty, and only a few "glued" to the Lord by free choice (Van Engen 2005, pp. 118, 132; 2010).

In a small community where work and routine were so important, and their religious identity so hard-won, a willful and literate mystic was profoundly challenging and even frightening for the order at large. In 1438, Alijt Bake (d. 1455) entered the Devout community at Ghent and promptly clashed with its formidable abbess, Hille Sonderlants. Alijt was a strong and charismatic personality herself and was difficult to handle precisely because of her broad knowledge of the mystical tradition: she knew the works of Mechthild of Hackeborn, Catherine of Siena, and Eckhart and had a deep working knowledge of the sermons of Tauler. Like Hadewijch or Marguerite Porete, she was impatient with the slow, externally focused work of the Devout community, advocating instead for the liberated soul leaving behind the virtues, which she likened to "taking off fourteen items of clothing." Alijt seems to have won the battle of wills against Hille Sonderlants, becoming prioress of the community on her death, but after seven years she was forced out of office and exiled in 1454, herself dying the next year. The same year, the Windesheim community, the public face of the Modern-Day Devout, banned women from copying mystical texts (Bollmann 2004, 2014; Van Engen 2005, p. 271).

One of the most famous religious images of the late Middle Ages is Jean Fouquet's 1450 painting of the Virgin Mary: absurdly young, alabaster-skinned, with downcast eyes and a conspicuously pert bare breast, with the Christ Child held at a certain distance from her body (see Figure 9.7). The model was the first official mistress of a French king, Agnès Sorel, consort of Charles VII. While the very existence of the painting is a testament to Agnès's ability to negotiate one kind of sexual and political space, her depiction, ironically, is very much as Mary rather than the Magdalene: submissive, pure, and silent. Christine de Pizan and Joan of Arc had died 20 years before. But the very next year a girl would be born who, in many ways, fully embodied and transformed the late medieval tradition of the female political visionary, this time as an anointed queen.

Isabella of Castile was the granddaughter of Catherine of Lancaster and the great-granddaughter of John of Gaunt. After her father's death, her mother became a kind of recluse, while Isabella's half-brother Enrique succeeded to the throne of Castile. Enrique was not particularly happy in the role, and indeed was largely expected to concede his power to his advisors. When no heir to the

**Figure 9.7** Jean Fouquet, Melun Diptych, Royal Museum of Fine Arts, Antwerp. *Source:* Jean Fouquet / Wikimedia Commons / Public domain.

kingdom was immediately forthcoming from his marriage, Isabella was made his successor in 1468, at the Treaty of the Guisando Bulls. Isabella stepped into her young adulthood with an absolute, unshakeable sense that she was an instrument of God, organizing her own marriage to her cousin Ferdinand of Aragon in the teeth of Enrique's ministers, and on terms of striking political equality (Tremlett 2017). The marriage was secretly carried out in October of 1469 – before the couple obtained a papal dispensation – and after 10 years of increasing financial desperation, Isabella came to the throne of Castile in 1479.

Although immediately faced with long years of war and uprising, Isabella seems rather to have enjoyed planning and supplying military campaigns and thrived on the adrenaline of leading troops in person. She saw herself as a latter-day Joan of Arc, in fact, and would view the conquest of Granada and her increasingly ferocious measures against Jews and Muslims as part of a holy crusade (Warren 2005, pp. 87–118). At the time, the church in Spain had half again as much wealth as the historically weak crown of Castile, and Isabella adroitly used the language of religious reform to consolidate her own power such that she more directly controlled the church. Combined with the power of the inquisition under her confessor, Torquemada, and the permission of a Spanish Borgia on the papal throne, she may have single-handedly prevented the Reformation from ever gaining momentum in Spain (Tremlett 2017, pp. 209, 385). Isabella never claimed to receive visions herself, and indeed, with Spain as her political vision, she did not really need to. She was as careful with her written legacy, however, as any late medieval mystic. In Spain it was Isabella who would control the printing press, and her court sponsored scholars to create an official, if semi-legendary, version of Spanish history, to which the highly colored heraldic fantasies of Christopher Columbus were tailor-made to appeal. In this sense, the discovery of the New World was only confirmation of Isabella as divine instrument, a mystic's vision made real.

# References

Anderson, W.L. (2006). Gerson's stance on women. In: *A Companion to Jean Gerson* (ed. B.P. McGuire), 293–315. Leiden: Brill.

Arnold, M. (2018). *The Magdalene in the Reformation*. Cambridge, MA: The Belknap Press.

Bainbridge, V. (2010). Syon Abbey: women and learning c. 1415–1600. In: *Syon Abbey and its Books: Reading, Writing, and Religion, c. 1400–1700* (ed. E.A. Jones and A. Walsham), 82–103. Woodbridge: Boydell Press.

Bell, D.N. (1995). *What Nuns Read: Books and Libraries in Medieval English Nunneries*. Kalamazoo: Cistercian Publications.

Blumenfeld-Kosinski, R. (2010). Holy women in France: a survey. In: *Medieval Holy Women in the Christian Tradition c. 1100–1500* (ed. A. Minnis and R. Voaden), 241–265. Turnhout: Brepols.

Blumenfeld-Kosinski, R. (2020). Saint Colette of Corbie (1381–1447): reformist leadership and belated sainthood. In: *Women Intellectuals and Leaders in the Middle Ages* (ed. K. Kerby-Fulton, K.A.-M. Bugyis and J. Van Engen), 303–317. Woodbridge: D.S. Brewer.

Bollmann, A. (2004). Being a woman on my own: Alijt Bake (1415–55) as reformer of the inner self. In: *Seeing and Knowing: Women and Learning in Medieval Europe* (ed. A.B. Mulder-Bakker), 67–96. Turnhout: Brepols.

Bollmann, A. (2014). The influence of the Devotio Moderna in northern Germany. In: *A Companion to Mysticism and Devotion in Northern Germany in the Late Middle Ages* (ed. E. Andersen, H. Lähnemann and A. Simon), 231–259. Leiden: Brill.

Bryan, J. (2008). *Looking Inward: Devotional Reading and the Private Self in Late Medieval England.* Philadelphia: University of Pennsylvania Press.

Bynum, C.W. (1987). *Holy Feast and Holy Fast: The Religious Significance of Food to Medieval Women.* Berkeley: University of California Press.

Campbell, B.M.S. (2016). *The Great Transition: Climate, Disease, and Society in the Late Medieval World.* Cambridge: Cambridge University Press.

Capgrave, J. (2011). *Life of Saint Katherine of Alexandria* (trans. K.A. Winstead). Notre Dame: University of Notre Dame Press.

Catherine of Genoa (1979). *The Spiritual Dialogue.* (trans. S. Hughes). New York: Paulist Press.

Catherine of Siena (1989). *The Dialogue* (trans. S. Noffke). New York: Paulist Press.

Coakley, J. (2006). *Women, Men, and Spiritual Power: Female Saints and Their Male Collaborators.* New York: Columbia University Press.

Coatsworth, E. and Owen-Crocker, G.R. (2018). *Clothing the Past: Surviving Garments from Early Medieval to Early Modern Western Europe.* Leiden: Brill.

Despres, D.L. (1996). Ecstatic reading and missionary mysticism: *The Orcherd of Syon.* In: *Prophets Abroad: The Reception of Continental Holy Women in Late Medieval England* (ed. R. Voaden), 141–160. Woodbridge: D.S. Brewer.

Duffy, E. (2006). *Marking the Hours: English People and Their Prayers.* New Haven: Yale University Press.

Dzon, M. (2017). *The Quest for the Christ Child in the Later Middle Ages.* Philadelphia: University of Pennsylvania Press.

Eckhart (1981). *Meister Eckhart: The Essential Sermons, Commentaries, Treatises, and Defense* (trans. E. Colledge and B. McGinn). New York: Paulist Press.

Elliott, D. (2010). Flesh and spirit: the female body. In: *Medieval Holy Women in the Christian Tradition c. 1100–1500* (ed. A. Minnis and R. Voaden), 13–46. Turnhout: Brepols.

Ellis, R. (1996). The visionary and the canon lawyers: papal and other revisions to the *Regula Salvatoris* of St. Bridget of Sweden. In: *Prophets Abroad: The Reception of Continental Holy Women in Late Medieval England* (ed. R. Voaden), 71–90. Woodbridge: D.S. Brewer.

Erler, M.C. (2002). *Women, Reading and Piety in Late Medieval England.* Cambridge: Cambridge University Press.

Falkeid, U. (2017). *The Avignon Papacy Contested: An Intellectual History from Dante to Catherine of Siena.* Cambridge: Harvard University Press.

Goodman, A. (2010). Margery Kempe. In: *Medieval Holy Women in the Christian Tradition c. 1100–1500* (ed. A. Minnis and R. Voaden), 217–238. Turnhout: Brepols.

Hamburger, J. (1997). *Nuns as Artists: The Visual Culture of a Medieval Convent.* Berkeley: University of California Press.

Hedlund, M. (2013). Nuns and Latin, with a special reference to the Birgittines of Vadstena. In: *Nuns' Literacies in Medieval Europe: The Hull Dialogue* (ed. V. Blanton, V. O'Mara and P. Stoop), 97–118. Turnhout: Brepols.

Herzig, T. (2007). *Savaranola's Women: Visions and Reforms in Renaissance Italy.* Chicago: University of Chicago Press.

Hobbins, D. (ed.) (2005). *The Trial of Joan of Arc.* Cambridge: Harvard University Press.

Huizinga, J. (2016). *The Autumn of the Middle Ages* (trans. R.J. Payton and U. Mammitzsch). Chicago: University of Chicago Press.

Jones, C.T. (2019). *Women's History in the Age of Reformation: Johannes Meyer's Chronicle of the Dominican Observance.* Toronto: PIMS.

Julian of Norwich (2015). *Revelations of Divine Love* (trans. B. Windeatt). London: Oxford University Press.

Karras, R.M. (1996). *Common Women: Prostitution and Sexuality in Medieval England*. New York: Oxford University Press.

Kempe, M. (2001). *The Book of Margery Kempe* (ed. trans. L. Staley). New York: W.W. Norton and Co.

Kerby-Fulton, K. (2006). *Books under Suspicion: Censorship and Tolerance of Revelatory Writing in Late Medieval England*. Notre Dame: University of Notre Dame Press.

Koch, B. (2010). Margaret Ebner. In: *Medieval Holy Women in the Christian Tradition c. 1100–1500* (ed. A. Minnis and R. Voaden), 393–410. Turnhout, Brepols.

Krafft, O. (2013). Many strategies and one goal: the difficult road to the canonization of Catherine of Siena. In: *Catherine of Siena: The Creation of a Cult* (ed. J. Hamburger and G. Signori), 25–45. Turnhout: Brepols.

Lerner, R. (1972). *The Heresy of the Free Spirit in the Later Middle Ages*. Notre Dame: University of Notre Dame Press.

Luongo, F.T. (2020). Catherine of Siena, *auctor*. In: *Women Intellectuals and Leaders in the Middle Ages* (ed. K. Kerby-Fulton, K.A.-M. Bugyis and J. Van Engen), 97–111. Woodbridge: D.S. Brewer.

Marguerite Porete (1986). *Speculum simplicium animarum: Le miroeur des simples âmes*. In: *Corpus Christianorum Continuatio Mediaevalis 69* (ed. P. Verdeyen and R. Guarnieri). Turnhout: Brepols.

Marguerite Porete (1999). *The Mirror of Simple Souls* (trans. E. Colledge, J.C. Marler, and J. Grant). Notre Dame: University of Notre Dame Press.

Marin, J. (2010). Annihilation and deification in beguine theology and Marguerite Porete's *Mirror of Simple Souls*. *Harvard Theological Review* 103 (1): 89–109.

Matter, E.A. (2010). Italian holy women: a survey. In: *Medieval Holy Women in the Christian Tradition c. 1100–1500* (ed. A. Minnis and R. Voaden), 529–555. Turnhout: Brepols.

Mazzi, M.S. (2020). *A Life of Ill Repute: Public Prostitution in the Middle Ages* (trans. J. Meyerson). Montreal and Kingston: McGill-Queen's University Press.

McNeill, W.H. (1976). *Plagues and Peoples*. New York: Anchor Books.

Mecham, J. (2014). *Sacred Communities, Shared Devotions: Gender, Material Culture, and Monasticism in Late Medieval Germany* (ed. A. Beach, C. Berman and L. Bitel). Turnhout: Brepols.

Mooney, C.M. (2013). Wondrous words: Catherine of Siena's miraculous reading and writing according to the early sources. In: *Catherine of Siena: The Creation of a Cult* (ed. J. Hamburger and G. Signori), 263–290. Turnhout: Brepols.

More, A. (2018). *Fictive Orders and Feminine Religious Identities, 1200–1600*. Oxford: Oxford University Press.

Mulder-Bakker, A.B. (2010). Holy women in the German territories: a survey. In: *Medieval Holy Women in the Christian Tradition c. 1100–1500* (ed. A. Minnis and R. Voaden), 313–341. Turnhout: Brepols.

Oberman, H. (1967). *Forerunners of the Reformation: The Shape of Late Medieval Thought*. London: Lutterworth.

O'Mara, V. (2013). The late medieval English nun and her scribal activity: a complicated quest. In: *Nuns' Literacies in Medieval Europe: The Hull Dialogue* (ed. V. Blanton, V. O'Mara and P. Stoop), 69–93. Turnhout: Brepols.

Piron, S. (2013). Marguerite, entre les béguines et les maîtres. In: *Marguerite Porete et le Miroir des simples âmes: perspectives historiques, philosophiques, et littéraires* (ed. S. Field, R. Lerner and S. Piron), 69–101. Paris: Vrin.

Reinburg, V. (2012). *French Books of Hours: Making an Archive of Prayer, c. 1400–1600*. Cambridge: Cambridge University Press.

Rollo-Koster, J. (2015). *Avignon and its Papacy, 1309–1407*. Lanham: Rowman and Littlefield.

Rubin, M. (2009). *Mother of God: A History of the Virgin Mary*. New Haven: Yale University Press.

Scanlan, S.M. (2018). *Divine and Demonic Imagery at Tor de'Specchi, 1400–1500: Religious Women and Art in Fifteenth-Century Rome*. Amsterdam: Amsterdam University Press.

Schirmer, E. (2005). Reading lessons at Syon Abbey: *The Myroure of Oure Ladye* and the mandates of vernacular theology. In: *Voices in Dialogue: Reading Women in the Middle Ages* (ed. L. Olsen and K. Kerby-Fulton), 347–376. Notre Dame: University of Notre Dame Press.

Schmidt, M. (1993). An example of spiritual friendship: the correspondence between Heinrich of Nördlingen and Margaretha Ebner. In: *Maps of Flesh and Light: The Religious Experience of Medieval Women Mystics* (ed. U. Wiethaus), 74–92. Syracuse: Syracuse University Press.

Simons, W. (2001). *Cities of Ladies: Beguine Communities in the Medieval Low Countries, 1200–1565*. Philadelphia: University of Pennsylvania Press.

Somerset, F. and Kerby-Fulton, K. (2005). "Eciam mulier: women in Lollardy and the problem of sources" and "Eciam Lolladi". In: *Voices in Dialogue: Reading Women in the Middle Ages* (ed. L. Olsen and K. Kerby-Fulton), 245–266. Notre Dame: University of Notre Dame Press.

Stargardt, U. (2010). Dorothy of Montau. In: *Medieval Holy Women in the Christian Tradition c. 1100–1500* (ed. A. Minnis and R. Voaden), 475–496. Turnhout: Brepols.

Stokes, L. (2011). *Demons of Urban Reform: Early European Witch Trials and Criminal Justice, 1430–1530*. London: Palgrave Macmillan.

Suerbaum, A. (2014). An urban housewife as a saint for Prussia. In: *A Companion to Mysticism and Devotion in Northern Germany in the Late Middle Ages* (ed. E. Andersen, H. Lähnemann and A. Simon), 179–204. Leiden: Brill.

The Paston Letters (2008). *The Paston Letters: A Selection in Modern Spelling* (ed. N. Davies). Oxford: Oxford University Press First edition, 1983.

Tremlett, G. (2017). *Isabella of Castile: Europe's First Great Queen*. London: Bloomsbury.

Tuchman, B. (1978). *A Distant Mirror: The Calamitous Fourteenth Century*. New York: Ballantine.

Turner, M. (2019). *Chaucer: A European Life*. Princeton: Princeton University Press.

Undset, S. (2009). *Catherine of Siena*. San Francisco: Ignatius Press.

Van Engen, J. (trans.)(1988). *Devotio Moderna: Basic Writings*. New York: Paulist Press.

Van Engen, J. (2005). *Sisters and Brothers of the Common Life: The Devotio Moderna and the World of the Late Middle Ages*. Philadelphia: University of Pennsylvania Press.

Van Engen, J. (2010). Communal life: the sister-books. In: *Medieval Holy Women in the Christian Tradition c. 1100–1500* (ed. A. Minnis and R. Voaden), 105–131. Turnhout: Brepols.

Van Engen, J. (2013). Marguerite (Porete) of Hainaut and the medieval Low Countries. In: *Marguerite Porete et le Miroir des simples âmes: perspectives historiques, philosophiques, et littéraires* (ed. S. Field, R. Lerner and S. Piron), 25–68. Paris: Vrin.

Van Engen, J. (2020). A woman author? The middle Dutch dialogue between a "good-willed layperson" and "Meister Eckhart". In: *Women Intellectuals and Leaders in the Middle Ages* (ed. K. Kerby-Fulton, K.A.-M. Bugyis and J. Van Engen), 155–168. Woodbridge: D.S. Brewer.

Voaden, R. (1999). *God's Words, Women's Voices: The Discernment of Spirits in the Writing of Late Medieval Women Visionaries*. York: York Medieval Press.

Warner, K. (2019). *Philippa of Hainault: Mother of the English Nation*. Stroud: Amberley.

Warren, A.K. (1985). *Anchorites and Their Patrons in Medieval England*. Berkeley: University of California Press.

Warren, N.B. (2001). *Spiritual Economies: Female Monasticism in Later Medieval England*. Philadelphia: University of Pennsylvania Press.

Warren, N.B. (2005). *Women of God and Arms: Female Spirituality and Political Conflict, 1380–1600*. Philadelphia: University of Pennsylvania Press.

Warren, N.B. (2010). *The Embodied Word: Female Spiritualities, Contested Orthodoxies, and English Religious Culture, 1350–1700*. Notre Dame: University of Notre Dame Press.

Watson, N. (1998). The trinitarian hermeneutic in Julian of Norwich's *Revelations of Divine Love*. In: *Julian of Norwich: A Book of Essays* (ed. S. McEntire), 61–90. New York: Garland.

Watson, N. (2005). The making of the Book of Margery Kempe. In: *Voices in Dialogue: Reading Women in the Middle Ages* (ed. L. Olsen and K. Kerby-Fulton), 395–434. Notre Dame: University of Notre Dame Press.

Watt, D. (1997). *Secretaries of God: Women Prophets in Late Medieval and Early Modern England*. Cambridge: D.S. Brewer.

Wickham, C. (2016). *Medieval Europe*. New Haven: Yale University Press.

Wieck, R.S. (1997). *Painted Prayers: The Book of Hours in Medieval and Renaissance Art*. New York: George Braziller.

Williams-Krapp, W. (2004). Henry Suso's *Vita*: between mystagogy and hagiography. In: *Seeing and Knowing: Women and Learning in Medieval Europe* (ed. A.B. Mulder-Bakker), 35–47. Turnhout: Brepols.

Winder, S. (2020). *Lotharingia: A Personal History of France, Germany and the Countries in Between*. London: Picador.

Winstead, K.A. (2020). *Fifteenth-Century Lives*. Notre Dame: University of Notre Dame Press.

Winston-Allen, A. (1997). *Stories of the Rose: The Making of the Rosary in the Middle Ages*. University Park: Pennsylvania State University Press.

Zieman, K. (2005). Playing *doctor*: St. Birgitta, ritual reading, and ecclesiastical authority. In: *Voices in Dialogue: Reading Women in the Middle Ages* (ed. L. Olsen and K. Kerby-Fulton), 307–334. Notre Dame: University of Notre Dame Press.

# 10

## Witness in Translation

Women in the Protestant Reformation, 1500–1600

After Marguerite Porete was burned at the stake in 1310, her book, *The Mirror of Simple Souls*, went on to have a strangely influential afterlife. Smuggled out of Paris and copied on both sides of the English Channel by the Carthusians, her *Mirror* survived and thrived as an anonymous treatise, with no one connecting book and author until Romana Guarnieri in the twentieth century. The thought of Marguerite was copied almost verbatim in an anonymous sixteenth-century Dutch work, *The Evangelical Pearl*, which was then translated by Catholic orders, the Carthusians and Franciscans, into Latin, German, and French (*La perle évangelique* 1997; Van Nieuwenhove et al. 2008). At the same time, another contemplative monastic order, the Celestines, preserved a sixteenth-century treatise, *Le Livre de la discipline d'amour divine*, whose author had clearly read Marguerite's work directly. *Divine Love's Discipline* traveled south, where it found a spiritual home in the Observant monastic reform undertaken by Mary of Brittany and the Fontevrist nuns at La Madeleine-les-Orléans. La Madeleine is not far from the Celestine house at Ambert, where the original French manuscript of the *Mirror* was also preserved (Hasenohr 2013; 2017). Marguerite of Navarre (1492–1549), sister of King Francis I, was a frequent visitor to La Madeleine, with the king a donor to the house in her name, and it is there that she encountered *The Mirror of Simple Souls*.

Marguerite of Navarre's own religious identity is deeply complex, both inescapably public as a result of her birth and position, and intensely personal, even solitary. Although she is traditionally known as a Huguenot, she remains difficult to categorize as a Protestant of either Lutheran or Reformed sympathies. Along with the French humanist Lefèvre d'Étaples, Guillaume Briçonnet, the reforming bishop of Meaux, was an immensely influential figure on Marguerite's early life. It was chiefly Briçonnet who encouraged in her a mystical bent that appears in all of her written work (Cholakian and Cholakian 2006, pp. 66–103). Although she corresponded with John Calvin, in practice, the aristocratic, inward-looking spirituality of Marguerite Porete was much closer to Marguerite's own temperament, social situation, and intellectual positions. Unwilling to attack Marguerite directly, Calvin fretted over the clergy the king's sister patronized at her court at Nérac. Dubbing them "the Navarran Network," Calvin wrote several treatises against those he saw as "French nicodemites" and "spiritual libertines" for their worrying fusion of evangelical teachings with secret mysticism and Joachimite apocalypticism (Calvin 1898; Thysell 2000, pp. 19–38, 99–106; Reid 2009, pp. 551–563).

Marguerite's final written work, *Prisons*, is arguably the culmination of a lifetime of thinking and writing about these themes, as well as the work where she is most explicit about her intellectual debt to Marguerite Porete. *Prisons* is said to be the first long narrative allegorical poem written by a woman. As the poem unfolds, Marguerite presents the reader with a kind of spiritual autobiography, as its male hero, Amy, escapes from a series of refuges-turned-prisons. First trapped and tortured by love, Amy then turns his energies toward worldly ambition, and finally, seeks solace in knowledge. In his windowless tower built of books, Amy literally becomes imprisoned by the seven liberal arts and ultimately by the pursuit of the virtues themselves (Marguerite of Navarre 1995, Bk. III). Only God the Far-Near, the *Loing-Près*, can free Amy, "till, brought at last to nothing by that power/I knew the One who truly is the All" (Bk. III, lns. 658–660).

Tragically, *Prisons*, with its explicit invocation and celebration of Marguerite's *Mirror*, would not see the light of day until the end of the nineteenth century. However, a much earlier published work of Marguerite of Navarre, *The Mirror of a Sinful Soul*, also reproduces elements of Marguerite Porete's thought. Marguerite grafted elements of the older, medieval *Mirror* into a narrative trajectory employed by many sixteenth-century evangelicals: blindness, sin, a secret conversion, followed by the outpouring of the grace of the Holy Spirit (Vance 2014, pp. 91–95, 102). Marguerite of Navarre retained from Marguerite Porete the radical juxtaposition of vehement, even violent debasement of herself with, after the action of grace, the exaltation of the soul made nothing, who becomes "sister to God." Marguerite often described herself in terms of nothingness or wishing to be nothing, and understood the influx of divine grace itself as a destructive force (Marguerite of Navarre 2008).

Even when massaged into a safer and more conventional narrative of Protestant conversion, the intensity of Marguerite's language suggests her lasting fascination with older, medieval beguine mysticism. *The Mirror of a Sinful Soul*, the first book to be printed in French by a woman, was initially published anonymously in 1531. Immediately it came under the censure of the Sorbonne for its use of the French psalter of Lefèvre d'Étaples, prompting the fury of Francis I, a hasty backtracking by the theological faculty, and a new edition in 1533. In somewhat mysterious circumstances, *The Mirror of a Sinful Soul* was the first translation project of a young Elizabeth I in 1545. Dedicated to her stepmother, Catherine Parr, the English title was *The Glass of a Sinful Soul* (Elizabeth 2009; see Figure 10.1). Catherine's own book, *The Lamentacion, or Complaint of a Sinner*, published two years later, was also modeled on *The Mirror*, and was so successful it went through three editions by 1563. Almost 50 years later in 1590, Elizabeth's translation was published by the former Carmelite turned Protestant pamphleteer John Bale.

How is it that the book for which Marguerite Porete died as a heretic in the fourteenth century became the great influence on the thought of Marguerite of Navarre, grandmother of the great defender of Huguenot liberties, Henry IV, and one of the first exercises in translation by a young Elizabeth Tudor? It could all simply be coincidence, a meeting of true minds, but it also suggests to what extent the evangelical critique of the late medieval church, which blossomed into what we now call the Protestant Reformation, combined aspects of late medieval mystical and devotional experience with fine-grained humanist textual criticism. Luther's famous "Tower Experience," which described his conviction of his own unworthiness and the outpouring of divine grace which followed, does not, in and of itself, sound so very different from the Far-Near in Marguerite Porete's *Mirror*. What is distinctive are the arguments over the nature and role of faith that Luther would make as a result of his experience and the close alliance of faith with the reading of scripture. In particular, a personal experience of divine grace encountered through scripture could become so paramount for an individual that, Luther argued, the rest of the complicated fabric of the late medieval devotional universe could be effectively discarded – or worse, seen as a golden calf to be destroyed.

**Figure 10.1**  Elizabeth I, *The Glass of a Sinful Soul* (1544), Bodleian Libraries, University of Oxford, MS Cherry 36. *Source:* Elizabeth I of England / Wikimedia Commons / Public domain.

## Women and the Reformation

What did this mean for women, who had been prominent in shaping both the conventions of mystical experience and the late medieval devotional universe? Did women have either a "Renaissance" or a "Reformation," and were such movements "good" or "bad" for women (Kelly 1984)? Unfortunately there can be no unilateral answer to these questions, not least because, as in the case of Marguerite of Navarre, in the early years of the Reformation clear-cut confessional boundaries between Protestant and Catholic identities did not always exist. Nor was there any single way for either to claim or to reject the past history and traditions of the medieval church. As with earlier religious dissent, "Protestant" was a label created mostly by its opposition; as a consequence many modern historians prefer to use the term "evangelical" until at least the seventeenth century. Moreover, the idiosyncratic example of Luther notwithstanding, Protestant identity was practically by definition various, multiplex, and shaped by local linguistic, social, and political context, as evidenced by the deep and early divisions between its Lutheran and Reformed branches.

Women in the Reformation had to negotiate this rapidly shifting landscape, and their reactions to the new teachings of the Reformation varied according to the personalities of the women themselves, their social circumstances, and their level of education. For some, the teachings of the Reformation were immediately embraced as a liberation; for others, they were scorned as a travesty. What was similar, however, were patterns of evangelical discourse around gender, affecting how women were treated by the theological leaders of the Reformation, by town councils, and by other forms of civic authority. Despite the complexity of the Reformation as a whole, the broad outlines of women's participation in the so-called "magisterial reformation" – the Lutheran and Reformed traditions – are fairly consistent and will be treated here in a single chapter. Women from the radical Reformation, or Anabaptist tradition, will also be included, as well as members of the Italian reforming movement known as the *spirituali*, although, like Marguerite of Navarre, many women here and in the next chapter defy easy confessional categorization.

The earliest years of the Reformation promised a radical, even apocalyptic transformation of society, and a return to a more egalitarian, Edenic past. In principle, Reformation teachings created several new avenues for women's spiritual experience and religious roles within the church. As in the early centuries of the church, there was now the opportunity for women to bear heroic witness before Catholic authority. Some testified to the grace they had received, even to the point of embracing martyrdom as so many early Christian women had done. The reformers' privileging of vernacular scripture encouraged women's literacy and education, as well as its expression in preaching and teaching within their own community. Finally, Luther's categorical rejection of celibacy led to reformers' elevation and exaltation of Christian marriage and child-bearing. This promised greater dignity to wives and mothers, so often seen as spiritual second-class citizens, as well as the embrace of marriage and human sexuality as an essential part of ordinary Christian life rather than a concession to the weak. These were the ideals of the Reformation, and for some women they may even have been realized.

More commonly, however, external factors limited the reach and power of these Reformation promises. For his movement to survive at all, Luther and other leaders of the magisterial reformation very quickly found themselves making common cause with aristocratic and civic authority, with all its vested interests. As with Luther's near-frantic disavowing of the Peasants' Revolt in 1524, reformers' encouragement of women's religious vocation was heavily qualified by the very real fear of being perceived as the cause of social disorder. In a fluid and competitive confessional environment, where religious discourse was polarized and often as sensational and scabrous as modern social media, women flouting social and religious mores made for easy targets and were, often as not, an embarrassment to the reformers. Far from wanting to appear as new or innovative, evangelicals couched the Reformation in terms of a conservative return to a more primitive and pure Christian tradition. With the evangelical rejection of the Apocrypha went such powerful biblical models for women as Judith and Susannah. Increasingly, the Reformed tradition in particular turned not to the New Testament or to the book of Acts but to the Old Testament for models by which to fashion God's chosen people and God's chosen clergy – and found, not least, the bearded patriarchs (MacCulloch 2003, pp. 254, 650). Marguerite of Navarre's distancing of Calvin stemmed in part from her rejection of the implicit hierarchy of authority and virtue she encountered in his thought, and she chose instead the radical isolation of the "simple soul."

Humanist thought, too, could be a double-edged sword. The same humanist scholarship which made classical and patristic texts accessible to ordinary people also revived classical discourses about gender, in particular Aristotelian conceptions of women's natural physiological inferiority, mental limitations, and the potentially unbridled nature of women's sexuality. These were accepted by most humanists and reformers without question, although the sixteenth century would also see increasingly articulate defenses of women's mental, moral, and spiritual capacity from both men and women (Jordan 1990, pp. 20–34). Ironically, this shared humanist hinterland, as well as the common emphasis on household instruction and education, meant that there was far more common ground between Protestant, Puritan, and Catholic social thought than one might initially suppose (Todd 1987, p. 98). At the same time, many women in the Reformation would turn their hands and their humanist education to the work of translating the bible, as well as other Latin and Greek texts, into the vernacular. Appearing as nearly invisible conduits of godly learning to the people, in effect, many were preaching publicly without appearing explicitly to do so. In this sense the Reformation translator was an equivalent strategy to the medieval visionary, by which women could shelter their vulnerable femininity behind the shield of the word of God. Ironically, as a consequence the number and influence of women translators in the Reformation has often been underestimated.

For centuries in the medieval church, religious women and their priests and confessors had formed alliances which, if they were not always symbiotic, were at least traditional by the sixteenth century. To Luther, however, celibate priest and celibate woman were dual and connected representatives of the clerical caste who had taken into Babylonian captivity the holy things of God and kept them from God's people. As such, he usually attacked them both together, and by and large, Luther's characterization of the medieval priesthood spilled over into his assessment of women's roles within the church. It cannot have helped that many religious women's spiritual authority rested on the power of their intercession over the fate of souls in purgatory, while wives were commonly assumed to be the chief participants in late medieval devotional ritual on behalf of their families (Peters 2003). Partly because of the threat posed by the Anabaptists, Luther fretted over even such traditional sacramental roles for women as the emergency baptism of infants by midwives (Wiesner 1989, pp. 24–25). In this way, paradoxically, women's religious vocation was collateral damage in Luther's revolutionary assertion of the priesthood of all believers.

In 1516, Erasmus had scandalized and thrilled the church with the publication of his Greek New Testament, which had notoriously translated the Isaiah 7 prophecy to read, not a virgin, but "a young woman shall conceive." In 1519, Marguerite of Navarre's friend, the French humanist Lefèvre d'Étaples, launched what would become known as the controversy of the Three Marys. Lefèvre argued against the harmonization and conflation by Gregory the Great of Mary Magdalene, Mary of Bethany, and the woman with the alabaster box from Luke's gospel (Lefèvre d'Étaples 2009). In this way, the humanists not only set themselves against Marian devotion, but also attacked the cult of the Magdalene.

Whatever the merits of both cases as textual criticism, whether they intended it or not, the humanists deconstructed the central models within the Christian tradition for women's active religious vocation. The reformers followed. Predictably, Luther and others rejected the traditional Catholic interpretation of Mary as "full of grace," seeing her not as Queen of Heaven and cosmic intercessor, but simply as a moral exemplar to the believer. Protestant polemicists gleefully seized on the brief exchange between Mary and Christ at the wedding at Cana, in which Christ seems almost to rebuke his mother, as well as the warnings of the Old Testament prophets against idolators who burn incense to the "Queen of Heaven" (Grindlay 2018). The Marian feasts in the church's calendar were rife with exactly the kind of elaborate music and liturgical ceremony that the reformers were trying to purge from the church (Rubin 2009, p. 367). Perhaps the most poignant loss of all was St. Anne, known only in apocryphal literature, but nevertheless a traditional model for the ministry of widows and older women in religious life and a patron of many late medieval guilds and confraternities.

Although Luther never went so far as to deny the virginity of Mary, for all the Reformation's emphasis on the early church, the virginity of so many of the early Christian women martyrs was so difficult a subject for evangelicals that they tended to ignore or avoid them (Peters 2003, pp. 209–210). As for Mary Magdalene, she was sufficiently scriptural for Luther to retain her feast day on July 22. But such an unavoidably sinful saint-turned-preacher made for awkward company, particularly for the first generation of reformers eager to purify and cleanse the church. In fact, Luther could embrace the example of Mary Magdalene as a penitent sinner relying solely on God's grace, and he even rather enjoyed pointing out her witness at the resurrection if it meant undercutting the primacy of Peter. However, he was not willing to go so far as to support those evangelical women who took the Magdalene for their model. Meanwhile, in the Reformed tradition, the doctrine of the universal total depravity of humanity did not leave much room for individual, sensational sinners-turned-saints. Calvin likewise rejected the emotionalism associated with and inspired by devotion to the Magdalene. Of all the reformers, Theodore Beza, originally from her cult center at Vézelay, was perhaps the most polite, but no one in the Protestant tradition felt particularly comfortable encouraging popular devotion either to the Virgin or to the Magdalene (Arnold 2018).

## Women and the Town Councils

In practice, Luther's joint attack on religious women and the clergy, as well as the gradual Protestant eradication of the confessional, led to a vacuum of spiritual authority in ordinary daily life. Into this vacuum expanded the values and authority structures of the late medieval guild and workshop. These were unambiguously patriarchal. For example, according to guild law, marriage was a matter not only of sexual morality but also of social status: marriage was the criterion which separated a master craftsman from a journeyman. Over time, the privileging of the married male householder by civic ordinance acted to restrict the economic opportunities of widows, poorer men, and surviving women's religious communities which still ran their own workshops (Roper 1989). As in the economic boom of the thirteenth century, the cheap wage labor of unskilled single women powered the growth of the early modern European economy (Weisner-Hanks 2019, p. 144).

On a larger scale, in regions where the Reformation took hold, noble and royal political authority was similarly strengthened. The evangelical redefinition of the sacrament of baptism eroded the old ties of spiritual kinship and godparenthood in favor of the nuclear family. The household was the new early modern civic unit, without the secondary support provided by a web of monastic institutions (Ozment 1983; Karant-Nunn 2000). The necessity of marrying a partner who shared one's particular religious convictions disrupted old family patterns of arranged marriages, which may not have always been beneficial to young women without significant personal resources (Bainton 1973, pp. 7–8). While the reformers' enthusiastic support of marriage may well have encouraged many women, it eliminated for them the possibility of a choice between a formal celibate and a married life, as well as the myriad forms of the medieval beguine or penitent community. Many of these, of course, had sheltered widows in the past; without them, what would become of former nuns, or even ordinary married women whose husbands had died, presented problems for which the evangelicals did not always have ready solutions.

In Lutheran cities, matters of public morality were handled directly by the town councils rather than by the reformers themselves. Needless to say, the translation by committee of reformers' teachings into pragmatic social policy often left much to be desired, and varied greatly from city to city. Inflation struck the European economy badly in the sixteenth century, driving many farmers off their land, and many town councils acted decisively with the primary goal of curbing vagrancy. Ironically, what had begun as a task of fostering virtue quickly centered on the question of whether a person's actions disrupted the social order, and by extension, if certain members of the poor were truly deserving of civic charity. In England after the dissolution of the monasteries, a range of institutions emerged to handle the subsequent shortfall in nursing and poor relief (Dinan 2016). Other traditional medieval institutions were reconfigured as well. In Germany, when town councils closed the older, medieval public brothels, for example, prostitution continued, but with more pointed attacks on the women's moral character, while men were usually dismissed with a fine. The civic suspicion of women living together unchaperoned extended not only to prostitutes but also to widows and to religious communities – and tended to lump them all together (Roper 1989, pp. 56, 81, 131, 225).

Reformation polemic made a particular point of attacking secret marriages, which reformers believed the medieval church had tacitly encouraged. Over the course of the Reformation, both Protestant and Catholic countries would require marriages to be increasingly formalized, public ceremonies. Ironically, however, this made it more difficult for rape victims or for pregnant women to argue for the legitimacy of sexual unions which were not formally witnessed as the regulations demanded. Town councils seem to have been more strict than the reformers themselves concerning the practice of divorce and remarriage, for example, and harangued parents for not teaching their children sufficiently strict self-discipline (Ozment 1983, pp. 30–38, 133–134). Not surprisingly, town councils do not seem to have been particularly skilled at marriage counseling, although that did not stop them from trying. In Huguenot Languedoc, the consistory at Nîmes was besieged by complaints from women hoping to use its authority to coerce men to keep broken promises of marriage, to seek compensation after rape or sexual violence, to escape brutal or abusive marriages, to redress insults and devastating gossip, or simply to adjudicate disputes over pews in church. The consistory did not set out to support women in particular, but its very existence in the city of Nîmes created one avenue or strategy which women might pursue (Lipscomb 2019).

Because so many social and religious pressures were civic and local, they were arguably felt by women as, or more, keenly than many former dictates from Rome, and most intensely of all, by Catholic women's religious communities in German-speaking lands. In 1521, Luther had published a pamphlet, *Judgment on Monastic Vows*, followed by another, even more pointed tract in 1523, *Why Nuns May Leave Cloisters with God's Blessing*. And yet, even in such cases, the range of outcomes which occurred in German cities attests to the variety of local and regional factors in play, the strength of individual personalities in both convents and on town councils, and ironically, the continuing social utility of women's religious communities. Not least, the quality of the education provided by the still-new Lutheran girls' schools was worse in many cases than that from the late medieval convents (Schlotheuber 2014). In some places, the transition appears to have been smooth enough. When the Reformation reached her in 1539, Anna von Stolberg, the abbess at the magnificent Ottonian foundation of Quedlinburg, simply released those of her nuns who chose to leave and opened a Lutheran school (Weisner-Hanks 2019, p. 246). It was not always so straightforward, however. Many of the women in religious communities were, by default, aristocratic or from prominent local families, and they often outranked the burghers attempting to regulate them. In some cases, such as at Augsburg, the fact that the councils had already extended the rights of citizenship to the women in an effort to usurp rights of jurisdiction from the local Catholic bishop meant that they could not then exile the women in question from their native city (Roper 1989, p. 211).

As a consequence, women's communities in Germany were frequently permitted to continue, although they were often not allowed to take on new members, and they were denied access to a priest and therefore to the sacraments. The nuns were often required to listen to evangelical preaching instead – a singularly unsuccessful missionary tactic, unless it was the abbess herself, like Anna von Stolberg or Lady Inger of Austraat in Norway, who brought in the Lutherans. More effective was the slow attrition of debt: the convents' endowment was gradually eaten up until they were forced to close. But at St. Katherine's in Augsburg, the convent continued under Lutheran leadership, with the town acting essentially as a board of trustees for what had become a largely civic organization made up of both Lutheran and older, Catholic nuns. In the city of Ulm, the Lutheran convent continued in this way until the nineteenth century.

In the Low Countries, the already ambiguous status of the beguinages meant that some were able to continue through the chaotic conditions of the Dutch war for independence. Some beguines were at least able to buy houses, or *kloppen*, where they could continue to live together; this was true in Germany as well (Marshall 1989; Kuijpers 2015; Deane 2016). "Evangelical nuns" did so as well under the leadership of the Lutheran Duke of Saxony, while an ostensibly Lutheran convent like the deeply learned foundation at Lüne continued to take on Catholic girls as pupils, with much depending on the personal convictions of individual abbesses (Plummer 2016). In Strasbourg in 1594, at exactly the moment when a holdout Dominican women's community, St. Nicholas-in-Undis, was about to collapse in a mountain of debt, factionalism, and highly colored charges of debauchery, pregnancy, witchcraft, and prostitution, the nuns rejected their bishop's governance in favor of their town council's. They and the other two Catholic foundations in Strasbourg continued in spite of everything, ultimately because both the women and the council needed them to do so (Leonard 2005).

In point of fact, the civic dimension of convent life was not so very incompatible with Lutheran theology. Ironically, the most vocal and articulate of the first generation of Protestant women reformers would be virtually all convent-educated, in much the same way that converted friars, like Luther himself or Martin Bucer in Strasbourg, became some of the most eloquent and passionate evangelicals. Most of the women to publish music in the early modern world, Protestant or Catholic, likewise came out of the convents. Ultimately, however, the reformers were most comfortable with women who practiced their religious vocation from within the household or at least as an obvious extension of it. As a consequence, amidst the ambivalence and complexity surrounding reformers' responses to women's religious vocation, one central figure or office emerged as the distinctive invention of the Reformation: the figure of the pastor's wife. The pastor's wife was the virtuous foil to the priest's concubine of late medieval anticlerical discourse (Stjerna 2009, p. 35; Plummer 2012). Despite the central place that many of these women held within their husband's ministry, however, their role remained unofficial and often unrecognized.

As a consequence, these women frequently found themselves in desperate straits when their husband died. It may then be partly for financial and partly for vocational reasons that the Reformation produced some spectacular cases of serial marriage. Wibrandis Rosenblatt (d. 1564), for example, married in succession John Oecolampadius, himself father-in-law to Thomas Cranmer, Wolfgang Capito, and Martin Bucer, already a widower (MacCulloch 2003, pp. 648–650).

**Figure 10.2** Katharina von Bora, portrait by Lucas Cranach the Elder, Wartburg Stiftlung. *Source:* Unknown source / Wikimedia Commons / Public domain.

### Doctor Katharina

Perhaps the most famous woman of the Reformation was Luther's own wife, the former nun Katharina von Bora (1499–1522; Stjerna 2009, pp. 51–70; see Figure 10.2). Convinced by Lutheran arguments, she had escaped dramatically from the convent of Marienthron with 12 other girls concealed in a fish-wagon. One was Magdalena, the sister of Luther's colleague-turned-Anabaptist Johann von Staupitz. Faced with the prospect of many such houseless former nuns, Luther was by then advocating for former monks and nuns to marry one another, a neat if often impracticable solution. More aristocratic than Luther, Katharina does not actually appear to have been required to marry the reformer. Certainly, given Luther's manifold and fluctuating mental and physical illnesses, Katherina was nothing if not a brave woman to have taken on the marriage. But on the whole it appears to have been a success: Katherina was a stable, practical, steadying influence on the mercurial Luther, and he fondly called her his "lord," as well as "teacher" and "doctor," a role that comes through most clearly in the work that most glorified the Protestant household, Luther's *Table-Talk* (Luther 2003, Sections 145, 156, 231, 402, 649, 715–754, 901). Katharina was also a formidable estate manager, and when the Luthers took over an abandoned Augustinian monastery – an irony of history the former friar and nun must have enjoyed – it was she who ran the farm. When Luther died, however, their children were removed from her care and Katherina was virtually dispossessed by the University of Wittenberg.

Much less well-known is Calvin's wife, Idelette de Bure (1506–1549). The widow of a former Anabaptist with two children, Idelette emerges only occasionally in Calvin's writings, although he deeply grieved her death (Bainton 1973, pp. 87–88; MacCulloch 2003, p. 251). Working alongside Martin Bucer in Strasbourg was the gentle but indomitable figure of Katharina Schütz Zell (1498–1562), married to the pastor Matthäus Zell (McKee 1999; Stjerna 2009, pp. 109–131). Both had converted in the early years of the Reformation, and were well-placed amidst the city's rich printing culture to be a kind of evangelical communications hub. Modeling herself on the Magdalene, Katharina wrote to virtually everyone who was anyone in the Reformation, and yet remained an ecumenical influence in the border town, likewise maintaining links with the Anabaptist Caspar Schwenkfeld and arranging Bucer's marriage to Wibrandis. Like Luther she wrote hymns, some 159 songs in all, which would be published as part of the first hymnbook of the Bohemian Brethren in German, and wrote her own devotional works, including a 1558 treatise, *Meditation on the Psalms and the Lord's Prayer* (McKee 1999, vol. II, pp. 305–366). Her works include a great deal of the feminine and maternal language used of Christ that had been characteristic of late medieval beguine literature, and indeed, Katharina seems once to have considered becoming a beguine before her conversion (Moss and Waite 2019). In later years, she called herself the "Kirchenmütter," or mother of churches, a particularly poignant title since all of her own children had died. And yet, when her husband died as well, she was in as desperate straits financially as Katharina von Bora. She continued her work, however, despite the fallout from her public criticism of a Strasbourg pastor with whose theology she disagreed, and ongoing allegations about whether she had written her own books.

## Reformation Magdalenes

The success of the Reformation is inseparable from the revolution caused by the printing press, and in turn from the web of humanists, pamphleteers, and printers who publicized evangelical teaching. Luther's "A Mighty Fortress Is Our God" was published by a woman printer, Kunigunde Hergott of Nuremberg, and he is known to have borrowed the work of another former nun and fellow evangelical hymnodist, Elisabeth Cruciger (Wilson 2016, p. 153). Another early evangelist, who like Katharina Schütz Zell modeled herself on the figure of the preaching Magdalene, was the Bavarian noblewoman Argula von Grumbach (1492–1563/8; Stjerna 2009, pp. 71–85). Highly aristocratic, she was a bible reader from a young age and converted in the early days of the Reformation. Argula began writing in 1523, and by her early thirties, she had nearly thirty thousand copies of her tracts in print (see Figure 10.3). Despite her husband losing his job over her work, she

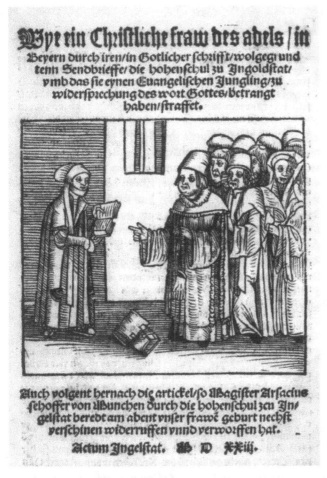

**Figure 10.3** Argula von Grumbach, frontispiece of *Wie ain Christliche Frau des Adels* (1523). *Source:* Argula von Grumbach / Wikimedia Commons / Public domain.

continued, corresponding with many of the leading reformers, including Luther, Bucer, Osiander, and Melancthon, and even attending the Diet of Augsburg. Luther, for one, seems have been somewhat intimidated by her rank, and the confidence her position lent her, combined with her driving sense of her own calling, led Argula to take up a one-woman defense of a student at the University of Ingolstadt who had been caught with evangelical pamphlets and was being threatened with the stake. While valiant, the verbal and written abuse she received as a result, akin to a modern doxxing campaign, drove her out of the public eye, her works were destroyed, and even her date of death is now unknown. Another Bavarian humanist and evangelist was Magdalena Heymair (c. 1535–1586), who served as a tutor in the household of an Augsburg Lutheran noblewoman, Catherine von Degenberg (Wilson 2016, pp. 102–104). After the invasion of Charles V, Magdalena and her husband Wilhelm moved first to Cham, and then to Regensburg, and then even further east to Košice in Slovakia, teaching all the way.

In a 1539 pamphlet entitled *A Most Beneficial Letter*, addressed to none other than Marguerite of Navarre, the Frenchwoman Marie Dentière (1495–1561) explicitly argued that women, following the example of the Magdalene, should also preach the liberation of the gospel (Arnold 2018, pp. 77–81; see Figure 10.4). A former Augustinian nun, Marie had converted in 1524 and married

**Figure 10.4**   The Reformation Wall, Geneva. *Source:* MHM55 / Wikimedia Commons / CC BY-SA 4.0.

first in Strasbourg. When her husband died, she married a second time, to another Frenchman who, like so many of Calvin's circle, emigrated to Geneva in 1526 to help Guillaume Farel in the conversion of the city. Calvin does not seem to have known what to do with Marie, any more than Luther did with Argula von Grumbach, and the two coexisted uneasily. Her 1536 treatise, *The War for and Deliverance of the City of Geneva*, was an early effort to set down the history of the Reformation in that sometimes turbulent city. Not surprisingly, as with Katharina Schütz Zell, many people suspected Marie's husband of writing it, and now no original copies of the book survive. *A Most Beneficial Letter* was published in the same year as Calvin's great theological summa, *The Institutes of Christian Religion*. Whether out of fear or frustration, he never mentions Marie (Stjerna 2009, pp. 132–149).

The most radical of the evangelical groups were the Anabaptists, hated and persecuted by magisterial Protestants and Catholics alike for their denunciation of infant baptism. Precisely because adult conversion and confession before the community was so central to Anabaptist identity, it is not surprising that they also had some of the most permissive attitudes concerning women's preaching and prophecy. Caspar Schwenkfeld corresponded not only with Katharina Schütz Zell but with many other women Anabaptists as well. Also from Strasbourg, the prophetess Ursula Jost received 77 visions between 1524 and 1530, published as *Prophetic Visions and Revelations of the Workings of God in These Last Days*, which in turn influenced her confessor, the radical Melchior Hoffman. The printer was the Anabaptist Margaretha Prüss (d. 1542), herself the daughter of a Catholic devotional printer whose trade had once been in breviaries. Margaretha married a total of three printers in her lifetime, circulating some of the hottest apocalyptic pamphlets in the literature. Perhaps frightened by the controversy, perhaps simply fed up by her family's radicalism, one of her daughters became a Catholic nun. The other, also called Margaretha, married the freethinker and mystic Sebastian Franck, also a friend of Schwenkfeld's (Wilson 2016, pp. 151–153).

With the establishment of the Anabaptist Kingdom of Münster, 1534 was the Anabaptist *annus mirabilis* turned nightmare. When the city was besieged by Catholic forces, its leader, Jan of Leiden, declared the kingdom of God to be imminent, himself the King and his wife, Divara van Haarlem, the Queen of Münster. Amidst the chaos, one woman, Hille Feicken, attempted to imitate the biblical Jael and Judith and personally assassinate the bishop in command of the siege. The prospect of so much martial female initiative getting out of hand appears to have so frightened Jan that he reinstituted biblical polygamy in an effort to keep the city's women under control (Moss and Waite 2019, pp. 168–171). In the horrific suffering which followed the capture of the city, some 278 women would die, and Münster became a byword across Europe for the utter breakdown of society to which Anabaptist doctrine would inevitably lead. One woman prophetess, Aeffgen Lystyncx, appears to have survived, however, and continued her ministry until she was banned from Holland three years later. In the persecutions which followed, Maria and Ursula van Beckum were two Dutch sisters who were burned at the stake in 1544, unmoved by any efforts to talk them out of their convictions.

## *Cuius regio*: Royal Women and the Reformation

On the opposite end of the social spectrum, noble and royal women with evangelical convictions negotiated a complex balancing act between their husbands' wishes, the reach of the fervently Catholic Habsburg dynasty, and their own desire to protect refugee reformers and to advance the faith. In a way, it was perhaps easier on the European frontiers: Isabella, the half-Polish, half-Italian wife of John Zápolya of Hungary, fended off Hapsburg aggression and became regent for her son in 1556, ruling Transylvania and installing Lutheran advisors there (Daniel 1989). In the heartland of the Reformation in Germany, Elisabeth von Brandenburg, also called Elisabeth of Denmark (1485–1555), was married to a brother of the same Albrecht Hohenzollern whose ecclesiastical pluralism had helped to launch the Reformation in 1517 (Stjerna 2009, pp. 87–108). Despite, or because of the closeness of these connections, in 1527 she converted, followed by her daughter, Elisabeth von Braunschweig, or Elisabeth of Brunswick (1510–1558). It would cost both women their marriages and positions. Poor and ill, Elisabeth von Brandenburg was even Luther's houseguest for a time, while her daughter chose a life of exile, writing evangelical hymns and pamphlets.

Meanwhile, the daughter of Marguerite of Navarre, Jeanne d'Albret (1528–1572), grew up a virtual prisoner of her uncle Francis I, with almost no relationship with her mother to speak of. Strong-willed and often ill, when her uncle attempted to marry her to the Catholic Wilhelm of Cleves, Jeanne physically refused to walk down the aisle and threatened to commit suicide. When she was overruled, Jeanne continued to rebel, this time with her mother's help, and eventually the unconsummated marriage was annulled. In 1548, she married the Huguenot Antoine de Bourbon instead. In 1560, she declared herself a full-blown Calvinist, supported by Calvin himself. Almost certainly the strength of her own convictions, as well as her experiences of powerlessness in following them, both as a child and as a young woman, shaped her respect for matters of conscience generally: it would be Jeanne d'Albret who was responsible for the *Ordonnances ecclésiastiques* of 1561 and *The Confession of La Rochelle*, the first attempts to create and foster religious toleration in early modern Europe (Stjerna 2009, p. 170). She died in 1572 of tuberculosis.

Jeanne's daughter, Charlotte de Bourbon (1546–1582), was placed in a convent, where she became abbess of the religious community. She left her vows behind, however, to become the wife of Duke William the Silent, the head of the Dutch cause for independence (Bainton 1973, pp. 89–109). Arguably, the movement was able to begin in the first place because of the long and ambivalent regency of Mary, Queen of Hungary (1505–1558). The sister of the Holy Roman Emperor Charles V, Mary, despite her Spanish connections and her Hapsburg family loyalties, respected the religious convictions of the Dutch and seems to have thoroughly loathed her position as her brother's enforcer (de Iongh 1958; Winder 2020, p. 181).

Renée de France (1510–1575), also called Renata di Ferrara, had the advantage of Jeanne, in that, while she too grew up under Francis I's control, it was a decade earlier, when his sister Marguerite's influence was at its strongest (Stjerna 2009, pp. 175–196). As a consequence, she and Marguerite would be far closer than mother and daughter ever were. Physically plain, Renée was married to Ercole d'Este of Ferrara, the son of the notoriously beautiful Lucrezia Borgia (see Figure 10.5). While never a love match, Renée appears to have held her own, despite never learning Italian and clinging resolutely to

**Figure 10.5** Renée de France, portrait by François Clouet, destroyed in World War II. *Source:* Ministry of Culture and Art / Wikimedia Commons / Public domain.

her French identity. Like Marguerite, Renée's precise religious beliefs are something of an enigma, and like Marguerite, she wrote to Calvin without explicitly taking sides with him, although she seems to have grown closer to his position over time. She provided her children with both Protestant and Catholic tutors, including the radical Pico della Mirandola and the equally free-wheeling leading light of the Italian *spirituali*, Bernardino Ochino. Neither could be said to be particularly law-abiding in their aiding and abetting of religious and political radicalism, and her husband eventually invited the Jesuits to Ferrara in 1548. In the summer of 1554, Renée was herself questioned by the inquisition. Imprisoned, she refused to admit anything until her children were taken away from her, when she finally submitted and recanted (Puaux 1997, pp. 210–218). Impressively, however, Renée lived for another 20 years, which, given the impossible circumstances in which she found herself, was in and of itself something of a diplomatic achievement.

## Italian *Spirituali*

One of the tutors assigned to Renée de France's children was the humanist and evangelical Fulvio Pellegrino Morato, whose daughter, Olimpia Fulvia Morata (1526–1555), would grow up as the childhood companion of Renée's daughter Anne. Surrounded by the Ferraran court, Olimpia was a petted child prodigy, and as such, was taught classical languages and formal academic debate. When the inquisition arrived she was 22, and her glittering life crumbled around her (Puaux 1997, pp. 204–205). Her friend Anne had become alarmingly Catholic, and when her father died she found herself truly desperate. In 1550, Olimpia married a German humanist, Andreas Grunthler, which in spite of her circumstances appears to have been a love match. In the next year Olimpia wrote *The Dialogue of Theophila and Philotina*, which captures something of the lost world most familiar to her – educated noblewomen teaching, talking, and writing to one another (Morata 1562, pp. 58–72). The young couple set out for Germany but found themselves caught up in Charles V's maneuvers against the Lutheran Schmalkaldic League, escaping from a besieged city in 1553 with only the clothes on their backs, leaving all their books behind. Andreas and, less officially, Olimpia seem to have finally found a haven teaching at the University of Heidelberg, but in 1556 she would die, tragically young, of tuberculosis.

Elsewhere in Italy, the lines between humanism, religious reform, mysticism, and evangelical religion were sometimes even more blurry than in the court of Ferrara, not least because few Lutheran treatises were translated into Italian and the humanist debates and dialogues evolved along independent, regional lines. The aristocratic Marchesa de Pescara, Vittoria Colonna (1490–1547), was a member of the *spirituali* and a friend of the moderate Venetian cardinal, Gasparo Contarini (see Figure 10.6). Like him, she managed to be highly critical of the often autocratic Renaissance papacy

**Figure 10.6** Vittoria Colonna, portrait by Sebastiano del Piombo, Museu Nacionale d'Art de Catalunya. *Source:* Vittoria Colonna / Museu Nacional d'Art de Catalunya / Public domain.

and yet escaped censure because of the status of her family. She modeled her own life on that of the Magdalene, whom she often described as the *annunciatrice* and "herald of the Divine Word." One poem describes how,

> Seized in her sadness by that great desire
> which banishes all fear, this beautiful woman
> all alone, by night, helpless, humble, pure,
> and armed only with a living, burning hope
> Entered the sepulchre and wept and lamented;
> ignoring the angels, caring nothing for herself,
> she fell at the feet of the Lord, secure,
> for her heart, aflame with love, feared nothing.
> And the men, chosen to share so many graces,
> though strong, were shut up together in fear:
> the true Light seemed to them only a shadow.
> If, then, the true is not a friend to the false,
> we must give to women all due recognition
> for having a more loving and more constant heart. (Colonna 1982, "Spiritual Poem no. 8";
> Murphy 2005, pp. 138–139; Rafanelli 2012; Brundin, Crivelli, and Sapegno 2016).

Caterina Cibo, the Duchess of Camerino (d. 1557), was another patroness of the ever-restless Ochino, while Giulia Gonzaga (d. 1566) presided over her court in Naples and patronized Ochino's mentor, the Spanish bible translator Juan de Valdés (Russell 2006; Ottaviani 2010). To what extent any of these figures, even Ochino, can be considered Protestant is highly conjectural; they represent, at most, only the seeds of an evangelical movement in Italy that would be swept up by the Catholic Reformation.

## The King's Great Matter and the Queen's Religion

The woman whose name is inextricably linked with the Reformation in England is, of course, Anne Boleyn (1501–1536). Henry's decision to divorce Isabella of Castile's daughter, Catherine of Aragon, and marry Anne led to the Act of Supremacy in 1534, made Henry the head of the church in England, and was a calculated act of political ambition. But by 1534, eight years into the affair, the King's Great Matter had become many things, political, religious, and sexual, inextricably tangled together: Henry's obsession with the fascinating Anne, vindication and revenge against Catherine, who had failed to bear a son and with whom, Henry had convinced himself, he had committed incest, vindication and revenge against the church which had signally failed to endorse Henry's plan, Henry's desperate need for a male heir to compensate for the instability of the still-fragile Tudor dynasty, a means by which to confiscate the wealth of the monasteries in the name of defending and purifying the church, and above all, the means to assert Henry's own will over and against any other authority in England.

It remains very difficult to see Anne clearly apart from all of this, not least because her reign, in the end, was very brief indeed. The daughter of ambitious and very new money, Anne was humanist- and French-educated; it was she who owned a copy of Marguerite of Navarre's *Mirror*. When she converted is not known, but the Boleyn family was from East Anglia, the region of England most intimately connected to the continent and the heartland of evangelical sympathies. Thomas Cranmer owed his position as Henry's archbishop of Canterbury to his time as Anne's father's chaplain, supported by the canny realpolitik of Henry's chancellor, the evangelical Thomas Cromwell. During her three-year reign, the trio of Queen Anne, Cranmer, and Cromwell were responsible for recruiting, promoting, and creating a circle of evangelical bishops who carried forward the Reformation in England under Henry and the reign of his son, Edward VI, the overall shape of whose Reformation Elizabeth retained (MacCulloch 1999, pp. 105–156; 2018, pp. 116–120, 205–230, 297–317). The Protestant cause was, in fact, perhaps the only thing Cromwell and Queen Anne sincerely agreed about; it is, ironically, their joint and lasting legacy, even while their own personality conflicts created rifts within the movement. Meanwhile, from the moment she consented to a sexual relationship with Henry, the pressure on Anne to produce a son, amidst the constant scrutiny and surveillance of the court, was suffocating. Elizabeth was her only surviving child. Anne would, in fact, miscarry three times in a little over two years, once when Henry was knocked unconscious on the jousting field, again soon after the death of Catherine of Aragon in January of 1536. This baby had been a son. Without him, Anne became disposable, as Henry's attentions turned elsewhere and her enemies closed in around her. Cromwell engineered the queen's downfall with a flurry of charges of adultery, witchcraft, and treason. The shocked Cranmer heard the queen's last confession before she went to her execution in 1536 (MacCulloch 1996, pp. 155–160; 2018, pp. 336–342).

Meanwhile, many evangelicals in England began to wonder if Henry wanted true religion after all. Nowhere was Henry's desire to control and limit the religious change he had unleashed more in evidence than in his conflicted attitude to vernacular scripture. It had been a woman printer, Françoise Le Rouge, who first published Tyndale's translation of the Old Testament into English; Lyon, because of its proximity to Geneva, would be a particularly important Huguenot printing center (Broomhall 2002). Tyndale himself had been forced into exile and then executed on the continent in 1535, and yet it was largely Tyndale's work, already circulating in thousands of copies in England, which was coopted into Henry's first authorized version of scripture, the Great Bible of 1539. In 1543, an Act of Parliament banned all women except gentry from vernacular bible reading. Ironically, however, it appears to have been a copy of the Great Bible which inspired a

Lincolnshire woman, Anne Askew (1521–1546), to defy her husband and read it anyway, demanding a divorce when he tried to stop her. Undaunted, she even set herself next to the bible on display in Lincoln Cathedral to preach and to debate with all comers. She claimed, as a woman, that she did not have the authority to interpret scripture, and yet it is very clear in Anne's case that, in practice, proclamation of the Word edged into precisely that. Questioned by the bishop of London, Anne was initially released in 1545, but the king's secretary, the Catholic bishop of Winchester, Stephen Gardiner, had her arrested and imprisoned in the Tower of London. There she would be the only woman put on the rack, but even there, she refused to recant. Anne was so debilitated as a result of her torture that she had to be carried to her execution, where she was burned at the stake in 1546 (see Figure 10.7).

The story of Anne's "examinations" was seized upon by the Protestant pamphleteer John Bale. For Bale, it was precisely Anne's gender which sensationalized her already gripping story, signaling both the urgency and the drama of the moment. Anne's witness spoke to a certain apocalypticism felt in evangelical circles, particularly in light of the resurgent conservative reaction spearheaded by Gardiner and his circle in the last, erratic years of Henry VIII. As a witness, Anne Askew triumphed, not with miracles, but as a conduit of the word of God. Bale even typeset his edition with headings to make it look as if it were printed abroad, placing Anne's story in a direct line of descent from Tyndale and Tyndale's friend John Frith, who had been executed in 1533 (Watt 1997, pp. 81–117; Dean 2018, pp. 37–53). The tactic worked: Bale's edition was hugely popular, and went through six editions before it became a centerpiece of Foxe's 1563 *Acts and Monuments*, more commonly called *The Book of Martyrs* (Coles 2008, pp. 4, 17–44). And yet, although it is clear that Bale saw the torture of Anne Askew and her suffering as akin to Christ's, he was also

**Figure 10.7** The burning of Anne Askew at Smithfield. *Source:* Lebrecht Music & Arts / Alamy Stock Photo.

discomfited by her forthright decision to leave her husband for the faith. By 1563, Foxe was also hesitant about Anne as an example of Protestant femininity, not least because of the precedent she seemed to set for so-called "gospelling sisters," Puritan women who would not be silent in church and who had become the targets of gleeful Catholic polemic (Hickerson 2005).

In this way, the very power of Anne Askew's witness almost immediately made her as polarizing a figure as Anne Boleyn herself. In fact, when Stephen Gardiner had arrested Anne in London, she was, in all likelihood, not his primary target. This was Henry's sixth and last wife, Catherine Parr (c. 1512–1548). The daughter of Northamptonshire gentry, her father had died and she had been raised and educated by her devout mother. Married young to a much older man who had already had children of his own, when he died she married a second time. But her second husband was also dying when, at the age of 31, she caught Henry's eye in 1543. The king by then was a volatile physical wreck of the perfect Renaissance prince he had once been, and Catherine does not seem to have been particularly joyful at the prospect of becoming queen, not least because she seems to have been in love with someone else. But she accepted the king's suit, and became a steadying influence on Henry and a good stepmother, particularly for the young Elizabeth but also for Mary (see Figure 10.8). Much as Anne Boleyn had once done, Catherine gathered around her a circle of like-minded evangelical ladies-in-waiting as part of her household. It was these women, with their sometimes radical tastes, with whom Anne Askew seems to have been in contact, and perhaps even with Catherine herself. At least, that was Gardiner's hope (Loewenstein 2013, pp. 69–101). But Catherine got wind of the trap before it was fully sprung, and took to her bed in quite sincere terror, loudly protesting her helplessness and undying loyalty to Henry. Mollified, the king refused to countenance Gardiner's accusations, and Queen Catherine was spared. She would even be made regent while Henry went on campaign in 1544.

When Henry died in 1547, Catherine Parr was finally able to marry Thomas Seymour, her former suitor when Henry had interposed himself. Even then the marriage was secret at first. The princess

**Figure 10.8** Princess Elizabeth Tudor, portrait attributed to William Scrots, Windsor Castle. *Source:* Juulijs/Adobe Stock.

Elizabeth was then 14, and although she spoke fondly of him in later years, Seymour may have attempted to molest the girl. It was certainly for this that the Privy Council executed him, and Catherine died in the next year of complications following the birth of her first child in four marriages (Dean 2018, pp. 54–71).

As well as *The Lamentacion of a Synner*, inspired by the work of Marguerite of Navarre, Catherine Parr also composed an immensely popular collection of devotions. Her *Prayers or Meditacions* would go through seven editions by 1550 and 20 by the end of the century. Part of the reason for its success was Catherine's ability to take up the forms of late medieval vernacular devotional literature and translate them into the new, evangelical spirit. In effect, she was acting as a sort of pastor's wife writ large, the wife of the head of the church in England. Her book was quite literally bound together with Cranmer's first English litany in 1545 (Coles 2008, pp. 45–74). As such, it represents an early version or attempt at creating an English prayer book, and in fact, after Catherine's death, it was her translation of the "Prayer for the Sovereign" which Cranmer would incorporate into the first Book of Common Prayer in 1549. Catherine would also translate part of Thomas à Kempis's *Imitation of Christ*, and she may well have translated John Fisher's treatise on the seven penitential psalms as well – an ironic possibility, given that Henry had beheaded Fisher alongside Thomas More for their refusal to countenance his divorce. In this way, while Henry may have remained profoundly ambivalent about Holy Writ in the vernacular for anyone to read, it was Catherine Parr who quietly and firmly advanced the witness of Anne Askew, and in a way, the religious legacy of Anne Boleyn as well.

Another of Catherine's evangelical protégées was the young Jane Grey (1537–1554), the great-granddaughter of Henry VII. When Edward VI lay dying, the boy king was still too young to make a valid will of his own to override his father's intentions, leaving his sister Mary next in the line of succession to the throne. All the potential claimants to the throne were women, in fact – a fitting irony of history, considering that it had been through a woman, Margaret Beaufort, that the Tudor dynasty had made its claim to the throne in the first place. Desperate to preserve evangelical reform in England, Edward, the Duke of Northumberland, and a circle of advisors drew up an improvisatory scheme in which the 16-year-old Jane, who was married to Northumberland's son, would be crowned queen. When Edward died, his death was concealed for three days, and Jane knew absolutely nothing of her fate until it was thrust upon her (Hoak 2015). Northumberland was captured by Mary's forces a week later, and pressured by Mary to re-convert to Catholicism before he was executed. It was Jane, the "nine days' queen," who refused to conform, and went to her death in 1554.

The daughter of one of the officials involved in Edward's plan was Lady Jane's cousin and exact contemporary, Lady Jane Lumley (1537–1578). Jane would go on to make the first complete translation of Euripides into English, which is also one of the first plays to be written in English by a woman. In fact, one can question to what extent the work is a "translation," as opposed to Jane Lumley's particular adaptation of the original source material. In *Iphigenia in Aulis*, in her description of the sacrifice of Agamemnon's daughter Iphigenia, the girl is transformed into a stag at the last minute before she can be sacrificed by her father. It is hard not to imagine that she was thinking of Jane (Knoppers 2009, pp. 249–250).

Under the reign of Mary, many of Catherine Parr's former circle were forced to go abroad. Stephen Gardiner, now made royal chancellor, smuggled his own goddaughter, Catherine Willoughby (1519–1580), Duchess of Suffolk and cousin of Lady Jane, out of England. Also called Catherine Bertie after her second marriage, Catherine was a redoubtable evangelical, even a kind of early Puritan. Landing on the Dutch coast in the fog, she would later call her son Peregrine, or "pilgrim," a particularly apt choice of name for a woman who would travel to Germany, Poland,

and even Lithuania with her husband, before returning to England under Elizabeth, of whom she did not always approve (Bainton 1973, pp. 253–276; Zahl 2001, pp. 75–91). In 1557, the Englishwoman Anne Locke (1530-bef. 1607) packed up her life and her two children and moved to Geneva. Her father had been a friend of both Tyndale and Cromwell, while her mother had been in Anne Boleyn's household, and in Geneva she would become one of the many women with whom John Knox would correspond, writing him some 15 letters by 1562. It is perhaps unfortunate that Knox is best known for his treatise against Mary Stuart, *A First Blast of the Trumpet against the Monstrous Regiment of Women*; Knox seems to have been much more comfortable than Calvin in writing to and maintaining friendships with women (MacCulloch 2003, pp. 655–656). One of the many links between the English Reformation and the Swiss, in Geneva Anne Locke would translate some of Calvin's sermons into English, as well as an English version of Psalm 51, and in 1560 would embark on a sonnet sequence (Felch 2011a, 2011b; Giselbrecht 2014). Her son, the poet Henry Vaughan, likewise used English verse to translate Calvin's teachings on the psalter for the English public (Coles 2008, pp. 113–148). Another woman who had been targeted by Gardiner in the 1546 plot was Elizabeth Tyrwhit (c. 1510–1578), a Sussex noblewoman who was, briefly, the princess Elizabeth's governess after Catherine's death. The teenage Elizabeth detested the older woman for the strictness of her piety, but despite her reputation she and her husband thrived in the reign of Mary. In 1574, she went on to publish a book of devotions, *Morning and Evening Prayers*, intended for use in private houses, as part of a charm offensive on the part of evangelicals with Elizabeth, now queen for a decade and more (Felch 2008). One wonders if it was a rather unfortunate choice of messenger.

The psalter had been the mainstay of late medieval lay devotion. Translated into English and sung, it became the mainstay of evangelical lay devotion in the English Reformation, ironically, its continuity with the past one of the chief reasons for its popularity (Gant 2017). However, there were those evangelicals who preferred the psalter of the Geneva Bible to the translation of Coverdale. Carrying on the cause of evangelical reform in the graceful English verse of the court was the Countess of Pembroke, Mary Sidney Herbert (1561–1621). When her brother the poet Philip Sidney died, Mary continued his unfinished translation of the psalter. Her near-constant process, both creative and spiritual, of meditation and revision renders it virtually impossible now to disentangle the countess's work from her brother's (Clark 2011; Full 2011).

Another English writer to bridge the late medieval and early modern devotional worlds was Grace Sharington, Lady Mildmay (1552–1620), the wife of Elizabeth's chancellor of the exchequer. Like Catherine Parr, she was the author of a book of meditations, as well as a kind of spiritual autobiography dedicated to her daughter and her grandson. Her work, as well as that of the writers Elizabeth Grymeston and Dorothy Leigh, represents a distinctive and emerging genre of Protestant devotional literature at this time: a kind of extended family meditation in which spiritual authority derived from and was shaped by a woman's role as the mother of her household (Knoppers 2009, p. 74; Warren 2010, pp. 77–95). It would be a woman, Anne Cooke Bacon (d. 1610), who would translate into English *An Apologia for the English Church*, the great work of Elizabeth's second archbishop of Canterbury, John Jewel. Precisely because her work was anonymous, Anne was able to make her work speak for, and on behalf of, the whole English church (Demers 2011; Magnusson 2011).

In this way, over the course of the Reformation Protestant women translators were able to make the most of the shelter of anonymity. By contrast, perhaps the least anonymous Protestant woman in the sixteenth century, the most polarizing figure in European politics, was the daughter of Anne Boleyn, Elizabeth I (1533–1603). Taught by her brother's tutors and by the learned Catherine Parr, Elizabeth had a magnificent humanist education and, in many ways, seems to have been at her happiest wrangling with Oxford scholars. Her court scholars loved to depict her as Queen Solomon, learned in Greek biblical manuscripts (Shenk 2010, pp. 21–54, 159–188; Petrina and Tosi 2011). After spending the five years of her sister's reign a conforming, if suspect, Catholic, when Elizabeth was free to declare her own spiritual convictions no one was in particular doubt that she would follow her mother, her stepmother, and her brother, if not quite with his reforming zeal. In many ways, however, over the course of her long reign the queen would come to resemble no one so much as her father: in her use of studied ambiguity, her refusal to commit herself too deeply to any particular religious ideology, and the assertion of her will made all the more ruthless because of the ongoing vulnerability and instability in her rule created by her gender. Whom would she marry? Who would succeed her? Targeted continually by Catholic assassins, Elizabeth's regime relied on a complex surveillance and intelligence network to anticipate the next plot. And yet, while the 39 Articles and the Book of Common Prayer all followed upon precedents from Edward VI's brief reign, Elizabeth always associated the Reformed tradition with John Knox and his unfortunate outburst originally directed at Mary Stuart, *A Monstrous Regiment of Women*, decrying a woman's ability to rule. By the end of the sixteenth century, persistent Catholic mockery of Elizabeth's more Calvinist subjects had, paradoxically, helped to create Puritanism as a religious identity (Alford 2012; Marshall 2017, p. 470).

Elizabeth came to the throne under the shadow of invasion from her sister's husband, Philip II, a threat that would not dissipate until the English defeat of the Spanish Armada in 1588. And yet, in her glittering public persona and the creation of her virtual cult at court, the woman Elizabeth most resembled was that most Catholic of monarchs, Isabella of Spain. Both women were, after all, distantly related descendants of John of Gaunt. Both oversaw a rapidly expanding Catholic and then Protestant European presence in the New World, alongside increasingly centralized and ambitious mechanisms of rule at home. Both to some extent are credited, for better or worse, with indelibly shaping the national character, respectively, of England and Spain. Both recognized the value of patronizing and thereby partly controlling the work of particular artists and playwrights and the nature of the national history that circulated in popular discourse. Both were highly adept creators of complex and ornate public images of themselves (Morgan 2021). Finally, to this end, both drew heavily on traditions of iconography and devotion to the Virgin Mary, which in turn drew on even older depictions of Sophia, Lady Wisdom. By chance, Elizabeth's birthday happened to be the eve of the feast of the nativity of the Virgin. Despite her Protestant beliefs or even because of them, as the Virgin Queen, Elizabeth sought to redirect older, medieval English devotion to Mary toward loyalty to the English crown (Warren 2005, p. 156). Under Catherine Parr's tutelage, Elizabeth may have begun as a translator of Marguerite of Navarre, and, unwittingly, of Marguerite Porete. She ended with her own political Assumption.

## References

Alford, S. (2012). *The Watchers: A Secret History of the Reign of Elizabeth I*. London: Allen Lane.

Arnold, M. (2018). *The Magdalene in the Reformation*. Cambridge, MA: The Belknap Press.

Bainton, R. (1973). *Women of the Reformation in France and England*. Minneapolis: Augsburg Publishing House.

Broomhall, S. (2002). *Women and the Book Trade in Sixteenth-Century France*. Aldershot: Ashgate.

Brundin, A., Crivelli, T., and Sapegno, M.S. (ed.) (2016). *A Companion to Vittoria Colonna*. Leiden: Brill.

Calvin, J. (1898). Épistre contre un certain Cordelier suppost de la secte des libertins lequel est prisonnier à roan. *Calvini opera* 7: cols. 341–364.

Cholakian, P.F. and Cholakian, R.C. (2006). *Marguerite of Navarre: Mother of the Renaissance.* New York: Columbia Press.

Clark, D. (2011). The Countess of Pembroke and the practice of piety. In: *The Intellectual Culture of Puritan Women, 1558–1680* (ed. J. Harris and E. Scott-Bauman), 28–41. London: Palgrave Macmillan.

Coles, K.A. (2008). *Religion, Reform, and Women's Writing in Early Modern England.* Cambridge: Cambridge University Press.

Colonna, V. (1982). *Rime* (ed. A. Bullock). Laterza: Rome.

Daniel, D. (1989). Piety, politics, and perversion: noblewomen in reformation Hungary. In: *Women in Reformation and Counter-Reformation Europe: Public and Private Worlds* (ed. S. Marshall), 68–88. Bloomington: Indiana University Press.

Dean, J. (2018). *To Gain at Harvest: Portraits from the English Reformation.* London: SCM Press.

Deane, J.K. (2016). Elastic institutions: beguine communities in early modern Germany. In: *Devout Laywomen in the Early Modern World* (ed. A. Weber), 175–195. London: Routledge.

Demers, P. (2011). "Neither bitterly nor brablingly": Lady Anne Cooke Bacon's translation of Bishop Jewel's *Apologia Ecclesiae Anglicanae.* In: *English Women, Religion, and Textual Production, 1500–1625* (ed. M. White), 205–217. Farnham: Ashgate.

Dinan, S. (2016). Nursing as a vocation or a profession? Women's status and the meaning of healing in early modern France and England. In: *Devout Laywomen in the Early Modern World* (ed. A. Weber), 69–88. London: Routledge.

Elizabeth I (2009). 1544: Marguerite de Navarre's *Le Miroir de l'âme pecheresse.* In: *Elizabeth I: Translations, 1544–1589* (ed. J. Mueller and J. Scodell), 25–125. Chicago: University of Chicago Press.

Felch, S.M. (2008). *Elizabeth Tyrwhit's Morning and Evening Prayers.* Aldershot: Ashgate.

Felch, S.M. (2011a). The exemplary Anne Vaughan Lock. In: *The Intellectual Culture of Puritan Women, 1558–1680* (ed. J. Harris and E. Scott-Bauman), 15–27. London: Palgrave Macmillan.

Felch, S.M. (2011b). "Halff a scripture woman": heteroglossia and female authorial agency in prayers by Lady Elizabeth Tyrwhit, Ann Lock, and Anne Wheathill. In: *English Women, Religion, and Textual Production, 1500–1625* (ed. M. White), 147–166. Farnham: Ashgate.

Full, M. (2011). "Theise dearest offerings of my heart": the sacrifice of praise in Mary Sidney Herbert, Countess of Pembroke's *Psalmes.* In: *English Women, Religion, and Textual Production, 1500–1625* (ed. M. White), 37–58. Farnham: Ashgate.

Gant, A. (2017). *O Sing Unto the Lord: A History of English Church Music.* Chicago: University of Chicago Press.

Giselbrecht, R. (2014). Religious intent and the art of courteous pleasantry: a few letters from Englishwomen to Heinrich Bullinger (1543–1562). In: *Women During the English Reformations: Renegotiating Gender and Religious Identity* (ed. J.A. Chappell and K.A. Kramer), 45–67. London: Palgrave Macmillan.

Grindlay, L. (2018). *Queen of Heaven: The Assumption and Coronation of the Virgin in Early Modern English Writing.* Notre Dame: University of Notre Dame Press.

Hasenhohr, G. (2017). The tradition of the *Mirror of Simple Souls* in the fifteenth century: from Marguerite Porete (d. 1310) to Marguerite of Navarre (d. 1549). In: *A Companion to Marguerite Porete and the Mirror of Simple Souls* (trans. Z. Kocher) (ed. R. Stauffer and W.R. Terry), 155–185. Leiden: Brill.

Hasenohr, G. (2013). La seconde vie du *Miroir du simples âmes* en France: le livre de la discipline d'amour divine (xv–xviiiième s.). In: *Marguerite Porete et le Miroir des simples âmes: perspectives historiques, philosophiques, et littéraires* (ed. S. Field, R. Lerner and S. Piron), 263–317. Paris: Vrin.

Hickerson, M.L. (2005). *Making Women Martyrs in Tudor England*. London: Palgrave Macmillan.

Hoak, D. (2015). The succession crisis of 1553 and Mary's rise to power. In: *Catholic Renewal and Protestant Resistance in Marian England* (ed. E. Evenden and V. Westbrook), 17–42. Farnham: Ashgate.

de Iongh, J. (1958). *Mary of Hungary: Second Regent of the Netherlands* (trans. M.D. Herter Norton). London: Faber and Faber.

Jordan, C. (1990). *Renaissance Feminism: Literary Texts and Political Models*. Ithaca: Cornell University Press.

Karant-Nunn, S. (2000). Reformation society, women, and the family. In: *The Reformation World* (ed. A. Pettegree), 433–460. London: Routledge.

Kelly, J. (1984). Did women have a Renaissance. In: *Women, History, and Theory*, reprinted ed., 19–51. Chicago: University of Chicago Press.

Knoppers, L.L. (ed.) (2009). *The Cambridge Companion to Early Modern Women's Writing*. Cambridge: Cambridge University Press.

Kuijpers, E. (2015). "O Lord, save us from shame": narratives of emotions in convent chronicles by female authors during the Dutch Revolt, 1566–1635. In: *Gender and Emotions in Medieval and Early Modern Europe: Destroying Order, Structuring Disorder* (ed. S. Broomhall), 127–146. Farnham: Ashgate.

Vidal, D. (ed.) (1997). *La perle évangelique (1602)*. Jérôme: Grenoble.

Lefèvre d'Étaples, J. (2009). *Jacques Lefèvre d'Étaples and the Three Maries Debates*. (ed. and trans S.M. Porrer). Geneva: Droz.

Leonard, A. (2005). *Nails in the Wall: Catholic Nuns in Reformation Germany*. Chicago: University of Chicago Press.

Lipscomb, S. (2019). *The Voices of Nîmes: Women, Sex, and Marriage in Reformation Languedoc*. Oxford: Oxford University Press.

Loewenstein, D. (2013). *Treacherous Faith: The Specter of Heresy in Early Modern English Literature and Culture*. Oxford: Oxford University Press.

Luther, M. (2003). *The Table-Talk of Martin Luther* (trans. W. Hazlitt). Fearn: Christian Focus Publications.

MacCulloch, D. (1996). *Thomas Cranmer: A Life*. New Haven: Yale University Press.

MacCulloch, D. (1999). *Tudor Church Militant: Edward VI and the Protestant Reformation*. London: Allen Lane.

MacCulloch, D. (2003). *Reformation: Europe's House Divided: 1490–1700*. London: Allen Lane.

MacCulloch, D. (2018). *Thomas Cromwell: A Life*. London: Allen Lane.

Magnusson, L. (2011). Imagining a National Church: election and education in the works of Anne Cooke Bacon. In: *The Intellectual Culture of Puritan Women, 1558–1680* (ed. J. Harris and E. Scott-Bauman), 42–56. London: Palgrave Macmillan.

Marguerite of Navarre (1995). *The Prisons of Marguerite of Navarre* (trans. H. Dale). Reading: Whiteknights Press.

Marguerite of Navarre (2008). The mirror of a simple soul. In: *Selected Writings: A Bilingual Edition* (ed. R. Cholakian and M. Skemp), 73–149. Chicago: University of Chicago Press.

Marshall, S. (1989). Protestant, Catholic, and Jewish women in the early modern Netherlands. In: *Women in Reformation and Counter-Reformation Worlds* (ed. S. Marshall), 120–139. Bloomington: Indiana University Press.

Marshall, P. (2017). *Heretics and Believers: A History of the English Reformation*. New Haven: Yale University Press.

McKee, E.A. (1999). *Katharina Schütz Zell: The Life and Thought of a Sixteenth-Century Reformer*, vol. 2. Leiden: Brill.

Morata, O.F. (1562). The dialogue of Theophila and Philotina. In: *Orationes, epistolae, carmina tam latina tam graeca*. Basel: Fernam.

Morgan, C. (2021). Mélusine: the myth that built Europe. *History Today* 71 (7): 76–83.

Moss, C. and Waite, G.K. (2019). Argula von Grumbach, Katharina Schütz Zell, and Anabaptist and Jorist women. In: *Protestants and Mysticism in Reformation Europe* (ed. R.K. Rittgers and V. Evener), 159–178. Leiden: Brill.

Murphy, C.P. (2005). *The Pope's Daughter: The Extraordinary Life of Felice della Rovere*. Oxford: Oxford University Press.

Ottaviani, M.G.N. (2010). Important ladies and important families: Lucrezia Borgia and Caterina Cibo Varano. In: *Medieval Italy, Medieval and Early Modern Women: Essays in Honour of Christine Meek* (ed. C. Kostick), 276–282. Dublin: Four Courts Press.

Ozment, S. (1983). *When Fathers Ruled: Family Life in Reformation Europe*. Cambridge: Harvard University Press.

Peters, C. (2003). *Patterns of Piety: Women, Gender and Religion in Late Medieval and Reformation England*. Cambridge: Cambridge University Press.

Petrina, A. and Tosi, L. (ed.) (2011). *Representations of Elizabeth I in Early Modern Culture*. London: Palgrave Macmillan.

Plummer, M.E. (2012). *From Priest's Whore to Pastor's Wife: Clerical Marriage and the Process of Reform in the Early German Reformation*, 2012. Farnham: Ashgate.

Plummer, M.E. (2016). Neither nun nor laywoman: entering Lutheran convents during the reformation of female religious communities in the Duchy of Braunschweig, 1542–1655. In: *Devout Laywomen in the Early Modern World* (ed. A. Weber), 196–218. London: Routledge.

Puaux, A. (1997). *La Huguenote: Renée de France*. Paris: Herman.

Rafanelli, L.M. (2012). Michaelangelo's *Noli me tangere* for Vittoria Colonna, and the changing status of women in Renaissance Italy. In: *Mary Magdalene: Iconographic Studies from the Middle Ages to the Baroque* (ed. M.A. Erhard and A.M. Morris), 223–248. Leiden: Brill.

Reid, J. (2009). *King's Sister, Queen of Dissent: Marguerite of Navarre (1492–1549) and Her Evangelical Network*, vol. 2. Leiden: Brill.

Roper, L. (1989). *The Holy Household: Women and Morals in Reformation Augsburg*. Oxford: Clarendon.

Rubin, M. (2009). *Mother of God: A History of the Virgin Mary*. New Haven: Yale University Press.

Russell, C. (2006). *Giulia Gonzaga and the Religious Controversies of Sixteenth-Century Italy*. Turnhout: Brepols.

Schlotheuber, E. (2014). Intellectual horizons: letters from a northern German convent. In: *A Companion to Mysticism and Devotion in Northern Germany in the Late Middle Ages* (ed. E. Andersen, H. Lähnemann and A. Simon), 343–372. Leiden: Brill.

Shenk, L. (2010). *Learned Queen: The Image of Elizabeth I in Politics and Poetry*. London: Palgrave Macmillan.

Stjerna, K. (2009). *Women and the Reformation*. Oxford: Blackwell.

Thysell, C. (2000). *The Pleasure of Discernment: Marguerite of Navarre as Theologian*. Oxford: Oxford University Press.

Todd, M. (1987). *Christian Humanism and the Puritan Social Order*. Cambridge: Cambridge University Press.

Van Nieuwenhove, R., Robert Faesen, S.J., and Rolfson, H. (ed.) (2008). *Late Medieval Mysticism of the Low Countries*. New York: Paulist Press.

Vance, J. (2014). *Secrets: Humanism, Mysticism, and Evangelicalism in Erasmus of Rotterdam, Bishop Guillaume Briçonnet, and Marguerite of Navarre*. Leiden: Brill.

Warren, N.B. (2005). *Women of God and Arms: Female Spirituality and Political Conflict, 1380–1600*. Philadelphia: University of Pennsylvania Press.

Warren, N.B. (2010). *The Embodied Word: Female Spiritualities, Contested Orthodoxies, and English Religious Culture, 1350–1700*. Notre Dame: University of Notre Dame Press.

Watt, D. (1997). *Secretaries of God: Women Prophets in Late Medieval and Early Modern England*. Cambridge: D.S. Brewer.

Weisner-Hanks, M.E. (2019). *Women and Gender in Early Modern Europe*, 4e. Cambridge: Cambridge University Press.

Wiesner, M. (1989). Nuns, wives, and mothers: women and the Reformation in Germany. In: *Women in Reformation and Counter-Reformation Worlds* (ed. S. Marshall), 8–28. Bloomington: Indiana University Press.

Wilson, D. (2016). *Mrs. Luther and Her Sisters: Women in the Reformation*. Oxford: Lion Hudson.

Winder, S. (2020). *Lotharingia: A Personal History of France, Germany and the Countries in Between*. London: Picador.

Zahl, P.F.M. (2001). *Five Women of the English Reformation*. Grand Rapids: Eerdmans.

# 11

# Women in the Catholic Reformation, 1500–1600

In 1516, the bishop of Winchester, Richard Fox, decided to translate the Benedictine Rule into English for the women's communities in his diocese. Fox's Rule deliberately used feminine language throughout and, with its mixture of translation and commentary, was intended to further, more or less gently, the twin causes of reform and good administration (Collett 2002). Fox had been a close advisor of Henry VII, the architect of the original marriage between Catherine of Aragon and the young prince Arthur, and the predecessor of Cardinal Wolsey, Henry VIII's flamboyant chancellor who would be brought low by his failure to bring about the king's divorce. Like his rival Wolsey, Fox was one of the new men of the Tudor bureaucracy, and like Wolsey, Fox cherished a vision of the renewal of the church coming out of the colleges. He was himself the founder of Corpus Christi College, Oxford, with Wolsey endowing his own, much larger foundation at Christ Church just across the street. Among his women's communities, Fox backed as abbess of the ancient foundation of Romsey Abbey the former schoolmistress Anne Westbrook. When he encouraged the abbesses within his jurisdiction to own their right and proper authority as delineated by the Benedictine Rule, he spoke from long experience.

Fox and his vernacular Rule represents one direction in which Catholic reform might have gone in England and elsewhere, were it not for Luther: humanist, Latinate, but with increasing room for the vernacular, particularly for literate women. Pastoral care would have been provided by university-trained clergy living in college-like accommodation, the smaller and less self-sufficient monastic communities allowed to die out naturally. It is not unrecognizable, but it is wildly different from the halting course the Reformation in England would eventually take, not to mention in the rest of Europe. It is also a reminder that the Catholic response to the Reformation, when it came, was itself qualitatively distinct and different from the shared late medieval world that had existed before, just as it cannot be seen as only a "counter-Reformation," an equal and opposite reaction to Luther (O'Malley 2009). Across sixteenth-century Europe, Protestant and Catholic churches could not help but evolve and define their own distinctive religious identities with each other in mind. In a process akin to corporate branding in the contemporary marketplace, what had begun as an inward-looking reassessment of the nature of faith and devotion, by the end of the sixteenth century increasingly revolved around external markers of religious identity: hymns and church music, attitudes to religious art, dress, particularly favored editions of the biblical text (Hsia 1989; Dixon 2016; Rummel 2000; Headley et al. 2016). And yet, this long-term process of religious differentiation, sometimes called confessionalization, can mask deeper similarities and continuities in society with regard to gender across confessional lines. In particular, both Protestant and Catholic traditions shared similar ideas about the nature and role of the godly household,

*A History of Women in Christianity to 1600*, First Edition. Hannah Matis.
© 2023 John Wiley & Sons Ltd. Published 2023 by John Wiley & Sons Ltd.

stemming partly from shared humanist presuppositions, partly from the desire on both sides to appropriate the late antique and patristic tradition, and partly simply from shared cultural norms in early modern Europe.

## The Council of Trent and the Catholic Reformation

At the same time, within the Catholic Church, the challenge and the success of the Protestant Reformation prompted a reevaluation of both clerical masculinity and forms of life for religious women. Central in articulating and defining the church of the Catholic Reformation was the Council of Trent, which began in 1545 but which would extend over nearly two decades, codifying church teaching and pronouncing on an enormous range of matters in the life of the church, not least the ratification of a revised and corrected edition of the Latin Vulgate Bible. The council's chief priority was the elimination of the absenteeism and pluralism in church offices so endemic to the late medieval church, and which had caused the vacuum in pastoral care around which the Protestant critique had revolved. The reestablishment of a consistent and well-educated pastoral presence throughout Europe, therefore, can be said to be the chief goal of the Council of Trent, with the papal approval of the Society of Jesus as an extension of this aim. Ignatius Loyola and the Jesuits, as well as the Cardinal Archbishop of Milan, Federico Borromeo, and the Florentine Philip Neri, best represent this muscular and extroverted reinvention of Catholic clerical masculinity (Strasser 2008; Milligan and Tylus 2010, pp. 13–40). As a corollary to this aim, the council dictated that women should be *aut maritus aut murus*, either married or enclosed. Many bishops aimed to eliminate the ambiguities and proliferating varieties of late medieval penitent spirituality in favor of a stripped-down administrative clarity that presented no vulnerable underbelly to Protestant polemical attacks.

Despite the forbidding connotations of Tridentine Catholicism, however, the council was, in fact, a fragile and conflicted creation (O'Malley 2013; Hsia 2005, pp. 10–25). From the point of view of the papacy, the Council of Constance a century before, which had resolved the Great Schism by dethroning three popes, had set a highly dangerous precedent in asserting conciliar over papal authority. Trent occurred, therefore, despite rather than with the full support of the head of Catholic Christendom, and the popes remained beset by political and familial rivalries. In particular, Italian nervousness around Hapsburg Spain, the richest and most powerful nation in Europe and ostensibly the spearhead of any unified Catholic response to Luther, in fact set a pope like Paul IV and Philip II of Spain often at cross-purposes. France profoundly mistrusted all things Hapsburg. This ensured that the Catholic Reformation, as much as the Protestant, would take on a regional, national quality, with no one party principally responsible for its implementation. With regard to its dictates concerning women in particular, Trent does not seem to have been enforced with particular success, any more than earlier legislation against the beguines had been, and for many of the same reasons – it was not always clear when and to what sort of women's community the legislation should apply. The 1563 *Decretum de regularibus et monialibus* and the 1566 decree *Circa pastoralis* represented yet more efforts to regulate monastic orders, particularly the lay, tertiary members of the Franciscans and Dominicans, by insisting that they make formal vows. However, these too were only irregularly followed. Fiercely independent Venice, for example, had a long tradition of well-educated and articulate women, in religious communities and beyond, and generally ignored both these measures and papal efforts to ban women from composing music.

In some cases, male clergy themselves supported the work of religious women, acting as sponsors of the new religious orders that would emerge in the Catholic Reformation, or recognizing the important work that many religious women did even if they were not enclosed. In other cases, socio-economic factors conspired to make *aut maritus aut murus* an ideal rather than the reality. In Spain, which sent huge numbers of fighting men to the New World in the sixteenth century, there were simply not enough men left behind to insist that women marry if they could not take formal vows. Throughout Europe, as women's economic fortunes slid and dowries inflated, there was not always enough money for marriage always to be a reasonable expectation for laywomen (Weber 2016). And finally, the slow and unfolding nature of Trent itself told in some ways against the rigorous enforcement of its own legislation: because the council had been so slow to begin, some women's orders, such as Angela Merici and the Ursulines, had already developed the particular nature of their vocation before Trent subsequently insisted on their enclosure. These women had to adapt and evolve in what they were already doing, but they had the advantage of the initiative.

Ironically, it was in its last moments that Trent approved a scattershot of measures which, in many ways, would become the hallmarks of Tridentine Catholicism for ordinary people: not least, it required a priest to be present for a marriage to be valid, but it did not require the consent of the parents of the couple. It affirmed the use of images and music, including polyphony, in worship. It affirmed the existence of purgatory and the efficacy of prayers for the dead, it embraced devotion to the saints, and it indirectly supported popular devotion to the Virgin Mary (Grindlay 2018). Taken together with Trent's emphasis on pastoral presence, the Catholic Baroque would be marked by an affective and emotional approach to devotion that was, if anything, democratic and even populist for its time. It aimed unabashedly to appeal to and to draw in the faithful, but as a consequence it verged at times on sentiment. In this vein, depictions of the Virgin Mary in particular tended to emphasize her beauty but also her youth, her humility, and her silence. In Guido Reni's 1610 Chapel of the Annunciation, for example, in the papal palace on the Quirinal in Rome, Mary is veiled with downcast eyes. Gabriel is depicted as equally young and feminized, and the two figures are surrounded by a veritable cloud of *putti*, or cherubs (Pepper 1984, pp. 24–25 and *passim*; see Figure 11.1). By contrast, the Carmelite women's community in Rome for whom Caravaggio made a characteristically unfiltered depiction of the death of the Virgin Mary sent back the painting. The Caravaggio now hangs in the Louvre; the painting by Carlo Saraceni which replaced it gives an idea of what was deemed acceptable for contemporary tastes.

## The Virgin and the Magdalene

Meanwhile, it would be devout Catholic women, like Angela Merici and Teresa of Avila, who tried to keep alive the voice of the Magdalene through the sixteenth century. Catholic devotion to the Magdalene preserved something of the tradition of penitence and tears which had been so important in the medieval world. To Tridentine clergy, the Magdalene evoked, not her own office in preaching the resurrection, but the laity's need for access to the sacraments. More often than not, in Baroque art, depictions of Mary Magdalene were also highly eroticized, often borrowing elements from the classical iconography of Venus, which rather undercut the spiritual authority she had once possessed. One of the great causes of both Protestant and Catholic social reform in the sixteenth century was the rehabilitation of prostitutes. While Mary Magdalene was an obvious choice of patroness, that particular aspect of her legend was sometimes emphasized to the exclusion of almost anything else. Caravaggio's depiction of the Penitent Magdalene is striking, not least because she is fully clad (Pepper 1984; Hunt 2012; Geshwind 2012).

**Figure 11.1** Guido Reni, Chapel of the Annunciation, Rome. *Source:* Guido Reni / Wikimedia Commons / Public domain.

Paradoxically, however, the older vision of the power and authority of the Virgin lingered and even found new expression in the waves of conversion, forcible and otherwise, which swept the early modern world on a global scale, and in the female sovereigns who drew on Marian iconography for their own political ends. Two generations before Elizabeth I, Isabella of Spain had portrayed herself as a latter-day Joan of Arc, but in her own political self-fashioning she also drew on aspects of Marian piety, culminating in the visit by her and Ferdinand to Guadalupe in 1477. In the early years of her reign, Isabella had portrayed herself as the immaculately conceived Mary in a deliberate effort to undermine her great rival to the throne of Castile, her brother's daughter Juana of Portugal, whom she attacked as illegitimate (Warren 2005, pp. 87–118). The Virgin of Guadalupe had been the battle patron of earlier kings of Castile and their fight for *reconquista*; Isabella invoked her in her own campaigns. After 1492 and the fall of Granada, Mary continued to be a potent model for the Catholic Monarchs as Isabella tightened restrictions and increased the pressure on Jewish and Islamic populations to seek conversion. Both "La Conquistadora" and "the mother of mercy," the Virgin Mary triumphed and welcomed, shifting seamlessly between hard and soft power as necessary (Remensnyder 2014, pp. 76–91).

## In the Shadow of Isabella: From the *Beatas* to Teresa of Avila

The legacy of Isabella's conquests and forcible conversions was a deep mistrust of Spain's *conversos* by the church, fueled in part by the lack of basic Christian education for those converted, and in part by the ongoing survival, unconscious or deliberate, of certain Jewish practices. Religious depictions of Jews and Muslims, already racialized, deepened discrimination (Ray 2006; Heng 2018; Schama 2013, pp. 423–487). As the Reformation took hold elsewhere in Europe, the fear of mass desertion to Luther on the part of the *conversos* mixed with the mistrust of the *alumbrados*, or the illuminated, the Spanish counterpart of the Italian *spirituali*. Over the course of Spanish history, with an often weak crown and regional, powerful overlords, Spanish aristocratic women's orders had often wielded significant religious authority, particularly the powerful abbesses at the royal Cistercian foundation of Las Huelgas. Beyond the cloisters, Spain had a lively penitent movement as well, with many *beatas* living in small communities, the *beaterios*, which like the beguines and third-order Franciscans, clustered around places to worship where the women could find pastoral care. One *beata*, María de Ajofrín (d. 1489), the so-called "scourge of Toledo," was a visionary who reenacted the events of Christ's passion in the role of the Virgin Mary and who railed both against clerical immorality and against "Judaizing" practices (Surtz 1995, pp. 68–84).

Isabella's confessor, the Franciscan cardinal Ximénes de Cisneros, had been a strong supporter of the *beatas*. Moreover, he recognized their need for devotional works in the vernacular. While vernacular biblical texts had been forbidden in Spain in 1492, Cisneros had sought to provide the *beatas* with works in translation from the medieval visionary tradition: Claire of Assisi and Angela of Foligno (pub. 1505 and 1510), Catherine of Siena (pub. 1512), Gerson (pub. 1505), and Mechthild of Hackeborn (pub. 1505; Surtz 1995, pp. 11–14; Weber 1990, p. 21). Teresa of Avila's favorite book, the Franciscan Osuna's *The Third Spiritual Alphabet*, also came from the Low Countries.

The farmer's daughter María de Santa Domingo, *beata* of Píedrahita (1485–1524), entered a Dominican community still in the process of reforming itself. When she went instead to a convent in Toledo, Cisneros himself interviewed her and was suitably impressed. But he died in 1517, and with the removal of the *beatas*' protector, almost immediately the local bishops and the Spanish Inquisition moved against them. As a prominent proponent of Observant reform in Spain, María would be interviewed by the inquisition some four times. When she published her book of prayers, her *Libro de la oración*, in 1518, its central theme was the witness of the Magdalene and how she was not believed (Surtz 1995, pp. 85–103; Giles 1990; Bastida 2014). Her contemporary, the visionary Juana de la Cruz (1481–1534), ran away from home dressed as man to enter a community of Franciscan tertiaries, where she would later become abbess. For 15 years, it was believed that she spoke the very words of the Holy Spirit, and her sermons were recorded by her companions, published as *El libro del conorte, or The Book of Consolation*. These include some rather racy tales of the budding womanhood of the Virgin, including one story in which Mary dances naked, rather more like Salome – and probably more like Juana herself – than the meek Virgin of Baroque tradition (Juana de la Cruz 2016; Surtz 1995, pp. 104–126; Thomas 2016).

Meanwhile, the inquisition seized on the potential associations and connections between *alumbradismo* and the mystical experiences of the *beatas*, vernacular scripture, and nascent Protestant experience. Isabel de la Cruz, who may have been influenced by the bible translator Juan de Valdés, was targeted by the inquisition for teaching from vernacular scripture, preaching a message of universal salvation and against anti-*converso* discrimination. She was imprisoned, her property seized, and she was sentenced to penance for the rest of her life, while her follower, Maria de Cazalla, was likewise tried and imprisoned from 1534 (Costa 1989, pp. 95–96; Weber 1990; Giordano 2016, pp. 94–95). Another laywoman, Marina de Saavedra, was herself illiterate but seems to have had connections to Spain's evangelicals. Marina lived a very beguine-like existence in a confraternity in Zamora until she was tried in 1558 and imprisoned from 1559 (Martínez 2016). One of the inquisition's most notorious cases was Magdalena de la Cruz, whose career as a *beata* in many respects resembled that of María de Santo Domingo or of Juana de la Cruz, until she was arrested in 1544 and her visions proved false. She was declared the devil's lover and imprisoned in 1546. Teresa of Avila was later believed to have said, "I can never remember her without trembling" (Costa 1989, p. 99; Eire 2019, pp. 38–39).

The death of such an overpowering figure as Queen Isabella created something of a spiritual and political vacuum in Spain which, in their way, the *beatas* were attempting to fill, even at the cost of too much attention from the inquisition. The woman who succeeded, in her own inimitable fashion, and was able to reconcile and reinvent the late medieval mystical tradition for Spain, and indeed for all of Europe in the Catholic Reformation, was Teresa of Avila (1515–1582). Herself the descendant of *conversos*, her Jewish grandfather had once been targeted by the inquisition as relapsed. He, his wife, and Teresa's father had been driven through the streets as penitents in the subsequent *auto da fé*. Her father may therefore be forgiven if he had an ambivalent or wary attitude to the church. In contrast with Catherine of Siena and her mother, Lapa, it is Teresa's father who emerges as her most complex and formative childhood relationship, partly because her mother died when she was 13. Teresa was clearly well aware that her father loved and was drawn to her; one wonders how much of Teresa's considerable charm and sense of humor she inherited from him. Teresa would blame her father for drawing her into what she later called frivolous company in her adolescence. He initially placed her in a convent, possibly to protect her reputation, where, like Julian of Norwich, she became so ill she was given last rites. However, her father was not at all pleased when she declared her intention to remain in religious life in 1535 (Teresa of Avila 2012; Weber 1990, pp. 8, 50; Medwick 2000, pp. 11–19).

Despite a long process of recovery punctuated by bouts of recurring illness, Teresa began her campaign to reform and even to reinvent the Carmelite order. Like Hildegard of Bingen, 25 years into her vocation she began to write. First was *The Book of My Life*, then *The Way of Perfection*, both of which she heavily revised under her confessor's instructions throughout the 1560s, followed by *The Interior Castle* in 1577. In 1581, she wrote *The Book of Foundations*, the year before she died, which one of her nuns, Ana de Jesús, helped to publish. "Nor did You Lord, when you walked in the world, despise women," she wrote in *The Way of Perfection*, in words very similar to those of Vittoria Colonna. "Rather, You always, with great compassion, helped them. And You found as much love and more faith in them than You did in men" (Teresa of Avila 2012, *Way of Perfection* Section 3). Teresa's books were very deliberately written for a female audience, grounded in her own spiritual experiences, with an extensive knowledge of spiritual direction and the pitfalls of religious life, both for women and for men. Her mystical experiences, particularly the reports of her ecstasies and levitations, captured the popular imagination – not least, that of the sculptor Bernini when *The Book of My Life* was translated into Italian. Sensational as they sound, however, these phenomena are arguably the most traditional aspect of Teresa of Avila, in firm continuity with the late medieval beguines and with the *beatas* who were her immediate predecessors. In comparison with these women, Teresa's originality lies rather with the wry acuity of her writing voice (see Figure 11.2). She insisted both that contemplation was for every woman in her community, and also that every woman might come to it in a different way. God's work in the soul happened when it would, and sometimes only after long stretches of routine, labor, and dryness (Williams 1991, pp. 54–75, 130–171; Eire 2019).

In a way, the inquisition replaced the role in Teresa's life once occupied by her father: the constant source of opposition that must be negotiated, got around, and, if possible, charmed. Ironically,

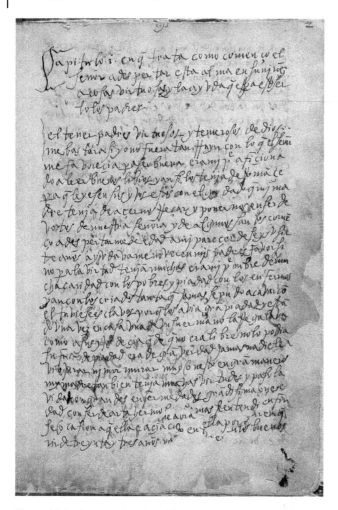

**Figure 11.2** Autograph letter of Teresa of Avila. *Source:* Album / Alamy Images.

it was men like her father, *converso* merchants, who would be the greatest financial supporters of her efforts to reform and reestablish the Order of the Discalced Carmelites (Weber 1990, pp. 124–125). Invoking Clare of Assisi's dictum that it was poverty which made great walls for a women's community, she refused formal enclosure and traveled constantly in the work of reform (Teresa of Avila 2012, *Way of Perfection* Section 2). But that work continued against the constant background noise of pushback from her own order and her own community, worry and censorship from her confessors, and, periodically, intrusions from the inquisition itself. This pressure has sometimes been dismissed, not least because Teresa proved well able to manage it, and even turn it to her own advantage. Others were not so fortunate, however, and the climate of opposition was arguably at its most acute before Teresa wrote *The Interior Castle* in 1577. Teresa was herself under investigation and house arrest and her confessor, John of the Cross, was likewise imprisoned that same year (Weber 1990, pp. 99–100; Ahlgren 1996, pp. 32–66).

In many ways, particularly given the additional suspicion her *converso* heritage inspired, it would have been easier for Teresa not to have written anything at all. She returned to it again and again, however, despite the fact that she potentially took her life – and the lives of her nuns and the future of her reform – into her hands every time she put pen to paper. It is possible that, like Hildegard of Bingen, once having begun, Teresa found she could not very well stop without undercutting her own reputation as a visionary. She also seems to have realized that a posture of constant, voluntary confession gave her a measure of agency and control, even self-protection, in setting her own narrative (Teresa of Avila 2012, *Way of Perfection* Section 7). But in Teresa's case, it also seems that she positively enjoyed the rhetorical challenge of teaching, even preaching, if only to her fellow sisters. Downplaying her own authority and long experience of religious life with her signature blend of humor and self-deprecation, she presented herself to the inquisition as an unlearned and harmless "little woman." Behind the folksy, chatty persona, however, Teresa positively delighted in tackling precisely those risky subjects, such as the bridal mysticism derived from the language of the Song of Songs which is such a feature of *The Interior Castle*, whose danger she felt she could defuse (Weber 1990; Ahlgren 1996, pp. 67–113). In so doing, as much or more than Cisneros, Teresa was able to bridge the worlds of late medieval women's mysticism and the early modern Catholic Reformation in a way that felt non-threatening in the new religious climate. Like Teresa herself, canonized less than 50 years after her death, innovation ultimately passed as tradition. She was made a doctor of the church in 1969.

As with so many other women reformers, Tridentine enclosure proved to be impossible for Teresa. Because her sanctity was recognized so soon after her death, other women were able to shelter in her example – up to a point. Many laywomen were drawn to make formal vows of virginity in the wake of the Council of Trent, but that also laid them open to discipline according to the council's mandates for women's religious communities, particularly its demands for formal enclosure (Weber 2016). Marina de Escobar (1544–1643) was a laywoman whom Teresa appointed to head up a community of 18 *beatas*. At the time of her death she seems to have been working to revive and reinvent the Bridgettine order for Catholic Spain. Less fortunate were Francisca de los Apóstolos and Isabel Bautista, two sisters from Toledo who also tried to reestablish their *beaterio* as something more official. Traveling to Rome to plead their case, Francisca was turned over to the inquisition, beaten, and banished in 1578. Catalina de Jesús amassed a significant crowd of some seven hundred supporters in Seville before she was sentenced by the inquisition in 1627. However, at the same time, in 1616 the inquisition also officially confirmed the existence of *beatas*, equivalent to recognizing their existence. As had Teresa herself, many of these women discovered the limits of the inquisition's toleration, but also, in so doing forced it to accommodate itself to them and necessarily shaped the course that the Catholic Reformation would take in Spain (Giordano 2016).

## "People are people": Caritas Pirckheimer

Ironically, precisely because of the legacy of efficient and effective Observant reform in Germany in the late Middle Ages, women's Catholic religious life remained healthy enough to survive even in the heartland of Luther's Reformation. Particularly in the early years of the reform, when many in society were actively trying to close down the convents completely, this took, not least, a great deal of nerve. One of the most engaging voices of the Reformation is that of the Catholic abbess of the community of St. Clare in Nürnberg, Caritas Pirckheimer (1467–1532). She and her brother, the humanist Willibald Pirckheimer, Albrecht Dürer's best friend, were the children of a career cleric who died a Franciscan. Caritas therefore learned Latin very young, which enabled her to join religious life early and to correspond with many of the leading humanists of the day herself (Robinson-Hammerstein 2010; see Figure 11.3).

**Figure 11.3** Caritas Pirckheimer and her chronicle of Nuremberg. *Source:* alchetron.

When the city of Nürnberg decided to throw in their lot with the Lutherans in 1524, Caritas had then been abbess of St. Clare's for over 20 years. The evangelicals of Nürnberg were presented, therefore, not with a Lutheran caricature of a nun, but with the formidable prospect of a highly educated, intellectually confident, and administratively competent abbess who could quote scripture, in Latin and the vernacular, right back at the town council, and who could hold her own in theological discussion with its Lutheran ministers. This did not shield her community from the divisive effects of evangelical rhetoric against the monastic life, however, and Caritas's journal records heart-rending scenes of families pulling their daughters out of the community, often when the girls were unwilling and had been in St. Clare's for a decade. "In this way," she wrote, "we argued with each other for a long time. Each believed the other was blind and mistaken" (Pirckheimer 2006, p. 49). Devastating rumors flew. Banned from taking new members, "we were, you see," she notes sarcastically, "in a state of damnation, heretics, idolaters, blasphemers, and would belong to the devil forever" (p. 63).

Caritas needed the city council to approve a Franciscan priest to act for the community, but instead "our dear fathers" sent in evangelical preachers to try to convert the remaining sisters. "We have now heard," Caritas reported dryly to the council, "111 of these sermons and for a while, as you wanted, we listened to Andreas Osiander for up to four hours . . . we are too insignificant to be able to enter into a discussion with such highly learned people. We like to say what we want; we must be wrong" (p. 112). In response to a deliberately offensive letter from a Lutheran on the monastic life, she wrote again to the town council, poignantly describing the plight of elderly ex-nuns thrown out of their convents but also including a balanced defense of the role of the communion and intercession of the saints. Her journal preserves the back and forth of her grinding negotiation with the council fathers. She liked to remind them that they had taken away her authority, so she could not possibly command her nuns to do anything herself. Tensions finally eased when the evangelical Philip Melanchthon was persuaded to pay the sisters a visit, and advised the council to stop browbeating St. Clare's. "People are people," Caritas wrote, "today as well as a thousand years ago, but the Word of God remains eternal" (p. 113).

In the Dominican communities of Strasbourg, the evangelicals attempted similar conversion tactics. In one community, the nuns screamed and fainted when the pastor began to speak. In the community of St. Margaret and St. Agnes, when the ex-Dominican Martin Bucer came to preach, the nuns, with their abbess's full knowledge, took to dressing up angel icons behind the cloister screen to listen on their behalf. The ruse was discovered when Bucer, carried away by the heat of his rhetoric, knocked over his pulpit and his inanimate audience did not respond. After that, the nuns, whom Bucer wittily nicknamed "the Margaret dragons," were given assigned seats by the town council (Leonard 2005, pp. 135–139). Ironically, in Strasbourg it seems to have been the families of the nuns who protested the loudest when the council attempted to make the nuns leave the convent. Gradually, the convent became a confessionally mixed community, administered largely by the city.

Caritas Pirckheimer spoke the truth about the desperate plight of many former nuns, who may not have had anywhere else to go. No one in religious life was really adequately pensioned off in the Reformation, particularly the elderly, but most former nuns were given a financial pittance compared with their male counterparts on which to live. If they could not live together, these women were almost bound to end up on the fringes of a society increasingly unwilling and unable to care for them. In the Holy Roman Empire, the combination of a society under profound stress with the ambitions of vying political authorities, Catholic and Protestant, constantly testing the limits of their authority, created a veritable powder keg of suspicion and scapegoating which began to find expression in chronic witchcraft panics. Contrary to popular belief, witchcraft charges had not been common in the Middle Ages until the very end of the period, and only then in very particular circumstances. Even then, it was not always a gendered charge, with men suspect as often as women in the medieval world. In the sixteenth century, however, somewhere between a hundred thousand and two hundred thousand people were tried and around fifty thousand executed on charges of witchcraft. The vast majority of these were women. Moreover, this was not only a Protestant obsession; in fact, many witchcraft panics appear to have been instigated by Catholic prince-bishops keen to suss out religious dissent (Weisner-Hanks 2019, pp. 278–279, 295–296; Zika 2015). In the Protestant world, the charge of witchcraft seems to have largely replaced that of heresy in early modern Europe, although the hermeneutic of suspicion when applied to women, particularly solitary women, remained very similar.

## English Women and the Old Religion

In the English Reformation, these discourses and suspicions ultimately would be applied both to Anne Boleyn and to the woman who was the most powerful source of religious and political opposition to her and Thomas Cranmer: Elizabeth Barton, the Maid of Kent (d. 1534). Elizabeth Barton had been a servant before a period of illness and a series of intense visionary experiences in 1525 thrust her into religious life in the community of St. Sepulchre in Canterbury, where she became a Benedictine nun. In 1527, she published her account of her own miraculous healing at the Marian shrine in Aldington in Kent, *A Marvelous Worke*. Modeling herself on Joan of Arc and Bridget of Sweden, Elizabeth became a kind of religious and political oracle by the 1530s, with religious and political connections to the Bridgettines at Syon Abbey in particular. The claim to Lancastrian descent was vitally important to the Tudor dynasty, and for Henry VIII, both Syon and Elizabeth Barton represented important potential political supporters (Warren 2010, p. 195). In the wake of the king's diplomatic coup at the Field of the Cloth of Gold, Henry was flush with his own success and still fixedly determined to marry Anne Boleyn. In 1532, Henry VIII declared himself to be Melchizedek, priest and king over both church and state, a title historically used by Roman emperors in the Byzantine world. In fact, Henry wanted Elizabeth to ratify his divorce and decision to break with Rome, even though her doing so would have meant a betrayal not only of Catherine of Aragon but also of the princess Mary. When Henry realized he could not get Elizabeth's approval, he turned on her (Warren 2005, pp. 119–138). Thomas Cromwell and Thomas Cranmer launched into a full-scale investigation of Elizabeth Barton and her religious and political contacts, which revealed the Maid of Kent to be a fraud. She was hanged at Tyburn with her confessor in April of 1534.

By extension the fall of the Maid of Kent discredited an entire ring of potential aristocratic and monastic opposition to Cranmer, Cromwell, and the cause of evangelical reform. It put Cranmer squarely in charge of the English church before the Act of Supremacy in 1534 (MacCulloch 1996, pp. 102–109). Four years later, the great Marian shrine at Walsingham was burned and sacked. In the same year, the king himself stood by while the shrine of Thomas Becket in Canterbury, with all its connotations of clerical martyrdom to royal power, was dismantled piece by piece; the body of the saint vanished without a trace, possibly burned (de Beer and Speakman 2021, pp. 222–230). The abbess of Syon, Agnes Jordan, as well as the confessor of the community and the neighboring community of Carthusians at Sheen, were all closely connected to Elizabeth Barton, and her death signaled the end of Syon's preeminence in English religious and political life (Watt 1997, pp. 51–80). Henry's treatment of the London Charterhouse became notorious: the imprisoned Carthusians were chained and (reputedly) starved in Newgate Prison when they refused to submit to the Act of Supremacy. Visiting them there, smuggling in precious aid and support, was Thomas More's adopted daughter, Margaret Giggs Clement (d. 1570) (Chappell and Kramer 2014, p. 3). The extensive monastic buildings remained intact at Syon for a time, with those nuns who accepted the Act of Supremacy remaining. Henry's luckless fifth wife, Katherine Howard, was kept there before her execution, and after his death, Henry's own body rested for a night there, where, so goes a famous story, as befell the biblical King Ahab, the dogs licked up his blood.

One of the most poignant victims of the deadly combination of religious reform with Tudor dynastic politics was Margaret Pole, née Plantagenet (1473–1541), the Countess of Salisbury. Her parents were the brother of Richard III, George, Duke of Clarence, and Isabella Neville. Margaret was made a ward of the king when her father was executed in the Wars of the Roses. Her brother was likewise executed in 1499 and his estates reclaimed by Henry VII. Margaret was quietly married to Richard Pole, a friend of Prince Arthur but otherwise a deliberately mediocre match. However, it was through this connection that Margaret became a friend of Catherine of Aragon. In 1512, she had proved herself sufficiently loyal to Henry VIII to petition successfully for the return of her brother's lands and estates. She was made godmother to the princess Mary and the head of Mary's household from 1525. However, over the course of her marriage to the nondescript Richard Pole, Margaret had had five children, which meant that over time, her political stock rose while the king's and Catherine's began to fall. A Plantagenet in close proximity with Henry VIII was a dangerous position in which to be. One of Margaret's five children was her son, Reginald Pole, who entered the church and even taught at Sheen Priory for a time. Margaret was staunchly loyal to both Catherine and Mary over the course of the rise of Queen Anne. In 1536, Reginald Pole was made a cardinal by the Vatican, not only to send a pointed message to the king but also to signal his potential claim to the throne over heretical Henry. As a consequence, Reginald would spend most of his life abroad as a friend to the *spirituali*, a would-be Catholic reformer who was unable to return to England. His mother, meanwhile, was banished from court, and in 1541, although she protested her loyalty, she was beheaded in a horrible debacle of an execution (Pierce 2013; Liedl 2014).

## Queen Mary

Even before she came to the throne, therefore, Mary Tudor and the man who would become her archbishop of Canterbury were linked from the beginning by Margaret's death. In addition, they were also deeply involved in the broader culture of humanist learning that they shared with Henry and Catherine of Aragon, Catherine Parr, and Elizabeth Tudor. The first printed edition of Christine de Pizan's *City of Ladies* was made jointly for Catherine of Aragon and the princess Mary in 1521 (Jordan 1990, p. 105; Schutte 2014). In 1523, the Spanish humanist Juan Luis Vives famously dedicated his treatise on Christian womanhood to Catherine, although it would be Mary who took its lessons most to heart. Unfortunately, these included the argument that women were to be essentially subordinate and that a female sovereign was, practically by definition, a contradiction in terms, a position with which John Knox would have agreed (Jordan 1990, pp. 117–119). In this way, for all her sophisticated education, Mary was taught from the beginning to rely first, on the authority of her father, and second, on that of her future husband (see Figure 11.4).

**Figure 11.4**  Mary Tudor, portrait by Antonis Mor, Museo del Prado. *Source:* DIRECTMEDIA Publishing GmbH / Wikimedia Commons / Public domain.

In 1531, Mary was incapacitated by an illness that seems to have affected her menstrual cycle – perhaps endometriosis – and which may have been connected to her notorious troubles later in life in conceiving a child. In 1533, to pave the way for Anne's future offspring, Mary was stripped of her rank, stigmatized as a bastard, and separated from her mother, who died without her in 1536. Forced by her father to conform with the new church under pain of execution, she found a temporary harbor under the wing of Catherine Parr. When Henry died in 1547, Mary began to push the boundaries of what was permitted in her own religious expression, her fervent eucharistic piety in strong contrast with her evangelical brother's reign.

When Mary came to the throne herself in 1553, she appointed Reginald Pole her archbishop, promptly restored traditional Latin worship, including the Mass, and reconstituted a celibate clergy, sending many married evangelicals into exile. The next year, she married the prince of the Catholic Reformation, Philip II of Spain. However, for a variety of reasons, none of these decisions amounted to the straightforward restoration of the way things had been before 1533. The wifely submission to her husband's authority which her education had counseled her was best was never actually possible for Queen Mary. Her courtly and sombre husband did not seem particularly enamored of either his bride or her country, and remained often in Spain. The pope, Paul IV, detested the *spirituali* in general and Pole in particular, a hatred surpassed only by his loathing for all things Spanish.

At the very moment, then, when the English people should have been welcomed back into the Catholic fold, they found themselves still shunned. Mary and Pole may well have been sympathetic to at least some of the humanist critiques of late medieval religion themselves. Mary restored only a few religious communities, one of which was the women of Syon, and she did not make a push to reinstate the major shrines at Canterbury and Walsingham. In defiance of Tridentine dictates, Mary never recalled or restricted the use of the English bible, and she refused to hand Pole over to the tender mercies of Paul IV (Loades 2006). East Anglia and London remained staunchly evangelical, internationally connected through networks of Protestant refugees, while the base of Catholic support in England came from the rural north and west. The three hundred Protestants she executed, beginning with Thomas Cranmer and his circle of evangelical bishops, were learning what an effective tool for proselytization public executions could be, and even in death were generally successful in winning public sympathy over the grim piety of "Bloody Mary" and her dictatorial Spanish husband. But England was a young nation, and for the generation immediately before that of Shakespeare, the Catholic catechism they received under Mary was their first (Gregory 1999, pp. 153–183; Marshall 2017, pp. 365–415). If Mary's reign had extended as long as Elizabeth's, had she been able to bear a child, and if, over time, she had gradually acquired a more practical political *nous*, she might have been able to lead a Catholic Reformation of her own. In the event, Mary's death of cancer after a reign as brief as her brother's, ending in her desperate, delusional belief in her own pregnancy, shows a monarch paradoxically boxed in by the strength of her loyalties.

## Recusant Women and the Jesuits

The reign of Elizabeth I coincided with the full strength of the Jesuit order, which, once it became clear a Catholic marriage was not in the offing for the queen, set about trying to create networks of political resistance against her. The Jesuits attempted to assassinate Elizabeth in the Babington Plot in 1586. Elizabeth's response to the Jesuits was no more merciful than her sister's had been to the evangelicals, and the system of surveillance she fostered helped to crystallize English recusant Catholicism along fervent, polarized lines. Central to recusant piety was the intimate and passionate alliance between devout Catholic women and individual Jesuit missionaries in England, whose bodies they sheltered, and after their execution, mourned and venerated as martyrs (Bossy 1975, pp. 11–48; Gregory 1999, pp. 272–303). Because women could not hold property in their own names, they were paradoxically difficult to target by the courts, and made ideal allies for priests precisely because the Elizabethan Settlement had already declared them to be, in effect, invisible (Lay 2016, pp. 2–17). From abroad, meanwhile, Syon continued to play a central and formative role in calling for Elizabeth's removal. In exile under Edward VI, the Syon Bridgettines had gone first to Antwerp, then to Termonde in Flanders. Under Mary they returned to England, but the reconstituted Syon had lasted for less than a year. Exiled again, this time to Rouen under Elizabeth, Syon finally ended its peregrinations at Lisbon with a pension from Philip II. Its abbesses, Elizabeth Sanders and Marie Champney, worked to overthrow Elizabeth and put Mary Stuart on the throne. Despite her support in England for the Jesuit martyr Edmund Campion and her multiple imprisonments, the abbess Elizabeth successfully protested her feminine helplessness and survived to return to her nuns in Portugal (Warren 2005, pp. 139–167).

Back in England, Margaret Clitherow determined that she would go on a kind of pilgrimage to the place where six Catholic seminarians had been executed in the 1580s. It is clear that this was very much her own idea and not that of her priests, who did not entirely know what to make of such a gesture and who were frightened by the ramifications of Margaret's open admission of her faith. Captured and interrogated, she was pressed to death in 1586, the first woman to be executed for not adhering to the new laws against Catholic recusancy (Peters 2003, pp. 286–290; Lake and Questier 2011; Chappell and Kramer 2014, p. 3). Anne Dacre Howard, the Countess of Arundel (d. 1630), harbored the Jesuit poet Robert Southwell and was married to the Earl of Arundel, Philip Howard, who returned to Catholicism even though it meant his execution in 1595 (Monta 2011). Ordinary women also sheltered priests, however. Dorothy Lawson in Newcastle acted to hide and help Jesuits, while the convert Anne Line (1567–1601) was known as "Mrs. Martha" and even as "Mrs. Magdalen" for her work running a safe house and staging-point for missionary Jesuits in London. Anne never took formal vows, and lived as a devout lay-sister until too many people were seen attending Mass at her house in 1601. She was executed that year (Scully and Robert 2016). Perhaps the most famous case of a woman's public conversion to Catholicism was Elizabeth Tanfield Cary, Vicountess Falkland (1586–1639), who was said to have converted in 1626 after she attempted to read Calvin's *Institutes*. In 1613, she had written the *Tragedy of Mariam*, the first original drama in English by a woman; it is possibly her portrait which now hangs in the Tate Gallery (Knoppers 2009, pp. 47–48). The sisters Eleanor Brooksby and Anne Vaux were the center of a ring of Catholic recusants that extended to the composer William Byrd and Ann Garnet, the niece of the head of the English Jesuits, Henry Garnet, executed in 1606 (Macek 2016).

Eleanor and Anne sheltered one of the strangest cases of would-be Jesuit martyrdom in Elizabethan England, Luisa de Carvajal y Mendoza (1566–1614; see Figure 11.5). Born of two extremely aristocratic Spanish lineages, her father was a lapsed abbot and her grandfather a bishop who had attended the Council of Trent, but she was orphaned by typhus in 1572. Raised by her great-aunt, who acted as governess to the children of Philip II, Luisa grew up alongside the royal children in a convent of Discalced Carmelites established by Philip's sister Juana – the only woman officially admitted, albeit secretly, into the Jesuit order. When her great-aunt died as well, Luisa came under the care of her uncle, the Marquis of Almazán. Luisa's uncle groomed and manipulated the 10-year-old girl in the name of the mortification of her body: he locked her up, encouraged her to scourge herself, made a servant beat her, and molded her into an early pattern of secrecy in which she concealed what was going on from the rest of the house. Luisa lived in the attic as a recluse until her uncle's death, when she moved to Madrid, within the immediate

**Figure 11.5** Luisa de Carvajal y Mendoza, portrait. *Source:* WordPress.com.

devotional purview of the Jesuits. There she founded what was essentially a *beaterio*, living a devout life without enclosure, seeking to reform the prostitutes of the city (Redworth 2008).

Throughout her life, Luisa was cheerfully, relentlessly practical. It is fair to say that, unlike Teresa, she was never drawn toward mystical experience, and indeed, never attempted to imitate her countrywoman in any noticeable way. Like Claire of Assisi, Luisa hung grimly on to her share of the family inheritance, if only so that she could donate it to the Jesuits. In 1598, Luisa made a vow of perfection akin to the one that Ignatius Loyola had taken, and moved alongside the Jesuits to Valladolid and the English College there, where the talk would have been almost constantly of martyrdom overseas. Campion had died in 1581, and Luisa knew at least two others who had been executed around the time of the queen's death in 1603. In the uncertain times for Catholics around James I's accession, Luisa decided to travel to England as a missionary apostle. Whose idea this was remains a mystery, although it is entirely possible that it was Luisa's own. It is certainly the case that no one had the authority or the ability to stop her once her mind was set. As a high-born Spanish aristocrat, if she were imprisoned she represented a potential political bombshell, and it is possible that Henry Garnet and the English Jesuits were courting precisely such an eventuality at that time. After the Gunpowder Plot in 1605, the Spanish ambassador kept Luisa virtually house-bound so that she could not amplify the tense situation even further.

As Luisa quickly discovered, however, whatever her ambitions, she could not make converts without knowing the English language. With Ann Garnet, she gradually started to build her own life in London. She began by visiting Catholics in prison, but gradually found herself agitating politically against James I's demands for an oath of loyalty from his citizens, writing some 180 letters in all, many to her aristocratic childhood friends who had married across the courts of Europe. She founded a small women's community, which she christened The Company of the Sovereign Virgin Mary Our Lady, and drew up a rule for it modeled on that of Ignatius. Whatever the order thought of her, Luisa certainly saw herself as one of the Jesuits, although her order also had strong parallels with the exiled sisters of Syon (Warren 2010, pp. 103, 135). Luisa continued her work despite arrest, running illegal books, invoking her family connections, and even, to the horror of the Spanish ambassador, receiving a belated papal blessing on her ad hoc mission. When several Jesuits were executed in 1610, Luisa gathered up what remained of their bodies and embalmed them in her house to send back to the continent as relics (Pando-Canteli 2016). She moved to Spitalfields, then the foreign quarter of London, and her house, called the Oran, acted to funnel young Catholic women with vocations to religious houses on the continent. Arrested by George Abbott, the archbishop of Canterbury, she was interrogated, but it was clear her health was failing. Luisa was released and died soon afterwards, her dream of martyrdom in the end unachieved. Fifty years later, just across the street from the Oran, Susannah Wesley would be born.

Luisa de Carvajal was not the only woman who modeled her vocation on that of the Jesuits, or who saw herself as a female Jesuit. Isabella Roser was a married Catalan noblewoman who corresponded with Ignatius, who once called her his spiritual mother (Ignatius 1960, pp. 262–295; 1991, pp. 327–332; Hufton 2001). The papacy, however, explicitly released the Jesuits from the spiritual care of women early in the order's history and even forbade it from 1558, on Ignatius's request. When Isabella sought papal approval in order to found an order of female Jesuits in 1630, Ignatius disavowed them, and their potential was never fully realized. Also known to Luisa was Mary Ward, who founded the Institute for the Blessed Virgin Mary, which also aimed to send women missionaries to England. Her schools, initially approved by the papacy, were very successful, but they were suppressed in 1630 alongside Isabella Roser. Ward herself and her "galloping Jesuitesses" came under inquisitorial suspicion. She was imprisoned for two months, and the Jesuit name was banned to women by the papacy in 1631 (Weisner-Hanks 2019, p. 251; Hsia 2005, pp. 38–39; Simmonds 2020; Goulding 2016).

## Mary and Martha: The New Catholic Orders

Insofar as women modeled themselves on the Jesuits, they invariably chose a form of active life with which the Jesuits, not to mention the papacy, could not be entirely comfortable. Jesuit spirituality continued to resonate, however, not least in the enclosed life of the Carmelite Maria Maddalena de'Pazzi (1566–1607). Only distantly related to those who famously plotted against the Medici, the girl Catherine joined the Carmelite convent at Santa Maria degli Angeli in Florence and took the name Maria Maddalena in religion. Like Catherine of Siena, from 1584, when she was only 18, she fell into periods of eucharistic ecstasy. She reenacted the Passion several times and received invisible stigmata, going on to have various and frequent visions that lasted throughout her life. In boarding school she had once been nicknamed "the Jesuitess" for her early habit of frequent silent prayer, and her confessors at the community were also predominantly Jesuit, encouraging her regimen of intense and vivid Passion meditation. They, in concert with the community's own formidable political connections, protected Maria Maddalena from the kind of inquisitorial examination Teresa had so frequently undergone; Filipo Neri and the Dominicans did the same for Caterina dei Ricci (1522–1590; Copeland 2006; Hsia 2005, pp. 145–146). In fact, the community carefully recorded whatever Maria Maddalena said in her visions, ostensibly to protect her and them, should it become necessary, but also because the community knew the value of having a saint in-house. Maria Maddalena's cult, therefore, was carefully guided and shepherded from the beginning. The campaign for her canonization began the year after her death, and was, in fact, a kind of community effort, culminating in her canonization in 1669. Alongside Francesca Romana, canonized in 1608, and Teresa of Avila in 1622, they were the first women canonized since Catherine of Siena herself a hundred and fifty years before.

One of the most innovative of the new Tridentine Catholic orders, who would be instrumental in channeling religious women's vocations toward teaching and practical charity, was Angela Merici (c. 1474–1540; see Figure 11.6). Originally a Franciscan tertiary, in 1535 in Brescia she founded a group of laywomen, which she called the Company of St. Ursula after the famous virgin saint with her eleven thousand companions. This might not have seemed so very different from the late medieval penitent communities in Italy, and indeed, the Ursulines built close relationships with reforming clergy much as Catherine of Siena or Angela of Foligno had once done. Angela was firm in her belief that each of her women had individual, personal access to Christ, however, and this streak of independence led her to place particular emphasis on a women's vocation in which women were understood to be, like evangelical translators, "repeaters" of the Holy Spirit. The vocation of the company centered particularly on education for girls (Mazzonis 2016). Angela herself was literate in both Latin and the vernacular, and seems to have read not only devotional works like Thomas à Kempis but humanist works by Erasmus and others. By the time of her death, her order had a hundred and fifty members (Mazzonis 2007, pp. 20–21, 27).

The early Ursulines were often of lower social class, drawn by the deliberately egalitarian structure of the order. Angela envisioned the order to be run exclusively by widows. Combined with their practical, educational bent, this largely kept them out of the high politics that drew the inquisition's attention. Despite Angela's early intention not to seek enclosure, however, the decades after Trent would see the church place institutional pressure on the Ursulines, who were then thriving. From the 1580s they were strongly encouraged to wear formal habits and to build even closer institutional relationships with their confessors. Gradually, precisely as the order grew and spread across national lines, the Ursulines grew more conventional in their acceptance of enclosure, which may even have been a selling point for those families who wanted their gently bred girls to be taught in Ursuline foundations.

In the city of Milan, then experiencing an economic and demographic boom, Countess Ludovica Torelli founded the confraternity of San Paolo in 1535 (Baernstein 2002). Ludovica had been

**Figure 11.6** *Sant'Angela Merici pellegrina* by Giuseppe Fali. *Source:* Giuseppe Fali / Wikimedia Commons / Public domain.

married twice, first to an invalid and then to an abusive husband, but had been widowed in 1527. Ludovica modeled her own piety on Mary Magdalene, but her career was also strongly reminiscent of Bridget of Sweden. Ludovica established a triple religious community, which included religious women, the Angelics, male clerics, who became known as the Barnabites, and a third order of married couples, the Paulines, who aimed to combine the active and contemplative lives. When they moved to Milan in 1532, like the Ursulines in their early years Ludovica and the Paulines were not enclosed, and they do not seem to have sought to make any kind of formal vows. Instead, the Paulines took over the management of hospitals and houses for the rehabilitation of prostitutes, particularly in the Veneto, and were known for their dramatic displays of public penitence. In 1535 the papacy approved the establishment of the Angelics, who adopted the Augustinian Rule.

As with the Bridgettines, the Angelics followed the leadership of a charismatic woman, the visionary abbess Paola Antonia Negri, who quickly came to control both the Angelics and the Barnabites, leading to dangerous rumors that she sought to celebrate Mass herself. In the next year, Pope Paul III likened them to the Waldensians, the medieval heretical group known for its women preachers. Despite these dangerous warning signs, the next decade would see the order only increase in popularity and in influence. But in 1551, Venice ousted the Paulines, and in 1552, the inquisition, led by the future Paul IV, began its investigation into Paola Antonia Negri. She attempted to escape but was imprisoned that year. The reeling Barnabites, meanwhile, quietly reinvented themselves as a much more conventional Tridentine order, conveniently blaming their brush with the inquisition on their former leader. The Angelics of San Paolo likewise adopted formal enclosure and became a much more traditional, well-connected women's community – Borromeo's favorite convent, in fact. In 1553, Ludovica left in disgust, taking her endowment with her.

As always, however, women's enclosure did not always mean the same thing to everyone, even between women's communities. In Paris in the wake of Henry IV's ruinous siege of the city, his subsequent conversion to Catholicism and his coronation left many dissatisfied whose fervent piety had been fostered under the Catholic League. Many were women for whom wartime conditions had created certain opportunities, including a kind of intensity and excitement of experience, and who now sought new forms of expression for their faith even while it reflected the trauma undergone by so many in the city. In many cases, this meant moving the older, rural women's communities, which had suffered worst in the Wars of Religion, inside the city walls, rebuilding a host of new foundations in the ruins: some 48 by 1650 (Diefendorf 2004). These included women's communities from reformed Fontevraud, from the reformed Franciscans, called the Capuchins, as well as the reformed Cistercians, called the Feuillants. Madeleine Luillier (1496–1548) brought the Ursulines to Paris. But the reorganization and rebuilding of Catholic religious life in Paris was truly spearheaded and bankrolled by a ring of aristocratic laywomen, chief of which was the charismatic Barbe Acarie (1565–1618; see Figure 11.7). Barbe Acarie's piety in many ways resembles that of the late medieval beguines and penitents whom she read, combining Mary and Martha in spiritual practices undergone while performing works of practical charity. It was she who made the contacts, petitioned the king, and found the donors – also aristocratic women – for Teresa's protégé, Ana de Jesús, to bring a group of Spanish Discalced Carmelites to Paris in 1604.

Despite the endless hours which Barbe Acarie lavished on the new foundation in preparation, which included her supervising the construction of the new building and her personally interviewing each and every new French postulant to the community, what ensued was an almost comical clash of cultural misunderstandings. The Spaniards did not speak French, and Ana de Jesús in particular seems to have embarked on the missional foundation believing herself to be surrounded by French heretics. She distrusted the size and lavishness of the new building and, on a deep and fundamental level, could not countenance the close interpenetration in Paris of women's religious

**Figure 11.7** Barbe Acarie. *Source:* Unknown / Wikimedia Commons / Public domain.

life with aristocratic *dévotes*, who wanted access to, and retreat in, the communities they patronized. No one could agree on who precisely had the prerogative of providing pastoral care to the women. Ironically, however, Ana passed on to the French Discalced Carmelites her own ironclad belief in the 1588 Constitutions of Alcalá as the final expression of Teresa's will for the order – which preserved a greater degree of autonomy for the abbesses of French Carmelite communities than the Spanish would ever retain (Diefendorf 2004, pp. 78–96, 102–118).

The new French offshoot of the Carmelite Order would spread rapidly, opening 37 houses in France by 1625. The community at Dijon would be where a young Jeanne de Chantal would find her religious vocation under the spiritual direction of Francis de Sales. In 1618, Jeanne would found the Visitandines, a women's order which took its name from the Lucan account of the Virgin's visit to Elizabeth, from which the text of the *Magnificat* derives. Encapsulated in this moment in the gospel, the Visitandines aimed to combine the active and contemplative lives, practical charity with praise and even a moment of prophecy. Along with the Ursulines, who likewise grew in the devotional footprint created by the Carmelites in Paris, the Visitandines were another case of a women's order channeling the ascetic, penitential piety of an earlier generation into teaching and nursing (Du Jeu 2001; Ravier 1989). Jeanne was canonized in 1767.

In fact, the explosion of women's communities in seventeenth-century France extends beyond the boundary of this study. To name only a few, these include the Filles de Ste. Marthe, who worked with reformed prostitutes, Louise de Marillac (1591–1660) who with Vincent de Paul established the Filles de la Charité, the Filles de Ste. Geneviève, the Dames de St. Maur, and the Filles de la Crois (Louise de Marillac 2005; Cohen 1989). By the end of the century, the transformation and reorientation of many women's orders in the Catholic Reformation was complete. In a tacit negotiation with male religious authority, and in a confessional context in which Catholic pastoral presence was vitally important in winning back hearts and minds lost during the Reformation, religious women were able to remain in the world insofar as they took up practical, "Marthan" service professions. Those orders which abided by Tridentine enclosure very swiftly became stratified along lines of class and gentrification, and far more dependent on aristocratic vocations for their economic survival.

The changing nature of women's religious vocation in the Catholic Reformation owed a great deal to the turbulent times through which Europe passed in the sixteenth and seventeenth centuries. War, trauma, and disease, and the competitive, polarized light of holy war colored Catholic religious identity throughout Europe in this period. For the first time, however, the Catholic Church in the west was also reaching beyond the boundaries of Europe, to the North and South Americas, and to India and Japan. The first African slaves who converted to Christianity became Catholic in Florida. Marie de l'Incarnation (1599–1672) established an Ursuline house in Quebec which accepted both European and Native American women. The first saint canonized from the New World was Rose of Lima (1586–1617). Of Indigenous and Spanish descent, she joined the Dominican Order and was canonized in 1671 (Weisner-Hanks 2019, p. 347; Maynard 1944; Hsia 2005, p. 146).

In Ethiopia, King Susenyos I (r. 1606–1632) attempted to introduce Catholic Christianity to his people with the help of the Jesuits. Ironically, however, his and their efforts directly created at least one woman Ethiopian Orthodox saint, and may well have provided the confessional historical context for several other fifteenth-century women saints who were recognized at that time. Described using many of the literary conventions of earlier monastic literature, these Ethiopian women saints were usually married before they began their religious vocations. The most famous of the group is probably Krestos Sämra, who, having borne 11 children, then became a nun, going off to form her own community as an ascetic on an island near Lake Tana. Like many of the monks of the late antique literature, she was supposed to have lived for an incredibly long time, and was even said to have attempted – only once – to make peace between God and the devil. This was too much for even the talents of Krestos Sämra, and she required the assistance of the archangel Michael to escape the devil's clutches. Even today, the lemon tree which bears her name is said to be a cure for infertility (Krzyzanowska 2015, p. 130). Fequertä Krestos was a child born to elderly parents on Christmas Day. As an adult, she lived in a chaste marriage with her husband until she received a personal angelic visitation, whereupon she became miraculously pregnant. When her son was born, the baby was seen to bear a cross on his face; she then became a nun. Zéna Maryam was a hermit who lived in two different caves in the Emfraz region, also near Lake Tana in northern Ethiopia, and was known for her penitential fasting. Most significant for the history of women's monasticism is Wälättä Pétros of Gojjam (now in Sudan), an Orthodox martyr from the reign of Susenyos. Visited daily by Jesuits who pressured her to convert, she refused and became an important monastic organizer for nuns in Ethiopia, founding seven communities which she made financially independent, her ministry supported both by elite women and by other nuns (Mecca 2006, pp. 153–167).

On the other side of the world, women were instrumental in the spreading of Christianity in early modern Japan (Ward 2016a; 2016b). The very terms used for religious women there suggest the complex discourses surrounding women's vocation present from the beginning for these Japanese converts: *jennhonin* (women lay preachers), *bicuni* (nuns), *virgens, caseras* (women who, like Anne Line in England, harbored priests in their homes), *beatas*, and *pinzochere* (a dialect name once used for the beguines). One of the most compelling of the early Japanese converts was Naitō Julia (1566–1627). When she converted to Christianity she had already been a Buddhist nun for 20 years, and she lent her leadership expertise, as well as her aristocratic background, wholeheartedly to the new religion. Called a "Jesuit evangelistic catechist-preacher," there do not seem to be many aspects of the life of the missionary church in which Naitō Julia, like Luisa de Carvajal, did not see herself participating. She too established a women's order which, like the Ursulines, originally centered around Christian education and the propagation of the faith. When she was tortured in 1613, however, the women's community, called the Nuns of Miyako, moved to the Philippines, where they gave up life in the world and became a contemplative community which survived through the seventeenth century. Oiwa Monica (d. 1624) and Hayashida Magdalena both chose a celibate life; Hayashida Magdalena became a martyr, burned at the stake in the same year that the Nuns of Miyako left Japan. Julia of Kami, like the English recusants, ran a safe house for priests and Christian converts and died in 1630. Lucía de Freitas, a laywoman born in Japan and married to a European, also sheltered Franciscan missionaries until she was arrested. In 1622, alongside 24 priests, she went to the stake in Nagasaki at the age of 80, singing the *Magnificat* (see Figure 11.8).

Despite the reputation of the Council of Trent, what is striking about so many religious women in the Catholic Reformation is the degree to which they, and not the papal curia, initiated reforms, reforms which were often later curtailed, adjusted, and adopted by the clerical hierarchy. The legacy of the late medieval church, its devotional practices and its complex traditions of penitent spirituality, continued to shape the church in the sixteenth century. Women's religious communities remained a necessary part of society even in Lutheran Germany, and flourished in new forms in Spain, Italy, and war-torn France. External factors and population pressures, while significant, do not entirely account for this appeal; many of the new orders, like the Ursulines, rejected Tridentine enclosure for a pragmatic, "Marthan" orientation to service, the ancestor of

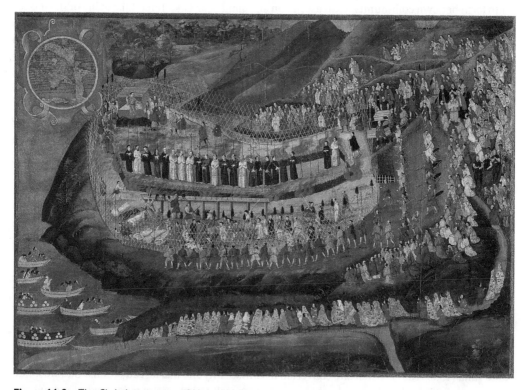

**Figure 11.8** The Christian martyrs of Nagasaki. *Source:* Unknown author / Martyrdom of Nagasaki / Public domain.

today's nursing and teaching professions. "Marian" contemplation survived as well, however, alongside "Magdalene" public witness; the women of the Catholic Reformation bequeathed a diverse and complex legacy.

## References

Ahlgren, G.T.W. (1996). *Teresa of Avila and the Politics of Sanctity*. Ithaca: Cornell University Press.

Baernstein, P.R. (2002). *A Convent Tale: A Century of Sisterhood in Spanish Milan*. London: Routledge.

Bastida, R.S. (2014). *Las Revelaciones de Maria de Santo Domingo (1480/6–1524)*. London: Department of Iberian and Latin American Studies, Queen Mary, University of London.

de Beer, L. and Speakman, N. (2021). *Thomas Becket: Murder and the Making of a Saint*. London: The British Library.

Bossy, J. (1975). *The English Catholic Community, 1570–1850*. London: Darton, Longman and Todd.

Chappell, J.A. and Kramer, K.A. (2014). Introduction. In: *Women during the English Reformations: Renegotiating Gender and Religious Identity* (ed. J.A. Chappell and K.A. Kramer). London: Palgrave Macmillan.

Cohen, S. (1989). Asylums for women in counter-Reformation Italy. In: *Women in Reformation and Counter-Reformation Europe: Public and Private Worlds* (ed. S. Marshall), 166–180. Bloomington: Indiana University Press.

Collett, B. (ed.) (2002). *Female Monastic Life in Early Tudor England: With an Edition of Richard Fox's Translation of the Benedictine Rule for Women*. Aldershot: Ashgate.

Copeland, C. (2006). *Maria Maddalena de'Pazzi: The Making of a Counter-Reformation Saint*. Oxford: Oxford University Press.

Costa, M.O. (1989). Spanish women in the Reformation. In: *Women in Reformation and Counter-Reformation Europe: Public and Private Worlds* (ed. S. Marshall), 89–119. Bloomington: Indiana University Press.

Diefendorf, B. (2004). *From Penitence to Charity: Pious Women and the Catholic Reformation in Paris*. Oxford: Oxford University Press.

Dixon, C.S. (2016). *The Church in the Early Modern Age*. London: I.B. Tauris.

Du Jeu, E. (2001). *Le témoignage de Jeanne de Chantal*. Paris: P. Téqui.

Eire, C. (2019). *The Life of St. Teresa of Avila: A Biography*. Princeton: Princeton University Press.

Geshwind, R. (2012). The printed penitent: Magdalene imagery and prostitution reform in early modern Italian chapbooks and broadsheets. In: *Mary Magdalene: Iconographic Studies from the Middle Ages to the Baroque* (ed. M.A. Erhard and A.M. Morris), 107–133. Leiden: Brill.

Giles, M. (1990). *The Book of Prayer of Sor Maria of Santo Domingo: A Study and Translation*. Albany: State University of New York Press.

Giordano, M.L. (2016). Historicizing the beatas: the figures behind the Reformation and counter-Reformation conflicts. In: *Devout Laywomen in the Early Modern World* (ed. A. Weber), 91–111. London: Routledge.

Goulding, G.K. (2016). *A Church of Passion and Hope: The Formation of Ecclesial Discipline from Ignatius Loyola to Pope Francis and the New Evangelization*. London: T&T Clark.

Gregory, B.S. (1999). *Salvation at Stake: Christian Martyrdom in Early Modern Europe*. Cambridge: Harvard University Press.

Grindlay, L. (2018). *Queen of Heaven: The Assumption and Coronation of the Virgin in Early Modern English Writing*. Notre Dame: University of Notre Dame Press.

Headley, J.M., Hillerbrand, H.J., and Papalas, A.J. (ed.) (2016). *Confessionalization in Europe, 1555–1700: Essays in Honor and Memory of Bodo Nischan*. London: Routledge.

Heng, G. (2018). *The Invention of Race in the European Middle Ages*. Cambridge: Cambridge University Press.

Hsia, R.P.-C. (1989). *Social Discipline in the Reformation: Central Europe, 1550–1750*. London: Routledge.

Hsia, R.P.-C. (2005). *The World of Catholic Renewal, 1540–1770*, 2e. Cambridge: Cambridge University Press.

Hufton, O. (2001). Altruism and reciprocity: the early Jesuits and their female patrons. *Renaissance Studies* 15 (3): 328–353.

Hunt, P. (2012). Irony and realism in the iconography of Caravaggio's *Penitent Magdalene*. In: *Mary Magdalene: Iconographic Studies from the Middle Ages to the Baroque* (ed. M.A. Erhard and A.M. Morris), 161–186. Leiden: Brill.

Ignatius of Loyola (1960). *Ignatius: Letters to Women* (trans. H. Rahner). Freiburg: Herder.

Ignatius of Loyola (1991). *Ignatius of Loyola: Spiritual Exercises and Selected Works* (ed. G.E. Ganss). New York: Paulist Press.

Jordan, C. (1990). *Renaissance Feminism: Literary Texts and Political Models*. Ithaca: Cornell University Press.

Juana de la Cruz (2016). *Mother Juana de la Cruz (1481–1534): Visionary Sermons* (ed. J. Boon and R.E. Surtz). Tempe: Arizona Center for Medieval and Renaissance Studies.

Knoppers, L.L. (ed.) (2009). *The Cambridge Companion to Early Modern Women's Writing*. Cambridge: Cambridge University Press.

Krzyzanowska, M. (2015). The *Gädlä Kiros* in Ethiopian religious practices: a study of eighteen manuscripts from eastern Tigray. In: *Veneration of Saints in Christian Ethiopia* (ed. D. Nosnitsin), 95–136. Wiesbaden: Harrassowitz Verlag.

Lake, P. and Questier, M. (2011). *The Trials of Margaret Clitherow: Persecution, Martyrdom, and the Politics of Sanctity in Elizabethan England*. London: Continuum.

Lay, J. (2016). *Beyond the Cloister: Catholic Englishwomen and Early Modern Literary Culture*. Philadelphia: University of Pennsylvania Press.

Leonard, A. (2005). *Nails in the Wall: Catholic Nuns in Reformation Germany*. Chicago: University of Chicago Press.

Liedl, J. (2014). "Rather a strong and constant man": Margaret Pole and the problem of women's independence. In: *Women during the English Reformations: Renegotiating Gender and Religious Identity* (ed. J.A. Chappell and K.A. Kramer), 29–43. London: Palgrave Macmillan.

Loades, D. (2006). The personal religion of Mary I. In: *The Church of Mary Tudor* (ed. E. Duffy and D. Loades), 1–29. Aldershot: Ashgate.

MacCulloch, D. (1996). *Thomas Cranmer: A Life*. New Haven: Yale University Press.

Macek, E.A. (2016). Devout recusant women, advice manuals, and the creation of holy households under siege. In: *Devout Laywomen in the Early Modern World* (ed. A. Weber), 235–252. London: Routledge.

de Marillac, L. (2005). *The Little Book of St. Louise de Marillac*. Dublin: Little Book Co.

Marshall, P. (2017). *Heretics and Believers: A History of the English Reformation*. New Haven: Yale University Press.

Martínez, D.M. (2016). Marina de Saavedra: a devout laywoman on a confessional frontier (Zamora, 1558–59). In: *Devout Laywomen in the Early Modern World* (ed. A. Weber), 219–234. London: Routledge.

Maynard, S. (1944). *Rose of America: The Story of St. Rose of Lima*. London: Sheed and Ward.

Mazzonis, Q. (2007). *Spirituality, Gender and the Self in Renaissance Italy*. Washington D.C.: Catholic University Press.

Mazzonis, Q. (2016). The company of St. Ursula in counter-Reformation Italy. In: *Devout Laywomen in the Early Modern World* (ed. A. Weber), 48–68. London: Routledge.

Mecca, S. (2006). Hagiographies of Ethiopian female saints: with special reference to Gädlä Krestos Sämra and Gädlä Fequertä Krestos. *Journal of African Cultural Studies* 18 (2): 153–167.

Medwick, C. (2000). *Teresa of Avila: The Progress of a Soul*. London: Duckworth.

Milligan, G. and Tylus, J. (ed.) (2010). *The Poetics of Masculinity in Early Modern Italy and Spain*. Toronto: Victoria University.

Monta, S.B. (2011). Anne Dacre Howard, Countess of Arundel, and Catholic patronage. In: *English Women, Religion, and Textual Production, 1500–1625* (ed. M. White), 59–82. Farnham: Ashgate.

O'Malley, J. (2009). *Trent and All That: Renaming Catholicism in the Early Modern Age*. Cambridge: Harvard University Press.

O'Malley, J. (2013). *Trent: What Happened at the Council*. Cambridge: Harvard University Press.

Pando-Canteli, M.J. (2016). Letters, books, and relics: material and spiritual networks in the life of Luisa de Carvajal y Mendoza (1564–1614). In: *Devout Laywomen in the Early Modern World* (ed. A. Weber), 294–311. London: Routledge.

Pepper, D.S. (1984). *Guido Reni: A Complete Catalogue of His Works with an Introductory Text*. Oxford: Phaidon.

Peters, C. (2003). *Patterns of Piety: Women, Gender and Religion in Late Medieval and Reformation England*. Cambridge: Cambridge University Press.

Pierce, H. (2013). *Margaret Pole, Countess of Salisbury, 1473–1541: Loyalty, Lineage, and Leadership*. Cardiff: University of Wales Press.

Pirckheimer, C. (2006). *Caritas Pirckheimer: A Journal of the Reformation Years, 1524–28* (trans. P.A. MacKenzie). Cambridge: D.S. Brewer.

Ravier, A. (1989). *Sainte Jeanne de Chantal: Noble Lady, Holy Woman*. San Francisco: Ignatius Press.

Ray, J. (2006). *The Sephardic Frontier: The Reconquista and the Jewish Community in Medieval Iberia*. Ithaca: Cornell University Press.

Redworth, G. (2008). *The She-Apostle: The Extraordinary Life and Death of Luisa de Carvajal*. Oxford: Oxford University Press.

Remensnyder, A.G. (2014). *La Conquistadora: The Virgin Mary at War and Peace in the Old and New Worlds*. Oxford: Oxford University Press.

Robinson-Hammerstein, H. (2010). *Bonae litterae* and female erudition in early sixteenth-century Nuremberg. In: *Medieval Italy, Medieval and Early Modern Women: Essays in Honour of Christine Meek* (ed. C. Kostick), 256–275. Dublin: Four Courts Press.

Rummel, E. (2000). *The Confessionalization of Humanism in Reformation Germany*. Oxford: Oxford University Press.

Schama, S. (2013). *The Story of the Jews: Finding the Words, 1000 BC–1492 AD*. New York: Ecco.

Schutte, V. (2014). "To the Illustrious Queen": Katherine of Aragon and early modern book dedications. In: *Women during the English Reformations: Renegotiating Gender and Religious Identity* (ed. J.A. Chappell and K.A. Kramer), 15–28. London: Palgrave Macmillan.

Scully, J. and Robert, E. (2016). The lives of Anne Line: vowed laywoman, recusant martyr, and Elizabethan saint. In: *Devout Laywomen in the Early Modern World* (ed. A. Weber), 276–293. London: Routledge.

Simmonds, G. (2020). Walking in Grandmothers' footsteps: Mary Ward and the medieval spiritual and intellectual heritage. In: *Women Intellectuals and Leaders in the Middle Ages* (ed. K. Kerby-Fulton, K.A.-M. Bugyis and J. Van Engen), 129–145. Woodbridge: D.S. Brewer.

Strasser, U. (2008). "The first form and grace": Ignatius Loyola and the reformation of masculinity. In: *Masculinity in the Reformation Era* (ed. S.H. Hendrix and S.C. Karant-Nunn), 45–70. Kirksville, MO: Truman State University Press.

Surtz, R.E. (1995). *Writing Women in Late Medieval and Early Modern Spain: The Mothers of St. Teresa of Avila*. Philadelphia: University of Pennsylvania Press.

Teresa of Avila (2012). *The Collected Works of Teresa of Avila* (trans. K. Kavanaugh and O. Rodriguez). Washington D.C.: ICS Publications First edition, 1980.

Thomas, G.A. (2016). *The Politics and Poetics of Sor Juana Inés de la Cruz*. London: Routledge.

Ward, H.N. (2016a). *Women Religious Leaders in Japan's Christian Century, 1549–1650*. London: Routledge.

Ward, H.N. (2016b). Women apostles in early modern Japan, 1549–1650. In: *Devout Laywomen in the Early Modern World* (ed. A. Weber), 312–317. London: Routledge.

Warren, N.B. (2005). *Women of God and Arms: Female Spirituality and Political Conflict, 1380–1600*. Philadelphia: University of Pennsylvania Press.

Warren, N.B. (2010). *The Embodied Word: Female Spiritualities, Contested Orthodoxies, and English Religious Culture, 1350–1700*. Notre Dame: University of Notre Dame Press.

Watt, D. (1997). *Secretaries of God: Women Prophets in Late Medieval and Early Modern England*. Cambridge: D.S. Brewer.

Weber, A. (1990). *Teresa of Avila and the Rhetoric of Femininity*. Princeton: Princeton University Press.

Weber, A. (2016). Introduction. In: *Devout Laywomen in the Early Modern World* (ed. A. Weber), 1–28. London: Routledge.

Weisner-Hanks, M.E. (2019). *Women and Gender in Early Modern Europe*, 4e. Cambridge: Cambridge University Press.

Williams, R. (1991). *Teresa of Avila*. London: Geoffrey Chapman.

Zika, C. (2015). Recasting images of witchcraft in the later seventeenth century: the Witch of Endor as ritual magician. In: *Gender and Emotions in Medieval and Early Modern Europe: Destroying Order, Structuring Disorder* (ed. S. Broomhall), 147–172. Farnham: Ashgate.

# 12

# Conclusion

> The queen is the piece that can carry on the best battle in this game, and all the other pieces help. There's no queen like humility for making the King surrender. Humility drew the King from heaven to the womb of the Virgin, and with it, by one hair, we will draw him to our souls. And realize that the one who has more humility will be the one who possesses Him more; and the one who has less will possess Him less. Teresa of Avila, *The Way of Perfection*

In the western adaptation of the Islamic game of chess, the vizier, the piece placed closest to the king at the beginning of the game, became the queen. As Teresa notes, the queen is the most obvious piece to spearhead offensive play. In both versions of the game, the essential juxtaposition survives between the limited range of play by the king and the much more flexible and deadly maneuverability of his second-in-command. In the Islamic world, the vizier encapsulates the political difference between a public figurehead and the more risky and dangerous ventures carried out in his name, which draw opponents' fire away from the king himself. In the west, not least because Europe for centuries had nothing comparable to the Persian civil service, the queen introduces a suggestively gendered component into the game. Had she but known about chess, an early medieval queen like the Merovingian Brunhild would probably have heartily agreed with its assessment of her role: its brutality, its fundamental vulnerability, and its capacity for innovation. Because she is not limited or constrained in her movements in the same way as the other pieces, it is as if the queen is both on and off the board simultaneously; she can move in every which way because in some ways she is never fully on the board in the first place.

Like chess queens, women, so often nameless in the Christian tradition, have been drawn to innovate, often driven out of necessity by their amorphous status within the church. Like the woman with the alabaster box, they have acted in a manner often unconstrained by secure institutional status. Because few of the regulations of the church were ever intended to apply directly to them, and could be brought to bear on them only with difficulty, women often drove processes of reform and change within the church by simple virtue of their persistent presence. Of course, this complex position, in which women were both institutionally marginal and doctrinally and spiritually experimental, made many desperately vulnerable. Not least, when formal theological discourse was not in their native language, women often employed the literary and social conventions of the vernacular in order to speak about God. Along the way, they created many of the first texts recorded in the modern vernacular languages and skirted the edges of both mystical and heretical discourse.

Conversely, many men whose vocation brought them into close proximity and who developed close friendships with religious women often used feminine language themselves. Maternal

*A History of Women in Christianity to 1600*, First Edition. Hannah Matis.
© 2023 John Wiley & Sons Ltd. Published 2023 by John Wiley & Sons Ltd.

language in particular was important for many men to articulate devotion that gendered differently from the conventional expectations placed upon aristocratic masculinity. Just as many women in the ascetic tradition had felt the need to step outside the social and cultural conventions of womanhood, many clergy modeled themselves on the religious women they encountered, and on saints like the Virgin Mary and the Magdalene. One of the most important texts in the history of Christian spirituality remains the Song of Songs, which dramatized the spiritual relationship between Christ and the believer as a dialogue between a bridegroom and a bride, and licensed countless monks and clergy to envision their souls, and their church, as feminine.

Most women in the Christian tradition, however, had to reckon with the social and cultural conventions of femininity, as well as the even less negotiable pressures of their own life cycles and persistent legal and economic inequality and instability. It was a rare woman who both chose to and could maintain her virginity – usually because she had considerable resources of her own. On the other hand, wealthy or aristocratic women often had as little choice about their own marriages, which met them at an even younger age than most. When poorer women, the vast majority, were a significant component of all manual, unskilled, or unpaid labor, the weight of debt and its concomitant pressures toward prostitution were difficult to avoid.

Religious communities of women have historically negotiated these dynamics amidst the particularity of their local regional context. As the orders of deaconesses and widows were enfolded into the emerging monastic movement, small women's houses often maintained close ties with men's houses and the local clergy, particularly if they already had relatives there. These communities were often endowed and underwritten by their aristocratic members and founders, perhaps located on former estates, and were by default usually very close to towns and cities, often for their own safety. The tension of this necessary proximity to society – without which all but a few women's houses withered eventually – with the near-constant and usually unsuccessful effort to keep religious women enclosed and separate from society, is the central drama of women's monasticism in the Latin west. In the Greek east, ancient traditions around the separation and segregation of the genders, which the Islamic world inherited but did not create, both limited women's liturgical participation in the church and paradoxically enabled it, particularly when strong traditions around adult baptism continued and the clerical status of the imperial family continued to be complex and ambiguous. In both east and west, queens and empresses continued to use religious patronage as a tool to shape the course of religious reform.

Women's religious communities performed a huge range of functions within society: they raised children and took in orphans, they educated young women, they said the divine office, they read scripture, they commemorated the dead, they copied books, they worked in wool and textiles, they made clerical vestments, they ran hospitals and supported the poor, and they provided a safe social environment for widows, the elderly, and aristocratic women in political retirement. Many women's communities would have been microcosms of their society, bridging generations and including all ages, from young children until death. Would-be saints, particularly young women with aggressive forms of ascetic self-discipline or loud and chaotic spiritual experiences, seem to have been divisive and disruptive as often as they were welcome signs of special grace. Meanwhile, the steadier heads of the widows, who often administered these communities, were far more important for the communities' survival in the long term.

The most popular forms of women's religious life were usually those that managed to combine Martha with Mary, the active and the contemplative lives. Again, this was partly down to economic necessity: it was a rare and aristocratic order which could afford and was well-educated enough to sustain a purely contemplative life. More common was an ideal which recognized and valued the contributions of ordinary women, with their range of literacies and life experiences. And yet, the beguine movement in particular, in all its diverse and local forms, brought together the old and deep connection between the commemoration of family and the dead with eucharistic contemplation and vernacular, visionary spirituality. Beguines and those orders like the Poor Clares and the Cistercians which paralleled the progress of the movement were unapologetically social and charitable in their orientation. Their concern was with feeding the poor, even while that concern was refracted in numerous ways, from establishing leper hospitals to the private reenactment of the crucifixion of Christ to praying for the souls in purgatory. The Virgin Mary was an important model and visionary companion for these women, but no less so was the penitent apostolate of Mary Magdalene.

For most of the Christian tradition, Mary and the Magdalene have been understood, in short, as *orans*: active figures of preaching, teaching, and ministry, alongside either a private life of penitence or spiritual sufferings which paralleled Christ's own. Both were coopted early in the church's history by gnostic teachers but could never be limited strictly to gnostic circles. In fact, popular devotion only increased as the threat of gnosticism receded, despite the fact that there was always more that the believer wanted to know about them than the gospels tell. The Virgin Mary has often been portrayed as either a priest or a bishop, Mary Magdalene as an apostle. Mary was always an important model for women in religious life, not least because her dual role as virgin and mother bound together two very different and potentially warring factions within any religious community. The Magdalene was the central devotional touchstone for religious women acting in the world – a priesthood without the name, all the more powerful because it was granted to a woman with past sexual experience. It was never too late to be the Magdalene.

And what of married mothers and sexually active women within the church? For many it will seem that Christianity has historically positioned itself in diametric opposition to sexuality. Sexual renunciation, after all, marked many of its earliest adherents, including the apostle Paul and the Syriac church. I have argued throughout this book that, from its inception, Christian practice was shaped by a world in which women's sexuality was indelibly marked by structures of slavery, prostitution, and sexual subordination. The glorious tragicomedy of Margery Kempe's bargain, by which she bought herself out of sexual relations within her marriage – after bearing 14 children – must be held to be far more normative in women's experience at that time than the experience of the modern western woman, supported by ready contraception and modern gynecology. In practice, as I have argued, virginity must have been a rare accomplishment; small wonder monastic writers frequently cautioned against the pride which inevitably accompanied it. It may well be that, in exalting celibacy, the church held women to an impossible and unachievable ideal and then faulted them for failing to live up to it. In the Greco-Roman world, however, the realistic historical alternative was to define women almost exclusively in terms of their sexual market value and their capacity for child-bearing. In its time, the church's support of women's asceticism created choices, however partial, privileged, and imperfect, by which women could opt out.

Women's work and labor, often invisible, made religious life possible in both the monastery and the ordinary parish. Unfortunately, neither liturgical books nor textiles survive well in the historical record, precisely because they were usually used until they fell apart. Modern women theologians have often turned to metaphors from the handicrafts to describe the process of piecing together the fragments of women's experience that do survive – a metaphor that itself comes from sewing and quilting (Chopp 1995, pp. 72–96). Some of the rarest and most poignant survivals of the participation of women in the life of the church are those examples of tablet weaving in which a medieval woman managed to record her own name within the textile itself, which was then incorporated into a vestment, adorned an altar, or formed part of a sacred object. In these, and in the books of life kept by religious communities, women recorded their presence and, implicitly or explicitly, asked to be remembered by the church. The commemoration of women across the history of Christianity resembles the archeological record in this regard: a few glittering fragments, leaving sometimes only traces of vast and living institutional structures in which women engaged with their faith, loved, failed, repented, and began again. A few names survive, sometimes by historical accident. But for better and for worse, Christianity and the church would not exist without them.

## References

Chopp, R.S. (1995). *Saving Work: Feminist Practices of Theological Education*. Louisville: Westminster John Knox Press.

Teresa of Avila (2012). *The Collected Works of Teresa of Avila* (trans. K. Kavanaugh and O. Rodriguez). Washington D.C.: ICS Publications First edition, 1980.

# Index

Page numbers in italics indicate figures.

*A History of Women in Christianity to 1600*, First Edition. Hannah Matis.
© 2023 John Wiley & Sons Ltd. Published 2023 by John Wiley & Sons Ltd.

Printed in the USA
CPSIA information can be obtained
at www.ICGtesting.com
LVHW080606211223
766828LV00009B/41